Computers in Railways XVIII

WIT*PRESS*

WIT Press publishes leading books in Science and Technology.
Visit our website for the current list of titles.
www.witpress.com

WIT*eLibrary*

Home of the Transactions of the Wessex Institute.
Papers contained in this volume are archived in the WIT eLibrary in volume 213 of WIT Transactions on the Built Environment (ISSN 1743-3509).
The WIT eLibrary provides the international scientific community with immediate and permanent access to individual papers presented at WIT conferences.
Visit the WIT eLibrary at www.witpress.com.

EIGHTEENTH INTERNATIONAL CONFERENCE ON RAILWAY ENGINEERING DESIGN & OPERATION

COMPRAIL 2022

Conference Chairmen

Giorgio Passerini
Marche Polytechnic University, Italy
Member of WIT Board of Directors

Jose Manuel Mera
Polytechnic University of Madrid, Spain

International Scientific Advisory Committee

Organised by
Wessex Institute, UK
Polytechnic University of Madrid, Spain

Sponsored by
WIT Transactions on the Built Environment
International Journal of Transport Development and Integration

WIT Transactions

Wessex Institute
Ashurst Lodge, Ashurst
Southampton SO40 7AA, UK

We would like to express thanks to all the conference Chairs and members of the International Scientific Advisory Committees for their efforts during the 2022 conference season.

Conference Chairs

International Scientific Advisory Committee Members 2022

Computers in Railways XVIII

Railway Engineering Design and Operation

Editors

Giorgio Passerini
Marche Polytechnic University, Italy
Member of WIT Board of Directors

Jose Manuel Mera
Polytechnic University of Madrid, Spain

WIT*PRESS* **Southampton, Boston**

Editors:
Giorgio Passerini
Marche Polytechnic University, Italy
Member of WIT Board of Directors

Jose Manuel Mera
Polytechnic University of Madrid, Spain

Published by

WIT Press
Ashurst Lodge, Ashurst, Southampton, SO40 7AA, UK
Tel: 44 (0) 238 029 3223; Fax: 44 (0) 238 029 2853
E-Mail: witpress@witpress.com
http://www.witpress.com

For USA, Canada and Mexico

Computational Mechanics International Inc
25 Bridge Street, Billerica, MA 01821, USA
Tel: 978 667 5841; Fax: 978 667 7582
E-Mail: infousa@witpress.com
http://www.witpress.com

British Library Cataloguing-in-Publication Data

A Catalogue record for this book is available from the British Library

ISBN: 978-1-78466-479-4
eISBN: 978-1-78466-480-0
ISSN: 1746-4498 (print)
ISSN: 1743-3509 (on-line)

The texts of the papers in this volume were set individually by the authors or under their supervision. Only minor corrections to the text may have been carried out by the publisher.

Preface

The present volume contains a selection of the papers presented at the 18th International Conference on Railway Engineering Design and Operation (COMPRAIL 2022) which was held online due to SARS-Covid pandemic. The Meeting, which started in Frankfurt in 1987, has been successfully reconvened every two years in different locations around the world. Unfortunately, this was the second online edition, but the large number of delegates joining from many countries and the quality of papers and presentations testified the worldwide interest and the success of the conference series.

COMPRAIL Conference aims at presenting and discussing the use of advanced technologies in railway systems, promoting wider understanding of new developments in the management, design, manufacturing and operation of railways and related transportation systems. It also emphasises the use of digital technologies such as Information and Communication Technologies in advanced cutting-edge railway engineering. Modern railway engineering requires access to a variety of disciplines and involves managers, consultants, train control system designers and IT specialists. This is reflected in the contents of this volume, which reveals the highly multidisciplinary and multinational approach of the works presented during the conference.

The papers contained in this Issue, as well as all others presented at the Wessex Institute Conferences are archived in the Institute's eLibrary (witpress.com/elibrary) where they are permanently available to the international community.

The Editors wish to acknowledge the authors, the members of the Scientific Committee, the Referees, the Institutional Partners, who supported the Conference, and Marta Graczyk, of the Conference Secretariat, who did an outstanding job of coordination together with the WIT Press staff, Isabelle Rham, in particular.

Finally, the Editors, the Chairmen, the Members of Scientific Committee and of the Wessex Institute wish to remember the late Professor Carlos Brebbia, founder of Wessex Institute and of WIT Press, who foresaw and established this series of meetings.

The Editors, 2022

Contents

Section 3: Operation of rail networks

Section 4: Advanced train control

Section 5: Energy-efficient design

Section 6: Traffic modelling and simulation

SECTION 1
TRAFFIC SAFETY, SECURITY AND MONITORING

ANALYSIS OF TRAM COMFORT USING THE UNE EN 12299:2010 STANDARD AND SPERLING METHOD (WZ)

GINA NOVILLO[1], NÉSTOR RIVERA[2], CÉSAR RICARDO SOTO-OCAMPO[1] & JOSÉ MANUEL MERA[1]
[1]Universidad Politécnica de Madrid, Spain
[2]Universidad Politécnica Salesiana, Ecuador

ABSTRACT

Vibration is a main factor in the driving comfort contribution and can affect the human body by being transmitted through the seats and backrests. The vibrations produced in transport are transferred to the human body, affecting passenger comfort in terms of physical health (amplitude, duration, frequency range) and psychological health (type of population, sex, age). Transport comfort is governed by evaluation tests, ISO 2631-1:1997 standard evaluates human exposure to vibrations, UNE EN 12299 standard is based on the previous one, allowing the evaluation of user comfort by calculating the average and continuous comfort index. Acquisition of acceleration data on the x,y,z axes is weighted in frequency with respect to its direction and weighting curves as a rule. Root mean square values (continuous comforts) are obtained, and the 50th and 95th percentiles for the subsequent calculation of mean comfort. The Sperling method obtains the ride quality and users comfort according to weights. The data has been extracted by the Freematics One+ device at various tram locations. The EN 12299 standard studies the acceleration behaviour (x,y,z), time, latitude, longitude, speed. It is possible to calculate the comfort index of the tram by means of norms and the Sperling method. The data was processed in Matlab obtaining favourable values in the two experimental trials, indicating that the tram in the city of Cuenca, Ecuador is very comfortable and the vibrations produced are slightly perceived by users.

Keywords: acceleration, accelerometer, comfort, EN 12299, frequency, Freematics, percentile, railway, Sperling, tram, vibrations, weighing.

1 INTRODUCTION

Railway vehicles have become systems of great importance, causing designers to be interested in achieving safe and comfortable operation [1]. Important criteria within the sustainability of the urban transport network, including the railway, are passenger satisfaction, travel time and comfort [2]. A comfortable environment involves enriching the performance of drivers and therefore the safety of users [3]. Several factors such as humidity, noise, temperature, seat design, vibrations, among others, can affect the trip or journey, and therefore driving comfort. Over the years, vibration has been the most studied factor due to railway demand the development of both experimental and theoretical studies is required [4], [5]. The vibrations produced by different types of transport are transmitted to the human body, affecting not only the comfort of passengers or train drivers, but also their physical and psychological health. Vibrations caused by the railway vehicle are the cause of different diseases, whether physical (amplitude, duration, frequency range) or psychological (type of population, gender, age, level of consciousness) [6]–[8]. Prolonged exposure to high-frequency vibrations of small amplitudes leads to concentration problems, while short-term exposure to low-frequency vibrations of large amplitudes causes damage to muscles and internal organs [9]. Vibration is a primary factor in contributing to driving comfort and can affect the entire body, as it is transmitted through the seats, backrests [10], [11]. Frequency is an important factor considering human beings as vibration systems with resonances at certain frequencies, each part of the human body with its respective masses, natural

WIT Transactions on The Built Environment, Vol 213, © 2022 WIT Press
www.witpress.com, ISSN 1743-3509 (on-line)
doi:10.2495/CR220011

frequencies, shock absorbers and elastic elements that act when stimulated by oscillatory phenomena [12], [13]. Comfort when traveling in a railway vehicle has increased in recent years due to social demand [14], [15], a main objective for train drivers is to guarantee quality service. Comfort assessment encompass methods, standards, or criteria to determine how users feel about comfort [16]. Comfort varies in different countries due to vehicle conditions, road conditions, speed restrictions, curve radii, among others [17]. There are several methods that relate passenger comfort and acceleration levels in an unbiased way, being accepted to assess driving comfort [18]. The established methods to evaluate the mean comfort and, the most used are: ISO 2631, EN 12299 and the Sperling's method. The comfort index varies according to the method used and according to the way of extracting and processing the acceleration data [19]–[21]. The evaluation of the data is acquired with an accelerometer located in the center of the surface of the seat cushion and the surface of the backrest proposed in ISO 10326-1 [22]–[24]. The EN 12299 standard is considered accurate in multiple countries for calculating the comfort levels of railway vehicles by obtaining three comfort evaluation indices: mean comfort (N_{MV}), continuous comfort index (Ccx, Ccy, Ccz), and complete comfort (NVA) [25]. In order to obtain the corresponding vibrations, a weighted general vibration level is used as an exposure metric, most of these curves are derived from the ISO 2631 standard [26].

2 MATERIALS AND METHODS

2.1 Experimental overview

UNE EN 12299 standard mentions that the measurement points established will be according to the method used and the type of vehicle. In single deck vehicles, three measurement points will be established: a point in the center and one at each end of the passenger compartment, as shown in Fig. 1 [27].

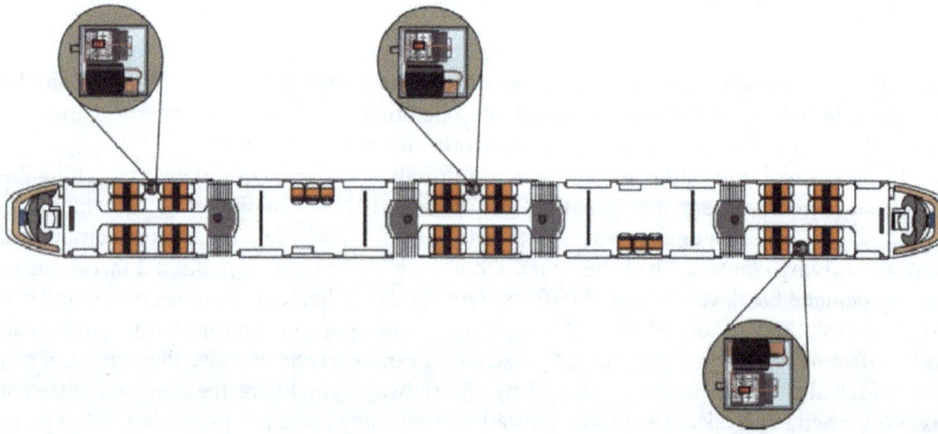

Figure 1: Measurement location points according to the UNE EN 12299 standard.

The UNE ISO 2631 standard establishes methods to quantify the vibration of the whole body in relation to human health and comfort, the probability of perceiving vibrations and the incidence of motion sickness [12], [28], [29] considering a frequency range of 0.5 Hz to

80 Hz for health and 0.1 Hz to 0.5 Hz for bad movement. Fig. 2 represents UNE ISO 2631 comfort analysis methodology.

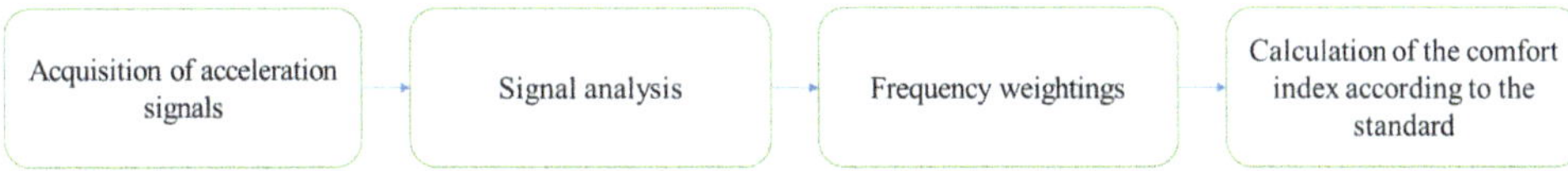

Figure 2: Comfort analysis methodology according to UNE ISO 2631-1, Vibrations and mechanical shocks.

2.2 Data acquisition

For data acquisition as mentioned in the EN 12299 standard, three Freematics One+ devices were organised as shown in Fig. 3. The acceleration data in the three axes extracted by the accelerometer measure with respect to the object inertial mass, allowing the movements of the railway vehicle to be identified during the journey, that is, the vibrations will be the Freematics One+ acquired data in addition to the maneuvers of drive and turns. The global positioning and location are acquired by means of the global positioning sensor (GPS) (M8030) obtaining data of latitude, longitude, altitude that allow knowing the route of the tram. The speed at which the tram circulated during the routes "Río Tarqui – Parque Industrial" and vice versa is obtained.

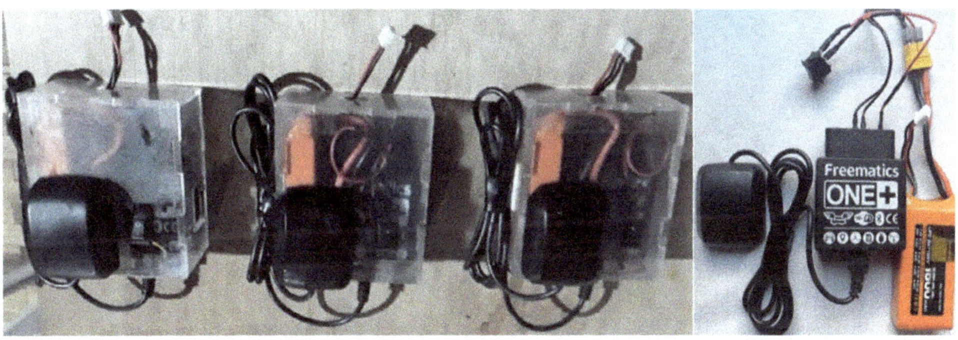

Figure 3: Freematics One+ and GPS devices used for data acquisition and Lipo battery power.

2.3 Data processing

Once the data is obtained, the microSD is connected to the computer to be able to process them. Freematics obtained data are stored in (.CSV) format, where eight files are obtained (round trip) for later processing in Matlab. By means of neural networks, a re-sampling of the GPS speed is performed to complete the speed matrix and relate these variables based on the accelerometers. The data of the three measurement points when applying the neural network are shown in Figs 4 and 5.

The latitude and longitude data sampled by the Freematics One+ device allow characterizing the behaviour of the tram route in Matlab using the Google Earth application, the green area indicates the route both outward and return.

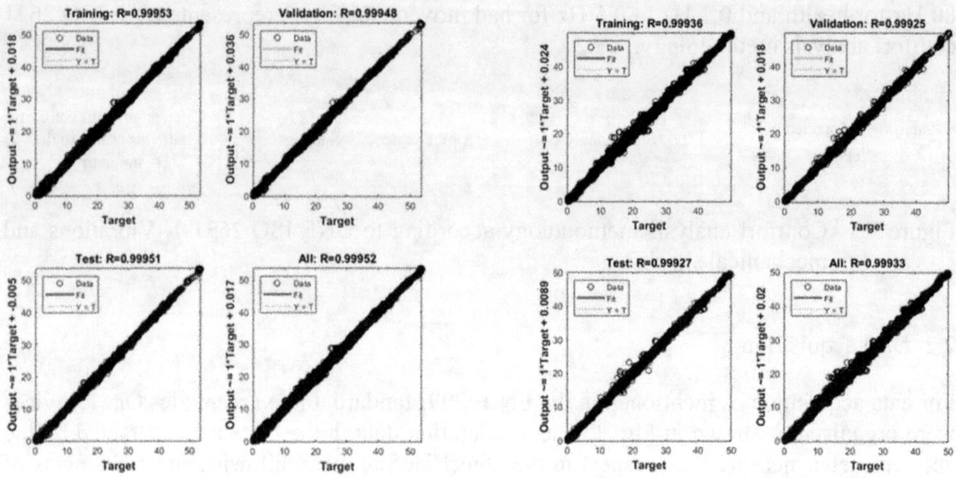

Figure 4: Neural networks: Front and middle measurement point respectively.

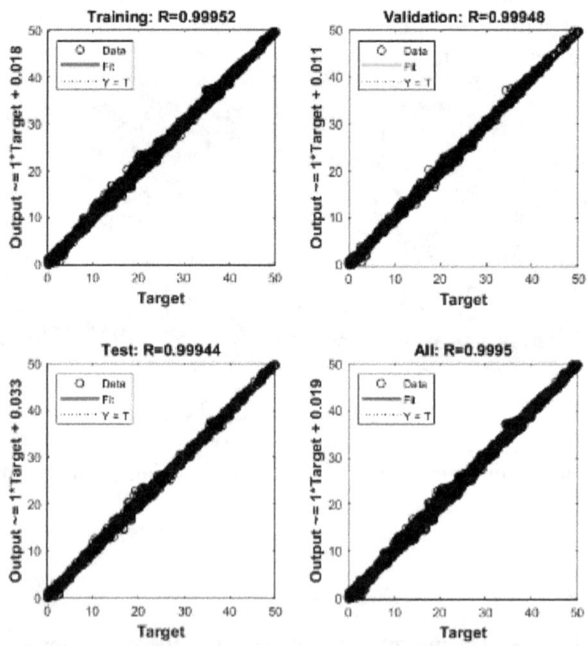

Figure 5: Neural networks: Front and middle measurement point respectively.

With the tram speed sampled on the route (tram routes are observed in Fig. 6), values of the maximum speed of the tram are obtained at the three measurement points, which oscillates around 48 km/h. The speed decreases when the tram is going to arrive at a station, therefore when the speed is equal to 0 km/h, that is, the tram has stopped because it has reached a station, as shown in Fig. 7.

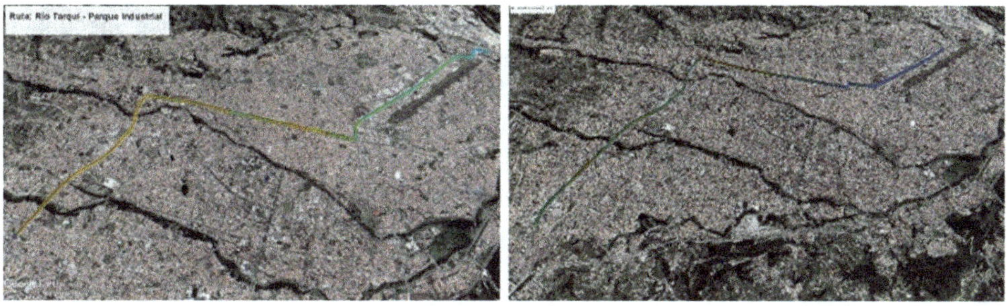

Figure 6: Characterization of the route Rio Tarqui – Parque Industrial/Parque Industrial – Rio Tarqui.

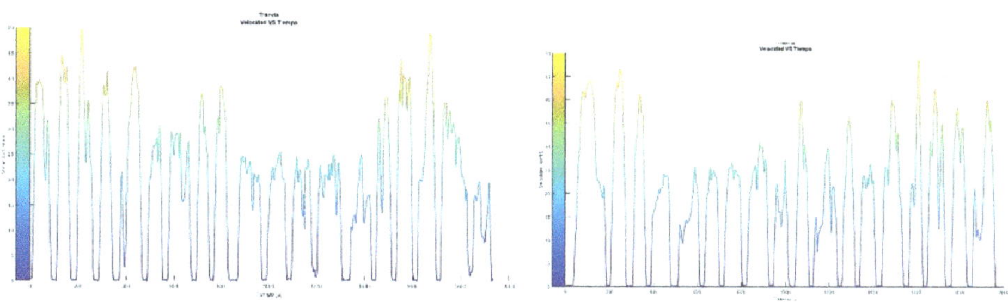

Figure 7: Round trip speeds respectively with measuring point forward.

2.4 Comfort evaluation

For the comfort evaluation according to the Sperling's method, vertical (Az) and horizontal (Ay) accelerations were used. The accelerations signals measured on the ground are transformed to cm/s^2. The power spectral density (PSD) is estimated through the vibration in each direction. It is weighted in frequency according to the vertical (passenger comfort) or horizontal (ride quality) direction. These weighting equations are:

Ride quality:

$$B\,(f) \;=\; 1.14\sqrt{\frac{[(1-0.056f_2)_2+(0.645f)_2*3.55f_2]}{[(1-0.252f_2)+(1.547f-0.00444f_3)_2](1+3.55f_2)}} \tag{1}$$

Passenger comfort:

$$(f) \;=\; 1.14\sqrt{\frac{1.911f_2+(0.25f_2)_2}{(1-0.277f_2)_2+(1.563f-0.0368f_3)_2}} \tag{2}$$

where $k = 0.588$ for vertical vibrations and $k = 0.737$ for horizontal vibrations.

When calculating the Wz index and comparing with the limit tables of this method, the index is evaluated by means of the integral of the product of the power spectral density and the weighting modulus.

Evaluation of comfort according to UNE EN 12299 standard was established to the tram analysis comfort from the measurement of the accelerations on the railway vehicles ground with an antistep filter. Weighting the accelerations in frequency according to the direction of the vibration, the calculation of the mean square values (rms) every 5 minutes represents the continuous comfort. Calculate the 50th and 95th percentile. The value of the mean comfort index (N_{MV}) is obtained for each location of the measurement points and a global.

3 ANALYSIS OF RESULTS

3.1 Evaluation according to Sperling

The comfort is represented by the red curves representing the weighting in the horizontal direction while the green color represents the vertical direction, the driving comfort index is used to obtain the ride quality and is given by the blue color (Fig. 8).

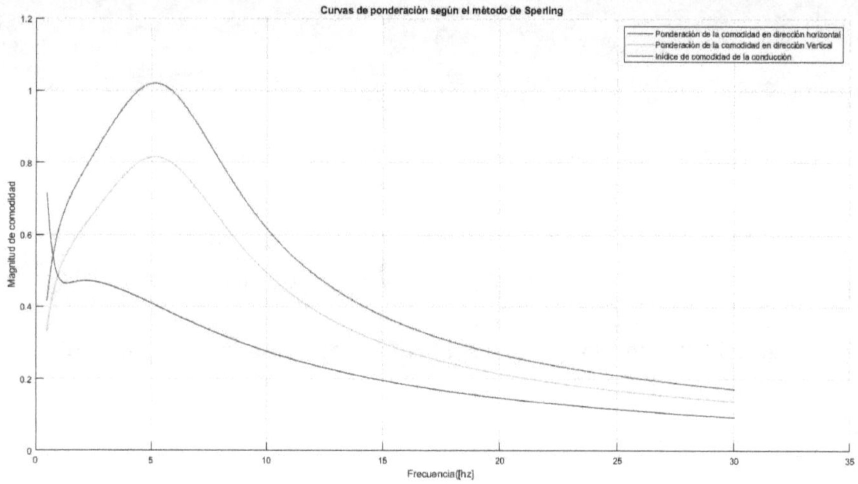

Figure 8: Sperling weighting curves depending on the measurement point forward, middle and back.

The Sperling method is evaluated according to the location of the measuring devices: forward, middle and at the other end of the tram. Defining as routes Río Tarqui – Parque Industrial (Route 1) and route Parque Industrial – Río Tarqui (Route 2). Comfort according to the Sperling method is reflected in Table 1. The values obtained are less than or equal to 1 in all directions and in the two study routes, according to the Sperling comfort index scale, the vibrations produced are "slightly perceptible" by tram users.

Table 1: Comfort index according to Sperling.

Route/Measurement point	Wzx	Wzy	Wzz
Route 1/Middle	1.01884	1.01884	0.82
Route 2/Middle	1.01793	1.01793	0.8147
Route 1/Back	1.01658	1.01658	0.8155
Route 2/Back	0.91862	0.91862	0.76
Route 1/Forward	0.9347	0.9347	0.761
Route 2/Forward	0.943	0.943	0.771

Gait quality according to the Sperling method is evaluated in Table 2. Ride quality results are the same for the three directions with values less than 1. According to the Sperling scale, driving is defined as "Very good".

Table 2: Driving quality according to Sperling (Wz).

Route/Measurement point	Wzx	Wzy	Wzz
Route 1/Middle	0.4	0.4	0.4
Route 2/Middle	0.4117	0.4117	0.4117
Route 1/Back	0.4132	0.4132	0.4132
Route 2/Back	0.45	0.45	0.45
Route 1/Forward	0.4517	0.4517	0.4517
Route 2/Forward	0.943	0.943	0.771

3.2 Evaluation according to UNE EN 12299 standard

Within the two tram routes there are different stations and each of them has been evaluated by means of the standard. Continuous comfort is calculated at the Río Tarqui – El Salado Interstation, considering the location of the Freematics One+: Forward. In Fig. 9, in the variable Ccx, values lower than 0.15 m/s^2 are obtained, the comfort in the transverse direction Ccy presents values of up to 0.17 m/s^2 except for the beginning of the route with a value of 0.33 m/s^2. Comfort in the vertical direction values range between 0.13 m/s^2, therefore, the preliminary scale defines it as "very comfortable" in that section.

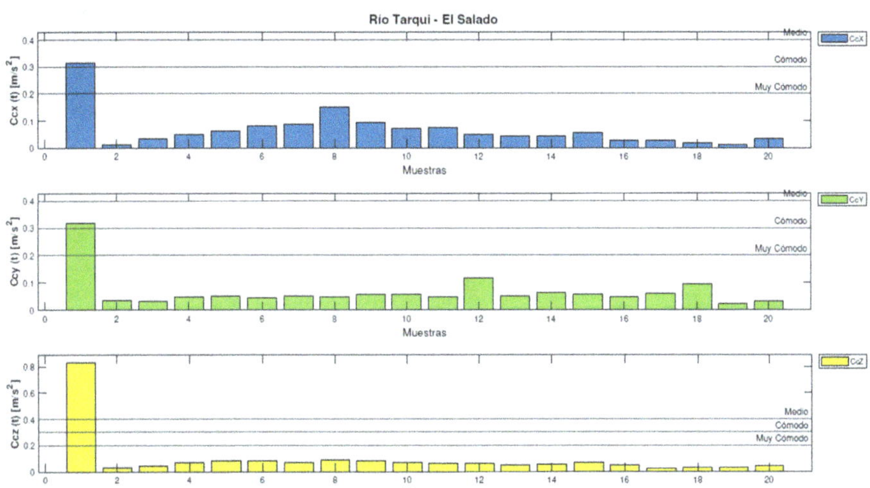

Figure 9: Continuous comfort: Ccx, Ccy, Ccz. Río Tarqui – El Salado. Measurement point: Forward.

The location of the measurement point was changed to medium as shown in Fig. 10. Obtaining a Ccx value of 0.16 m/s^2 and Ccy in the transverse direction of 0.18 m/s^2 establishing by the indices as "very comfortable". In the vertical direction Ccz, the first peak is identified as the starting moment with a value of 0.7 m/s^2 while the other values are less than 0.3 m/s^2, which according to the preliminary scale is "comfortable".

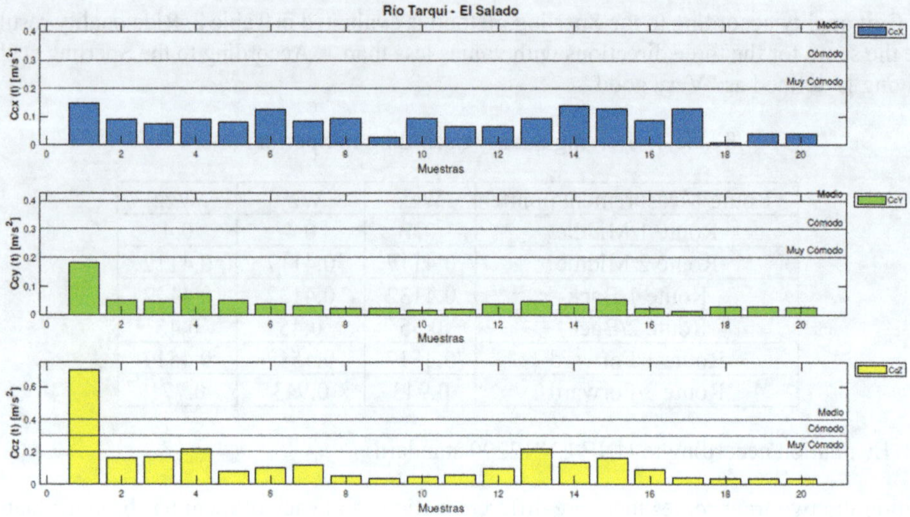

Figure 10: Continuous comfort: Ccx,Ccy,Ccz. Río Tarqui – El Salado. Measurement point: Medium

In Fig. 11, the location of the measurement point is modified to the back, where the values of both Ccx and Ccy take values less than 0.2 m/s^2, so according to the standard they are "very comfortable". In the vertical case, the same inconvenience is presented as in the previous case, where a value of 0.7 m/s^2 appears at the start, so that the other values satisfy the "very comfortable" scale.

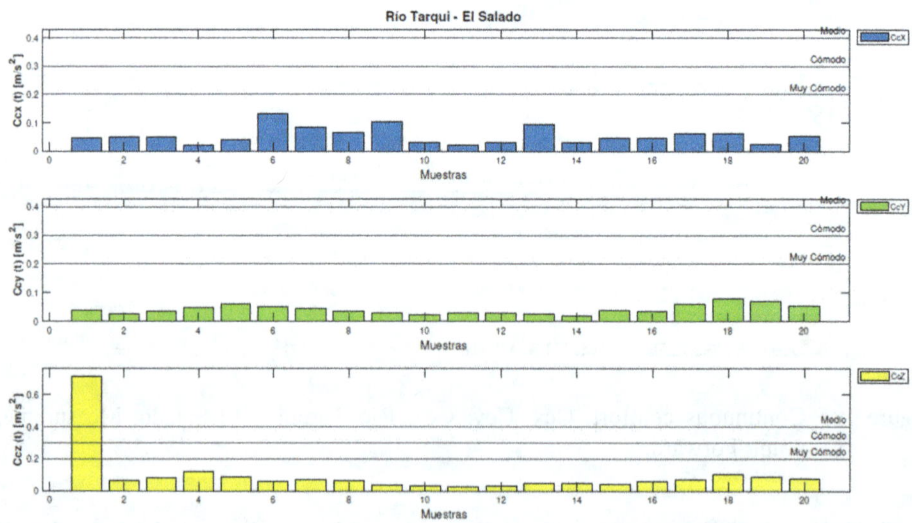

Figure 11: Continuous comfort: Ccx,Ccy,Ccz. Río Tarqui – El Salado. Measurement point: Back

The N_{MV} comfort index of standard EN 12299 is calculated by the normal method, the values were calculated for each direction (x, y, z). Table 3 shows that all the values of $N_{MV\ x}$, N_{MV} and y $N_{MV\ z}$ are less than one. Therefore, according to the scale for the comfort index of standard EN-12299, it is "very comfortable". Similarly, the global average comfort values, N_{MV}, are less than 1.5. These values correspond to the entire journey of the two routes.

Table 3: N_{MV} comfort index according to EN 12299.

Route	Measurement point	$N_{MV\ X}$	$N_{MV\ Y}$	$N_{MV\ Z}$	N_{MV}
Route 1	Forward	0.7449	0.4915	0.9708	1.3187
Route 2	Forward	0.6351	0.5595	0.7635	1.1399
Route 1	Middle	0.6205	0.5161	0.5229	0.9617
Route 2	Middle	0.4874	0.6148	0.5478	0.9569
Route 1	Back	0.6268	0.6907	0.5775	1.097
Route 2	Back	0.6615	0.6047	0.521	1.0367

4 CONCLUSIONS

Railway vehicle comfort has been evaluated by different methods and guidelines applying the Sperling method and the UNE EN 12299 standard. Comfort index allows to obtain the quality of the ride from the Sperling method by identifying the road infrastructure while the EN 12299 standard evaluates the comfort of a user in discrete events. Both the Sperling method and the UNE EN 12299:2010 standard consider certain scales to assess the comfort of the railway vehicle, in this case they coincide in their evaluation of the tram as a comfortable transport. Data collection in low-cost devices such as the Freematics One+ compared to other more sophisticated equipment has shown similarity due to its fast and reliable data extraction for subsequent processing. The most influential extracted variables in the comfort analysis are given by the acceleration in the three axes, speed, time, altitude, latitude, among others. The level of comfort of the Cuenca tram is characterized as comfortable and safe after the evaluation of the indices by regulation.

As future work, a frequent data sampling can be applied in the tram, corridors, vehicle fleets and estimate a comfort analysis using the ISO 2631 standard, in addition to modifying the location of the data acquisition device in the Bogie.

REFERENCES

[1] Cheng, T.-C. & Hsu, C.-T., Running safety and comfort analysis of railway vehicles moving on curved tracks. *International Journal of Structural Stability and Dynamics*, **14**(4), 1450004, 2014.

[2] Mohammadi, A., Amador-Jimenez, L. & Nasiri, F., Review of asset management for metro systems: Challenges and opportunities. *Transport Reviews*, **39**(3), pp. 309–326, 2019.

[3] Gameiro Da Silva, M.C., Measurements of comfort in vehicles. *Measurement Science and Technology*, **13**(6), R41, 2002.

[4] Kim, Y.G., Kwon, H.B., Kim, S.W., Kim, C.K. & Kim, T.W., Correlation of ride comfort evaluation methods for railway vehicles. *Proceedings of the Institution of Mechanical Engineers, Part F: Journal of Rail and Rapid Transit*, **217**(2), pp. 73–88, 2003.

[5] Suzuki, H., Effects of the range and frequency of vibrations on the momentary riding comfort evaluation of a railway vehicle. *Japanese Psychological Research*, **40**(3), pp. 156–165, 1998.

[6] Özkaya, N., Willems, B. & Goldsheyder, D., Whole-body vibration exposure: A comprehensive field study. *American Industrial Hygiene Association Journal*, **55**(12), pp. 1164–1171, 1994.

[7] Sevencan, F., Vaizoglu, S., Telatar, T. & Gler, C., The measurement of whole body vibration levels to which shuttle bus drivers. 2009.

[8] Lakušić, S. & Ahac, M., Vibracije od željezničkog prometa. *Gospodarenje Prometnom Infrastrukturom*, pp. 371–416, 2009.

[9] Bonin, G., Cantisani, G., Carbonari, M., Loprencipe, G. & Pancotto, A., Railway traffic vibrations: Generation and propagation – Theoretical aspects. *4th International SIIV Congress*, Palermo, 2007.

[10] Mansfield, N.J., *Human Response to Vibration*, CRC Press, 2004.

[11] Groenesteijn, L., Hiemstra-van Mastrigt, S., Gallais, C., Blok, M., Kuijt-Evers, L. & Vink, P., Activities, postures and comfort perception of train passengers as input for train seat design. *Ergonomics*, **57**(8), pp. 1154–1165, 2014.

[12] Knothe, K. & Stichel, S., *Rail Vehicle Dynamics*, Springer, 2017.

[13] Bodén, H., Carlsson, U., Glav, R., Wallin, H.P. & Abom. M., Ljudoch vibrationslära. *Lecture Notes* (in Swedish). The figure is taken from information materials of the company Brüel and Kjaer GmbH), Markus Wallenberg Laboratory for Noise and Vibration Research, 1999.

[14] De Ona, J., de Oña, R., Eboli, L. & Mazzulla, G., Heterogeneity in perceptions of service quality among groups of railway passengers. *International Journal of Sustainable Transportation*, **9**(8), pp. 612–626, 2015.

[15] Nathanail, E., Measuring the quality of service for passengers on the Hellenic railways. *Transportation Research Part A: Policy and Practice*, **42**(1), pp. 48–66, 2008.

[16] Suzuki, H., Research trends on riding comfort evaluation in Japan. *Proceedings of the Institution of Mechanical Engineers, Part F: Journal of Rail and Rapid Transit*, **212**(1), pp. 61–72, 1998.

[17] Tengku Munawir, T.I. et al., A comparison study on the assessment of ride comfort for LRT passengers. *IOP Conference Series: Materials Science and Engineering*, **226**(1), 012039, 2017.

[18] Thompson, C., Hardie, G., Shamandi, A., Wakeling, C. & Buscuttil, M., Continuous measurement of passenger ride comfort and track condition on the VLine network. *CORE 2018: Rail: Smart, Automated, Sustainable, Conference on Railway Excellence*, 30 Apr.–2 May, Sydney, Australia, 2018.

[19] Deng, C., Zhou, J., Thompson, D., Gong, D., Sun, W. & Sun, Y., Analysis of the consistency of the Sperling index for rail vehicles based on different algorithms. *Vehicle System Dynamics*, **59**(2), pp. 313–330, 2021.

[20] Lupiáñez, S.A., Modelización de la interacción vía-tranvía. PhD thesis, 2009.

[21] Pradhan, S. & Samantaray, A.K., Integrated modeling and simulation of vehicle and human multi-body dynamics for comfort assessment in railway vehicles. *Journal of Mechanical Science and Technology*, **32**(1), pp. 109–119, 2018.

[22] Ittianuwat, R., Fard, M. & Kato, K., Evaluation of seatback vibration based on ISO 2631-1 (1997) standard method: The influence of vehicle seat structural resonance. *Ergonomics*, **60**(1), pp. 82–92, 2017.

[23] Kufver, B., Persson, R. & Wingren, J., Certain aspects of the CEN standard for the evaluation of ride comfort for rail passengers. WIT Transactions on The Built Environment, vol. 114, pp. 605–614, 2010.

[24] International Organization for Standardization, ISO 2631-1:2008: Vibraciones y choques mecánicos Evaluación de la exposición humana a las vibraciones de cuerpo entero Parte 1: Requisitos generales. Standard C, International Organization for Standardization: Spain, 2018.
[25] CEN, UNE EN 12299: Aplicaciones Ferroviarias. Comodidad de viaje para los pasajeros. Medición y evaluación. Standard. Brussels: European Committee for Standardization, 2010.
[26] Zapfe, J.A., Saurenman, H. & Fidell, S., Human response to ground-borne noise and vibration in buildings caused by rail transit: Summary of the TCRP D-12 study. *Noise and Vibration Mitigation for Rail Transportation Systems*, Springer, pp. 25–32, 2012.
[27] Comite Europeo de Normalizacion CEN, UNE EN 12299: Aplicaciones ferroviarias. Comodidad de viaje para los pasajeros. Medición y evaluación, AENOR: Spain, 2009.
[28] Colella, G., Response of the human body to vertical vibration: Critical assessment of the frequency weighting curve for comfort evaluation of a railway vehicle. Master's thesis, Politecnico Milano, 2021.
[29] Schulte-Werning, B. et al. (eds), Noise and vibration mitigation for rail transportation systems. *Proceedings of the 9th International Workshop on Railway Noise*, 4–8 Sep, Munich, Germany, 2007.

PUBLICATION ANALYSIS OF CONCEPTS FOR TRAIN INTEGRITY MONITORING SYSTEMS

RASMUS RÜDIGER* & UWE BECKER†
Institute for Intermodal Transport and Logistic Systems, Technische Universität Braunschweig, Germany

ABSTRACT
Experts anticipate a significant increase in the globally transported rail freight volumes for years to come. A promising solution approach to this challenge is to implement the European Train Control System (ETCS) at level 3. In this way, the distances between trains would no longer depend on infrastructural fixed block sections and thus trains could follow at shorter intervals one after the other. For this approach to increasing the capacity of tracks, a demanding challenge is to realise a continuous train integrity monitoring system (TIMS) especially for freight trains, as there is no continuous electrical line in many of those trains. Within this challenge, the purpose of our publication is to present the methodical approach and the results of a publication analysis of approaches and concepts for TIMSs. For this goal, we researched and analysed intellectual property right documents (patents, utility models, patent application documents, etc.), scientific and business publications, etc. During our project work as part of smartrail 4.0 for Swiss Federal Railways SBB in 2018 and 2019, we contributed results first to the report Zwischenbericht Technologie PoC Lokalisierung as a part on safe train length and train integrity based on the research of in total 609 publications. Building on this, we have classified and enhanced the results. The solution concepts found cover fields like axle counters and track circuits as well as the main brake pipe, a continuous electrical line and coupling concepts. Furthermore, we researched concepts based on global navigation satellite systems, distributed acoustic sensing (DAS), optical systems or wireless data transmission. In conclusion, we have identified three promising solution classes for the future: digital automatic coupling, DAS and end-of-train device. Since we could not find a comparable publication, we contribute with this publication an up-to-date overview of concepts for TIMSs and in particular a corresponding classification.
Keywords: train integrity monitoring systems, TIMS, European Train Control System, ETCS level 3, CTCS level 4, moving block, virtual block, localization, digitalisation of freight trains, DAC.

1 INTRODUCTION

In the rail sector, a number of railway infrastructure companies around the world may need to increase the capacity of their tracks in the next years (see [1], [2]). Specialists expect that the entire global freight and logistics market will grow by 5% p.a. in the years to come [3]. In its "Sustainable and Smart Mobility Strategy" [4], the European Commission calls for rail freight transport to grow by 50% by 2030 compared to 2015 and to double by 2050 [4].

In order to achieve these goals, increasing the density of trains on tracks is a promising basic approach. By contrast, in many cases an extension of train lengths or an increase of train heights is not possible or only possible to a limited extent [1], [2].

A promising approach to increase train density on tracks is the introduction of the European Control System (ETCS) at level 3 or the similar Chinese Train Control System (CTCS) at the corresponding level 4. The highest level 3 of the ETCS differs from all other levels in the side where train completeness monitoring, which is also referred to as train integrity monitoring, is performed. In the lower levels of the ETCS, two consecutive trains are protected from each other by having fixed block sections on the track side. Only one train may be in a block section at a time [5], [6]. On the one hand, these fixed block sections result

* *ORCID: http://orcid.org/0000-0002-2979-9122*
† *ORCID: http://orcid.org/0000-0003-0184-1226*

WIT Transactions on The Built Environment, Vol 213, © 2022 WIT Press
www.witpress.com, ISSN 1743-3509 (on-line)
doi:10.2495/CR220021

in a limitation of the track capacity and, on the other hand, high infrastructure costs for the installation and maintenance of track-sided monitoring technology [7]. The ETCS level 3 is associated with the significant advantage that the train integrity monitoring is no longer performed on the track side, but on the train side [5], [6]. As a consequence, track-sided technology becomes superfluous and two trains can follow one after the other in the braking distance of the succeeding train, which is also referred to as *moving block* and can lead to an increase in track capacity [5], [6].

The introduction of the ETCS at level 3 is not yet feasible on the main routes of European rail traffic, as there is no sufficiently practicable, reliable and safe solution for train-sided train integrity monitoring, especially for freight trains [5], since these trains often lack a continuous electrical line [7]. As a result, there is still the challenging research area of developing a train-sided train integrity monitoring system (TIMS) that meets the requirements of European mainline rail traffic (see [1], [2]).

In this research area, the purpose of our publication is to outline the methodical approach and the results of a publication analysis of approaches and concepts for TIMSs. For this objective, we researched and analysed intellectual property right documents (patents, utility models, patent application documents, etc.) as well as scientific and business publications, etc. During our project work as part of smartrail 4.0 for Swiss Federal Railways SBB in 2018 and 2019, we contributed our results first to the report Zwischenbericht Technologie PoC Lokalisierung [8] as a part on safe train length and train integrity based on the research of in total 609 publications. In 2022, we updated our work by expanding the results and classifying them. As a result, we give a brief overview of the main concept classes for TIMSs with this publication.

In continuation of our previous work (see [1], [2], [8], [9]), this publication is structured as follows: After this introduction in Section 1, we present in Section 2 our methodical research approach. In Section 3, we provide an overview of the results of our in total broad publication analysis. Finally, in Section 4, we draw a conclusion and give an outlook on future work.

2 METHODICAL APPROACH

In this section, we expound our methodical research approach to search concepts for train integrity monitoring. For this purpose, we first explain the document types considered in Section 2.1. Based on this, we elucidate our search strategy in Section 2.2.

2.1 Document types

In this section, we present the two classes of researched documents: intellectual property documents in Section 2.1.1 and further publications in Section 2.1.2.

2.1.1 Intellectual property documents

In the case of intellectual property documents, we considered the following three document types as part of our research:

- Patent applications;
- Patents;
- Utility models.

Patent applications are usually published by default a certain time after filing, unless the patent has already been granted before the end of this period. In the case of utility models, there is usually no distinction between the application and the published utility model.

2.1.2 Further publications
Apart from intellectual property documents, we considered all other documents that were publicly available, especially online. These include e.g. scientific publications, popular scientific articles, documents published by companies, associations, etc.

2.2 Search strategy

In this section, we describe the two search strategies applied depending on the document type. We explain the one for intellectual property documents in Section 2.2.1 and the one for further publications in Section 2.2.2.

2.2.1 Intellectual property documents
In the case of intellectual property documents, we used the DEPATISnet database of the German Patent and Trade Mark Office, which is regularly updated internationally. Within the DEPATISnet database, we applied the expert mode with wildcards. Generally speaking, due to the patent examination procedure, patent applications can be more extensive than patents. Accordingly, if we had the choice between a patent application and a patent in the results, we used the patent application.

In the years 2018 and 2019, we conducted a total of three research passes, each building backwards on the results of the preceding one. During the three research passes, we found a total of 414 documents of relevance. In the year 2022, we perform an update.

2.2.2 Further publications
In the case of further publications, we used the search engines Google and Google Scholar in particular. In addition, we applied further databases such as SpringerLink, ScienceDirect, Eurailpress, etc. Moreover, we also searched in the local literature collections of the university and the institute.

In the years 2018 and 2019, we found a total of 195 further publications of relevance in this way. In the year 2022, we also perform an update.

3 RESULTS OVERVIEW
In this section, we give a structured overview of the results of our publication analysis. For this, we perform a top-level classification of the results in Section 3.1. In the following Sections 3.2 to 3.7, we explain each of the six main classes defined in Section 3.1.

3.1 Top-level classification

In this section, we introduce a top-level classification for the researched solution concepts. Since a train-sided TIMS is required for using the ETCS at level 3 [5], we differentiate fundamentally between track-sided and train-sided solution concepts in our classification. In practice, we have found numerous concepts that are not, or not only, applicable on one side. As a result, there are various combinations, so that we have defined six main classes as shown in Fig. 1.

For the six main classes according to Fig. 1, there are various examples. A track-sided TIMS can be e.g. an axle counter, whereas a train-sided concept can be based on the use of the main brake pipe, for example. There are also concepts with system parts that can be applied only on the track side or only on the train side, such as some optical systems. In addition, there are two-sided concepts that require system parts on both the track side and the train side, such as a system comprising a balise in a track and a transponder on a train.

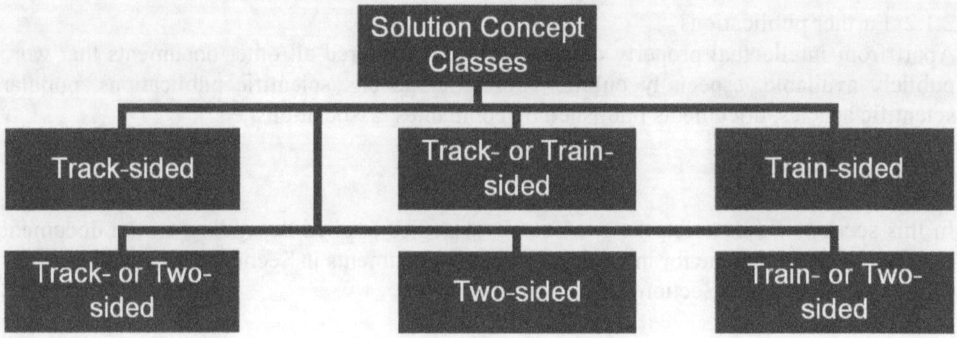

Figure 1: Top-level classification of solution concepts.

Moreover, there are also concepts for implementation either on the track side or on both sides, as well as concepts for implementation either on the train side or on both sides.

Overall, the researched concepts are very heterogeneous in terms of their kind. Some concepts represent an approach to a complete TIMS, while others can be, for example, a technique for measuring, especially for localization. As a result, the subclasses of the six main classes are correspondingly heterogeneous. They are considered in more detail in the following Sections 3.2 to 3.7.

3.2 Track-sided solution concept classes

In this section, we present three only track-sided solution concept classes. These classes are axle counter in Section 3.2.1, track circuit in Section 3.2.2 and distributed acoustic sensing (DAS), which is also referred to as fibre-optic sensing (FOS), in Section 3.2.3.

3.2.1 Axle counter

This section comprises the solution concept class of axle counters. After a general explanation of the class, we present researched options and enhancements.

Generally speaking, an axle counter is a track-sided track vacancy detection system based on the counting of entering and leaving wheelsets at both ends of a track section. By calculating the difference of those two numbers, the axle counter can determine the vacancy of that track section. An axle counter includes rail contacts usually realised as inductive sensors and implemented twice at each end of a track section in order to detect the direction of travel. In Germany, railway infrastructure companies prefer axle counters for new installations since the mid-1990s [5].

During our work, we have found a patent application for the use of diversity in axle counting systems. In this patent application, the author explains the usage of different variants of diversity, such as spatial diversity, time diversity, wheel diversity by detecting both wheels of a wheelset, and processing diversity [10].

In addition, we have found publications on the enlargement of axle counters by measuring distances between axles or differences in weights [11], [12]. One patent application comprises a procedure for gaining the number of axles, the number of vehicles, the axle distances, the vehicle lengths, and the lengths of coupled vehicle groups with only two track means and an evaluation unit [11]. In another patent, the writers expound an invention to identify engines or locomotives in a moving train by counting and weighing axles at different points along a track [12].

From our point of view, axle counters have the advantages of their many years of proven experience and the possibility of any block section length. In contrast, the disadvantages are the high costs and in particular the necessity to implement track-sided fixed block sections. As a consequence, axle counters are not suitable as an essential concept for a TIMS when using the ETCS at level 3.

3.2.2 Track circuit

This section covers the solution concept class track circuit. Based on a general introduction to track circuits, we give the researched results.

The solution concept class track circuit together with the solution concept class axle counter presented in Section 3.2.1 form the two conventional solution concept classes for train integrity monitoring (see [13]) and have high costs in common [7].

For a track circuit, an electrical voltage is applied to both rails of a track. If a rail vehicle is on such a track, there will be a short circuit via the wheelsets. Therefore, the rail vehicle becomes detectable. Traditionally, this method requires that sections of a track are electrically isolated from each other. Due to the electrical resistance of tracks, the length of the sections is currently mostly limited to about 2 km (see [13]).

A significant disadvantage of track circuits compared to axle counters is the limited length of block sections of about 2 km when using track circuits. As a consequence, there are different concepts to increase the length of track circuits. For example, to extend the transmission length of the signal of a track circuit in the track and thus the length of track circuits, the authors of a patent application propose the use of capacitors connected in parallel between the rails [14].

The authors of other publications propose concepts to determine the length of trains using e.g. track circuits. For example, one patent application covers an approach for calculating roughly the length of a train by using more than two consecutive track vacancy detection sections. This approach is based on detecting the chronological sequence of the occupancy of the individual track vacancy detection sections and on the section lengths [15].

In our opinion, the advantages and disadvantages of track circuits are largely comparable to those of axle counters. The long-term probation in use is advantageous. By contrast, the high costs and in particular the need for track-sided fixed block section lengths are significant disadvantages. Consequently, track circuits are not suitable as a basic TIMS for the implementation of ETCS at level 3. In addition, there is the disadvantage of limited block section lengths.

3.2.3 Distributed acoustic sensing

DAS is also referred to as FOS sometimes. Specifically, DAS is the application of special FOS methods e.g. relevant to rail systems. For this reason, the designation DAS is used in the following [16].

In general, DAS is a relatively new technology that has not yet been approved for European mainline traffic and is currently still under development (see [17]). In order to use DAS, the main requirement is a fibre-optic cable running alongside a track. Laser light is pulsed into that cable from one end and reflected at natural impurities. If a train drives on the track, the train will cause vibrations in the track bed and the surrounding area. The vibrations perpendicular to the cable also influence the reflection behaviour of the laser light in the cable. As a consequence, the backscatter pattern of the laser light changes at the end of the cable. By evaluating these changes, the train can be localized [18].

From our perspective, DAS is linked to several advantages, such as the ability to use existing fibre-optic cables [17], the possibility to detect unequipped people and vehicles [8], the ability to continuously monitor, and the non-necessity of a vehicle migration strategy. Nevertheless, DAS suffers from disadvantages such as difficulties in detecting slow-moving vehicles and the inability to detect stationary vehicles [8], difficulties in distinguishing between axles of a train and parallel tracks [8], [18], and the susceptibility to vibrations from e.g. road traffic in the vicinity [8].

3.3 Train-sided solution concept classes

In this section, we consider the eight only train-sided useable solution concept classes in Sections 3.3.1 to 3.3.8. These solution concept classes are based on the techniques main brake pipe, continuous electrical line, coupling, force evaluation, wireless sensor network (WSN), eddy current sensor, inertial sensor and gyroscope, and end-of-train device (EOT).

3.3.1 Main brake pipe

There are quite a number of approaches dealing with train integrity monitoring via the main brake pipe. Various concepts are based, for example, on monitoring the air pressure and/or volume flow on the traction vehicle or using an EOT at the end of a train [19], [20]. In addition, there is the approach for determining train length e.g. by measuring and evaluating air pressure, air-mass flow and temperature of the main brake pipe [20]. In our opinion, the evaluation duration in the literature sources available to us is very long with a target value of e.g. 30s [19], so that we cannot currently see any breakthrough with concepts based on the main brake pipe.

3.3.2 Continuous electrical line

With regard to a continuous electrical line in trains, there is e.g. a method to monitor the breakage of such a line [21]. Another concept proposes how the existing electrical wiring in passenger trains can be used for integrity monitoring [22]. Due to the great effort involved, we expect that a continuous electrical line in freight trains can only be implemented in practice on the basis of the digital automatic coupling (DAC).

3.3.3 Coupling

In the area of couplings, the DAC is currently the main topic as a replacement for the screw coupling in freight trains. With the introduction of a DAC, a continuous electrical line and, depending on the DAC type, possibly also a continuous data line would become reality in freight trains and form the basis for a TIMS in those trains. Additionally, the DAC would offer various logistical advantages, such as automatic coupling, better traceability of freight wagons, etc. The expected costs of EUR 6.6 to 8 billion presently represent a significant risk for a Europe-wide implementation. Moreover, a demanding migration strategy would become necessary [23]. Currently, as the goal of the DAC4EU project, experts are researching how a DAC can be designed for Europe [24]. Independent of the DAC, there is e.g. also a concept for the monitoring of couplings by detecting the inclination angle of screw couplings [25].

3.3.4 Force evaluation

In the field of force evaluation, there are concepts on the basis of measuring e.g. tensile and compressive forces between the locomotive and the first wagon. During a journey, a device compares the force curve with previously recorded force curves and evaluates the data with regard to the integrity of the train [26].

3.3.5 Wireless sensor network

There is also the approach of wireless train integrity monitoring based on a WSN. For example, a concept deals with a train-specific protocol for communication between a locomotive as the master unit and wagons as slave units [27].

3.3.6 Eddy current sensor

An eddy current sensors allows for precise relative train location from a known starting point [28]. In our opinion, this sensor technique seems to be very useful for traction vehicles, while we do not expect equipment costs to be realisable for freight wagons.

3.3.7 Inertial sensor and gyroscope

In the area of inertial sensors and gyroscopes, there are publications to use an inertial sensor as part of an EOT [8], [19]. The authors of a further publication propose to utilize gyroscopes track-sided to detect the path of a train in a switch [29].

3.3.8 End-of-train device

An EOT can be a module of a TIMS. After completing assembling of a train, railway workers can attach an EOT to the end of the last wagon of that train. An EOT includes different submodules, e.g. a telematics submodule for communication with the traction vehicle and a sensor module for self-localization. A sensor module can, for example, comprise a global navigation satellite system (GNSS) sensor and an inertial sensor [7], [8], [30]. Moreover, there is the approach of supplying energy to an EOT via the main brake pipe [31].

From our point of view, EOTs offer various advantages such as the ability to be relatively inexpensive to implement without expensive changes to infrastructure or vehicles, the feasibility without a migration strategy, and the possibility of simply replacing devices in the event of a defect. In contrast, there are disadvantages such as the possibly technically difficult communication with the traction vehicle, the potentially challenging energy supply, reliable attachment at the end of the last wagon and reliable pairing with the right traction vehicle, and limitations in the choice of sensors compared to a locomotive.

3.4 Track- or train-sided solution concept classes

In this section, we describe the track- or two-sided solution concept classes in the three Sections 3.4.1 to 3.4.3: optical sensor, acoustic sensor, and vibration sensor.

3.4.1 Optical sensor

In the area of optical systems, there are both train-sided systems for recording the track side [7], [8] and vice versa [32]. In our opinion, optical systems have potential for the future.

3.4.2 Acoustic sensor

In the field of acoustic systems, there are concepts for detecting trains on the track side [33] as well as for monitoring the own train or the track side on the train side [34].

3.4.3 Vibration sensor

In order to detect trains on the track side, there is e.g. an approach on the basis of vibration detection to initiate safety measures such as closing a gate [35].

3.5 Two-sided solution concept classes

In this section, we present two-sided solution concept classes in Sections 3.5.1 to 3.5.4: balise, radio-frequency identification (RFID), GNSS, and mobile communications.

3.5.1 Balise

A balise is a device installed in the track and working in accordance with the transponder principle. Correspondingly, a balise does not require its own energy supply [5], [13]. There is also the approach to use this punctiform information transmission for train integrity monitoring, e.g. by equipping trains with a transmitter at the front and at the end [36].

3.5.2 Radio-frequency identification

According to a researched concept, the installation of RFID transponders on freight wagons, for example, allows for identifying the freight wagons when driving past a track-sided detection device [37].

3.5.3 Global navigation satellite system

In the area of GNSS, there are e.g. different concepts to utilize a GNSS sensor as part of an EOT [7], [8], [19]. GNSS can also be combined with mobile communications [38].

3.5.4 Mobile communications

Regarding mobile communications, there are concepts with telematics modules for various e.g. also logistical applications [38], [39]. The concepts also pertain to the combination with GNSS in an EOT to monitor the integrity of a train [40].

3.6 Track- or two-sided solution concept classes

In this section, we consider the two track- or two-sided solution concept classes in the Sections 3.6.1 and 3.6.2: magnetic field sensor and waveguide.

3.6.1 Magnetic field sensor

In the area of magnetic field sensors, there are e.g. concepts for trackside detection of rail vehicles using anisotropic magnetoresistive (AMR) sensors, which allow also for measuring speed [41].

3.6.2 Waveguide

For an electrical waveguide along a track, there is a concept according to which a train sends a signal into the waveguide. A track-sided receiving device processes the signal to locate the train [42].

3.7 Train- or two-sided solution concept classes

In this section, we describe the three train- or two-sided solution concept classes in the Sections 3.7.1 to 3.7.3: ultrasound, radio detection and ranging (radar), and radio.

3.7.1 Ultrasound

With regard to ultrasound, there is a concept on the basis of track-sided devices to detect train-sided ultrasound transmitters at EOTs [43]. In addition, there are train-sided concepts such as sending ultrasound signals from an EOT through the main brake pipe to the traction vehicle or sending ultrasound signals from the traction vehicle into the main brake pipe and measuring the reflection patterns both on the traction vehicle and with an EOT [44].

3.7.2 Radio detection and ranging

In terms of radar, there is a concept for identifying track-sided reflectors from a train and thus improving the self-localization of the train [45]. Conversely, there is also a concept for monitoring train integrity with track-sided radar devices, e.g. at train stations [46].

3.7.3 Radio

In the field of radio, there is e.g. a concept that includes a transmitting and receiving module on the traction vehicle and in an EOT. Based on this, for train integrity monitoring, one module sends an electromagnetic wave to the other one at a defined point in time and the receiving module measures the transmission duration and signal strength [47]. Additionally, there are further concepts that deal, for example, with communication between trains and track-sided devices, e.g. with regard to the positioning of transmitter and receiver units [48].

4 CONCLUDING PART

In this section, we draw a conclusion of our publication analysis and give an outlook on future research work.

In general, we conclude that we have developed a classification for TIMSs with this publication. The classification is based on the idea to distinguish between track-sided and train-sided solution concept classes. Since in reality there are many mixed forms, the classification comprises a total of six main classes and 23 subclasses.

On the basis of the developed classification, we have identified two particularly proven and three especially promising solution concept classes. These classes are the proven subclasses axle counter and track circuit on the one hand and the promising subclasses DAC, DAS and EOT on the other hand.

With regard to the two proven solution concept classes axle counter and track circuit, we consider in particular that they require track-sided fixed block section lengths. Consequently, they are not suitable for the ETCS at level 3 or only suitable as a supporting system in train stations, at level crossings, etc.

Regarding the three promising solution concept classes, there are different advantages and disadvantages. From our point of view, the best long-term solution for European rail freight transport is certainly the implementation of the DAC, but the financing of the high investment costs and the need for a migration strategy still seem to be associated with considerable risks. DAS is a promising technique, although the inability to detect stationary vehicles will require a supporting solution. From our perspective, the further development of DAS and the answers to the current questions will be important. The concept class on the basis of an EOT presently seems to be the best solution for short- to medium-term implementation. In particular, the relatively low implementation costs and the fact that there is no need for a migration strategy allow us to regard the class of EOT as a promising bridge technique to the DAC.

In addition, various further solution concept classes, such as eddy current sensor and optical system, appear promising to support the implementation of the ETCS at level 3.

In the future, in order to be able to evaluate the presented concepts in more depth, we intend to continue researching the requirements for future TIMSs. In this process, we will focus in particular on the reliability, availability and safety of possible future solutions.

With our structured analysis of publications on concepts for TIMSs, we contribute a new classification of concepts for TIMSs and a current overview of corresponding concepts. During our literature research in the last years, we could not find a comparable publication comprising a similar scientific overview. As we attribute great importance to this research field, we close this gap with our present publication.

ACKNOWLEDGEMENTS

We would like to thank Anna-Lena Müller and Michael Kücker for their support in conducting our research for publications.

REFERENCES

[1] Rüdiger, R., Lan, T., Geffert, A. & Becker, U., Formalization of localization units for train integrity monitoring. *Book of Abstracts of the 27th ITS World Congress*, pp. 2563–2578, 2021.

[2] Rüdiger, R. & Becker, U., Formalization of train integrity monitoring systems. *Proceedings of the 3rd International Railway Symposium Aachen 2021*, pp. 428–447, 2022.

[3] Mordor Intelligence Private Limited, Freight and logistics market: Growth, trends, COVID-19 impact, and forecasts (2022–2027). https://www.mordorintelligence.com/industry-reports/freight-logistics-market-study. Accessed on: 31 Aug. 2022.

[4] European Commission, Sustainable and smart mobility strategy: Putting European transport on track for the future. COM(2020) 789 final. https://eur-lex.europa.eu/resource.html?uri=cellar:5e601657-3b06-11eb-b27b-01aa75ed71a1.0001.02/DOC_1&format=PDF. Accessed on: 31 Aug. 2022.

[5] Pachl, J., *Systemtechnik des Schienenverkehrs: Bahnbetrieb planen, steuern und sichern*, Springer Fachmedien Wiesbaden: Wiesbaden, Germany, 2021.

[6] Pachl, J., *Railway Signalling Principles*, Technische Universität Braunschweig: Braunschweig, 2021.

[7] Technologiebericht PoC GLAT, smartrail 4.0. https://www.voev.ch/de/System/Suchen?term=smartrail+Technologiebericht+GLAT&submit=Suchen. Accessed on: 31 Aug. 2022.

[8] Zwischenbericht Technologie PoC Lokalisierung (updated edition of Zwischenbericht Technologie PoC GLAT), smartrail 4.0. https://docplayer.org/160608243-Zwischenbericht-technologie-poc-lokalisierung.html. Accessed on: 31 Aug. 2022.

[9] Rüdiger, R. & Becker, U., Comparison of concepts for possible future train integrity monitoring concepts. *Proceedings of the 5th International Conference on Railway Technology*, 22–25 Aug. 2022, Montpellier, France, 2022 (accepted for publication).

[10] Southon, B.N., Vital wayside train detection system. Canadian patent application CA 2 685 575 A1. 2011-06-08, 2011.

[11] Deutsche Reichsbahn, Forschungs- und Entwicklungswerk, Blankenburg, Verfahren zur Anzahl- und Längenermittlung bewegter Eisenbahnfahrzeuge. East German patent application DD 229 657 A1. 1985-11-13, 1985.

[12] Mangood Corporation, Method and apparatus for identifying engines in a train of railway vehicles. United States Patent US 3,659,261. 1972-04-25, 1972.

[13] Maschek, U., *Sicherung des Schienenverkehrs: Grundlagen und Planung der Leit- und Sicherungstechnik*, Springer Fachmedien Wiesbaden: Wiesbaden, Germany, 2018.

[14] Siemens AG, Device for detecting the occupied or free status of a section of track. International patent application WO 2007/134992 A1. 2007-11-29, 2007.

[15] Alcatel, Verfahren und Anordnung zur Bestimmung der Länge eines Zuges. German patent application DE 197 43 631 A 1. 1999-04-08, 1999.

[16] Rohwetter, P., Eisermann, R., Großwig, S. & Krebber, K., Fibre-optic distributed acoustic and vibration sensing for monitoring of industrial plants and installations. *Proceedings of the ICSIC International Conference on Smart Infrastructure and Construction*, pp. 63–68, 2016.

[17] ITK Engineering GmbH, Distributed acoustic sensing for railway technology. https://www.itk-engineering.de/en/story/innovation-distributed-acoustic-sensing/. Accessed on: 31 Aug. 2022.

[18] Rosenberger, M. & Hall, A., Distributed acoustic sensing as a base technology for railway applications. *SIGNAL + DRAHT*, **108**(9), pp. 73–84, 2016.

[19] Heitmann, R., Ptok, F.-B. & Quante, F., Machbarkeitsuntersuchungen zu Strategien in der Zugvollständigkeitsüberwachung. *SIGNAL + DRAHT*, **91**(1+2), pp. 5–11, 1997.

[20] DaimlerChrysler AG, Verfahren zur lokbasierten Bestimmung der Zuglänge. German patent application DE100 09 324 A 1. 2001-09-06, 2001.

[21] SAB WABCO S.p.A., A safety system for checking continuously the integrity of a railway train. European patent application EP 1 316 489 A2. 2003-06-04, 2003.

[22] Deutsche Bundesbahn, Anordnung zur ständigen Überwachung der Vollständigkeit eines Zuges. German patent application DE38 40 844 A 1. 1990-06-07, 1990.

[23] Lang, H.P., Anforderungen an das System Bahn und Konsequenzen für die Strategie. *HANDBUCH Das System Bahn*, PMC Media House: Leverkusen, Germany, pp. 119–147, 2021.

[24] Deutsche Bahn AG, Digital automatic coupling in rail freight traffic. https://www.dac4.eu/en/. Accessed on: 31 Aug. 2022.

[25] Siemens Aktiengesellschaft, Verfahren zum Ermitteln des Kupplungszustands einer Eisenbahnkupplung, Eisenbahnkupplung sowie Anordnung mit einer Eisenbahnkupplung. German patent DE 10 2008 034 018 B3. 2009-07-30, 2009.

[26] Deutsches Zentrum für Luft- und Raumfahrt e.V., Einrichtung zur Überwachung der Zugvollständigkeit. German patent DE 10 2006 005 206 B3. 2007-09-13, 2007.

[27] Scholten, H., Westenberg, R. & Schœmaker, M., Trainspotting, a WSN-based train integrity system. *Proceedings of the 8th International Conference on Networks*, pp. 226–231, 2009.

[28] Geistler, A., Train location with eddy current sensors. *WIT Transactions on the Built Environment*, vol. 61, WIT Press: Southampton and Boston, pp. 1053–1062, 2002.

[29] Broquetas, A., Comerón, A., Gelonch, A., Fuertes, J.M., Castro, J.A., Felip, D., López, M.A. & Pulido, J.A., Track detection in railway sidings based on MEMS gyroscope sensors. *Sensors*, **12**, pp. 16228–16249, 2012.

[30] Kunze, M.D., Chelobanov, D., Vlasenko, S., Rosenberger, M., Schubert, M., Theeg, G. & Pachl, J., Detection. *Railway Signalling and Interlocking*, PMC Media House: Leverkusen, Germany, pp. 123–179, 2020.

[31] VEB Braunkohlewerk Welzow, Elektropneumatische Zugschlusswarnanlage fuer Schienenfahrzeuge. East German patent 213 638. 1984-09-19, 1984.

[32] Servo Corporation of America, Identifikationssystem für sich bewegende Objekte. German patent application DE 31 36 925 A 1. 1982-06-24, 1982.

[33] Deutsche Aerospace AG, Verfahren zur Erfassung von Gefahrenquellen. German patent application DE 42 14 271 A 1. 1993-11-04, 1993.

[34] Detlef Riemer, Akustische Überwachung von Schienenfahrzeugen, insbesondere von Hochgeschwindigkeitszügen der Art ICE. German patent application DE 198 25 580 A 1. 1999-12-16, 1999.

[35] Suharjono, A., Wardihani, E.D. & Hardani, Y.F.K., Analysis of the vibration signal detection for rail train arrival. *Proceedings of the IEEE International Conference on Communication, Networks and Satellite*, pp. 85–87, 2017.

[36] Standard Elektrik Lorenz AG, Einrichtung zur Zugschlußüberwachung. German patent DE 29 02 238 C 2. 1980-07-31, 1980.

[37] DVV Media Group, RFID-transponder für DB AG; EI, 01/2019. https://eurailpress-archiv.de/SingleView.aspx?show=570455. Accessed on: 31 Aug. 2022.

[38] Moreno, J., Riera, J.M., de Haro, L. & Rodriguez, C., A survey on future railway radio communications services: Challenges and opportunities. *IEEE Communications Magazine*, **53**(10), pp. 62–68, 2015.

[39] Faubel, P. & Windolf, W., Online-monitoring von Eisenbahn-Güterwagen. *SIGNAL + DRAHT*, **100**(9), pp. 40–46, 2008.

[40] Kreis, W. & Bastin, A., Einrichtung und Verfahren zur Überwachung von Schienenfahrzeugen, insbesondere von Güterwaggons. German patent application DE 44 08 261 A 1. 1995-09-14, 1995.

[41] Temic Telefunken microelectronic GmbH, Verfahren zur Detektion von Straßen- und Schienenfahrzeugen. German patent application DE 44 19 355 A 1. 1995-12-07, 1995.

[42] CSF-Compagnie Générale de Télégraphie Sans Fil, Funkortungssystem für entlang einer gerichteten Bahn laufende Züge. German patent application DE 1 591 043. 1970-04-09, 1970.

[43] Dinter, K., Ingenieurbüro und Laboratorium für neue elektronische Produkte, Zugkontrolleinrichtung. German patent application 23 29 341, 1975-02-13, 1975.

[44] Pellerano, A., Next generation train detection. *IRSE NEWS*, **132**(3), pp. 6–10, 2008.

[45] Siemens Aktiengesellschaft, Positionsbestimmung eines Schienenfahrzeugs. German patent application DE 10 2013 219 805 A1. 2015-04-02, 2015.

[46] Schön, S. & Streitzig, C., Additional methods to detect train integrity under ETCS level 3 and the effects on capacity and control of movement. *Proceedings of Euro: Žel 2013: 21st International Symposium*, pp. 202–207, 2013.

[47] DB Cargo AG, Einrichtung zur Erkennung der Zugvollständigkeit bei aus einem Triebwagen und Wagen bestehenden Zügen. German patent DE 199 51 259 B4, 2001-04-05, 2001.

[48] Siemens AG, Schienenfahrzeug mit einer Überanstreckungsstrecke für Daten und/oder Befehle. German patent application DE 10 2004 032 015 A1. 2006-01-26, 2006.

STUDY FOR THE COMPATIBILITY OF BOTH CYBERSECURITY AND FUNCTIONAL SAFETY STANDARDS FOR RAILWAY SIGNALLING APPLICATIONS

JUN YOSHINAGA
National Traffic Safety and Environment Laboratory, Japan

ABSTRACT

A new railway sector technical specification for the cybersecurity of railway applications was issued in July 2021 as CENELEC/TS 50701. Until now, the concept of development and design of railway applications related to safety have been based on conformity with functional safety standards such as IEC 62278, IEC 62279, and so on. In this paper, we discuss the new issues caused by the scope overlap of functional safety standards and the scope of CLC/TS and by the difference between the lifecycle span of CLC/TS and the functional safety standards argued from the configuration of some typical railway signalling applications. And it is described that CLC/TS requirements raise some new issues that may need some configuration reformation not only the separation of processing programs and its data and data preparation tools kits (this is required by IEC 62279) but also it might need to make some configuration changes by manufacturer and its management method changes by infrastructure managers. In addition, we propose a reasonable validation measure based on functional safety and CLC/TS when railway applications have changed such as creating a preliminary plan to achieve satisfying both viewing points at the same time.

Keywords: cybersecurity, CLC/TS 50701, functional safety, operation phase, vulnerability.

1 INTRODUCTION

With the development of technologies such as railway digitalisation and driverless operation, safety and cybersecurity risk tolerance are becoming more necessary. In 2021, CENELEC issued technical specifications of cybersecurity for railway applications. Cybersecurity threats may increase gradually.

Since technological progress is too rapid in cybersecurity than safety technology, it is essential to pay close attention to cybersecurity information in other industries in order to maintain the performance of railway products.

In this paper, we focus on vulnerabilities which had hidden behind the railway signalling system countermeasures though sometimes suddenly arising from the characteristics of CLC/TS short-term life cycle during the operation phase on the basis of some configuration of recent railway signalling systems. And we argue our proposal against vulnerabilities.

2 METHOD

The methodologies and know-how to achieve the safety of functional safety standards, general information can be referred to from the existing signalling systems which have already developed and operating now. Based on these information, our evaluation experiences, and researching CLC/TS articles, we identify issues related to compatibility between functional safety and cybersecurity and consider appropriate measures to ensure both compatibility.

WIT Transactions on The Built Environment, Vol 213, © 2022 WIT Press
www.witpress.com, ISSN 1743-3509 (on-line)
doi:10.2495/CR220031

3 FUNCTIONAL SAFETY STANDARDS AND CYBERSECURITY STANDARD

3.1 Functional safety standards for railway sector

The aim of functional safety standards is to archive functional safety required for the railway product [1], [2].

In functional safety standards, they assumed that the hazard sources are random failures not cybersecurity risks. Whether or not the target product can achieve safety is determined by risk assessment, and the factors to be examined are:

1. frequency of occurrence of some risk; and
2. its impact (seriousness).

It is common to investigate these factors rate from existing similar products and use them as input of safety risk assessment, and these are known information to some extent, and their values tend to be stable.

The achieved safety is expressed by SIL (safety integrity level). In the case of railway signalling products, it is common to achieve the highest level of SIL (SIL4) because it is important for railway safety.

3.2 CLC/TS requirement

Concerning CLC/TS and IEC 62443(cybersecurity for industrial automation and control system), a design method which called "security design" is applied to a target system [3].

In the security design, the required security levels are classified into SL (security level) 1 to SL4 according to the assumed security risk. SL1 assumes an accidental attack, and SL4 assumes an attack using advanced technology. SL0 is also defined, but it is not discussed here because it is a "No protection system" and is not used for safety equipment.

In IEC 62443-3-3 and CLC/TS, the target system is classified into "zone" and "conduit" from the viewpoint of cybersecurity.

There are some examples of Likelihood evaluation factors in CLC/TS, but the impact is calculated based on the evaluation indicators of "exposure(EXP)" and "vulnerability(VUL)" on a scale of 3 to 5 degrees (see 6.3.2 of CLC/TS)) is mentioned. It is also characteristic that vulnerabilities and expertise are liable to fluctuate depending on the situation.

3.3 Study of differences between safety and cybersecurity risk

There are many differences, of course, but I would like to raise some issues regarding maintaining the cybersecurity and safety functionality of the railway product during the operation phase.

First, the evaluation scales stability shown in Fig. 1. Because using the scale of EXP and VUL is one of methods in CLC/TS, other scales are possible. In any case, these scale values are change rapidly as technology advances or security incidents occur, and so on.

Second, cybersecurity and safety factors sometimes overlap, but CLC/TS requires the separation of the two. In the case of a system that considers cybersecurity from the beginning, it is supposed to evaluate how cybersecurity threats adversely affect the safety of the system.

However, many functional safety standards-based systems currently in operation are usually designed in a mixed manner, as described in Section 4.1 below. At that time for updates to apply a patch of security risks, it may be sometimes difficult to identify an impact in the view of safety.

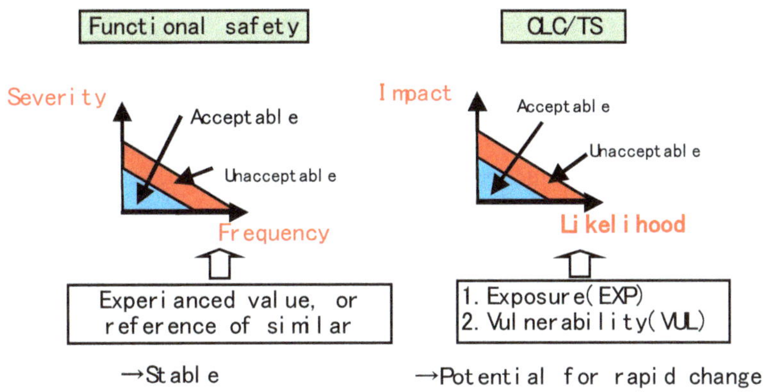

Figure 1: Comparison about evaluation scales.

The third point is that although SIL is examined for the target product in functional safety standards, the CL of cybersecurity risk is not applied to each product but is required for the zone as one group. The target CL is achieved as a whole zone, the vulnerability of one device may or may not be cybersecurity risk.

4 STUDY OF COMPATIBILITY ISSUES

4.1 General network structure of signalling system

Fig. 2 shows a recent typical network configuration of general railway signalling systems. As shown in Fig. 1, the network is mainly constructed from three networks. It is considered that these networks correspond to the zone mentioned in CLC/TS [3].

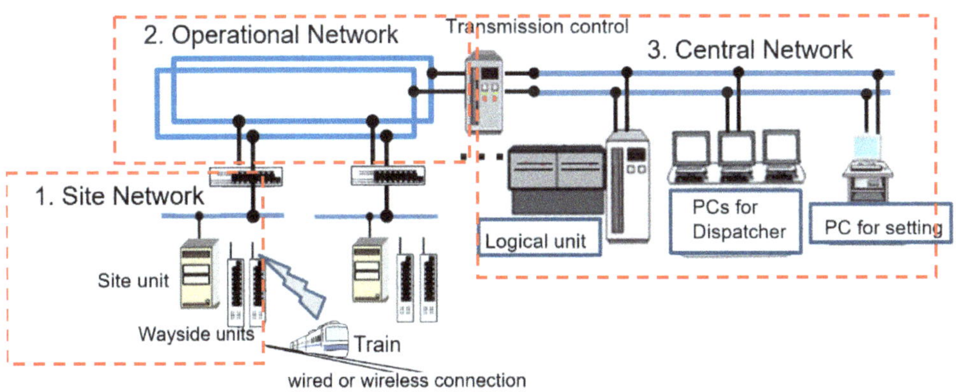

Figure 2: Typical signalling system network structure.

The "1. Site Network" in that figure is the on-site network. Generally, it is installed at each interlocking station separately. The "3. Central Network" is like OCC, and "2. Operational Network" lies along a railway wayside and connecting other networks.

Currently, most of railway lines are using connections between trains and wayside equipment via track circuits, but the number of systems using a wireless connection is increasing.

When using wireless, there is also a network between a train and on-site equipment. In this case, more strong safety measures are generally taken based on IEC 62280 (one of functional safety standard for information and communication) or IEEE 1474.1 than a wired connection.

Although not shown in the figure, security measures such as locking buildings doors and granting system usage rights are also taken in networks other than along the railway lines. Therefore, physical access to the network is considered to be extremely difficult.

4.2 Adopted measures of current signalling system

Since railway products have sometimes decades of life cycle, CLC/TS also stipulates recommendations for legacy systems (Annex B Handling legacy systems) until cybersecurity considerations are widespread.

Table 1 shows CLC/FS description. The mid column in the table shows corresponding measures that can find in the actual signalling product design and deployed materials [4]–[6]. In addition, the applicable provisions of the functional safety standard are described in the right column. These items shown here are main ones, many measures have actually been taken.

Table 1: Examples of measures adopted for products based on functional safety standards.

	Measures for legacy system described in CLC/TS Annex B	Typical measures adopted in signalling products	Related terms of the functional safety standards
1	Closed network (B.4.4)	• Not use open network	• IEC 62280 7.3.7 • IEC 62425 B.4.6, etc.
2	Network segmentation/ restricted data flow (B.4.5)	• Checking right of access to system • Components segmentation • Data encryption, technical sophistication, etc.	• IEC 62425 B.4.6 • IEC 62425 B.3.2 • IEC 62280 C.2
3	Redundant communication (B.4.9)	• Providing fault tolerance	• IEC 62425 3.1.38
4	Security gateway (B.4.10)	• Protection against unauthorized access • Choice and use of safety codes and cryptographic techniques	• IEC 62425 B.4.6 • IEC 62280 C.2

Concerning hazardous mistakes, measures have been taken for some kinds of handling mistakes. As shown in Table 2, countermeasures are taken assuming in current SIL4 of functional safety signalling systems such as wrong machine installation with mistakes, etc. Although these are not measures that directly assume cybersecurity risks, they are also considered to function as security risk measures.

Table 2: Examples of hazard assumptions of current signalling systems for cybersecurity.

Estimating hazards	Example of countermeasures
Wrong handling by human error	To void wrong data
Unexpected system configuration	Rejecting data of illegal equipment
Illegal data receiving	To void To design adopting high confidential connection

From these present conditions, it can be said that measures for cybersecurity threats have actually been taken even for existing signalling system.

Therefore, even if some devices in the zone become vulnerable for cybersecurity threats, it is considered that cybersecurity risks can be protected due to these strong countermeasures. And such cybersecurity accident has not occurred in Japan.

4.3 Possibility of vulnerability

Although strong measures have been taken in railway signalling system, it has been reported that the number of APT attacks is increasing [7], one day a vulnerability may be exploited.

Even in a railway system, it is common that general-purpose software and general-purpose communication equipment are partially used in a non-safety function mainly.

General-purpose products are considered to have a higher risk of being subject to zero-day attacks after vulnerability information is revealed because they are used more widely [8]. We assume a case where the vulnerabilities associated with such general-purpose equipment become a problem.

However, it is unlikely that it will interfere with safety as described above, but there may be some risk to be out of operation. For example, it is possible that a combination of these events will lead to vulnerabilities.

Fig. 3 is not actual system but only imaginary situation. Thought it shows that a device that is temporarily connected as tool for maintenance is equipped with a Wi-Fi connection that is never use normally.

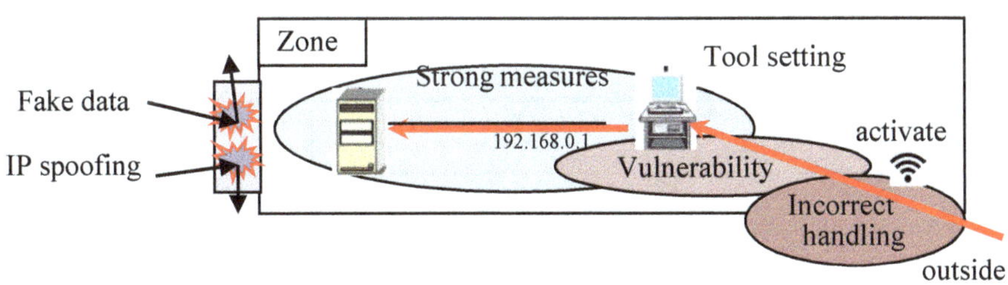

Figure 3: Concept of unauthorized access due to two causes.

It does not pose a threat to safety immediately, though it is not desirable to be able to access it from outside by incorrect handling. We would like to consider measures to prevent such vulnerabilities from being exploited.

Many of the products currently in use have strong countermeasures, so there is a concern that they will continue to be used with these vulnerabilities, so we would like to consider this countermeasure.

4.4 Our proposal of vulnerability evaluation method

The issue of vulnerability Section 4.3 mentioned occurred in the operation phase of the railway product life cycle. Vulnerabilities were sometimes rapidly changed as a result of being received from various channels such as security incidents from worldwide.

This kind of vulnerability may be temporary until measures until patching security holes are taken.

On the other hand, the measures that shown in Table 1 (specifically, functions such as passwords and keys) are defined by the signalling system manufacturer or integrator for secure design, the reduction of this vulnerability also affects the usability of the product. It is thought that the nature is different from the former vulnerability and later because the former vulnerability is considered to be more than a temporary effect and it has the potential to recover.

To manage vulnerability factor more simply in operation phase, our propose is to divide into two scales, like temporary vulnerability and system vulnerability.

We think that the proposed scaling has the following advantages than not separated.

1. After receiving cybersecurity information from the manufacturer of general-purpose products, it is possible to record that there is a problem with the vulnerability all at once, and it is possible to take prompt measures. Table 3 shows to change Temporary Vulnerability of Unit A immediately.
2. Since the current state of vulnerabilities is quantified, it is possible to compare vulnerabilities with similar systems and examine the order of countermeasures within the system (IEC62443 states that the simultaneous update function is desirable). The current use of railway products is considered to be extremely limited).

Table 3: Example of updating a vulnerability revealed in a general-purpose product.

	Unit A	Main unit B	…	Zone total (weakest value)
System vulnerability (stable factor)	1	1	…	1
Temporary vulnerability (variable factor)	1→3	1	…	3
Total vulnerability (by multiple)	1→3	1	…	3

4.5 Measures for incorrect handling in operation phase

Next, we will consider how to deal with human handling incorrectness. Most vulnerabilities occur after deployment product to the user (operation phase) and are not considered to be the first responsibility of the manufacturer and integrator. Therefore, we think that a mechanism that allows users to evaluate their own current situation is necessary.

In the functional safety standard, if a security risk due to the handling of the user is assumed at the product development stage, the user (IM, RU) should comply by notifying the user as a product handling rule books (SRAC, user manual, etc.). Therefore, it is not certain that user manages in the best condition or not.

4.5.1 Ideal solution

ISMS (ISO/IEC 27001) has control measures. It is desirable to evaluate this control measure and the following (1)–(4) view point (in addition, this is one of analysis methods for ISMS control measures) of deficiencies as Table 4, though it seems difficult to list all the devices using in the system that fall under the control measure especially legacy system. That is described 3.3 second point above.

1. Physical (stolen, lost);
2. Unauthorized access;
3. Loss of availability (disaster, breakdown);
4. Mistakes (operational mistakes, rule violations, omission of security measures).

Table 4: Desirable GAP analysis method based on ISMS.

ISMS control measures	Detailed control measures	Concerned equipment of system	View (1)	View (2)	View (3)	View (4)
A11.1.2 Management of room enter/exit checking	Item a: Restriction for visitor move	AR01, AR01a, AR02e …	1. … 2. … 3. … 4. …	1. … 2. … 3. … 4. …	1. … 2. … 3. … 4. …	1. … 2. … 3. … 4. …
	Item b:	…				
	….	…				

4.5.2 Suggestion of solution

If the railway system gradually becomes unprotected over time, a mechanism to prompt detection and optimization might effective.

The GAP analysis method is known for evaluating the difference between the ideal state and the actual state. It is possible to weigh the questions and survey results for the influential factors and evaluate the degree of impact when the event occurs.

1. Key questions about cybersecurity handling

To list up all assets is difficult mentioned above, then it is conceivable that the user performs periodical self-check by answering to the relevant key questions. This requires the cooperation of the manufacturer or integrator as shown in Fig. 4.

2. Evaluation of vulnerabilities and threats

Vulnerability values (five levels from 1 to 5) are assigned with reference to Table 5. This is to make it easier to answer and to see tendency.

This advantage is it is not required specialised knowledge, and it is easy to check current situation visibly.

4.6 Necessity of safety evaluation

In the functional safety standards, to validate modified system is described in its the maintenance plan, however cybersecurity updates are frequent as shown in Fig. 5.

If the impact range can be identified and modification like patch for cyber security, it is reasonable to plan by limiting the test range.

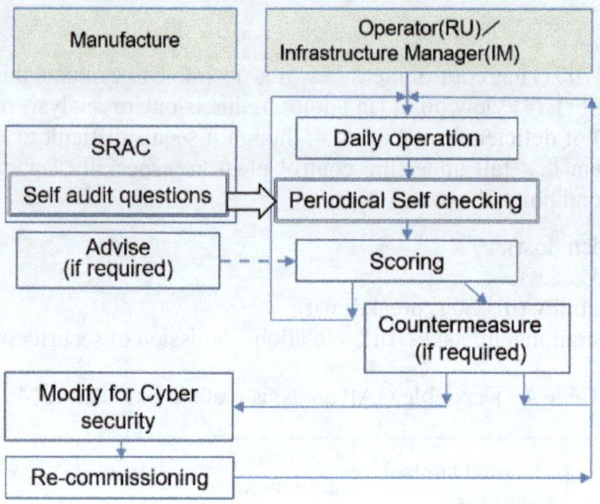

Figure 4: Proposal of a scheme that provides key questions making by manufacturer or integrator.

Table 5: An example of answer options for signalling system user.

Answer option		Weight	Explanation
Total execution	Regulated	1	Requirements are regulated and conducted surely
	Clearly	2	Requirements are not regulated but conducted definitely
Partial execution	Partial	3	Partially conducted for requirements
	Depend on person	4	Implemented irregularly for requirements
	Few	5	It has not been implemented at all
Void	Not required	–	Determined that it does not need to be implemented

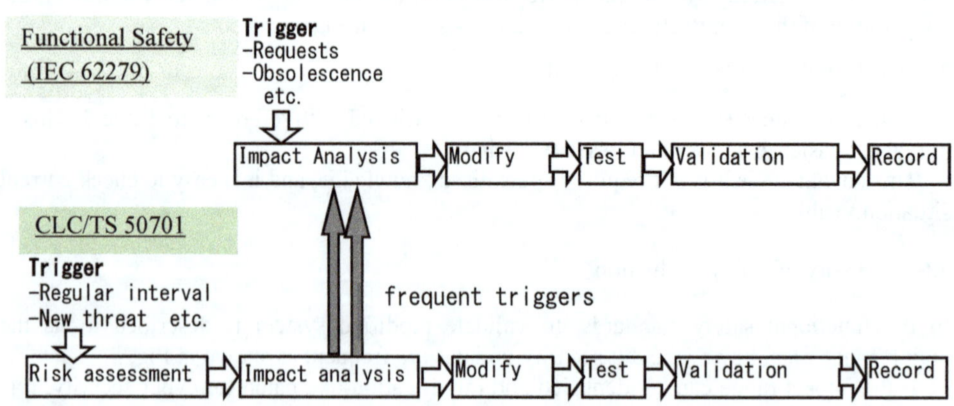

Figure 5: Modification procedure of software in operation phase.

5 CONCLUSION

In this paper, we discussed the differences between functional safety standards and CENELEC/TS 50701. CLC/TS has a concept to assess each zone against cybersecurity threats, we argued evaluation scales of CLC/TS has rapidly changed described by the configuration of a typical signalling system.

In order to match the characteristics, we proposed to manage vulnerabilities separately into two parameters. And proposed a method based on GPA analysis that makes it easy for product users to aware the current situation of their handling management regarding handling.

Regarding the direction of research, we would like to demonstrate the advantages of the proposed method and to improve a question database based on ISMS controls.

REFERENCES

[1] IEC 62425, Ed. 1.0 Railway applications – Communication, signalling and processing systems – Safety related electronic systems for signalling, September 2007.

[2] IEC 62279, Ed.2.0 Railway applications – Communication, signalling and processing systems – Software for railway control and protection systems, June 2015.

[3] European Union Agency for Cybersecurity, Zoning and Conduits for Railways, February 2022.

[4] Baba, Y., Radio train control system (ATACS). *JR East Technical Review*, **3**, 2003.

[5] Kurita, A., Radio communication network for train control of SPARCS (safety-infrastructure), STECH/1C11 RADIO, 2015.

[6] Nakashima, K., New CBTC System for smart operation latest developments for safe and reliable railways. *Hitachi Review*, **67**(7), 2018.

[7] National Institute of Standards and Technology (NIST), Information security. NIST Special Publication 800-137, p. B-1, 2011.

[8] ENISA threat landscape 2021, April 2020 to mid-July 2021, October 2021.

ATO OVER ETCS: A SYSTEM ANALYSIS FOR FREIGHT TRAINS

PHILIPPE BON[1], SIMON COLLART-DUTILLEUL[1] & RACEM BOUGACHA[2]
[1]Univ. Eiffel, COSYS/ESTAS, France
[2]Institut de Recherche Technologique Railenium, France

ABSTRACT

Automatic train operation under the supervision of a human driver is sometimes presented as a first step toward autonomous trains. This paper provides a system analysis of the available norms dealing with automatic train operation under driver supervision. Clarifications that have to be introduced to make it compatible with an autonomous train module are highlighted. Then, the work focuses on the collaboration between an automatic software for braking and accelerating in the European normative and technological context, known as ATO over ETCS. The study of the available documents allows proposing an architectural model of this global system containing on board automation and on track automated specific devices. The main motivation behind using this technical architecture is to trace a future implementation that preserves the high-level goals. This technical contribution is a first step for building an integrated approach to specify a correct system by construction, conforming to the industrial norms of automated train. In this paper, we explain how it is relevant to use a norm based technical architecture, providing intellectual references that allows drivers to identify various functioning phases where, depending on the overall context, they can let an automatic system drive the train or not.

Keywords: ERTMS, automatic train operation (ATO), ATOoETCS, grade of automation (GoA), autonomous freight train.

1 INTRODUCTION

Checking the closed door is not as critical for a freight train as for a passenger train. Nevertheless, in both cases, the beginning of a train mission mostly starts with a phase where a human has to manage with the situation's uncertainty until it reaches an ERTMS beacon. At this point, its position is perfectly known and the train can receive a Movement Authority (MA) and use a "Full Supervision" mode (FS). Under this particular functioning, the behaviour of the driver is supervised. It means that a warning, then service brakes, then emergency brakes will be triggered. As a consequence, they are several kind of phases in a train mission. In some of them, the main conditions of a safe functioning can be automatically checked and maintained, in other ones, a human actor is needed. In order to perform an industrial implementation of the above concepts, automatic and non automatic phases must be clearly identified. A preliminary condition seems to be the definition of a normative framework. Moreover, a methodology ensuring the rigorous implementation of this framework is an important contribution to its industrial efficiency.

The presented paper proposes a system analysis of a functioning which is automated in some phases and driven by a human in other phases on the basis of normative documents. Corresponding UNISIG Subsets will be mentioned all along the current document to explain how an Automatic Operation System (ATO) can be supervised by ETCS. The second section presents main high level requirements for automatic train operation. the third section details the architecture of ATO over ETCS on the basis on available normative or pre-normative documents. In a fourth part of the paper, a SysML model of the described architecture is introduced as a starting point for an automated software generation, this model being by construction conform to the modelled normative framework.

WIT Transactions on The Built Environment, Vol 213, © 2022 WIT Press
www.witpress.com, ISSN 1743-3509 (on-line)
doi:10.2495/CR220041

2 TECHNICAL MOTIVATION FOR AN ATO SYSTEM

There are several Grades of Automation (GoA) for trains. The highest one, the level 4 does not require any human contribution for driving trains and is called GoA4. The French VAL system (Véhicule Automatique Léger) which is operating on the Lille Metro since 1983, is a fully automated GoA4 system. A similar ATO system is also used with conventional rolling stock on the Paris Metro Line 14 and Line 1. The Swiss Lausanne Metro line 2 uses the same system too.

2.1 GoA2 and GoA4

Considering a freight train running with a GoA2 system, a human driver drives the train "when needed" and handles emergencies. "When needed," may corresponds to particular operational test cases. A wide list of classical emergency cases can be found in the Section F of the RCL [1]. The RCL is a more than 1300 pages document describing principles for a French driver behaviour. It is used and periodically updated by teachers in learning centres. It is assessed by various railway experts. To give an example, in Section F of the RCL, the procedure "obstacle protection" is documented. It details what to do when a rock or a fallen tree is laying on the railway tracks. In case of GoA2 functioning, the driver identifies the problem and switch off the ATO. Then, he applies the specific procedure. In case of GoA4 functioning, new procedures have to be introduced as there are no driver able to apply the existing procedure. In terms of requirements, it means that the driver should be able to take the control of the train efficiently while it was running automatically. In the case of a pure GoA2 functioning, the driver is mainly in charge of its own awareness. In other words, he is supposed to supervise the automatic driving such a way that he is fully able to operate when it is needed. To give an example, in a case of an emergency braking, the driver is supposed to know if the emergency brake is not occurring because of the train has passed through a red light, but for another reason. An information missing can lead to a wrong evaluation of the current situation, and then to a wrong decision.

Let us introduce a deeper illustration about awareness. Let us suppose a car driver drives using a function of its car known as "autopilot", corresponding to GoA2. When the driver takes back control in order to manage a situation of emergency:

- He is supposed to know whether there is a vehicle just behind his car;
- He is supposed to be aware of the presence of an emergency stopping lane adjacent to the road;
- He is supposed to know if he is driving on a high-way or on a two-way traffic road.

These three piece of information are instances of data, which have to be available, because they are needed to take an emergency decision for obstacle avoidance. For all these reasons, a GoA2 car driver is regularly required to put his hands on the steering wheel of the car. This is expected to be a sufficient measure to ensure the driver's attention.

When the emergency management is provided by a software entity, the situation has to be analysed deeper. There are two classes of emergency scenarii:

- When the automatic driving GoA2 system identifies that it is not able to manage the current situation;
- When it identifies no problem, but an outside monitoring loop diagnoses the need of an emergency management.

The first case corresponds to an obstacle detection, which a GoA2 train driving system may knows that it is not able to handle: in the current existing procedure, a real human has to put warning devices on the tracks in order to prevent another train to collide the obstacle. The second case may correspond to the vision of a ball crossing the railway track, at five o'clock in the neighbourhood of a school building. The GoA2 system may identify the ball as a non-dangerous entity when it has the sensors and associated software able to do so, because a collision with a ball does not damage the train at all. Moreover, if the ball is damaged, its commercial value can be neglected. Nevertheless, an experimented driver, may know that a ball in the neighbourhood of a school, at this moment of the day and in the current range of date is linked to a high probability of children running after the balloon. In the considered use case, the emergency management need is identified using a knowledge, which is not embedded in a common GoA2 driving system.

To conclude this section, authors want to highlight that the definition of a GoA2 automation system being compatible with GoA4 is difficult to establish, because it is not standalone. It depends clearly on the GoA4 monitoring services that are running in parallel in order to diagnose difficult scenarios. When the monitoring GoA4 layer does not build its own knowledge on history, the GoA2 system has to share its needed variable states in order to complement the knowledge of the GoA4 system. Today the state variables needed for the management of a GoA4 train system are not formally defined in the literature. Therefore, complementing this undefined set of variable cannot be formally achieved, on the basis on normative or pre-normative documents that we have consulted. Nevertheless, this is a work to perform, before being able to specify a GoA2 system "compatible with GoA4." It would be a step forward towards the autonomous train.

2.2 GoA2 train

In the literature of requirement engineering, "goals are desired system properties that have been expressed by some stakeholders" [2]. The main motivation of their usage in requirement engineering is justifying requirements by linking them to higher-level goals. A railway system has to be safe. As a consequence, the first high-level goal named G1 is needed to receive an authorisation of commercial exploitation from the National Safety Agency.

- **G1: "The system should be safe."**

In the subset 125 normative document proposing a GoA2 framework [3], the driver is in charge of managing safety related events, whereas the autopilot software deals with non-critical situations.

From the previous analysis, it is proposed to specify a GoA2 services, potentially compatible with a GoA4 system on a main line. The goal G2 and G3 can be expressed as follow:

- **G2: The GoA2 system should respect signals and speed limits. When it is not able to do so, it should formally specify its situation.**
- **G3: The GoA2 system should take into account timetables and condition of traffic in order to respect the timetables of the global system.**

Analysing G2, respecting signals and speed limit is a necessary safety condition. Nevertheless, in case of default of the braking system, it may happen that a common braking distance cannot be applied [4]. In this case, values of last signals and last braking distances associated to well defined control orders should be communicated. The best contribution of the GoA2 system is to share its knowledge. In other words, values of the variables allowing to identify that the limit of the GoA2 functioning has been over-passed should be accessible for the GoA4 system. Moreover, the semantic of the considered state variable has to be formally defined. Let us recall to mind that a common ontology of all actors of the railway system, named Ontorail (https://ontorail.org/wiki/), has been introduced by the International Union of Railway (UIC). Nevertheless, concept definition is not sufficient for scenario identification. In order to characterize a given situation in a professional railway context, the RailTopoModel (http://www.railtopomodel.org/en/) standard may be used. Finally, when a precise and rigorous description is needed, the dynamic scenario can be specified by the mean of Goro [5]. Examples of using ontology engineering in order to model railway accidents can be found in the state of the art [6]. All these considerations lead to claim that state variables leading a GoA2 system to the self-characterization of its own limits of functioning should be formally defined, as they can technically be formally defined.

The following of the document focuses on the specification of a GoA2 services, potentially compatible with GoA4 of a freight train while running ERTMS.

3 ATO GOA2 POTENTIALLY COMPATIBLE WITH A GOA4?

The fact that the implementation of an ATO is implementing ERTMS does not have any influence on the global goals. ERTMS can be seen as an implementation constraint. This implementation constraint makes things simpler, as the functional specification of a rolling stock behaviour is provided in the subset 26 [7]. The component in question is called EVC (European Vital Computer) and its communication with peripheral components is specified too. The interface specification defines the form fit functional interface between the ERTMS/ETCS on-board equipment and the vehicle [8]. On the web site of the European Commission, we can read: "The railway interoperability Directive 2008/57/EC of 17 June 2008 [9] sets out the conditions to be met to achieve interoperability within the Union rail system." Interoperability is a way of providing better performance of the global European railway system, and it is a means to provide safety while managing the diversity of European railway infrastructure and European rolling stocks.

3.1 ERTMS System

ATO operates under ETCS supervision and does not affect safety [10]. The basic principle for insuring safety while providing interoperability embedded into the ERTMS architecture is to split responsibilities between operation stakeholders.

- Trackside system (under the responsibility of the infrastructure manager) sends track description, which content has to be semantically aligned with "ETCS language" and ETCS rules.
- ETCS on-board systems implement ETCS-specified behaviour, according to messages received from the trackside system.

3.2 ATO Over ETCS (ATOoE)

In order to fulfil high-level goals G2 and G3, the track, i.e. the global system management of the infrastructure holder, provides two different set of data being specified respectively in subset 131 [UNI131] and in Subset 132 [UNI132] as presented in the final conference presentation of X2Rail-1 (https://projects.shift2rail.org/s2r_ip2_n.aspx?p=X2RAIL-1, slides 16 and 17). The global architecture of the system (see Fig. 1) in a nominal functioning can be seen as a three layered one.

On the top, there is the ETCS supervision. Particularly in Full Supervision (FS) mode, the ETCS OB system may apply a "service braking" in case of small over speed. In case of heavy over speed, the ETCS OB system will trigger an emergency braking, triggering the TRIP

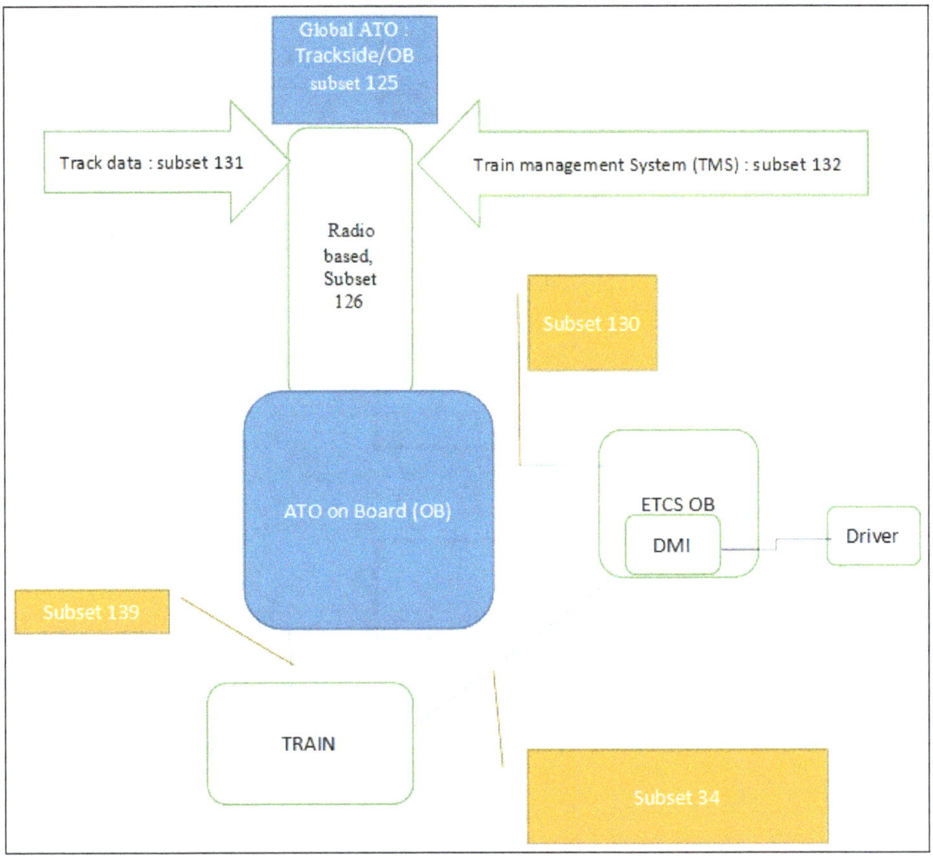

Figure 1: ATO over ETCS, partial architecture.

mode. At a second level, the driver sends a message to get in Automatic Driving mode, by the means of the Display Machine Interface (DMI): the DMI is the normalized human interface using ERTMS. This message asks to trigger the process towards ATO mode. As detailed in [11], the Subset 126 details The ATO OB (On-Board) – Vehicle Interface, allowing the ATO OB to control the vehicle. ATO over ETCS specifies the interface between the ATO on board and and the physical vehicule in the Subset 139. ATO OB – ETCS OB Interface defines the needed data and the corresponding operational protocol allowing exchanges between a software entity running in the automatic train and the hardware and software entities corresponding to the ETCS technical specification. It is detail in the Subset 130.

This interface includes:

- ATO Status ("AD Mode request," "ATO Engaged").
- ETCS Train Data (e.g., "Train length," "Maximum Train Speed," "operational train running number").
- Dynamic ETCS Data (e.g., "EB is requested," "Positioning Information," "MA Information," "Speed Information").

As an example, ATO OB needs to receive train data, which are provided by the driver running the ERTMS/ETCS procedure called "data entry." Among other information, a data

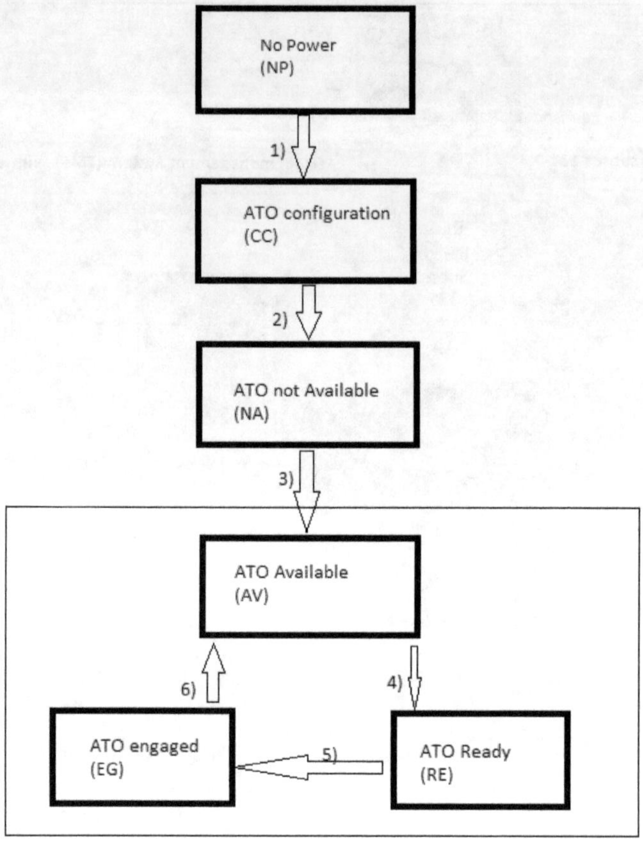

1)	The ATO-OB is powered on. The ATO state changes from NP to CO. The "**ATO Selected**" indication is displayed
2)	ETCS data entry process (including ATO Specific Data Entry) is completed and the ATO-OB receives the required data. The ATO state changes from CO to NA. The "**ATO Selected**" indication is displayed.
3)	When all the ATO Engagement Conditions are fulfilled, the ATO state changes from AV to RE and the "**ATO Ready for Engagement**" indication is displayed to the driver.
4)	When all the ATO Engagement Conditions are fulfilled, the ATO state changes from AV to RE and the "**ATO Ready for Engagement**" indication is displayed to the driver.
5)	The driver selects "**ATO Engage**," the ETCS changes to AD Mode. The ATO state changes from RE to EG. The "**ATO Engaged**" indication is displayed to the driver and the ATO-OB starts driving the train automatically
6)	The ATO-OB drives the train. When the train stops, the ATO-OB requests the "**Train Holding Brake**" application and the "ATO Selected" indication is again displayed to the driver. The state changes from EG to AV. The train is stationary waiting until the ATO Engagement Conditions are fulfilled again.
7)	Return to step 4) and repeat the sequence until the end of the journey

Figure 2: ATO states for a nominal scenario, out of draft of subset 125.

entry provides the length and the nature of the train. Obviously, this information is needed to smartly control the train. In the context of a GoA2 functioning, the driver may send the following orders to ATO OB through the human interface of ETCS OB called DMI:

- ATO Engage: Used by the driver to request the start of automatic driving (departure of the train or engagement on the move).
- ATO Disengage: Used by the driver to disengage ATO while the ATO OB is engaged.

The "ATO Disengage" input is considered as enabled by the ETCS OB when the "ATO engaged" or when the "ATO Disengaging" indication is displayed. Some national signalling system may benefit from the normalization of interfaces between trackside and on-board systems [3], [12]–[15]. The table presented on the Fig. 2 may be consulted for more information on the ATO mode state management.

3.3 Functional analysis conclusion

What are the advantages of using subset 131 and 132 under AoE, using a GoA2 autopilot?

1. The computer is more efficient at processing dynamic information in real time without making any error.
2. The driver is in charge of other safety goals, he is therefore not supposed to make heavy calculations in real time which may create loss of attention. Functions such as "monitoring the environment" are clearly specified in the "RCL" line repository as being the driver's tasks. The work-load of a driver adapting his driving strategy to a continuously changing environment including timetables real time adaptation with regards to delays of ongoing missions of other trains, decreases his ability for checking the safety of his mission.

As such, it is the driver who guarantees that the context of the GoA2 operation ("No safety function other than compliance with signs") is fulfilled. When the ATO is running, the work-load of the driver is decreased in such a way that his level of awareness of environmental evolutions may increase.

4 ATO OVER ETCS SYSTEM ARCHITECTURE

As presented in the previous section, when the system switches from a human driver to an automatic system, abilities of the driving agent change. A consequence is that configuration changes on the track-side and on the on-board system, using the communication means provided by the subset 126.

The current section provides a global description of the corresponding architecture using SysML block-diagrams [16]. It is detailed by presenting state machines of each of the 3 first layers. The last layer and sequence diagrams are not presented in the current paper. To model the GoA2 ATO over ETCS System architecture, the system is broken down into 4 levels (see Fig. 3).

The first one (see Fig. 4) "ATOoETCS_GOA2SystemL0" represents the abstract system, that contains only one element named "ATOoETCS_GOA2SystemL1."

The second one (see Fig. 5) "ATOoETCS_GOA2SystemL1" represents a refinement of the Level 0. It introduces two components, Track and On board, as specified in subset 125 [3] and can be seen in the blue components of Fig. 1.

In the level 2 there are 2 subsystems "Track" and "OnBoard" as components of "ATOoETCS_GOA2System" element of level 0. The third level (see Figs 6 and 7) is a

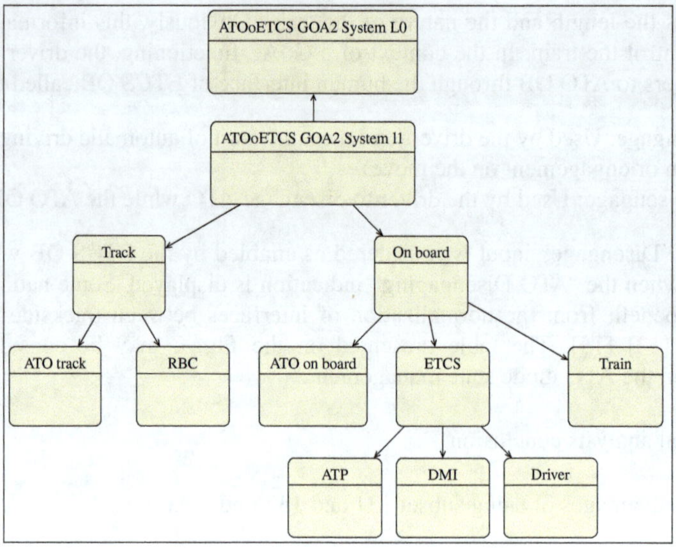

Figure 3: Modeling architecture.

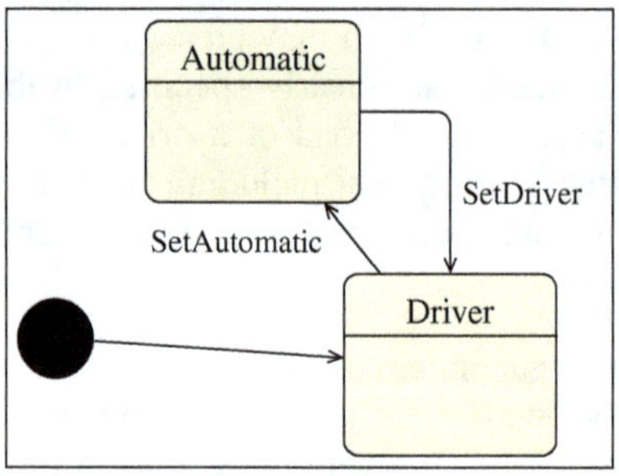

Figure 4: Level 0.

decomposition of the second level into five components. Track is decomposed into (ATO-Track, RBC) and Onboard is decomposed into (ATO-Onboard, ETCS and Train). One can notice that in the two first levels, a logical architecture able to manage the various functioning phases is presented. This specification concerns mainly software and automation. At this level, the mechanical part of the system appears with the component *train*. Messages exchanged between components of *Onboard* are normalized respectively by subsets 130, 34 and 139 as shown in the lower part of Fig. 1. This specification can be integrated in the port definitions of corresponding Block definition Diagrams modelling the on board system description at level 2.

In the last level, ETCS is decomposed into (ATP, DMI, DRIVER), which are not presented here. We have to notice that the driver may not be a component of the system, because in a Jacobson schema he would be an agent triggering functions by the mean of the DMI. A more relevant analysis consider the driver to be a component of a GoA2 system (see Fig. 1). Adopting this point of view, the human is not only an agent triggering functions; he is one of the components of the global system (see Fig. 3). As a consequence, his operational ability has to be ensured by the system. It means that interactions with the autopilot induce a sufficient

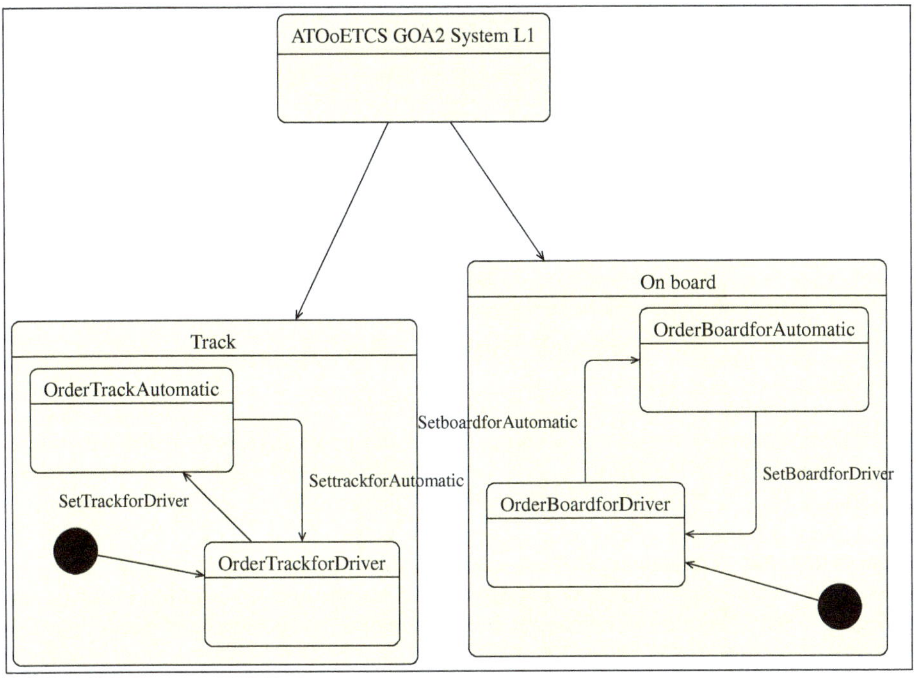

Figure 5: Level 1.

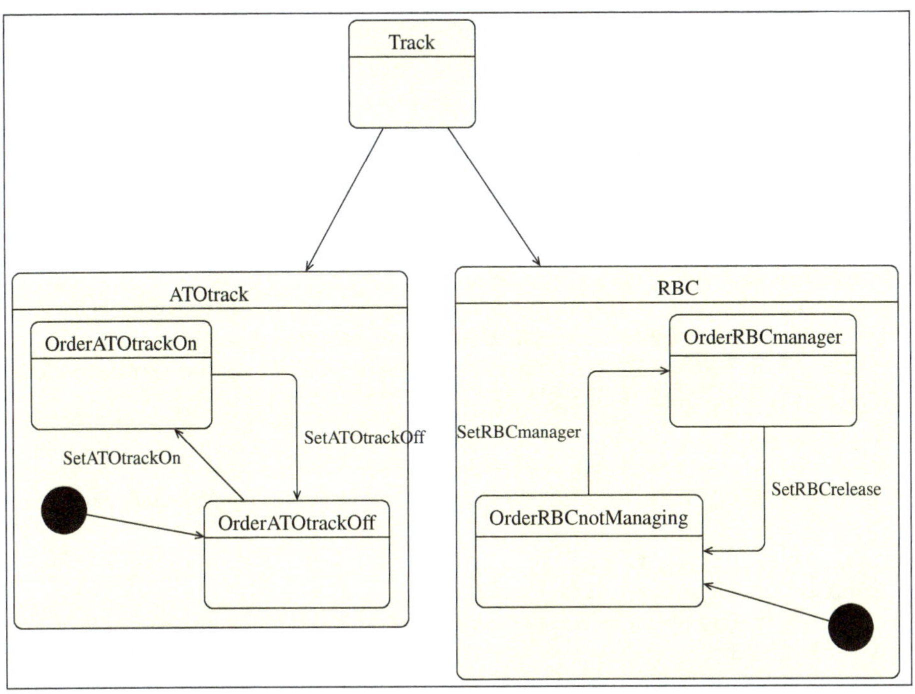

Figure 6: Track at Level 2.

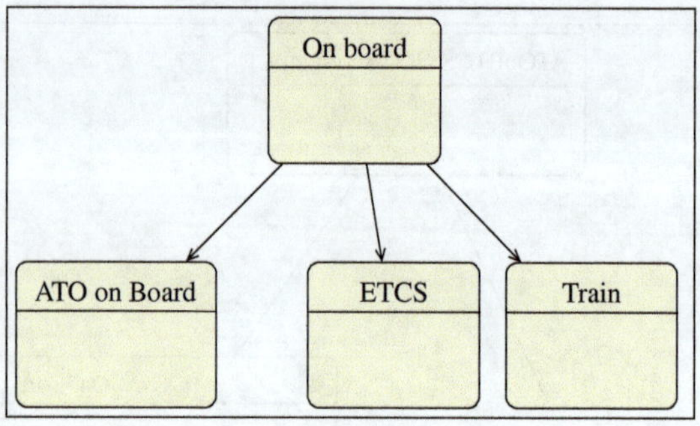

Figure 7: On board at Level 2.

level of attention and a coherent understanding of the operating context. By adopting this point of view for the ATO GoA2 system analysis, a high level goal, in the sense of Kaos methodology [2] is elicited. In this methodology, goals are expressed by requirements. As an example, periodic task has to be allocated to drivers in order to maintain their attention and the system has to provide to drivers necessary information for transient mode handling. Consequently, this goal produces specific proof obligation injections in the event-B model that insures a fully compliant implementation with regard to this high level need.

5 CONCLUSION AND FUTURE WORKS

The paper presented a system analysis of a pre-normalized technical solution for ATO GoA2 functioning. It consists of using an automatic operation system over ETCS, while a driver is in charge of safety relevant operations. Analysing normative or pre-normative documents, assumptions of functioning are explained in a first part of the paper. In a second part, a SysML model of the higher levels of the architecture is provided. This is a first step of an approach which is "correct by construction". Using a Kaos methodology [2], some event B abstract machines [17] may be generated from the SysML architecture, where some invariants modelling the main goals of the architecture can be proved. Thorough the whole paper, some high level goals were presented. Moreover, going out of an ATO supervised functioning is not a simple shift from a functioning to another and the awareness of the driver – this driver can be a human or a intelligent GoA4 software – is a problem to be considered. Focusing on this technical challenge, new specific goals (in the sense of the KAOS approach) have to be introduced. These Goals are to be translated in Event B invariant insuring that the initial need are tracked toward a safe ATO software implementation. Clearly, further works concerning model engineering still need to be undertaken.

REFERENCES

[1] SNCF specific driver rulebook for operating train in France, *Référentiel conducteur de ligne*.

[2] Matoussi, A., Gervais, F. & Laleau, R., An event-b formalization of kaos goal refinement patterns. Technical report, HAL CCSD, 2010.

[3] Subset-125: ATO over ETCS – system requirements specification. (issue: 0.1.0). Std, UNISIG, 2018.

[4] Technical investigation report on the rail accident that occurred at longueville on 16 february 2005. Technical report, BEATT, 2008. http://www.bea-tt.developpement-durable.gouv.fr/longueville-english-summary-a178.html.

[5] Bernabé, C.H., Souza, V.E.S., de Almeida Falbo, R., Guizzardi, R.S.S. & Silva, C., Goro 2.0: Evolving an ontology for goal-oriented requirements engineering. *Advances in Conceptual Modeling – ER 2019 Workshops FAIR, MREBA, EmpER, MoBiD, OntoCom, and ER Doctoral Symposium Papers*, Salvador, Brazil, 4–7 Nov., Proceedings, eds G. Guizzardi, F. Gailly & R.S.P. Maciel, Springer, volume 11787 of *Lecture Notes in Computer Science*, pp. 169–179, 2019.
[6] Debbech, S., Bon, P. & Dutilleul, S.C., Towards semantic interpretation of goal-oriented safety decisions based on foundational ontology. *J. Comput.*, **14**(4), pp. 257–267, 2019.
[7] Subset 26: "system requirements specification". Std, UNISIG, 2016. https://www.era.europa.eu/content/set-specifications-3-etcs-b3-r2-gsm-r-b1_en.
[8] Subset 119: "train interface fffis". Std, UNISIG, 2020. https://www.era.europa.eu/content/informative-set-specifications-3-etcs-b3-r2-gsm-r-b1_en.
[9] European Commission, Directive 2008/57/EC on the interoperability of the rail system. Technical report, European Union, 2008. https://eur-lex.europa.eu/eli/dir/2008/57/oj.
[10] Bienfait, B., ATO over ETCS, 2016. https://slideplayer.com/slide/14324166.
[11] Kuhn, M., System architecture description, smartrail 4.0 architecture. Technical report, Smartrail 4.0, 2019.
[12] Subset-126: ATO over ETCS – ato-ob/ato-ts fffis application layer specification. (issue: 0.0.16). Std, UNISIG, 2018.
[13] Subset-130: ATO over ETCS – ato-ob/etcs-ob ffis application layer. (issue: 0.1.0). Std, UNISIG, 2018.
[14] Subset-139: ATO over ETCS – ato-ob/ vehicle interface specification fis. (issue: 0.0.8). Std, UNISIG, 2018.
[15] Buurmans, K., Automatic train operation over legacy automatic train protection systems, a case study on the groningen-buitenpost line. Technical report, Delft University of Technology, 2019. Master of science in civil engineering at the faculty of Civil Engineering and Geosciences, department Transport and Planning of Delft University of Technology. https://repository.tudelft.nl/islandora/object/uuid:dffc21d9-936c-4286-9611-a2a846cfc416?collection=education.
[16] Holt, J. & Perry, S., *SysML for Systems Engineering*. Computing and Networks Series, Institution of Engineering and Technology, 2008.
[17] Abrial, J.R., Butler, M., Hallerstede, S., Hoang, T.S., Mehta, F. & Voisin, L., Rodin: An open toolset for modelling and reasoning in Event-B. *International Journal on Software Tools for Technology Transfer*, **12**(6), pp. 447–466, 2010.

SECTION 2
TRAIN AND RAILWAYS ANALYSIS

CONSTRUCTION OF FAULT EVOLUTION MAPS FOR DAMAGE LEVEL ASSESSMENT OF RAILWAY BEARINGS

CÉSAR RICARDO SOTO-OCAMPO[1], JUAN DAVID CANO-MORENO[2] & JOSÉ MANUEL MERA[1]
[1]Railway Technology Research Center (Centro de Investigación en Tecnología Ferroviaria-CITEF), Universidad Politécnica de Madrid, Spain
[2]Escuela Técnica Superior de Ingeniería y Diseño Industrial, Universidad Politécnica de Madrid, Spain

ABSTRACT

The diagnosis of the state of machinery is becoming increasingly important in a more competitive industrial sector. Therefore, maintenance strategies are essential to ensure the correct and continuous operation of equipment. In the last decade, the application of condition based monitoring (CBM) has increased significantly in the detection of bearing faults. CBM is based on the characterisation of equipment behaviour and focuses on preventing a machine from failing. Therefore, fault characterisation and the construction of health indicators is a fundamental issue in CBM. This study evaluates the performance of the diagnostic methodology based on the construction of contour maps from envelope spectra. This allows the construction of visual maps that characterise the evolution of the amplitude of a fault frequency and its harmonics. They also serve as a reference to establish health indicators of future equipment conditions. The results suggest that the methodology holds promise for bearing condition classification. Furthermore, the use of contour maps is a visually intuitive tool for the analyst.

Keywords: contour map, condition monitoring, bearing diagnosis, envelope analysis.

1 INTRODUCTION

Increasing industrial progress has driven the development and evolution of maintenance strategies. These are focused on ensuring the correct and continuous operation of machinery, especially of the most critical components, such as bearings [1], [2]. One of the maintenance strategies with the greatest projection in the diagnosis and prognosis of the condition of mechanical equipment is condition based monitoring (CBM) [3]–[5], due to the availability of data processing techniques.

Using mainly vibration signals [6], CBM studies the state of the machine during its entire operating interval, to extend the life of the different components, reduce downtime and optimise the maintenance schedule. In other words, CBM focuses on identifying the cause of the failure to prevent it from occurring. Therefore, the characterisation of behavioural patterns and the construction of health indicators plays an important role in machine condition assessment tasks. This has created many studies focused on the extraction of features that allow the construction of classifiers of the state of a machine, mainly based on artificial intelligence or signal processing [7].

In recent years, studies developed using artificial intelligence have increased significantly, where surface learning and deep learning algorithms are protagonists in the detection, diagnosis, and prognosis of bearings [2], [3], [8]–[11]. On the other hand, an increase in studies associated with traditional vibration signal processing techniques is also evident in the literature [7], [12]–[14]. In these studies, envelope analysis takes centre stage in the demodulation of resonant zones of signals associated with frequencies of bearing failures. Moreover, a novel methodology based on contour maps has been presented for the characterisation and construction of fault evolution maps, which serve as a reference in the diagnosis of bearings [14].

WIT Transactions on The Built Environment, Vol 213, © 2022 WIT Press
www.witpress.com, ISSN 1743-3509 (on-line)
doi:10.2495/CR220051

The main objective of this work focuses on the evaluation of the performance of the bearing diagnosis methodology based on contour maps, presented in Soto-Ocampo et al. [14]. Contour maps are graphical illustrations used to represent spatial functions by incorporating isolines. This criterion has allowed characterising the behavioural pattern of a bearing defect, considering the changes experienced by the amplitude of the fault frequency and harmonics over time. Therefore, the construction of these fault evolution maps makes it possible to establish a relationship with any machine condition.

2 METHODOLOGY

2.1 Basis of the methodology

The approach of using contour maps as a method of vibration mode characterisation arises from considering the oscillatory fundamentals of rolling bearings.

2.1.1 Vibration mode of rolling bearings

Bearings are mechanisms that have their own mode of vibration, generated by the contact of the components that make them up and interpreted through their frequencies. From this, a relationship is established between the geometry of the components and the energy developed in the passage of the rolling elements through the load zone [15]. Consequently, irregularities in the surface generate changes in the contact stresses of the components of a bearing, resulting in the generation of very short duration pulses that excite the natural frequencies of the entire structure [6], [16], [17]. Thus, the vibration signature of a bearing establishes the relationship between the magnitude of the irregularity and the amplitude of the generated pulse, manifested in the characteristic frequency of the failure component (Fig. 1).

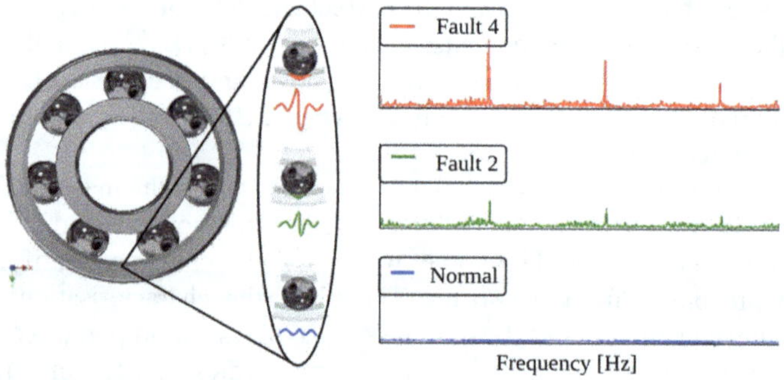

Figure 1: Envelope spectra representation of fault evolution.

2.1.2 Contour maps

As mentioned above, signal spectra can identify frequencies associated with a fault component and its respective amplitude. However, the main drawback arises at the time of diagnosis. There is a lack of criteria to evaluate the state of the components of a bearing and to relate them to a fault level. However, the use of contour maps [14] allows to characterise the behavioural pattern of a bearing defect, by relating the failure frequency of a component to the amplitude changes it experiences as the failure level increases.

Contour maps are graphical illustrations used to represent spatial functions by incorporating isolines [18]. Each isoline has a constant and equally spaced contour value (associated with an amplitude value) [19], [20]. In this way, the isolines allow to classify and separate the points of the underlying space, generated by amplitude changes of a fault, establishing a direct relationship between the fault frequency, its amplitude and the corresponding fault level. Fig. 2 represents the contour map characterising the amplitude changes of a fault frequency over time.

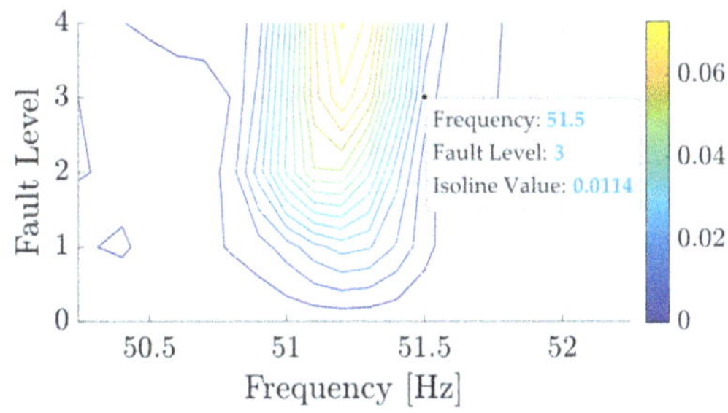

Figure 2: Representation of the coordinates of the points that form the isolines.

In the spectral analysis of a record to be evaluated, information is obtained from two of these components (fault frequency and amplitude) named analysis points from now on. The objective of the methodology is to determine the relationship of the analysis points of a spectrum with the fault level to which it corresponds within the fault evolution map. Therefore, the spectrum to be compared in the contour map must be evaluated according to the values of the isolines of the fault evolution map, thus obtaining the analysis points.

2.2 Basis of the methodology

The development of the proposed methodology is structured in six phases, which have been detailed in Soto-Ocampo et al. [14]. However, this article presents changes in obtaining the threshold value and considers measures of central tendency to estimate the relationship of a spectrum with its failure level. The methodology is presented below in the flow chart in Fig. 3.

2.2.1 Data acquisition

The data acquisition phase comprises the instrumentation of the equipment under study and the capture of vibration records. This phase is carried out in two scenarios. Initially, it is necessary to have records describing the evolution of the failure of a bearing component over time. These should allow the construction of the failure evolution maps. In this scenario it is important to determine up to what level the deterioration of a failure is considered permissible for continued operation. On the other hand, the second scenario refers to the records that are analysed or related to the fault evolution maps.

2.2.2 Determination of representative samples

It is important to ensure that the samples of the records that make up the fault evolution map and the record to be diagnosed, have:

1. Constant rotational speed,
2. Homogenisation of fault frequency, and
3. Same frequency resolution.

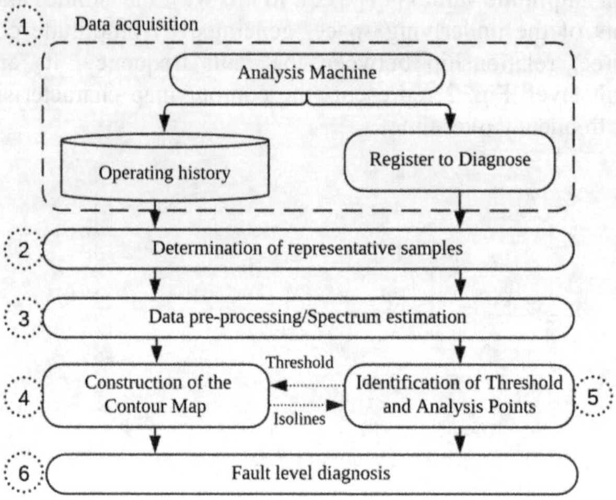

Figure 3: Structure of the methodology.

Fernández-Francos et al. [21] stresses the importance of maintaining a constant rotational speed in record capture. This is to eliminate frequency lags and variations in impact force. Regarding the homogenisation of the failure frequency, this criterion reduces the uncertainty in the identification of the failure frequency. Smith and Randall [22] consider a variation of the frequency calculation between 1% or 2%. It is also important to maintain the same frequency resolution, so the samples that make up the fault evolution map and the one to be evaluated must have the same length in time [23].

2.2.3 Data preprocessing

Gupta and Pradhan [17], suggest that the data processing technique used in the analysis should be selected according to the component under study. Therefore, considering the oscillatory fundamentals of the bearing, this study uses the "Envelope Analysis" technique, as it mainly seeks to detect resonant zones excited or modulated in amplitude by periodic impact forces, whose repetition frequency is an indicator of the location of the defect and its amplitude a measure that characterises the state of the component [24]. The application of this analysis technique includes:

1. Frequency band selection,
2. Signal filtering,
3. Extraction of the envelope signal (using Hilbert Transform), and
4. Construction of the Envelope Spectrum.

Some studies describe the importance of identifying the frequency band with the most information about the condition of a bearing [16], [25]. However, in this study, a constant filtering band of 1.8–6.1 kHz is considered [26]; this is to avoid signal attenuation due to changes in the selection of the filtering band.

2.2.4 Construction of the fault evolution map

In the construction of fault evolution maps there are three key parameters to consider, as follows:

1. Lower limit or threshold
2. Upper limit,
3. Contour interval.

The estimation of the *Threshold* corresponds to the lowest isoline value and allows the identification of the most representative amplitudes of the signal. Since the main objective of the methodology is to evaluate records of different fault levels, it is considered that this value should be adapted to the behaviour of the record under study. Therefore, the Threshold value is provided by the record to be diagnosed. In Soto-Ocampo et al. [14], the estimation of this parameter was performed by implementing a series of processes, however this process entails a higher computational expense. In this work, the estimation of the Threshold value is performed in three steps:

1. Determination of the mean ($\bar{x}$) of the sample (x), corresponding to the data of the spectrum with length N,

$$\bar{x} = \frac{\sum_{i=1}^{N} x_i}{N} \tag{1}$$

2. Identification of the peaks (P_e) of the sample, whose amplitude exceeds the mean of the signal ($\bar{x}$),

$$P_e = Peak(x) \geq \bar{x} \tag{2}$$

3. Threshold estimate, equivalent to the median (M_e) of the amplitude of the peaks identified in (6), where N_{P_e} represents the number of peaks identified.

$$M_e = \begin{cases} P_{e\frac{N_{P_e}+1}{2}} & N_{P_e}\ odd \\ \dfrac{P_{e\frac{N_{P_e}}{2}} + P_{e\frac{N_{P_e}+1}{2}}}{2} & N_{P_e}\ even \end{cases} \tag{3}$$

The *Upper Boundary* ($Upper_{Boundary}$) is associated with the maximum amplitude of the fault frequency, or harmonics, of the spectra that make up the fault evolution map. This limit represents the maximum value for isolines fault evolution map.

The Contour Interval (C_i) represents the spacing value between isolines. It is therefore important to define the number of isolines (N_{iso}) used in the construction of the contour maps, which in turn allows to define the values of each isoline ($Isoline_{value}$). This process is carried out in three stages:

1. In the determination of the N_{iso} the Sturges rule [27] is considered, this rule is simple and is adjusted to the number of samples (N) of the spectrum analysed,

$$N_{iso} = 1 + 3.322 \cdot log_{10}(N) \tag{4}$$

2. Calculation of the contour interval,

$$C_i = \frac{Upper_{Boundary} - Threshold}{N_{iso}} \tag{5}$$

3. The value of each isoline ($Isoline_{Value}$) is defined by a set of values, set by the multiples of the contour and threshold interval, without exceeding the upper limit. This relationship is presented below, where k = 0,1,2,3,..., represents the multiple of the spacing value.

$$Isoline_{Value} = Threshold + k \cdot C_i \tag{6}$$

2.2.5 Treatment of the record to be evaluated

As in the construction of the fault evolution maps, the record to be diagnosed is evaluated according to the estimated isoline values. This makes it possible to identify the analysis points associated with the intersection of the isoline values and the amplitude of the frequency under study, as shown in Fig. 4.

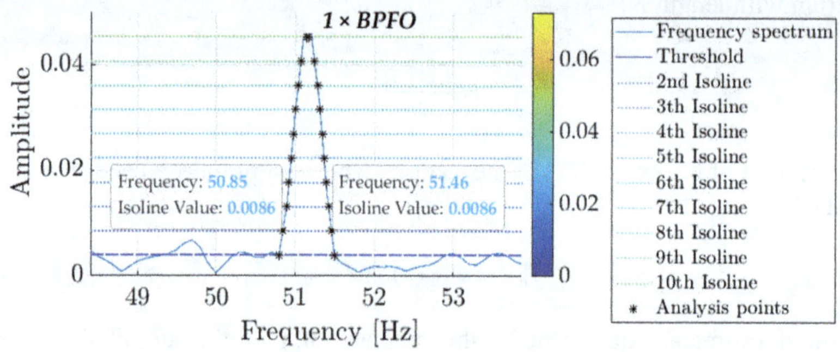

Figure 4: Identification of the analysis points (recording at 500 rpm and fault level F2).

In this way, the analysis points identify two coordinates, frequency and amplitude, associated with each isoline value. Fig. 5 presents the coordinates of two of the analysis points P1 (50.85, 0.0086) and P2 (51.46, 0.0086), associated with the intersection of the fault frequency amplitude with the second isoline.

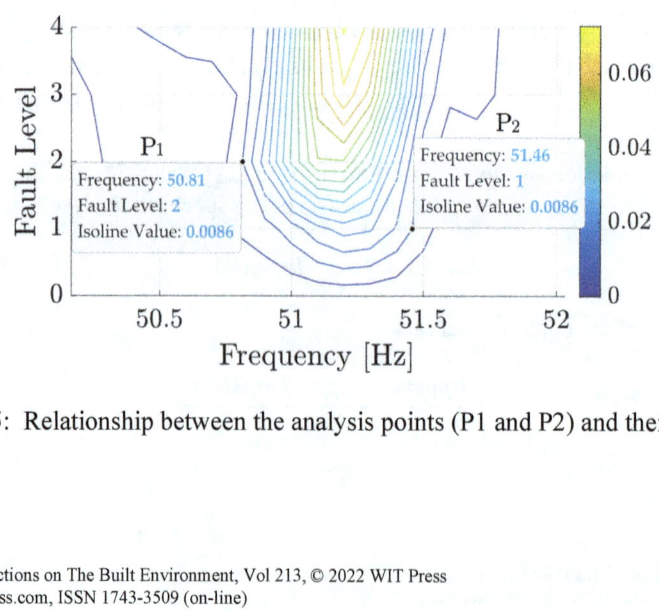

Figure 5: Relationship between the analysis points (P1 and P2) and their isoline.

2.2.6 Fault level diagnosis

It is known beforehand that each of the isolines of the fault evolution map is associated with an amplitude level, and that the points that form it have coordinates in frequency and fault level. Therefore, by defining the isoline of the fault evolution map to which each point of analysis corresponds and identifying its frequency, the relationship with the corresponding fault level is visualised.

Fig. 5 presents the relationship between the analysis points P1 and P2 (see Fig. 4), and the corresponding isoline points of the fault evolution map. This analysis was carried out by frequency approximation. Once the isoline was selected, the frequency coordinate of the analysis points was identified in the coordinates of the isoline points, looking for the corresponding frequency or the closest frequency. From this analysis, a relationship of P1 and P2 was established with a fault level of 2 and 1 respectively.

The isolated analysis of points P1 and P2 could be considered confusing, given their relationship with different fault levels. However, when considering the totality of the analysis points for each harmonic of the fault frequency, the trend over a fault level F2 is clearly observed, as presented in Fig. 6.

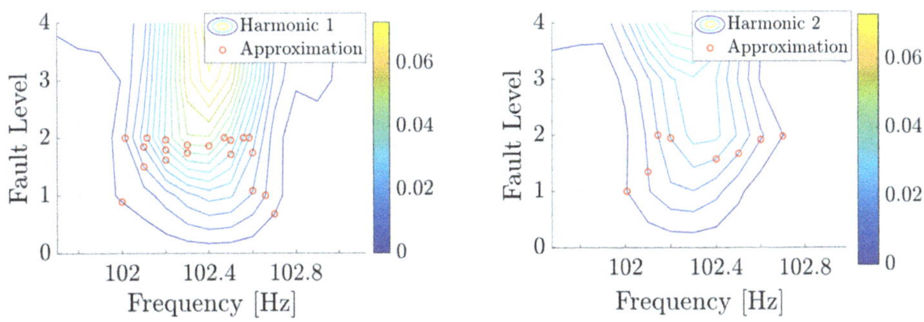

Figure 6: Relationship between the analysis points and the fault evolution map.

As observed in Fig. 6, the diagnosis of a spectrum on a fault evolution map is visually intuitive, as the fault level trend of each harmonic is marked by a point cloud. In the quantification of the fault level trend, central tendency measures, such as mean and median, are considered. Thus, from the data set defined by the point cloud of each harmonic the trend or fault level is established. The evaluation of the trend of the fault level of the spectrum at 500 rpm and labelled with fault level F2 (see Fig. 4), is estimated at 1.93 and 1.87 by means of the mean and median respectively.

3 EXPERIMENTAL DATA

The data set used in this study to evaluate the performance of the proposed methodology was obtained from the bearing test rig of the Railway Technology Research Center (CITEF) [28]. Since the methodology has been devised for the diagnosis of railway axlebox bearings, the bearings in the test rig housings have a similar configuration. Also, the evaluation regimes have been considered according to the angular velocity profile of the wheels of a metro train.

The test bearing used is a double row spherical roller bearing. The records were evaluated at three different speeds (200, 350, 500 rpm). Their characteristic failure frequencies as ball pass frequency inner (BPFI), ball pass frequency outer (BPFO), ball spin frequency (BSF) and fundamental train frequency (FTF), are presented in Table 1.

Table 1: Estimating the level of failure by measures of central tendency.

22205E1KC3				Units
Regime	200	350	500	rpm
BPFO	20.62	36.08	51.54	Hz
BPFI	29.38	51.42	73.46	Hz
BSF	18.01	31.52	45.03	Hz
FTF	1.37	2.41	3.44	Hz

A combined rolling element (RE) and outer race (OR) failure was induced in the bearing, evaluated at five failure levels including the normal state (F0, F1, F2, F3, F4). The generated damage ranged in depth from 0.006 to 0.027 mm for RE, and 0.007 to 0.028 (mm) for OR. Each case study was repeated three times, where the most representative replica was used to construct the failure evolution map.

The data acquisition equipment used is based on low-cost components developed for condition monitoring of rotating machinery [26]. The acceleration signals were obtained at a sampling frequency of 45 kHz. Each record has a length of 45 seconds.

4 RESULTS

This section presents the results of the bearing diagnosis using the proposed methodology. Given the length of each record (45 seconds) and considering the criteria for selecting representative samples, each record was evaluated in a window with a length of 5 seconds, which allows several samples to be available for each record. In addition, with the proposed window length, a frequency resolution of 0.1 Hz is obtained, which guarantees to distinguish between close frequencies. It should be noted that the samples used in the construction of the fault evolution maps are not considered for the diagnosis and validation of the methodology.

Although the records are associated with a combined fault (ORRE), in this study the evaluation of the performance of the methodology focuses on the fault associated with the outer track.

4.1 Use of isolines for spectra evaluation

The arrangement of the isolines that make up the fault evolution map establishes a pattern of scales that allow the amplitudes of the spectrum under study to be analysed.

Fig. 7 presents the use of the isoline values as a scaling pattern on which to evaluate the record under study (record at 500 rpm and fault level F2). As can be seen, the maximum peak of the evaluated spectrum intersects with the tenth isoline. Therefore, from this analysis a pre-diagnosis can be established, concluding that the evaluated spectrum is associated with a considerable fault level, since the maximum amplitude of the fault frequency has reached 66.6% of the isolines of the fault evolution map.

4.2 Diagnostic spectra

Bearing vibration signals are not periodic, but stochastic. Therefore, throughout a record there are segments associated with different energy values for the same fault level. This causes changes in the behaviour of the spectrum, especially in the amplitude of the fault frequency and its harmonics.

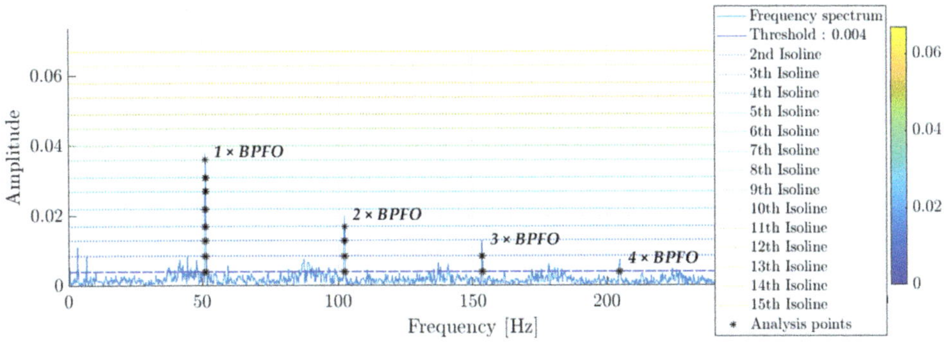

Figure 7: Use of isolines as a fault level scaling pattern (500 rpm recording and fault F2).

Fig. 8 shows two samples of the same record with spectra of different behaviour, at 500 rpm and catalogued with fault level F2. As previously mentioned, the database used corresponds to a combined rolling element (BSF) and outer track (BPFO) fault. Therefore, the spectrum in Fig. 8(a) shows higher energy associated with the BSF component, compared to the spectrum in Fig. 8(b), and vice versa for the BPFO component.

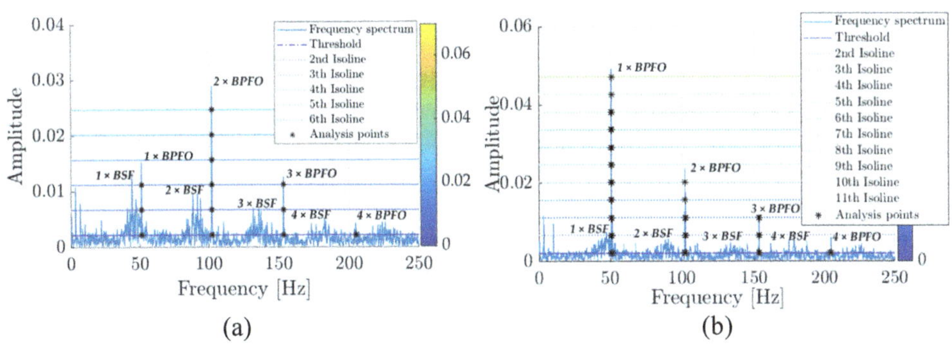

Figure 8: Spectra of two samples (record at 500 rpm and fault F2).

Fig. 9 presents the diagnosis of the spectra presented in Fig. 8. In this figure, despite the differences in the behaviour of the spectrum, the diagnosis has been feasible, which demonstrates the versatility and accuracy of the methodology presented. Fig. 9(a) presents the spectrum diagnostic presented in Fig. 8(a), where the measures of central tendency establish a ratio of 1.95 and 2.08 for the mean and median, which is consistent with the fault level to which more samples correspond. The same is true for the diagnostic spectrum in Fig. 8(a) presented in Fig. 9(a), where a ratio of 2.23 and 2.24 is observed for the mean and median respectively.

4.3 Evaluation of the methodology

In order to estimate the performance of the proposed methodology, the 45 records of the database were diagnosed in their respective fault evolution maps, associated to speeds of 200,

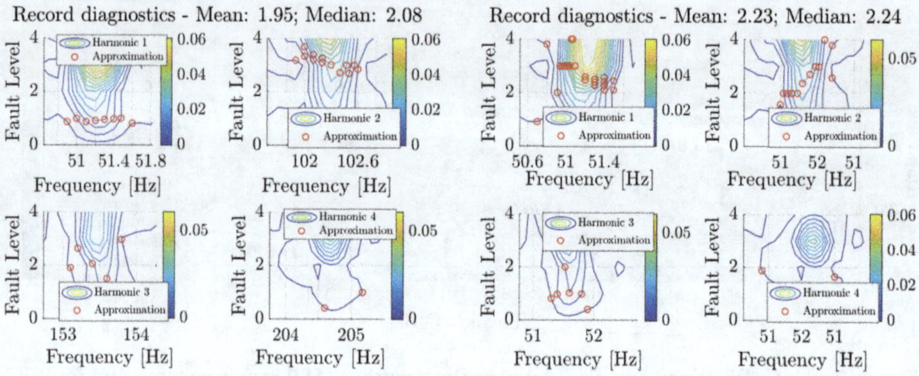

(a) (b)

Figure 9: Spectrum diagnostics.

350 and 500 rpm. In each of the records, five samples (of 5 seconds) have been identified that meet the conditions presented in Section 2.3.2. Therefore, the fault evolution maps associated with each rpm will be evaluated using 75 samples, comprising the five fault levels (F0, F1, F2, F3, F4) analysed, including the normal state.

Fig. 10 presents the confusion matrices to evaluate the measures of central tendency used in the estimation of the corresponding failure level. Fig. 10(a) shows that the "mean" has a higher accuracy in the diagnosis of the different samples, reaching 79.11% correct. The samples with failure level F0, F1 and F2 present an error in diagnosis of 13.3, 6.7% and 15.6% respectively. For the misdiagnosed samples, samples with fault level F0 and F1 are associated with a higher fault level, while samples with fault F2 are associated with a lower and higher fault level. In the case of the samples with fault F3, all have been correctly diagnosed. Finally, the samples with fault level F4 are the most problematic, with 68.9% of failures in the diagnosis. A similar behaviour is observed in the median confusion matrix Fig. 10(b), reaching 78.22% correct.

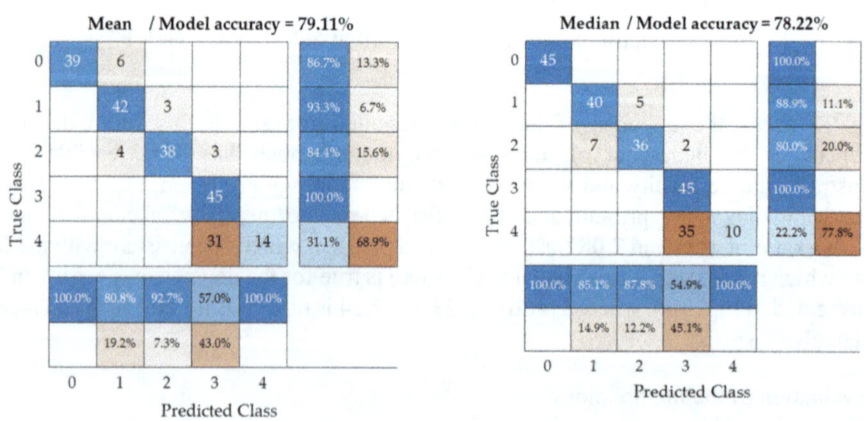

(a) (b)

Figure 10: Confusion matrix of measures of central tendency. (a) Mean; and (b) Median.

5 CONCLUSIONS

This paper documents the evaluation of the bearing diagnosis methodology proposed in Soto-Ocampo et al. [14]. It concludes that the implementation of contour maps allows the construction of maps that characterise the evolution of a fault. In addition, it allows future records to be evaluated and associated to a fault level according to the behaviour of the fault frequency and harmonics.

Regarding the process of evaluation and diagnosis of a record, two phases have been distinguished. The first is associated with the consideration of the value of the isolines as a scale map to evaluate the amplitudes of the fault frequency and harmonics of the spectrum under analysis. In this way, a visual analysis of the trend of the amplitudes is carried out, to subsequently carry out the diagnosis and establish the corresponding fault level. In the second phase, the relationship between the analysis points and the coordinates (frequency, amplitude and fault level) of the points of the isolines that make up the fault evolution map can be seen. This, based on the behaviour of the fault frequency amplitudes and harmonics, establishes the corresponding fault level when implementing the measures of central tendency.

The methodology has been validated using 225 samples associated with 45 vibration records obtained from a test bench. In the evaluation of the methodology, an accuracy of around 79% has been observed. It should be noted that this value was obtained by processing all the analysis points of 6 harmonics. Therefore, if an analysis to identify which of the harmonics has the highest relationship with the fault level is considered, the accuracy would be improved. This will be considered in future works.

REFERENCES

[1] Behzad, M., Feizhoseini, S., Arghand, H.A., Davoodabadi, A. & Mba, D., Failure threshold determination of rolling element bearings using vibration fluctuation and failure modes. *Appl. Sci.*, **11**, p. 160, 2021. DOI: 10.3390/app11010160.

[2] Shao, H., Jiang, H., Lin, Y. & Li, X., A novel method for intelligent fault diagnosis of rolling bearings using ensemble deep auto-encoders. *Mech. Syst. Signal Process*, **102**, pp. 278–297, 2018. DOI: 10.1016/j.ymssp.2017.09.026.

[3] Zhang, W., Li, C., Peng, G., Chen, Y. & Zhang, Z., A deep convolutional neural network with new training methods for bearing fault diagnosis under noisy environment and different working load. *Mech. Syst. Signal Process*, **100**, pp. 439–453, 2018. DOI: 10.1016/j.ymssp.2017.06.022.

[4] Liu, R., Yang, B., Zio, E. & Chen, X., Artificial intelligence for fault diagnosis of rotating machinery: A review. *Mech. Syst. Signal Process*, **108**, pp. 33–47, 2018. DOI: 10.1016/j.ymssp.2018.02.016.

[5] Moshrefzadeh, A., Condition monitoring and intelligent diagnosis of rolling element bearings under constant/variable load and speed conditions. *Mech. Syst. Signal Process*, **149**, 107153, 2021. DOI: 10.1016/j.ymssp.2020.107153.

[6] Randall, R.B. & Antoni, J., Rolling element bearing diagnostics: A tutorial. *Mech. Syst. Signal Process*, **25**, pp. 485–520, 2011. DOI: 10.1016/j.ymssp.2010.07.017.

[7] Brusa, E., Bruzzone, F., Delprete, C., Di Maggio, L.G. & Rosso, C., Health indicators construction for damage level assessment in bearing diagnostics: A proposal of an energetic approach based on envelope analysis. *Appl. Sci.*, **10**, p. 8131, 2020. DOI: 10.3390/app10228131.

[8] Hamadache, M., Jung, J.H., Park, J. & Youn, B.D., A comprehensive review of artificial intelligence-based approaches for rolling element bearing PHM: Shallow and deep learning. *JMST Adv.*, **1**, pp. 125–151, 2019. DOI: 10.1007/s42791-019-0016-y.

[9] Liu, Z.-H., Lu, B.-L., Wei, H.-L., Chen, L., Li, X.-H. & Ratsch, M., Deep adversarial domain adaptation model for bearing fault diagnosis. *IEEE Trans. Syst. Man Cybern. Syst.*, pp. 1–10, 2020. DOI: 10.1109/TSMC.2019.2932000.

[10] Sun, J., Yan, C. & Wen, J., Intelligent bearing fault diagnosis method combining compressed data acquisition and deep learning. *IEEE Trans. Instrum. Meas.*, **67**, pp. 185–195, 2018. DOI: 10.1109/TIM.2017.2759418.

[11] Lei, Y., Jia, F., Lin, J., Xing, S. & Ding, S.X., An intelligent fault diagnosis method using unsupervised feature learning towards mechanical big data. *IEEE Trans. Ind. Electron.*, **63**, pp. 3137–3147, 2016. DOI: 10.1109/TIE.2016.2519325.

[12] Kwak, D.-H., Lee, D.-H., Ahn, J.-H. & Koh, B.-H., Fault detection of roller-bearings using signal processing and optimization algorithms. *Sensors*, **14**, pp. 283–298, 2013. DOI: 10.3390/s140100283.

[13] Qiu, H., Lee, J., Lin, J. & Yu, G., Robust performance degradation assessment methods for enhanced rolling element bearing prognostics. *Adv. Eng. Inform.*, **17**, pp. 127–140, 2003. DOI: 10.1016/j.aei.2004.08.001.

[14] Soto-Ocampo, C.R., Cano-Moreno, J.D., Mera, J.M. & Maroto, J., Bearing severity fault evaluation using contour maps: Case study. *Appl. Sci.*, **11**, p. 6452, 2021. DOI: 10.3390/app11146452.

[15] Ghafari, S.H., A fault diagnosis system for rotary machinery supported by rolling element bearings. PhD dissertation, University of Waterloo, 2007.

[16] Yu, K., Lin, T.R., Tan, J. & Ma, H., An adaptive sensitive frequency band selection method for empirical wavelet transform and its application in bearing fault diagnosis. *Measurement*, **134**, pp. 375–384, 2019. DOI: 10.1016/j.measurement.2018.10.086.

[17] Gupta, P. & Pradhan, M.K., Fault detection analysis in rolling element bearing: A review. *Mater. Today Proc.*, **4**, pp. 2085–2094, 2017. DOI: 10.1016/j.matpr.2017.02.054.

[18] Guilbert, E., Multi-level representation of terrain features on a contour map. *GeoInformatica*, **17**, pp. 301–324, 2013. DOI: 10.1007/s10707-012-0153-z.

[19] Jeong, M.-G., Lee, E.-B., Lee, M. & Jung, J.-Y., Multi-criteria route planning with risk contour map for smart navigation. *Ocean Eng.*, **172**, pp. 72–85, 2019. DOI: 10.1016/j.oceaneng.2018.11.050.

[20] Hahmann, T. & Usery, E.L., What is in a contour map? S.I. Fabrikant, M. Raubal, M. Bertolotto, C. Davies, S. Freundschuh, S. Bell (eds), Springer: Cham, 2015.

[21] Fernández-Francos, D., Martínez-Rego, D., Fontenla-Romero, O. & Alonso-Betanzos, A., Automatic bearing fault diagnosis based on one-class ν-SVM. *Comput. Ind. Eng.*, **64**, pp. 357–365, 2013. DOI: 10.1016/j.cie.2012.10.013.

[22] Smith, W.A. & Randall, R.B., Rolling element bearing diagnostics using the Case Western Reserve University data: A benchmark study. *Mech. Syst. Signal Process*, **64–65**, pp. 100–131, 2015. DOI: 10.1016/j.ymssp.2015.04.021.

[23] IS/ISO 13373-2, Condition monitoring and diagnostics of machines: Vibration condition monitoring, Part 2: Processing analysis and presentation of vibration data. Bureau of Indian Standards: New Delhi, India, p. 38, 2005.

[24] Samanta, B. & Al-Balushi, K.R., Artificial neural network based fault diagnostics of rolling element bearings using time-domain features. *Mech. Syst. Signal Process*, **17**, pp. 317–328, 2003. DOI: 10.1006/mssp.2001.1462.

[25] Liu, Z., Jin, Y., Zuo, M.J. & Peng, D., ACCUGRAM: A novel approach based on classification to frequency band selection for rotating machinery fault diagnosis. *ISA Trans.*, **95**, pp. 346–357, 2019. DOI: 10.1016/j.isatra.2019.05.007.

[26] Soto-Ocampo, C.R., Mera, J.M., Cano-Moreno, J.D. & Garcia-Bernardo, J.L., Low-cost, high-frequency, data acquisition system for condition monitoring of rotating machinery through vibration analysis-case study. *Sensors*, **20**, p. 3493, 2020. DOI: 10.3390/s20123493.
[27] Rizzo, M.L., *Statistical Computing with R*, CRC Press: Ohio, 2007.
[28] Soto-Ocampo, C.R., Cano-Moreno, J.D., Mera, J.M. & Maroto, J., Bearing database: Combined failure, 2021. DOI: 10.5281/zenodo.5084405.

STUDY ON THE INFLUENCE OF THE MODELLING STRATEGY IN THE CALCULATION OF THE WORN PROFILE OF RAILWAY WHEELS

NICOLA BOSSO[*], MATTEO MAGELLI[†] & NICOLÒ ZAMPIERI[‡]
Politecnico di Torino, Department of Mechanical and Aerospace Engineering, Italy

ABSTRACT
As changes in the wheel and rail profiles strongly affect vehicle dynamics, running stability and safety, maintenance operations such as wheel turning and rail grinding are necessary. The availability of numerical models for wear prediction can be a huge support to optimize the scheduling of such operations. Thanks to the computational power of modern computer architectures, allowing parallelization and co-simulation, the typical strategy is based on a dynamic module performing the vehicle dynamics simulation, usually developed in commercial multibody (MB) software packages, and on a wear module for the calculation of the worn material. The latter can be implemented in the same MB code or in a separate software, such as Matlab/Simulink, which exchanges data with the MB code. Wear modules rely on wear laws relating the amount of worn material to the normal load and sliding distance or to the energy dissipated at the contact interface. Both types of law can be applied locally, calculating the worn depth in each cell of the discretized contact patch from the contact pressures and sliding speeds, or globally, hence calculating the worn volume or mass starting from the global forces and creepages. In the latter case, the worn material is calculated on the whole contact patch rather than only on the slip zone, and a proper distribution is required to relate the worn depth to the worn volume. The present work aims to further investigate the differences between the two approaches in the computed worn profiles in a specific case study in terms of reference vehicle and track, carrying out the dynamic simulations through the Simpack MB code. The paper is intended to highlight the differences in both the numerical results and computational efforts, comparing the wear computed by a local model with the outputs of the Simpack wear module.
Keywords: wheel wear, worn profiles, wheel–rail tribology, wheel–rail contact, Archard wear law, dynamic simulation, multibody simulation.

1 INTRODUCTION

Uniform wear, i.e., the change in the wheel transversal profile shape due to wear, has a strong impact on the running behaviour of railway vehicles. To ensure safety, the wheel profiles undergo periodical maintenance so that the original profile shape can be restored thanks to machining operations. Such maintenance operations are typically scheduled at fixed travelled distances, but this strategy neither prevents possible premature failures of the wheel nor it ensures that turning is indeed necessary when performed. Therefore, modelling the wear of the wheel transversal profile is crucial to predict the damage of the wheels and to optimally schedule the maintenance interventions, with obvious economic benefits.

Currently, the typical strategy adopted to predict wear of wheel profiles is based on numerical tools that include a module for the vehicle-track dynamic simulation, usually implemented in a commercial multibody (MB) software package, and a module that computes the worn profile starting from the outputs of the dynamic simulation [1]. In the past, the wear module was implemented in the MB code used for the dynamic simulation in

[*] *ORCID: https://orcid.org/0000-0002-5433-6365*
[†] *ORCID: https://orcid.org/0000-0002-2962-7873*
[‡] *ORCID: https://orcid.org/0000-0002-9197-1966*

WIT Transactions on The Built Environment, Vol 213, © 2022 WIT Press
www.witpress.com, ISSN 1743-3509 (on-line)
doi:10.2495/CR220061

the form of a user-written routine, while nowadays several wear computation tools rely on co-simulation approaches, with the wear module implemented in a different computational environment [2]. Moreover, all commercial MB codes are currently provided with add-ons for the calculation of the wheel worn profile. These built-in modules ensure a fast setting of the wear computation thanks to user-friendly graphical interfaces (GUIs). Commonly, wear is computed at discrete steps, so that the wheel profile is considered unchanged during a single dynamic simulation, but at the end of each step of the wear calculation the profile is updated and fed back to the dynamic simulation module. This strategy is far more accurate with respect to the simplified approaches adopted in the past, in which the wheel profile was updated at discrete steps without launching new dynamic simulations [3], [4].

The amount of worn material is computed as a function of the main contact patch quantities by means of wear laws obtained from experimental campaigns. Two main types of wear laws are available in the literature, namely laws that relate the worn material to the normal load acting on the contact patch and laws that relate wear to the dissipated energy. The most common wear law based on the normal load is the Archard law [5], [6], while examples of wear laws based on the dissipated energy include equations proposed by British Railway Centre (BRR) [7], University of Sheffield (USFD) [8], Krause and Poll [9] and Zobory [10].

Most of the above-mentioned wear laws can be applied either globally or locally. In the first case, the worn material is computed directly from the global forces and creepages acting at the contact patch, while with the second approach, the wear depth is computed in each cell of the contact patch grid. Clearly, the first approach ensures a faster computation, but it requires the development of a strategy to spread the worn material along the profile transversal coordinate. On the other hand, the second solution allows to directly compute the wear depth locally, but it demands a local contact module that performs the discretization of the contact patch to obtain the distribution of the tangential pressures and slip velocities.

In a recent paper, Peng et al. [11] suggested that a global application of the wear laws is not suitable when the wear computation focuses on irregular wear along the circumferential direction ("wheel polygonization"), due to the generation of sharp points in the wear depth distribution. Nonetheless, for what concerns uniform wear of the wheel profile, different works in the literature indicate that the global approach might be the best compromise solution in a trade-off between numerical accuracy and computational efficiency. Researchers from USFD and Alstom Ferroviaria found that that the wheel worn transversal profiles computed with local and global applications of the USFD law were in good agreement with each other, with a maximum error of 20% [12]. Nevertheless, the investigation was not extended to other wear laws, therefore there is still a lack of knowledge for what concerns different equations.

Furthermore, based on the authors' experience and industrial collaborations, there is still a big need to assess the validity of the wear computed by the built-in modules implemented in commercial MB codes. This aspect was not addressed by USFD and ALSTOM researchers, as both global and local approaches were implemented in a post-processing in-house Matlab routine. To gain further insights into the problem, Ignesti et al. [13] compared the results computed by the Simpack wear module, which adopts a global approach, with the outputs of a local wear model implemented in a user-written Matlab routine. The authors of the cited reference found a generally good agreement between the two models, with Simpack predicting slightly larger wear. However, the main drawback of this work is that while the Simpack global wear model used the Krause–Poll law, the local wear model relied on the USFD wear law. Therefore, the cited reference did not directly compare the implementation of the same wear law in a global application of a MB code and in a local application in a user-written routine.

The present work aims at gaining a better understanding of the differences due to global and local applications of wear laws in the calculation of the wheel worn profile, adopting the Simpack wear module as the reference for the global calculation. The wear law considered in the present paper is the Archard wear law in the implementation of the Swedish Royal Institute of Technology (KTH). Such law is available in the Simpack wear module and it can be applied locally.

Often, when using local approaches, the dynamic simulation calculates the wheel–rail forces by means of fast heuristic methods [14]–[16], while the discretization of the contact patch is carried out only by the local contact model implemented in the wear module. Nonetheless, this approach can lead to inconsistent results as different algorithms for the computation of the tangential forces rely on different relations between forces and creepages, and correction factors should be introduced in the local contact model to improve accuracy [17], [18]. Therefore, in the present paper, the tangential forces are computed implementing the FASTSIM [19] algorithm in both the dynamic simulation and in the local wear model.

The paper is organised as follows. The next section describes the numerical model of the vehicle and track considered in the present work, also giving focus to the algorithms adopted to compute the worn profile with global and local approaches. Then, the results of the proposed numerical activity are shown and discussed, and finally a last section highlights the main conclusions and suggests possible future developments of the proposed activity.

2 NUMERICAL MODEL

2.1 Vehicle-track dynamic model

The vehicle considered in the present work is the diesel powered Aln 663 railcar, which is a vehicle running mainly on secondary lines. The railcar is equipped with a hydromechanical 5-gear manual transmission, and it reaches a maximum speed of 120 km/h. The vehicle includes two FIAT bogies, with primary and secondary suspensions realized with helical springs. For each bogie, the inner wheelset is powered, while the outer one is trailed.

The railcar model was developed in the Simpack MB software package, and it consists of one coach, two bolsters, two bogie frames, four wheelsets and eight axle-boxes. A sketch of the model structure is given in Fig. 1. Each axle-box features a single degree of freedom (d.o.f.), i.e., the relative rotation with respect to the corresponding wheelset, and it is connected to the bogie frame via two force elements. The first force element is a flexicoil spring, with axial and shear stiffnesses, while the second force element is used to simulate the rubber joint connecting the axle-box control arm to the bogie frame. The secondary suspension is simulated by introducing another set of flexicoil springs, that connect the bogie frame to the bolster. Each bolster is rigidly connected to the railcar coach via proper bushing elements, with large stiffness values along each direction except for the rotation along the vertical direction, which is free. Moreover, the secondary suspension incudes two lateral bumpstops that provide a reaction force when the lateral displacement between the bolster and the bogie frame exceeds a prescribed threshold value. Finally, two lateral and two vertical linear dampers are added between each bolster and bogie frame, as a part of the secondary suspension.

Since the scope of the present work is the comparison between the local and global approaches in the calculation of the worn wheel profile, the simulated track is a simplified

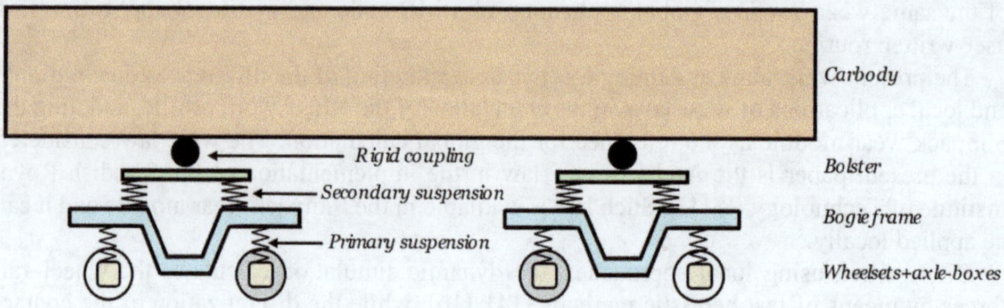

Figure 1: Sketch of the MB model architecture (powered wheelsets are coloured in grey).

track rather than a real track. The simplified track includes four different curves, with prescribed superelevation values, that are faced in both left and right-hand direction. All curves are separated by straight sections. Fig. 2 shows the curve radius along the track and the speed profile superimposed to the vehicle, while Table 1 presents the values of curve radius and superelevation for each curve. To directly compare the global and local approaches in wear computation, the track is modelled without irregularities and the rail profiles (UIC60) are considered as unworn along the whole reference track length. Please note that since curves are faced in both left and right-hand direction and that the wheel profiles (S1002) are considered as unchanged during the simulation, the wear of the left and right wheels belonging to the same wheelset is extremely similar. In the present work, wear is computed on the right wheel of the leading wheelset, which is a non-powered axle. The speed profile is followed by applying braking torques to the powered axles of the vehicle, thus simulating dynamic braking operations. The value of these torques is computed during the simulation taking into consideration the adhesion limit.

The determination of the wheel–rail contact points and the solution of the normal problem, i.e., the computation of the normal force and of the shape and size of the contact patch, is

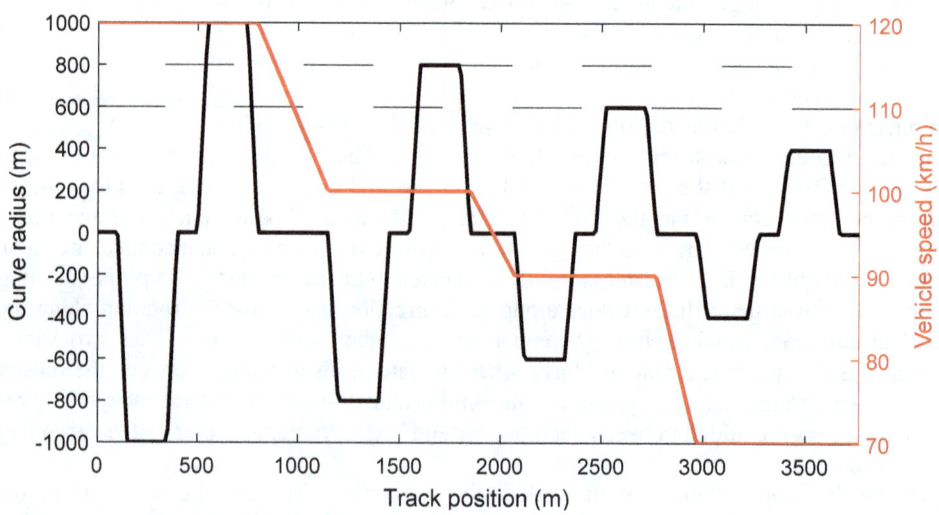

Figure 2: Speed profile and curve radius along the simulated track.

Table 1: Curves included in the simulated simplified track.

Curve radius (m)	Main curve parameters	
	Superelevation (mm)	Vehicle speed (km/h)
1000	150	120
800	150	100
600	160	90
400	160	70

carried out by means of Simpack built-in algorithms. The normal problem is solved using the equivalent elastic approach [20], which transforms the actual shape of the contact patch, obtained using the Kik–Piotrowski method [21], into an equivalent ellipse. The tangential problem, i.e., the calculation of the tangential forces, is solved using the FASTSIM algorithm by Kalker, directly available in Simpack. The profiles of wheels and rails are the standard S1002 and UIC60 profiles, respectively, and the friction coefficient is assumed constant and equal to 0.4, so that falling friction [22]–[24] and adhesion recovery phenomena [25]–[27] as well as curve lubrication are neglected.

2.2 Wear computation

The worn wheel profile is computed using the Archard wear law in both global and local forms. The global computation of wear is performed using the Simpack wear module, while the local computation is carried out by means of a dedicated Matlab routine, which reads the contact patch data obtained from the dynamic simulation.

The Simpack wear module computes the worn volume ΔW in each contact point position for each time step according to eqn (1), in which N is the normal load, H is the hardness of the softer material, s is the total sliding distance and k_{Arch} is the wear coefficient, which is a function of sliding speed and contact pressure. The wear coefficient is obtained from the KTH wear map as a function of the contact pressure and of the sliding speed, with a reduction of the nominal values by a factor 7 to account for natural contamination at the wheel–rail contact, as suggested by Jendel [28] and Jendel and Berg [29]. Fig. 3 shows the Archard wear map and the wear coefficients adopted in the present work. The hardness of the wheel and rail steels is assumed to be equal to 300 HB.

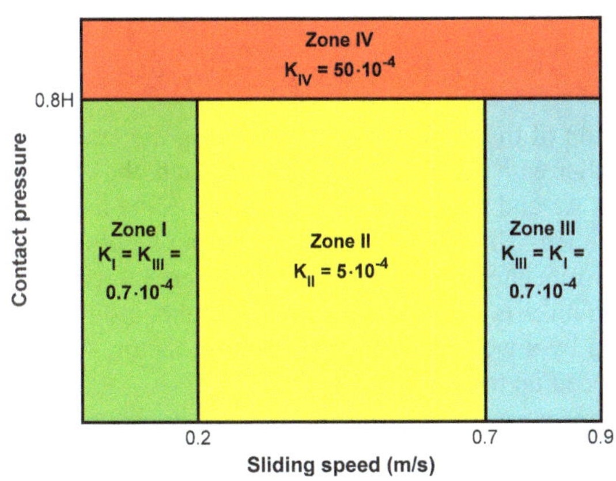

Figure 3: Archard map adopted in the present work.

When the Archard law is applied globally in the form of eqn (1), a distribution of the normal wear depth along the contact patch lateral coordinate must be assumed a priori. The algorithm implemented in the Simpack wear module is transparent for the user, as it is intellectual property of the software house. However, from the total worn volume, Simpack calculates the removed area in a radial section of the wheel ΔA with eqn (2), in which R_{cp} is the wheel radius at the contact point position. Finally, the normal worn depth Δz_n in each lateral position of the contact patch y is calculated introducing an a priori distribution, which unfortunately is not specified by the software developers. In the present work, a global wear algorithm was developed and implemented in a dedicated Matlab routine to compare its results with the outputs of the Simpack wear module. The normal wear depth distribution considered in the in-house Matlab algorithm is semi-elliptic, see eqn (3), in which b is the lateral semi-axis of the contact ellipse and δ is the contact angle.

$$\Delta W = k_{Arch}\frac{Ns}{H}, \tag{1}$$

$$\Delta A = \frac{\Delta W}{2\pi R_{cp}}, \tag{2}$$

$$\Delta z_n(y) = \frac{2}{\pi}\frac{\Delta A}{b\cos\delta}\sqrt{1-\left({}^{y}/_{b}\right)^2}. \tag{3}$$

To avoid the introduction of an a priori distribution of the wear depth along the contact patch and to increase the numerical accuracy, the Archard wear law can be applied locally in the form of eqn (4) to directly compute the normal wear depth Δz_n in each point of the contact patch, identified by the local coordinate set (x,y), as a function of the normal contact pressure p_z and of the sliding distance s_{el} of an element in the contact patch grid. Please note that the local form of Archard law expressed by eqn (4) is derived from eqn (1) by dividing the left-hand and right-hand sides by the area of an element in the contact patch grid. The sliding distance and sliding speed in each element of the contact patch are computed from by means of a dedicated Matlab function implementing the FASTSIM algorithm.

$$\Delta z_n(x,y) = k_{Arch}\frac{p_z(x,y)s_{el}(x,y)}{H}. \tag{4}$$

To obtain a uniform wheel worn profile, the normal depth distribution is summed along each longitudinal strip and then spread along the circumferential direction, see eqn (5), in which Σ_x represents the summation along the longitudinal strip, V_{ref} is the wheel translational speed and finally Δt is the sampling time of the output results.

$$\Delta z_n(y) = \frac{\Sigma_x \Delta z_n(x,y)}{2\pi R_{cp}}\cdot V_{ref}\Delta t. \tag{5}$$

Once the distribution of the normal wear depth along the lateral coordinate of the wheel profile is obtained, either with the local or global approach, the wear depths along the lateral and vertical directions ΔY and ΔZ can be calculated according to eqns (6) and (7), in which γ is the local profile gradient. Finally, the worn profile can be obtained by applying the worn depths to the proper profile lateral coordinates, and the vertical wear depth can be interpolated with respect to the original array storing the profile lateral coordinate. The vertical wear depth can then be multiplied by a wear multiplier or distance factor, which magnifies the amount of worn material to speed up the simulation time.

$$\Delta Y = \Delta z_n\frac{1}{\sqrt{1+\gamma^2}}, \tag{6}$$

$$\Delta Z = \Delta z_n\frac{\gamma}{\sqrt{1+\gamma^2}}. \tag{7}$$

3 RESULTS

The current section presents the results of the investigation on the effects of local and global approaches in the computation of the wheel worn profiles. The dynamic simulation was run considering the vehicle and track described in the previous section, and the computation of the worn profile was carried out using both the Simpack wear module, implementing a global algorithm, and the dedicated Matlab routine for the direct computation of the worn depth in each cell of the contact patch. Furthermore, an additional computation of the worn profile was carried out with the in-house Matlab global wear model, relying on a semi-elliptic distribution of the normal wear depth along the contact patch lateral direction. The in-house global model was developed as an alternative to the Simpack wear module with the aim to be used in future works in which the worn profile is fed back to the dynamic simulation, in order to improve the numerical stability of the computation, using a strategy similar to the one described by Bosso and Zampieri [2].

The wear depth computed from the dynamic simulation was magnified introducing a wear multiplier equal to 20, as if the wear computed on the simulated track, with a length of 3.77 km, could be extended to a track with a length of 75.4 km. Obviously, the introduction of wear multipliers can lead to a loss of accuracy of the method and to numerical instabilities, because wear is always assigned to the same positions on the wheel profile. Nonetheless, as the goal of the present work is the comparison between global and local approaches in the same scenario, the wear multiplier is just adopted as a mean to increase the wear depth.

Fig. 4 shows the results of the wear computation performed with the three models, namely the Simpack global module, the in-house Matlab global model and the in-house Matlab local model, while Table 2 presents the worn volume computed by the three methods. Please note that the Simpack wear module does not provide the value of the total worn volume as an output, while the local algorithm directly provides the wear depth rather than the removed volume. Nonetheless, the worn volume can be estimated from the Z coordinates of the original (Z_{or}) and worn (Z_{worn}) profiles according to eqn (8), in which Y_s and Y_f are the limit coordinates of the wheel profile and R_w is the wheel radius evaluated in each lateral position Y.

$$\Delta W = \int_{Y_s}^{Y_f} [Z_{or}(Y) - Z_{worn}(Y)] \cdot 2\pi R_w(Y) dY. \tag{8}$$

As noticeable from Fig. 4(a), all three models compute the maximum wear depth in the zone near the flange, where large creepage values arise during curve negotiation. Fig. 4(b) shows a zoomed view in the flange zone, while Fig. 4(c) presents a zoom in the tread zone. The local model is the one that computes the largest peak in the flange zone, while in the tread zone, the global approaches calculate higher values of wear depth, and this explains why the local model is the one that computes the lowest worn volume. The explanation to this behaviour can be given by observing the wear regime calculated in each element of the contact patch grid for a contact position in the flange zone, see Fig. 5(a), and for a contact position in the tread zone, see Fig. 5(b).

The wear regime computed for both cases by the global wear model corresponds to zone I of the KTH wear map, see Fig. 3. As shown in Fig. 5(a), in the flange contact point, one element in the contact patch falls in the catastrophic regime. As the coefficient for the catastrophic regime is 10 times higher with respect to the coefficient of the mild zone, a local generation of catastrophic wear can indeed lead to a wear peak. On the other hand, in the tread contact, see Fig. 5(b), a large portion of the contact patch is in full adhesion conditions, and wear zone I is detected for a small number of elements, while the global wear model

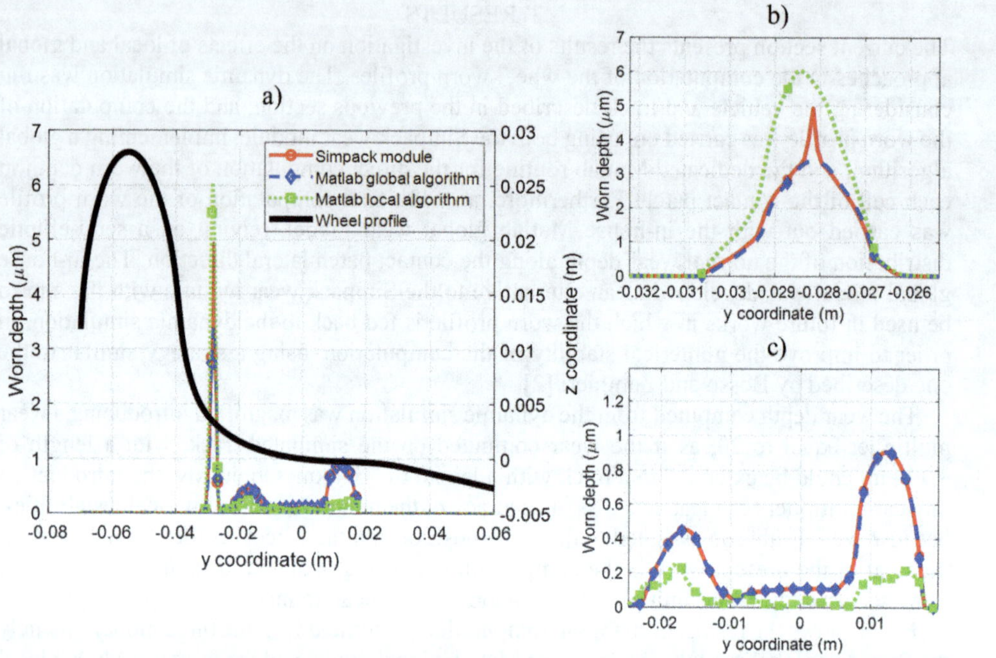

Figure 4: Results of the wear computation. (a) Wear depth along the lateral coordinate; (b) Zoomed view in the flange zone; and (c) Zoomed view in the tread zone.

Table 2: Worn volume computed by the three algorithms.

Model	Worn volume (mm^3)
Simpack wear module	57.9
Matlab global model	56.3
Matlab local model	47.0

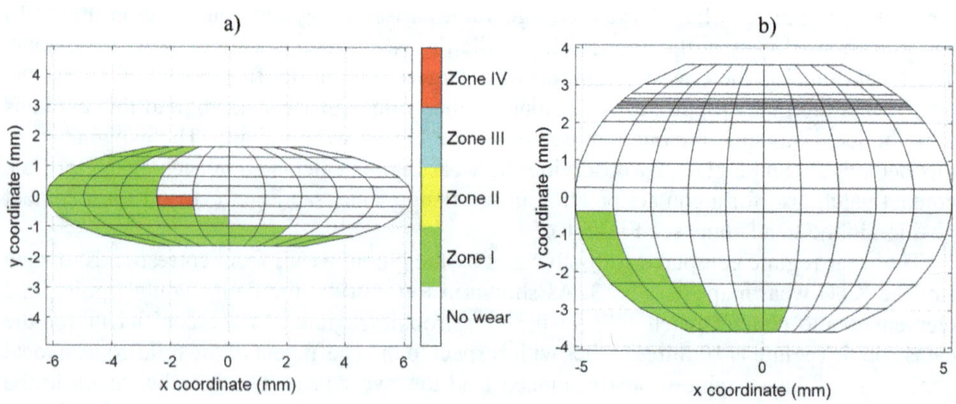

Figure 5: Wear regime computed in the contact patch. (a) Contact near the flange; and (b) Contact in the tread zone.

considers a wear loss on the whole patch. Therefore, the wear depth computed with the local approach is lower with respect to the wear depth computed with the global model for a contact position in the tread zone. Please note that another source of discrepancy between the global and local approaches is the assumption of the distribution of the traction bound. In the global approach, the Hertzian pressure is used to determine the wear regime, while in the local approach, a parabolic distribution is assumed. The parabolic distribution is preferred over the elliptic one as it gives a more accurate division between the adhesion and slip zone in the contact patch when using the FASTSIM algorithm [30].

Focusing again on Fig. 4, the global model developed by the authors is in excellent agreement with the wear depth provided by Simpack in the tread zone, while in the flange zone the Matlab global algorithm misses the wear peak computed by the Simpack algorithm at the lateral position of −0.028 m. This discrepancy can be mainly related (but not limited) to the two possible reasons listed below:

1. The a priori distribution of the wear depth adopted by the Simpack wear module is not known and it may differ from the semi-elliptic distribution implemented in the in-house Matlab wear module, especially in case the Simpack module considers the penetration distribution and the real shape of the contact patch.
2. The Matlab global wear routine uses interpolation strategies that may differ with respect to the ones adopted by the Simpack algorithm.

Finally, for what concerns the computational times, several runs were launched with both the Matlab global and local algorithms, as the code is not run in real-time, and the global method proved to ensure a speedup by a factor equal to 1.58. Obviously, the global method is faster because it saves the time required to discretize the contact patch.

4 CONCLUSIONS

The main outcomes of the numerical activity presented in the previous sections are summarized in the following bulleted list.

- The application of the Archard wear law in the global form overestimates wear in the tread zone, while slightly underestimating wear in the flange.
- The generation of catastrophic wear in even a small number of elements in the contact patch grid can lead to high wear peaks, because the wear coefficient in the catastrophic regime is ten times higher compared to the wear coefficient in the mild regime.
- In the tread zone, the global approach calculates wear on the whole extension of the contact patch, but a local analysis shows that typically only a small number of elements produces wear, as most of the contact patch is in full adhesion.
- The global method developed by the authors provides results in good agreement with the outputs of the Simpack wear module, although in the flange zone a wear peak is missed, probably due to differences in the interpolation strategies and in the wear depth distributions.
- The global approach speeds up the computation by a factor equal to approximately 1.58 compared to the local method. As the local approach is clearly more accurate, because it distinguishes between slip and adhesion zones in the contact patch and it directly computes the wear depth, the local approach is the better choice when the goal of the simulation is a detailed prediction of the wheel life. On the other hand, if the computation only aims at assessing the influence of several parameters on wear, the global method can be a reliable solution to ensure fast simulation times.

To gain a better understanding of the problem, further investigations, should be carried out, see the bulleted list below.

- The numerical activity performed in the context of the present work should be extended to consider different types of vehicles and different track layouts.
- The comparison between local and global approaches should be extended to the Krause–Poll law, which is the energy-based wear law available in Simpack. To the authors' knowledge, the adoption of the Krause–Poll law in local form is currently not witnessed in the literature, but the authors recognize that this wear equation can be easily written in local form if the dissipated energy is computed locally in each cell of the contact patch grid.
- Numerical simulations relying on a loop of dynamic simulations with worn profiles should be performed, to investigate how the differences between local and global approaches increase during the simulation.

REFERENCES

[1] Bosso, N., Magelli, M. & Zampieri, N., Simulation of wheel and rail profile wear: A Review of numerical models. *Railway Engineering Science*, in print.

[2] Bosso, N. & Zampieri, N., Numerical stability of co-simulation approaches to evaluate wheel profile evolution due to wear. *International Journal of Rail Transportation,* **8**(2), pp. 159–179, 2020. DOI: 10.1080/23248378.2019.1672588.

[3] Abeidi, A.S., Bosso, N., Gugliotta, A. & Somà, A., Numerical simulation of wear in railway wheel profiles. *Proceedings of the 8th Biennial ASME Conference on Engineering Systems Design and Analysis, ESDA2006*, pp. 963–977, 2006. DOI: 10.1115/ESDA2006-95571.

[4] Bosso, N., Gugliotta, A. & Abeidi, A.S., Influence of vehicle dynamics on wear of railway wheel profiles. *International Journal of Applied Engineering Research,* **13**(6), pp. 3540–3549, 2018.

[5] Archard, J.F., Contact and rubbing of flat surfaces. *Journal of Applied Physics,* **24**(8), pp. 981–988, 1953. DOI: 10.1063/1.1721448.

[6] Archard, J.F., Hirst, W. & Allibone, T.E., The wear of metals under unlubricated conditions. *Proceedings of the Royal Society of London Series A: Mathematical and Physical Sciences*, **236**(1206), pp. 397–410, 1956. DOI: 10.1098/rspa.1956.0144.

[7] McEwen, I.J. & Harvey, R.F., Interpretation of wheel/rail wear numbers. Railway Technical Centre, Report No. TM VDY 004, 1986.

[8] Lewis, R. et al., Integrating dynamics and wear modelling to predict railway wheel profile evolution. Presented at the *6th International Conference on Contact Mechanics and Wear of Rail/Wheel Systems: CM2003*, Gothenburg, Sweden, 2003.

[9] Krause, H. & Poll, G., Wear of wheel–rail surfaces. *Wear,* **113**(1), pp. 103–122, 1986. DOI: 10.1016/0043-1648(86)90060-8.

[10] Zobory, I., Prediction of wheel/rail profile wear. *Vehicle System Dynamics,* **28**(2–3), pp. 221–259, 1997. DOI: 10.1080/00423119708969355.

[11] Peng, B., Iwnicki, S., Shackleton, P. & Crosbee, D., Comparison of wear models for simulation of railway wheel polygonization. *Wear,* **436–437**, 2019. DOI: 10.1016/j.wear.2019.203010.

[12] Lewis, R., Kuka, N., Ariaudo, C., Dwyer-Joyce, R., Tassini, N. & Quost, X., Predicting railway wheel wear starting from multi-body analysis: A preliminary study. Presented at the *IEEE/ASME/ASCE 2008 Joint Rail Conference*, Wilmington, DE, 2008. DOI: 10.1115/JRC2008-63021.

[13] Ignesti, M., Innocenti, A., Marini, L., Meli, E. & Rindi, A., Development of a model for the simultaneous analysis of wheel and rail wear in railway systems. *Multibody System Dynamics,* **31**(2), pp. 191–240, 2014. DOI: 10.1007/s11044-013-9360-0.
[14] Shen, Z.Y., Hedrick, J.K. & Elkins, J.A., A comparison of alternative creep force models for rail vehicle dynamic analysis. *Vehicle System Dynamics,* **12**(1–3), pp. 79–83, 1983. DOI: 10.1080/00423118308968725.
[15] Polach, O., A fast wheel–rail forces calculation computer code. *Vehicle System Dynamics,* **33**(sup1), pp. 728–739, 1999. DOI: 10.1080/00423114.1999.12063125.
[16] Bosso, N. & Zampieri, N., A novel analytical method to calculate wheel–rail tangential forces and validation on a scaled roller-rig. *Advances in Tribology,* **2018**, 2018. DOI: 10.1155/2018/7298236.
[17] Enblom, R. & Berg, M., Impact of non-elliptic contact modelling in wheel wear simulation. *Wear,* **265**(9), pp. 1532–1541, 2008. DOI: 10.1016/j.wear.2008.01.027.
[18] Kaiser, I., Poll, G. & Vinolas, J., Modelling the impact of structural flexibility of wheelsets and rails on the wheel–rail contact and the wear. *Wear*, 2020. DOI: 10.1016/j.wear.2020.203445.
[19] Kalker, J.J., A fast algorithm for the simplified theory of rolling contact. *Vehicle System Dynamics,* **11**(1), pp. 1–13, 1982. DOI: 10.1080/00423118208968684.
[20] Vollebregt, E.A.H., Use of "CONTACT" in multi-body vehicle dynamics and profile wear simulation: initial results. *Proceedings of the 22nd International Symposium on Dynamics of Vehicles on Roads and Tracks*, 2013.
[21] Piotrowski, J. & Kik, W., A simplified model of wheel/rail contact mechanics for non-Hertzian problems and its application in rail vehicle dynamic simulations. *Vehicle System Dynamics,* **46**(1–2), pp. 27–48, 2008. DOI: 10.1080/00423110701586444.
[22] Monk-Steel, A.D., Thompson, D.J., de Beer, F.G. & Janssens, M.H.A., An investigation into the influence of longitudinal creepage on railway squeal noise due to lateral creepage. *Journal of Sound and Vibration,* **293**(3), pp. 766–776, 2006. DOI: 10.1016/j.jsv.2005.12.004.
[23] Spiryagin, M., Polach, O. & Cole, C., Creep force modelling for rail traction vehicles based on the Fastsim algorithm. *Vehicle System Dynamics,* **51**(11), pp. 1765–1783, 2013. DOI: 10.1080/00423114.2013.826370.
[24] Vollebregt, E.A.H., Numerical modeling of measured railway creep versus creep-force curves with CONTACT. *Wear,* **314**(1), pp. 87–95, 2014. DOI: 10.1016/j.wear.2013.11.030.
[25] Bosso, N., Gugliotta, A., Magelli, M., Oresta, I.F. & Zampieri, N., Study of wheel–rail adhesion during braking maneuvers. *Procedia Structural Integrity,* **24**, pp. 680–691, 2019. DOI: 10.1016/j.prostr.2020.02.060.
[26] Bosso, N., Gugliotta, A., Magelli, M. & Zampieri, N., Experimental setup of an innovative multi-axle roller rig for the investigation of the adhesion recovery phenomenon. *Experimental Techniques,* **43**(6), pp. 695–706, 2019. DOI: 10.1007/s40799-019-00327-x.
[27] Bosso, N., Magelli, M. & Zampieri, N., Investigation of adhesion recovery phenomenon using a scaled roller-rig. *Vehicle System Dynamics,* **59**(2), pp. 295–312, 2021. DOI: 10.1080/00423114.2019.1677922.
[28] Jendel, T., Prediction of wheel profile wear: Comparisons with field measurements. *Wear,* **253**(1), pp. 89–99, 2002. DOI: 10.1016/S0043-1648(02)00087-X.
[29] Jendel, T. & Berg, M., Prediction of wheel profile wear. *Vehicle System Dynamics,* **37**(sup1), pp. 502–513, 2002. DOI: 10.1080/00423114.2002.11666258.

[30] Vollebregt, E.A.H. & Wilders, P., FASTSIM2: A second-order accurate frictional rolling contact algorithm. *Computational Mechanics,* **47**(1), pp. 105–116, 2011. DOI: 10.1007/s00466-010-0536-7.

INFLUENCE OF MODIFIED POWERTRAIN MASSES ON THE RIDE COMFORT OF A LIGHT RAIL VEHICLE

LUKAS LEICHT, LEONIE HECKELE & PETER GRATZFELD
Institute of Vehicle System Technology, Rail System Technology, Karlsruhe Institute of Technology, Germany

ABSTRACT

Lower powertrain masses and new integration possibilities can be accomplished by using high-speed machines. Since a changed powertrain means a change of the overall system, the aim of this paper is to examine the effects on the system property passenger comfort. This is done using a simulative approach. First, a multi-body model of a Flexity Zurich, a low-floor vehicle that has been operating in Zurich since 2020, is created using the software Simpack. Subsequently, a run on line 9 is simulated and evaluated according to common methods for determining the passenger comfort of rail vehicles. In detail, these are the Sperling method and the Continuous Comfort method according to DIN EN 12299. In order to investigate how powertrains with high-speed machines affect passenger comfort, the model is modified. Machines and gearboxes are replaced by new components that lead to a significant reduction in the mass of the powertrain. It is shown that a concept that leads to a 13% reduction in the primary suspended mass does not have any significant impact on passenger comfort in the simulated vehicle on the specified route. Neither does a concept that leads to a 35% reduction in primary suspended mass and a 38% increase in unsprung mass. In order to gain an insight into the influence of the unsprung and primary suspended mass on passenger comfort, a series of simulations are carried out to investigate this relationship on a broadband basis on the above vehicle. The results show that there is no evidence of a correlation between the unsprung and primary suspended masses and passenger comfort in the lateral direction. However, there is a slight trend towards better comfort values in the vertical direction with lower unsprung and primary suspended masses.
Keywords: comfort, unsprung, primary suspended, powertrain, mass, light rail, tram.

1 INTRODUCTION

Public transport operators want to shift the modal split in favour of their modes of transport. To achieve this in the light rail sector, the vehicles must meet certain requirements. These include the use of energy efficient powertrains as well as providing a high passenger comfort [1].

Powertrains with high-speed machines can contribute to this, as they promise higher efficiency and thus lower energy consumption compared to conventional machines. This leads to lower operating costs. Furthermore, powertrains with high-speed machines can be realised smaller and lighter than conventional machines [2].

Heckele et al. [3] investigate how much energy can be saved if a Flexity Zurich, a low floor tram operating in Zurich, is equipped with a powertrain with high-speed machines. They show that energy consumption can be reduced by up to 29% to 3.5 kWh/km. According to the authors, this is due to both the 21% reduction in powertrain mass and the use of components which lead to an increase in powertrain efficiency of 9 percentage points to 84%.

The mass of a railway vehicle can influence the vibrations of railway vehicles [4]. Therefore, we expect that the passenger comfort will also be influenced. The aim of this paper is to investigate the extent of this influence in order to assess whether mass reduction through high-speed machines can contribute to higher passenger comfort. To the authors' knowledge, there are no publications thus far that have investigated this relation.

In order to determine this, a simulative approach is taken. In the field of rail vehicles, simulations are commonly used as an analytical investigation of the behaviour of entire

WIT Transactions on The Built Environment, Vol 213, © 2022 WIT Press
www.witpress.com, ISSN 1743-3509 (on-line)
doi:10.2495/CR220071

vehicles is not possible. Therefore, multi-body simulation software is used to assess the dynamic behaviour [5].

On the one hand, manufacturers use multi-body simulation to meet safety criteria such as protecting the vehicle from derailing or overturning. On the other hand, it can be used to ensure that freight and passengers are not exposed to unacceptable vibrations, i.e., to guarantee sufficient comfort [6].

We create a multi-body model of the Flexity Zurich using the software Simpack. Different configurations of this model are subjected to a run on the line 9 and are evaluated according to common methods for assessing passenger comfort.

In Haladin et al. [7], various methods for determining passenger comfort in rail vehicles were investigated for their suitability in light rail vehicles. The authors conclude that the Sperling method is convenient for assessing tramway infrastructure and ride comfort. However, they criticize that it cannot evaluate comfort in longitudinal direction, although recurring start–stop driving is of great importance for ride comfort. Furthermore, they reckon the valid frequency range to be not sufficient to properly reflect excitations caused by welding irregularities. They also examined the methods provided by EN 12299 for determining passenger comfort in rail vehicles. The Mean Comfort methods are not suitable for light rail vehicles as the standard demands 5-minute-long test sections with constant speed which is too long for light rail track sections. Nonetheless, the authors consider the Continuous Comfort method suitable as vibration levels are averaged over five seconds, and it provides a sufficient valid frequency range up to 100 Hz. They cite the resolution of the scale as a disadvantage of this method. In their measurement, 95% of all comfort values already fall in the highest comfort category which makes it inconvenient to compare different test sections to one another [7].

In this paper, we use both the Sperling method and the Continuous Comfort method to evaluate the different configurations of the model to obtain findings about the influence of powertrain masses on the passenger comfort.

2 METHODS FOR DETERMINING PASSENGER COMFORT

The most common methods to determine passenger comfort of rail vehicles in general are:

1. the Sperling method; and
2. the methods according to EN 12299, which is based on ISO 2631 [6].

Each of which were originally developed for the heavy rail sector, but according to Haladin et al. [7], both the Sperling method and the Continuous Comfort method in EN 12299 are suitable for the light rail sector. In the following, a brief overview of the mentioned methods will be given. Both methods consider the accelerations and frequencies a human is exposed to as the only relevant factors for comfort.

2.1 Sperling method

Sperling developed a method for evaluating the ride quality of passenger and freight wagons [8], [9]. In this method, a ride index Wz, which describes the comfort, is calculated using eqn (1):

$$Wz = \sqrt[10]{B(f)^3 \hat{a}^3}. \tag{1}$$

This is an empirically established correlation between the ride index Wz and a perceived excitation with the acceleration amplitude $\hat{a}$ in $\mathrm{m/s^2}$ and the frequency f in Hz. In $B(f)$, the frequency is weighted to consider that humans perceive different frequencies differently.

$B(f)$ is valid in a frequency range from 0.5 Hz to 20 Hz and is calculated as follows for the lateral and vertical direction:

$$B_{\text{vert}}(f) = 0.588\sqrt{\frac{1.911f^2+(0.25f^2)^2}{(1-0.277f^2)^2+(1.563f-0.0368f^3)^2}}, \tag{2}$$

$$B_{\text{lat}}(f) = 1.25 \cdot B_{\text{vert}}(f). \tag{3}$$

There is no weighting curve for the longitudinal direction [10].

The lower the ride index Wz, the better the comfort. Table 1 shows which ride index corresponds to which perception.

Table 1: Ride index evaluation scale [10].

Wz	Description in words
1	Just noticeable
2	Clearly noticeable
2.5	More pronounced but not unpleasant
3	Strong, irregular, but still tolerable
3.25	Very irregular
3.5	Extremely irregular, unpleasant, annoying; prolonged exposure intolerable
4	Extremely unpleasant; prolonged exposure harmful

Eqn (1) is only valid for accelerations with a single frequency. Since in reality accelerations occur with multiple frequencies, the whole spectrum must be considered. This is done with eqn (4) [6]:

$$Wz = \left[2\sum_{i=1}^{n}\left(B(f_i)a_{i,\text{RMS}}\right)^2\right]^{0.15}, \tag{4}$$

with

$$a_{\text{RMS}} = \sqrt{\frac{1}{2}\hat{a}^2}. \tag{5}$$

2.2 Continuous Comfort according to EN 12299

This method uses the time-dependent accelerations a to determine the Continuous Comfort C_{C}. Depending on the direction, the values are calculated according to the following equations:

$$C_{\text{Cx}}(t) = a_{\text{XP}}^{\text{W}_\text{d}}(t), \tag{6}$$

$$C_{\text{Cy}}(t) = a_{\text{YP}}^{\text{W}_\text{d}}(t), \tag{7}$$

$$C_{\text{Cz}}(t) = a_{\text{ZP}}^{\text{W}_\text{b}}(t). \tag{8}$$

The accelerations are RMS values averaged over 5 seconds. W_d and W_b refer to weighting curves in a frequency range between 0.1 Hz and 100 Hz. P indicates the location where the measurement is made, in this case on the floor. The calculated values for $C_{\text{Cy}}(t)$ and $C_{\text{Cz}}(t)$ can be classified on the evaluation scale shown in Table 2.

However, this evaluation scale is only preliminary, and the standard does not provide a scale for $C_{\text{Cx}}(t)$ thus far [11].

Table 2: Evaluation scale for C_{Cy} and C_{Cz} [11].

$C_{Cy}(t), C_{Cz}(t)$ in $\frac{m}{s^2}$	Description in words
<0.2	Very comfortable
0.2–0.3	Comfortable
0.3–0.4	Medium
>0.4	Less comfortable

3 SIMULATION OF PASSENGER COMFORT

This section presents the models of the chosen track and vehicle. Next to the baseline, the changes made on it are explained.

3.1 Track

The track the vehicle is simulated on is the tramline 9 in Zurich. A cartographic track is created with the track and height profile shown in Fig. 1. *x*, *y* and *z* are spatial coordinates and *s* refers to the length of the track.

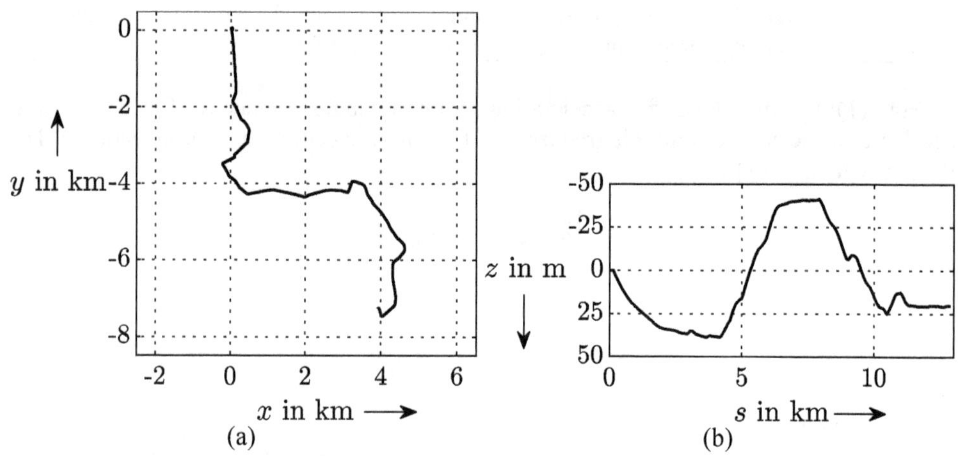

Figure 1: (a) Track profile; and (b) Height profile.

In accordance with the official planning guideline [12], superelevation is added. Furthermore, track irregularities are added as these are mainly responsible for the excitation of a rail vehicle [6]. These irregularities are modelled small according to [13].

3.2 Vehicle configurations

Subsequently, the multi-body model of the Flexity Zurich created in Simpack is presented. Furthermore, the mass-related changes that are made to the vehicle are explained.

3.2.1 Baseline

Fig. 2 shows the model of the topology of the model of the Flexity Zurich. It is based on dimensions and mass properties available to the authors as well as the spring and damper constants of the force elements. The cars 1, 3, 5 and 7 have bogies, all of which are powered expect for car 3. Each bogie consists of two wheelsets which have a force element that models the wheel–rail contact based on FASTSIM. The wheelsets are connected to the bogie frame via the primary suspension. In car 1, 5 and 7, the machines and gearboxes are modelled as rigid bodies that are mounted on the frame. The railcar bodies are connected to the bogie via the secondary suspension, and they are connected to one another using joints and force elements. Between the railcar body pairs 1–2, 3–4, 5–6 and 6–7, there are joints that allow rotations about the vertical axis. The force elements there represent yaw dampers. The joints between the other railcar body pairs allow rotations about the transverse axis. This model serves as the baseline further changes are compared with.

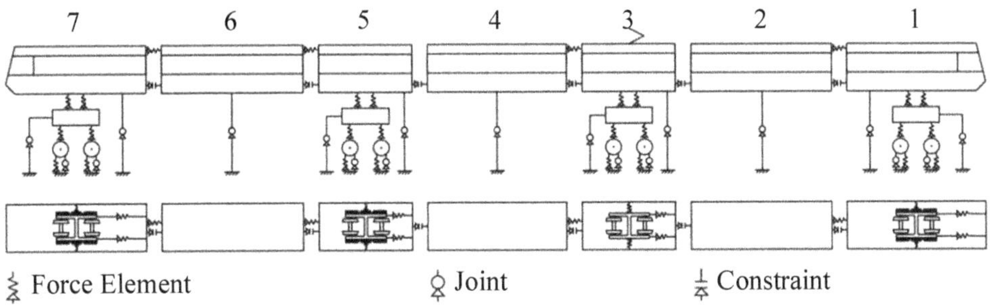

Figure 2: Topology of the Simpack model of the Flexity Zurich.

The model is equipped with acceleration sensors according to the standard [11], see Fig. 3. An end module, an intermediate car and a drive-less car are chosen to represent each type of car used in the vehicle.

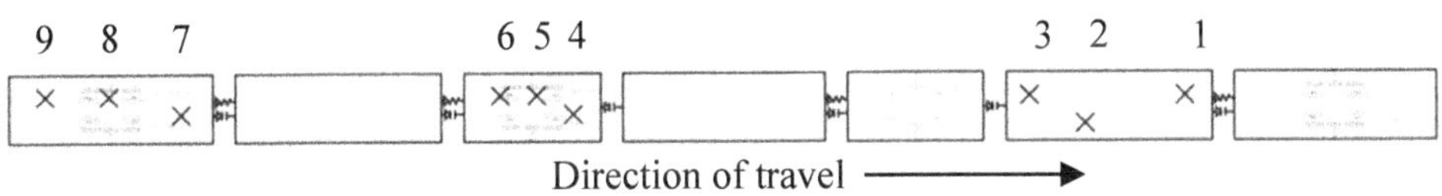

Figure 3: Placement of the acceleration sensors in the model, numbered from 1–9 starting at the head of the train.

The vehicle is placed on the track shown in Fig. 1 and pulled with the speed profile shown in Fig. 4. The speed profile corresponds to the real speeds at which the Flexity Zurich runs on line 9. However, the waiting times at the stops are shortened from 20 s to 10 s to save simulation time.

3.2.2 Concepts with high-speed machines

Two concepts with high-speed machines in the powertrain are simulated. This is achieved by changing the masses of the baseline vehicle according to Table 3.

There are two machines and two gearboxes per powered bogie. All bogies except the second one from the direction of travel are powered, see Fig. 3. In the baseline, the bogie

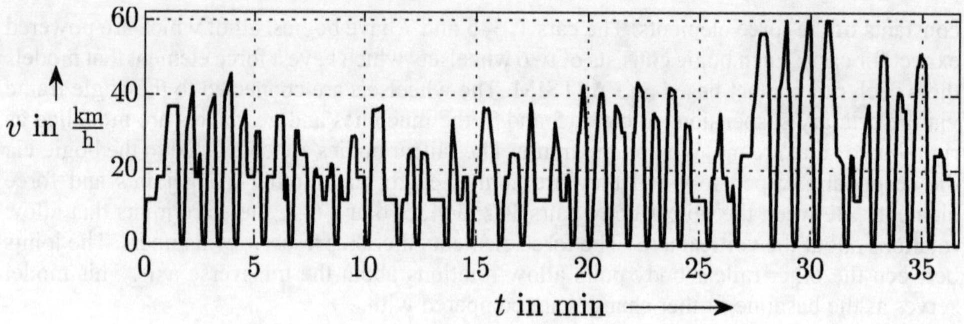

Figure 4: Speed profile of the Flexity Zurich on line 9

Table 3: Masses of the parts of the powertrain and the total masses from the baseline and two concepts.

Part	Baseline	Concept 1	Concept 2
Machine	336 kg (p)	125 kg (p)	125 kg (p)
Gearbox	285 kg (p)	310 kg (p)	310 kg (u)
Total mass (u)	1640 kg	1640 kg	2260 kg
Total mass (p)	2857 kg	2485 kg	1865 kg

Note: u = unsprung, p = primary suspended.

frame carries the machines and gearboxes, what makes them part of the primary suspended masses.

In concept 1, the conventional machines are replaced by high-speed machines which are significantly lighter than those of the baseline. However, the gearboxes require one stage more due to the higher revolution speed of the machines. Therefore, they are heavier than those of the baseline.

Concept 2 uses the same parts as concept 1. The difference, however, is that the gearboxes are attached to the swingarm of the wheelsets and not to the bogie frame. Hence, the gearbox masses are unsprung in this concept.

For concept 1, the primary suspended mass decreases by 13% per powered bogie. For concept 2, the changes lead to a reduction of the primary suspended by 35%. However, the unsprung mass increases by 38% in this concept.

3.2.3 Variation of unsprung und primary suspended masses

To determine the influence of unsprung and primary suspended masses on passenger comfort, two series of simulations are carried out. In the first simulation series, all unsprung masses are varied within a range of ± 40% in 10% steps. In the second simulation series, the same is done with the primary suspended masses.

4 RESULTS

This section presents the results of the simulations from Section 3. First, it shows the results of the baseline model, as these serve as a benchmark for its variations. Second, it presents the results of the two concepts. Finally, it shows the results of the simulation series in which the unsprung and primary suspended masses vary.

4.1 Baseline

Fig. 5 shows the ride index Wz both in lateral and vertical direction. The dashed line and the number above indicate the 95th percentile. In lateral direction, Wz according to sensor 1 was chosen and in vertical direction sensor 9, as these sensors detect the highest level of the ride index.

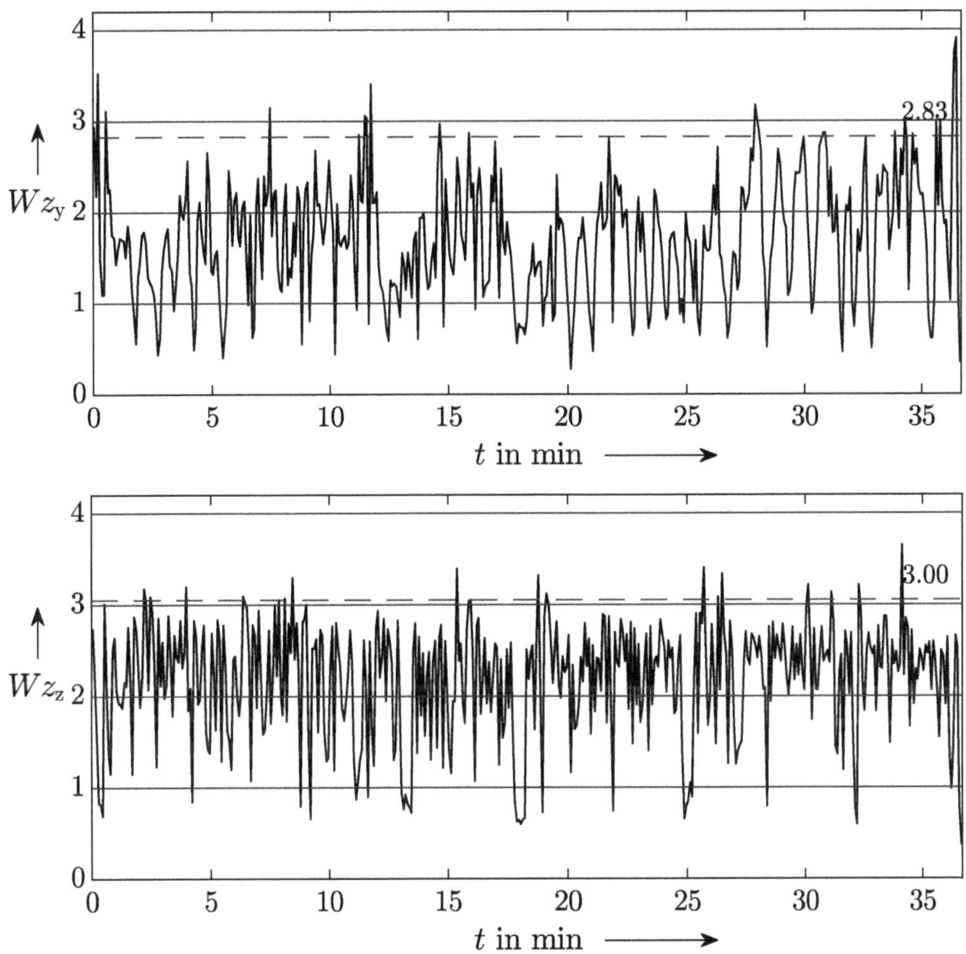

Figure 5: Course of ride index Wz of the baseline.

Most values are below 3.0 which corresponds to *Strong, irregular, but still tolerable* or better, see Table 1. Peak values higher than 3.5, which corresponds to *Extremely irregular, unpleasant, annoying; prolonged exposure intolerable,* are reached in lateral direction towards the end of the run. At this point, the vehicle travels through a turnaround loop. In vertical direction, this is the case on a hilltop the vehicle travels over.

Fig. 6 shows the course of the Continuous Comfort according to the same sensors.

Most values are below 0.2 and fall into the category *Very comfortable*, see Table 2. Peak values on this scale correspond to the same track events as on the Sperling scale in Fig. 5.

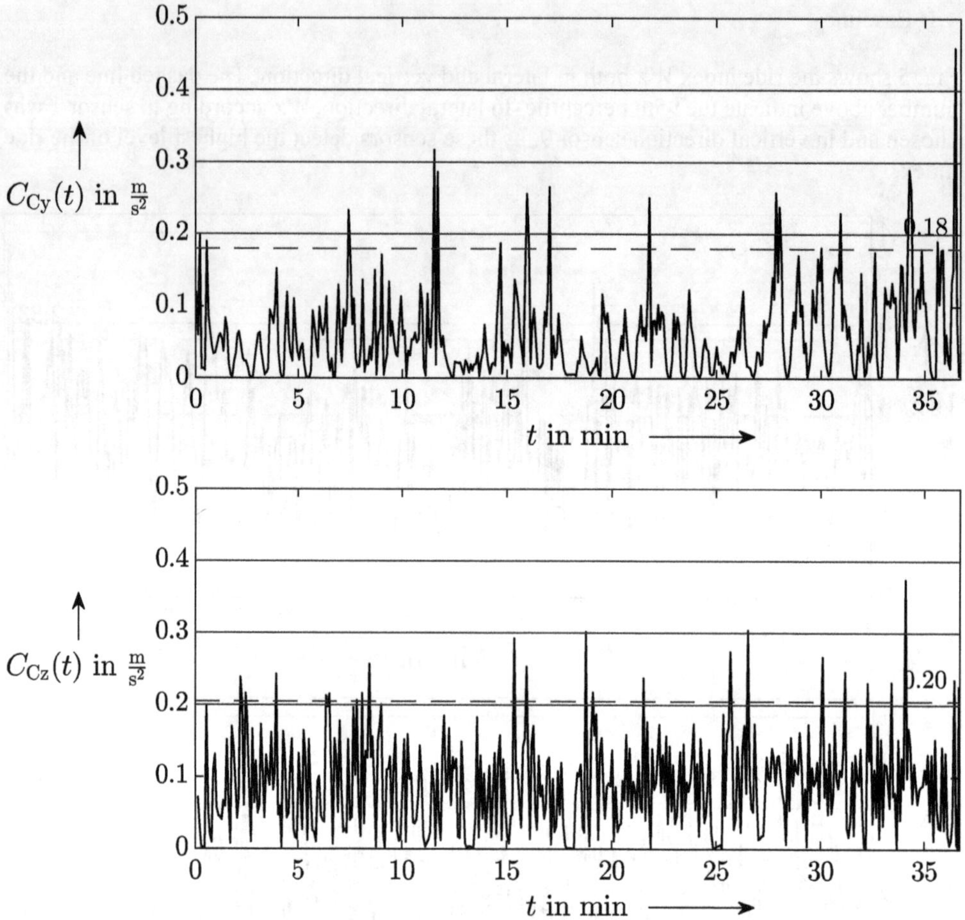

Figure 6: Course of Continuous Comfort C_C of the baseline.

4.2 Concepts with high-speed machines

To compare the concepts with the baseline with respect to the passenger comfort, the 95th percentiles of the comfort values of the sensors with the highest difference to the baseline are used. In lateral direction, this is the case for sensor 9 and in vertical direction for sensor 2. Table 4 gives the 95th percentiles both for the values on the Sperling scale and the scale of the Continuous Comfort.

Table 4: 95th percentiles of the ride index Wz and the Continuous Comfort C_C for the baseline and the concepts.

	Baseline		Concept 1		Concept 2	
	y	z	y	z	y	z
Wz	2.52	2.40	2.56	2.38	2.56	2.41
C_C in $\frac{m}{s^2}$	0.12	0.09	0.12	0.09	0.12	0.10

The biggest difference on the scale of the Continuous Comfort is 0.01 m/s^2 and on the Sperling scale 0.04. Therefore, the comfort values of the two concepts fall into the same categories as those of the baseline, so no noticeable changes are to be expected.

4.3 Variation of unsprung masses

In order to determine the passenger comfort as a function of the unsprung masses, the 95th percentiles of the ride index Wz are used. Sensor 1 reacts most sensitively to changes of the unsprung masses in the lateral direction, and sensor 4 in the vertical direction. Fig. 7 shows the ride index Wz as a function of the factor applied to the unsprung mass.

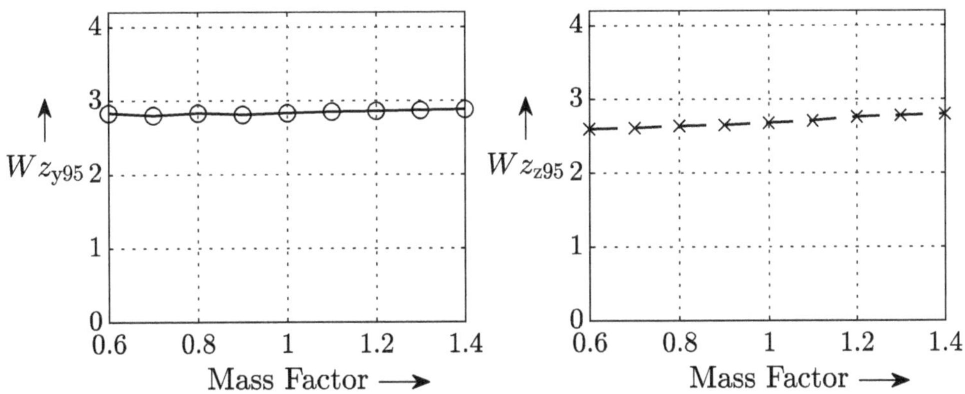

Figure 7: Course of Wz as a function of the unsprung mass in lateral and vertical direction.

In lateral direction, the values for Wz are in a range of 2.80 and 2.88, but no trend can be identified. In vertical direction, the values range between 2.60 and 2.80, and they fall steadily with decreasing unsprung mass. However, the extent is too low to cause perceivable changes in passenger comfort, as all the values remain in the same comfort category.

The scale of the Continuous Comfort turns out to be not suitable, as the changes are barely resolvable on this scale.

4.4 Variation of primary suspended masses

For determining the passenger comfort as a function of the primary suspended mass, the same procedure is used as in Section 4.3. Fig. 8 gives the ride index Wz as a function of the factor applied to the primary suspended mass.

In lateral direction, the values for Wz range between 2.84 and 2.87 with no discernible relationship to the primary suspended masses. Vertically, the values are between 2.62 and 2.85 with a trend towards better comfort values the lower the primary suspended mass becomes. However, like in Section 4.3, the differences of Wz are too low to cause perceivable changes in passenger comfort.

As for the unsprung masses, the scale of the Continuous Comfort turns out to be not suitable, as the changes are barely resolvable on this scale.

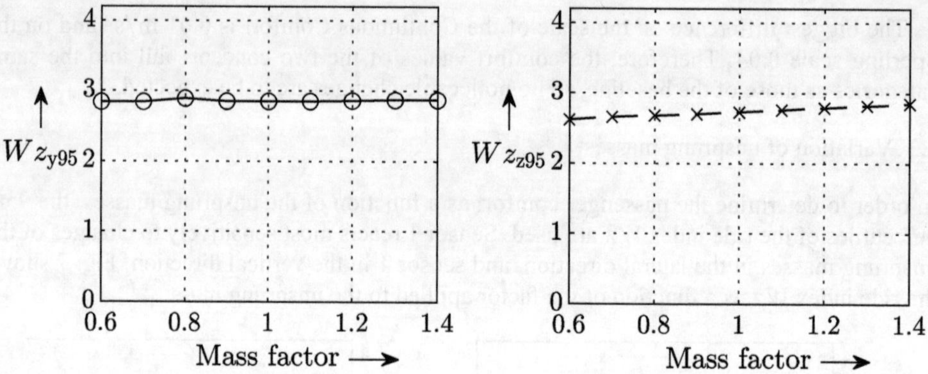

Figure 8: Course of Wz as a function of the primary suspended mass in lateral and vertical direction.

5 VALIDATION

To adequately validate the results, a field trial would be necessary. This is not possible within the scope of this paper, but the plausibility of the baseline model can be checked using literature values.

In Haladin et al. [7], acceleration measurements were carried out in two trams in the Croatian cities Osijek and Zagreb and evaluated according to the Sperling method and the Continuous Comfort method, as in this paper. With a length of 12.5 km, slopes up to 60‰ and velocities up to 50 km/h, the conditions of the section in Zagreb are most comparable to those of this paper and are used to evaluate the plausibility of the results of the baseline model.

In Table 5, the distribution of the measured comfort values from the TKM2200, the vehicle in Zagreb, and the distribution of the simulated comfort values from the Flexity Zurich is shown on both the Sperling scale and the Continuous Comfort scale.

Table 5: Distribution of the measured comfort values from the TKM2200 in comparison to the simulated comfort values of the Flexity Zurich, percentage values.

	TMK2200		Flexity Zurich			TMK2200		Flexity Zurich	
Wz	Wz_y	Wz_z	Wz_y	Wz_z	C_C in $\frac{m}{s^2}$	C_{Cy}	C_{Cz}	C_{Cy}	C_{Cz}
<1.0	0.1	0.1	15.9	7.2	<0.2	97.8	86.4	97.3	94.5
1.0–2.0	33.9	35.6	51.6	26.6	0.2–0.3	2.2	13.6	2.3	4.8
2.0–3.0	65.9	64.2	29.8	60.7	0.3–0.4	0.0	0.0	0.2	0.7
3.0–3.25	0.0	0.0	1.8	4.1	>0.4	0.0	0.0	0.2	0.0
3.25–3.5	0.0	0.0	0.2	1.1					
3.5–4.0	0.0	0.0	0.7	0.2					

The majority of both the measured values and the simulated values fall into similar comfort categories. The values of the Flexity Zurich tend to a shift towards better comfort values. This is to be expected as it is a more modern vehicle. However, the model tends to rare but high peaks of bad comfort. This is considered unrealistic as bad comfort values do not occur at all in the vehicle in Zagreb. This can be due to uncertainties in the track model.

From the given track data, there were no information about transition curves and superelevations. These had to be assumed according to the official planning guideline in Verkehrsbetriebe Zürich [12], which does not necessarily represent real conditions.

6 CONCLUSION

This paper investigated the influence of modified powertrain masses on the ride comfort of a light rail vehicle. A multi-body model of Flexity Zurich, a tram operating in Zurich, was created using the software Simpack. The model was exposed to a run on the tramline 9 and evaluated according to common methods for determining ride comfort. These are the Sperling method and the Continuous Comfort method according to EN 12299.

The baseline model, which serves as a benchmark, reaches comfort values of which 95% fall into the category *Strong, irregular, but still tolerable* and better on the Sperling scale. On the Continuous Comfort scale, 95% of all values fall into the highest category, *Very comfortable*.

The concepts did not cause relevant changes in ride comfort in comparison to the baseline. This was the case although concept 1 leads to a reduction in primary suspended mass of 13% per powered bogie and concept 2 of 35%, but a 38% increase in unsprung mass per powered bogie.

In order to examine the effects of unsprung and primary suspended masses on the ride comfort, two simulation series were carried out in which both the unsprung masses and primary suspended masses were varied in a range of ± 40%. Even in this range, there is no relevant influence on ride comfort in lateral direction. However, a slight trend towards better comfort values with lower masses in vertical direction could be detected. But this influence is too small to cause perceivable changes in comfort, as all comfort values remain in the same category.

The model could not yet be validated, but in comparison with values from literature, it could be shown that it provides plausible results. However, the model tends to rare but high peaks which can be considered unrealistic.

To increase comfort, track irregularities and the suspension are probably of greater importance. Those factors were investigated in Dumitriu and Gheti [14] and correlated with the ride index Wz.

For validation purposes, measurements of the real vehicle could be taken and compared with the results of the baseline to evaluate the model.

REFERENCES

[1] Verband Deutscher Verkehrsunternehmen e.V. (VDV), *Stadtbahnsysteme, Grundlagen – Technik – Betrieb – Finanzierung*, DVV Media Group GmbH/Eurailpress: Hamburg, pp. 38–48, 2014.

[2] Heckele, L. et al., Steigerung der Leistungsdichte und des Wirkungsgrades von Straßenbahnantrieben durch den Einsatz hochdrehender Maschinen. *Elektrotech. Inftech*, 2022. DOI: 10.1007/s00502-022-01011-6.

[3] Heckele, L., Tesar, M. & Gratzfeld, P., Wirkungsgradsteigerung von elektrischen Antriebssträngen mit hochdrehenden Maschinen. *Elektrische Bahnen*, **6**(2), pp. 282–289, 2020.

[4] Fontanel, É. & Christeller, R., *Rolling Stock in the Railway System,* vol. 2, PMC Media House GmbH: Leverkusen, p. 218, 2020.

[5] Jänsch, E., Lang, H. & Nießen, N., *Das System Bahn: Handbuch,* PMC Media House GmbH: Leverkusen, p. 162, 2021.

[6] Knothe, K. & Stichel, S., *Schienenfahrzeugdynamik*, Springer-Verlag: Berlin, pp. 139–166, 2003.
[7] Haladin, I., Lakušić, S. & Bogut, M., Overview and analysis of methods for assessing ride comfort on tram tracks. *Građevinar*, **71**, pp. 901–921, 2019. DOI: 10.14256/JCE.2731.2019.
[8] Helbig, W. & Sperling, E., Verfahren zur Beurteilung der Laufeigenschaften von Eisenbahnwagen. *Organ Für Die Fortschritte Des Eisenbahnwesens*, **96**, 1941.
[9] Sperling, E., Beitrag zur Beurteilung des Fahrkomforts in Schienenfahrzeugen. *Glasers Annalen*, **80**, 1956.
[10] Garg, V.K. & Dukkipati, R.V., *Dynamics of Railway Vehicle Systems*, Academic Press: Toronto, pp. 68–71, 1984.
[11] Railway Standardisation Committee, Railway applications: Ride comfort for passengers: Measurement and evaluation. German version EN 12299:2009.
[12] Verkehrsbetriebe Zürich, Empfehlungen für die Planung von Strassenbahnanlagen auf dem Netz der Verkehrsbetriebe Zürich, 2014.
[13] Specification for a bogie with improved curving characteristics. Bogies with steered or steering wheelsets. *ORE (ERRI)*, **176**(2), 1989.
[14] Dumitriu, M. & Gheti, M., Evaluation of the ride quality and ride comfort in railway vehicles based on the index W_z. *Annals of Faculty Engineering Hunedoara – International Journal of Engineering*, 2016.

COMPUTER SIMULATION TO PREDICT THE SLIDING WEAR OF PEARLITIC RAILS IN CONTACT BETWEEN CAST AND FORGED RAILWAY WHEELS

JOÃO V.R. SILVA E SILVA[1], LUIZ F.V. CORRÊA[1], RUBSON M. CAMPOREZ[2], CHERLIO SCANDIAN[2] & GUILHERME F. M. DOS SANTOS[1]
[1]Tribology and Railway Dynamics Laboratory, Federal University of Espírito Santo, Brazil
[2]Tribology, Corrosion and Materials Laboratory, Federal University of Espírito Santo, Brazil

ABSTRACT
This work aims to implement and evaluate the effectiveness of the semi-analytical computational method global incremental wear model (GIWM) in predicting the sliding wear of rails in contact with the flange of railway wheels during curves, which is a parameter of great importance for the efficiency of railway operation. The method validation was performed by comparing the wear depth calculated using the GIWM algorithm to the experimental results published in previous work. The data was obtained in dry (relative humidity: 55% ± 10%) pin-on-disc tests carried out on a universal PLINT TE67 tribometer under a normal load of 24.6 N, representing 1.5 GPa of contact pressure. The specimens, hemispherical pins, were extracted from a pearlitic steel rail and the discs were extracted from two different, forged and cast, Class C railway wheels. The tangential sliding speeds were 0.1 m/s and 0.9 m/s, the latter being the most representative according to the literature. The wear model was based on Archard's law for sliding wear and the algorithm was implemented in Python. The results showed good agreement of the wear depth values between the computational and experimental methods for the cast wheel material under higher sliding speed, partial agreement for both wheel materials at lower speed and inconsistency for the forged wheel material under higher sliding speed. Furthermore, the algorithm is computationally efficient, presenting simulation time up to 180 times less than the finite element methods reported in the literature. Therefore, it was concluded that the GIWM method has potential for application in the freight railway sector, which uses cast wheels extensively, to guide technical areas regarding the wear behavior of rails under sliding contact during curves.
Keywords: tribology, railway, sliding wear, Archard, computer simulation, GIWM.

1 INTRODUCTION

Heavy-haul railways development is highly associated with economic growth since it increases transportation efficiency of raw materials [1]. Besides, according to the National Association of Rail Carriers [2], railway cargo transport is responsible for 21.5% of the Brazilian national transportation matrix and there is still plenty of space to grow, indicating the importance in destinate efforts on railway improvement.

However, rail transport operation is subject to wear, especially in the vehicle and rail contact. Miranda et al. [3] emphasizes the relationship between the efficient management of such contact and lowering maintenance costs of rolling and track components. Thus, modelling and predicting the wear mechanisms present in this system is crucial to improve railway operation efficiency.

The wheel–rail contact is the core of scientific researches in respect to the vehicle–track interaction. According to Lewis and Olofsson [4], this contact assumes three basic configurations, as shown in Fig. 1. Region A illustrates the wheel tread–rail head contact that occurs in straight tracks. Further, Region B delineates the wheel flange–rail gauge corner contact that takes place in curved track, exhibiting a large sliding component on the contact patch. Finally, Region C, the most improbable, represents the contact between field sides of

WIT Transactions on The Built Environment, Vol 213, © 2022 WIT Press
www.witpress.com, ISSN 1743-3509 (on-line)
doi:10.2495/CR220081

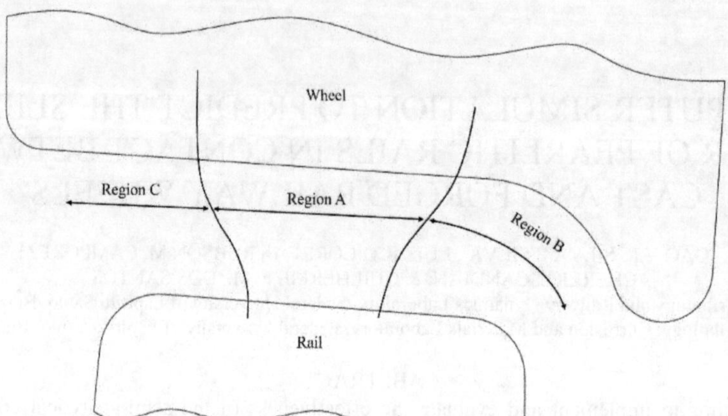

Figure 1: Wheel–rail contact zones. *(Source: Adapted from [4].)*

wheel and rail. In this work, the B case will be scrutinized in view of the fact that this contact condition has a higher potential to cause severe wear compared to the other two [5].

Provided that the appropriate conditions are applied and controlled, laboratory tests may be used to investigate wear mechanisms. The pin-to-disc geometry correctly reproduces the sliding conditions. Furthermore, the nature of the contact is asymmetrical, which means that the pin experiences a continuum contact while the disc experiences an intermittent contact [6].

Hence, this experimental method is extensively employed [7]–[9] to study wear in the contact between the wheel flange, characterized by the disc, and the corner of the track head gauge, characterized by the pin.

Nonetheless, to carry laboratory tests may be onerous and time-consuming resulting in considerable delays in the scientific investigations. Thereupon, simulation tools are interesting solutions for predicting wear. Several researches [11]–[13] were executed to investigate the application of finite element method (FEM) in emulating laboratory tests response.

However, Bastola et al. [11] has shown the necessary precondition of results extrapolation in order to obtain sufficiently accurate results as a consequence of the exorbitant computational time required in the FEM method. Development of more efficient and less time-consuming methods are therefore required.

Regarding sliding wear, Bortoleto et al. [14] cite that several formulations have been investigated in order to describe the different mechanisms involved in this phenomenon. In the 1950s, Archard [15] demonstrated his sliding wear model which according to Liu et al. [16] is widely employed to measure the worn volume as well as the wear depth of body and counter body of the system.

Based on Archard's wear law, Hegadekatte et al. [17] coined a simulation tool named global incremental wear model (GIWM). It is a computationally inexpensive algorithm for predicting pin wear depth or disc wear depth in pin-on-disc tests. This method uses global quantities and updates the contact geometry at each sliding interval with the aim to efficiently determine wear depth. Therefore, the aim of this work is to examine the applicability of the GIWM in efficiently predicting wheel flange–rail gauge corner contact wear depths prevalent in curved tracks and guide engineering decisions.

2 MATERIALS AND METHODS

2.1 Materials

Rail and rail wheel were used to manufacture the pin and disc samples (Fig. 2), respectively. The rail wheels are produced in cast and forged steel class C following the standard of the Association of American Railroads (AAR) and, the rail is conventional pearlitic steel used in railways. The chemical composition of the pins and discs are shown in Table 1 [7].

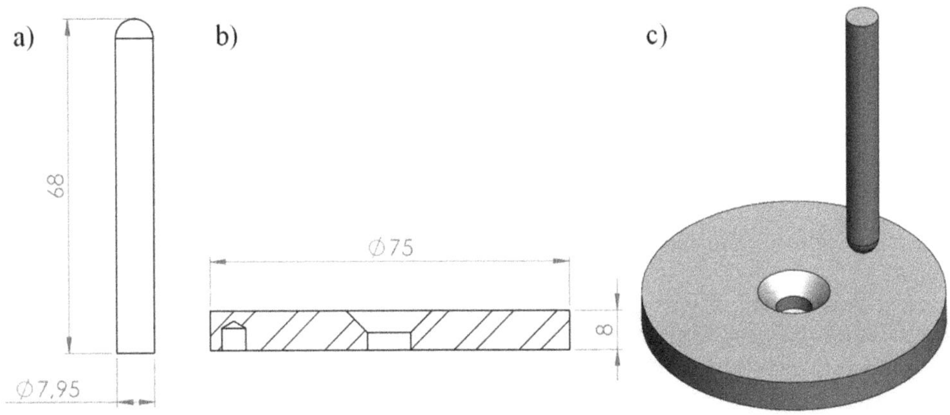

Figure 2: Dimensional, in millimeters, of (a) Pin; and (b) Disc samples; and (c) Schematic assembly. *(Source: Adapted from [7].)*

Table 1: Chemical composition of discs and pins [7].

Materials	C (wt%)	Mn (wt%)	Si (wt%)	P (wt%)	S (wt%)	Cr (wt%)
Pin–Rail	0.72–0.82	0.80–1.25	0.10–0.50	< 0.03	< 0.02	< 0.25
Disc–Wheel	0.67–0.77	0.60–0.90	0.15–1.00	< 0.03	0.005–0.04	–

2.2 Wear tests

Wear tests without lubrication (relative humidity: 55% ± 10%) were performed in pin-on-disc configuration on the PLINT TE67 universal tribometer. For each pair of materials, a normal load of 24.6 N was applied in order to achieve an initial mean contact pressure of 1.5 GPa. The test lasted 1 h and two sliding speeds, 0.1 m/s and 0.9 m/s, were applied. The initial mean contact pressure of 1.5 GPa along with the 0.9 m/s sliding speed constitute the most representative condition for the in the wheel flange–rail gauge corner contact [7].

To this work, only the wear of the pin will be considered, and the results are based on the work by de Almeida et al. [7]. The equations for calculating the wear height (h_p) and consequently the volume (V_p) removed from the pin follow the ASTM G99 standard and will be described ahead in eqns (1) and (2), respectively [18].

$$h_p = R_b - \sqrt{(R_b^2 - r_b^2)}, \tag{1}$$

$$V_p = \frac{\pi h_p}{6}(3r_b^2 + h_p^2), \tag{2}$$

where: R_b: pin end radius;r_b: wear scar radius.

Specific wear rate, k_p, is calculated from volume loss, V_p, total sliding distance, s_{max}, and normal load, W, applied, eqn (3):

$$k_p = \frac{V_p}{s_{max}W}. \tag{3}$$

In this work, the wear of the pin was evaluated in continuous and interrupted tests. Continuous tests were used to obtain the specific wear rate, and the results of the interrupted tests helped in the comparison with the GIWM model. The wear depth of the pin, interrupted tests, was obtained by eqn (1), the specific wear rate was calculated from the combination of eqns (1), (2) and (3).

2.3 Global incremental wear model (GIWM) for pin-on-disc tests

The term "global" indicates that global quantities are used in the model, i.e., nominal quantities, e.g., average contact pressure or nominal contact pressure, not considering the real contact pressure and in this model, the contact area considers the contribution of elastic deformation and wear, from the pin, orthogonal to the contact surface.

The term "incremental" means that at each step, within the algorithm, variables such as the contact area are being updated, as with each iteration of a predetermined slipped distance, wear changes it and therefore the contact pressure varies, and this will influence the next wear depth [17].

2.3.1 GIWM for wear pin

It is known that the pin and the disc wear out simultaneously during sliding, but for the computer modeling it will be assumed that the disc wear is negligible and that practically all the wear occurs on the pin [17], [19].

To obtain the wear depth of the pin along the slid distance, it is necessary to use the iterative computational model presented in Fig. 3(a), where p is the contact pressure, W is the normal load, a is the radius of contact from elastic deformation and wear, h is the total displacement of the hemispherical tip of the pin, R_p is the radius of the pin, h^e is the deformation elastic, h^w is the wear depth, k_p is the dimensional wear coefficient, Δs is the distance increment, s_{max} is the maximum slip distance, and E_c is the combined modulus of elasticity [6]. The implementation of this computational model was carried out in Python, a high-level, scientific, free, and open-source programming language.

The combined modulus of elasticity, E_c, and the initial contact radius, a_0, are calculated from eqns (4) and (5), respectively [6]:

$$E_c = \left(\frac{1-v_p^2}{E_p} + \frac{1-v_d^2}{E_d}\right)^{-1}, \tag{4}$$

$$a_0 = \left(\frac{3WR_p}{4E_c}\right)^{\frac{1}{3}}, \tag{5}$$

where: v_p: Pin Poisson's ratio; v_d: Disc Poisson's ratio; E_p: Pin elastic modulus; E_d: Disc elastic modulus.

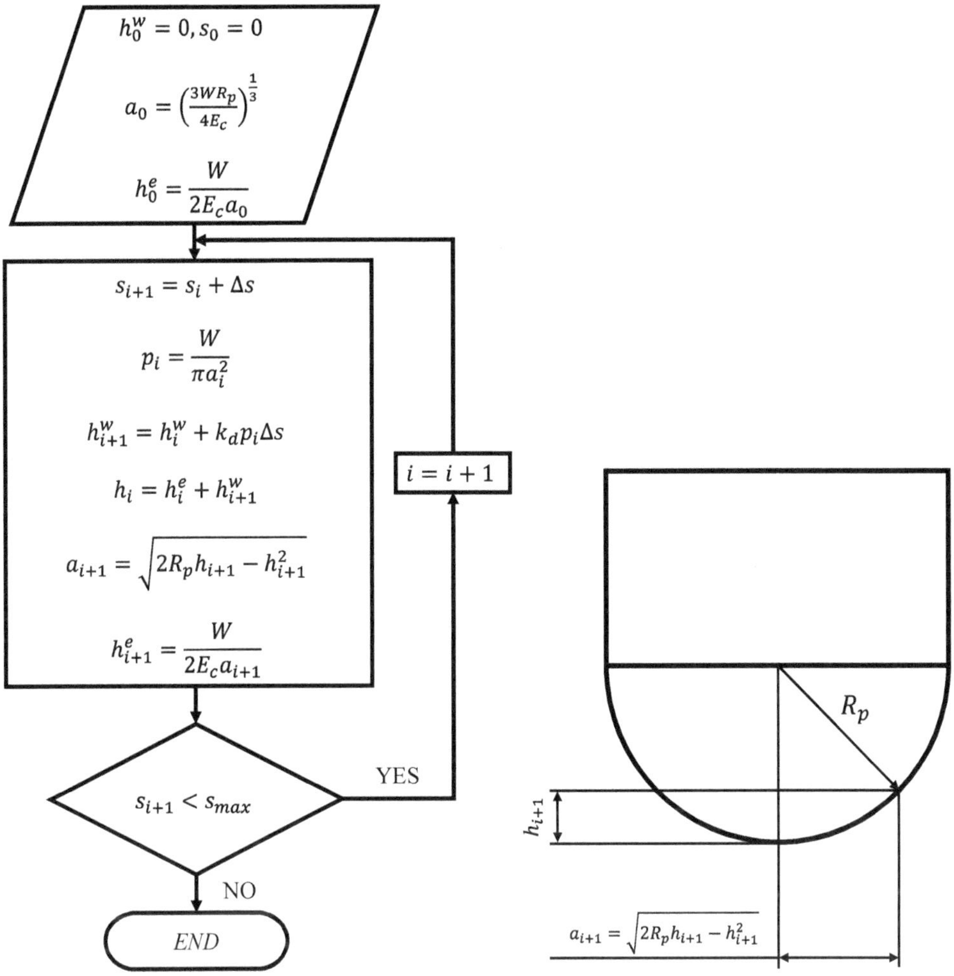

Figure 3: (a) Flow chart of GIWM for pin; and (b) Schematic drawing of the contact radius each Δs and with the combination of elastic deformation and pin wear [17], [19].

The elastic deformation orthogonal to the surface is obtained through eqn (6) [10]:

$$h^e = \frac{W}{2E_c a}. \tag{6}$$

The update of the contact radius, a_i, with each increment of the slipped distance, Δs, is obtained by the sum of the elastic deformation and the wear depth from the contact geometry (Fig. 3(b)) and the wear depth is calculated with Euler explicit model integrated over sliding distance on eqn (7) till the end of the algorithm [17], [19].

$$h_{i+1}^w = k_d p_i \Delta s_i + h_i^w. \tag{7}$$

3 RESULTS AND DISCUSSIONS

Fig. 4(a) and (b) show the comparative results of the semi-analytical GIWM computational simulation with the experimental results found in de Almeida et al. [7], for pearlitic steel pin sliding against forged steel disc with a microstructure of colonies of pearlite interspersed with bainite, under velocities of 0.1 m/s and 0.9 m/s, respectively.

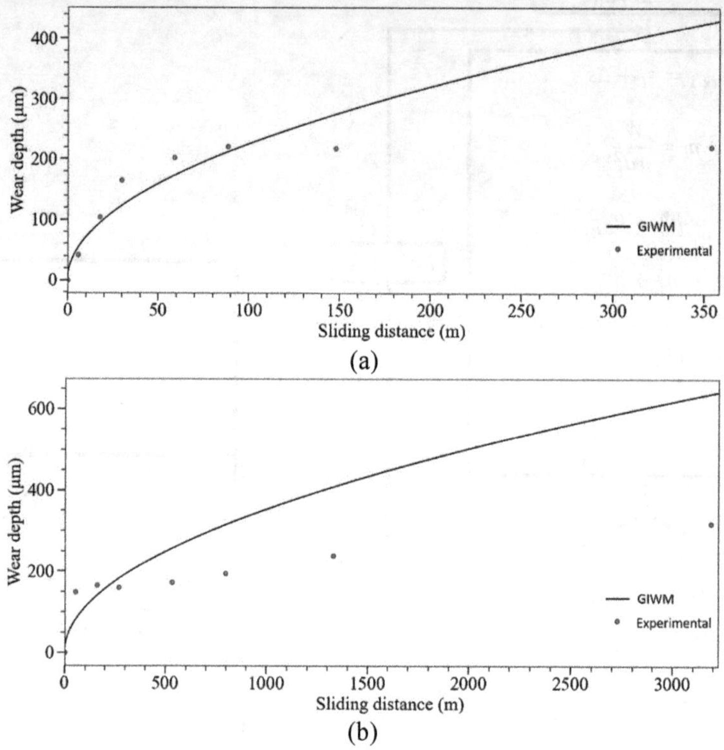

Figure 4: GIWM computer simulation results compared with pin-on-disc tribometer experimental results from de Almeida et al. [7] for the normal load of 24.6 N. (a) Forged steel wheel under sliding speed of 0.1 m/s; and (b) Forged steel wheel under sliding speed of 0.9 m/s.

It can be noted that the semi-analytical method has good agreement with the experimental method until approximately 90 m of sliding distance (running-in), in the case of the lowest sliding speed (Fig. 4(a)). However, after this distance, the GIWM method has low assertiveness.

According to the experimental study under which this paper was based, particles removed from the disc surfaces were highly deformed and had a considerable specific surface area which, according to the researchers, is convenient for the occurrence of rapid oxidation.

The oxidized particles in turn adhere to the disc surface, exponentiated by debris formation, and can cause micro abrasive events on the pin, changing the wear mechanism seen before [7].

It is likely, then, that the GIWM method did not work well from a certain sliding distance, as it does not have the ability to work under a possible oxidative episode that occurred after initiating the experimental test.

For the case of the highest sliding speed (Fig. 4(b)), it can be seen that the semi-analytical method has good agreement with the experimental method only between 100 m and 300 m sliding distance (running-in). After this range, the GIWM method does not work well to simulate the wear of the pearlitic rail.

The result of the computer simulation corroborates the literature and the simulation for cast wheels itself, with regard to the formation of debris and the consequent favoring of the modification of the wear mechanism to oxidative.

Similarly, Fig. 5(a) and (b) show the comparative results of the semi-analytical GIWM computational simulation with the experimental results found in de Almeida et al. [7], for pearlitic steel pin sliding against predominantly pearlitic cast steel disc, under velocities of 0.1 m/s and 0.9 m/s, respectively.

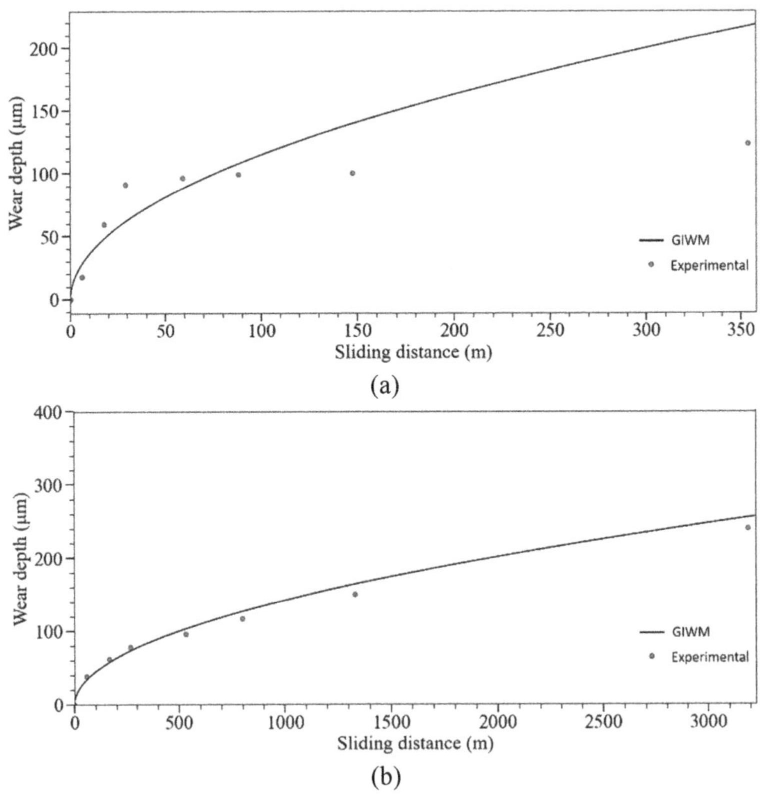

Figure 5: GIWM computer simulation results compared with pin-on-disc tribometer experimental results from de Almeida et al. [7] for the normal load of 24.6 N. (a) Cast steel wheel under sliding speed of 0.1 m/s; and (b) Cast steel wheel under sliding speed of 0.9 m/s.

In Fig. 5(a), where the sliding condition was tested under speed of 0.1 m/s, a consonance of GIWM result with the same condition for forged wheels is observed, where the method proved assertive only in initial ranges of sliding distances.

A possible reason for the low assertiveness of the method is the high adhesion and plastic deformation observed by de Almeida et al. [7] since the method is based on the stiffness of the materials under unloading conditions and thus the GIWM does not have the ability to act predictively in plastic regime [17], [19]. In addition, de Almeida et al. [7] observed that when the plastic limit was reached, the wear mechanism changed from adhesion to fatigue, which might be another possible reason for the low assertiveness of the method in these cases.

For the case of the higher sliding speed (Fig. 5(b)), it is possible to note a good assertiveness of the GIWM method in the whole extension of the test both in running-in and steady state in comparison with the experiments performed by de Almeida et al. [7].

Probably, the method adapted better due to a lower amount of material adhesion on the pins under this sliding condition, as stated by the researchers. Therefore, a better agreement of the GIWM with laboratory experiments is perceived when the actual conditions of the pair of materials do not favors a change in the wear mechanism involved, as it was said that it occurred for the other three cases tested. Evidence that helps to corroborate this theory can be found in Kurzenhäuser et al. [20].

For all cases tested, simulations via GIWM were considerably faster than analogous simulations via FEM reported in the literature. Bastola et al. [11], for example, performed analyses in their recent work that demanded 12 hours of simulation to reach 0.2% of the total sliding distance. The GIWM simulations of the present work were up to 180 times faster, due to its semi-analytical method of easy computational iteration.

4 CONCLUSIONS

The work in question proposed to evaluate the assertiveness of the semi-analytical method global incremental wear model (GIWM) in predicting the wear behavior of railway tracks, when in curved contact with cast and forged wheels.

The method is based on the incremental calculation of the evolution of the body's worn height through the contact area with the counter-body. The results of the algorithm were compared with results of sliding experiments in the pin–disc configuration present in the literature, where the pin was made with rail sample (body) and the discs with wheel sample (counter–body).

The analysis showed that the GIWM can predict satisfactorily, quickly and cheaply the wear behavior in the running-in period. This is a surprising result because the method was not designed to be sensitive to the switch from running-in to steady state.

However, at steady state the GIWM exhibit erroneous wear predictions in three of the four tests. The only exception was the last case, which represents real operating conditions. Possible reason for that is the abrupt changes in the wear mechanisms involved observed in those tribosystems, since this method only works when the active wear mechanism remains the same [20]. Future investigations on interrupted tests shall be taken in order to inspect the wear mechanism change and inspect the correlation between it and the method's accuracy.

All tests with GIWM were exorbitantly more computationally efficient than similar simulations in FEM listed in the literature, in addition to having very equivalent responses between them [21]. This fact shows that the semi-analytical method has the potential to quickly orient the railway sector in constant relation to the materials and the dynamics of use it has already known and constant use.

ACKNOWLEDGEMENT

The authors are grateful for the support of Vale S.A. (Cátedra de Vagões Program).

REFERENCES

[1] Bai, W., Zhou, L., Wang, P., Hu, Y., Wang, W., Ding, H., Han, Z., Xu, X. & Zhu, M., Damage behavior of heavy-haul rail steels used from the mild conditions to harsh conditions. *Wear*, **496–497**, 204290, 2022.

[2] ANTF, National Association of Railway Carriers, General information. Brasilia, Brazil, 2022. www.antf.org.br/informacoes-gerais/. Accessed on: 31 Jul. 2022.

[3] Miranda, R.S., Rezende, A.B., Fonseca, S.T., Fernandes, F.M., Sinatora, A. & Mei, P.R., Fatigue and wear behavior of pearlitic and bainitic microstructures with the same chemical composition and hardness using twin-disc tests. *Wear*, **494–495**, 2022.

[4] Lewis, R. & Olofsson, U., Basic tribology of the wheel–rail contact. *Wheel–Rail Interface Handbook*, 1st ed., pp. 34–57, 2009.

[5] Lewis, R. & Olofsson, U., Mapping rail wear regimes and transitions. *Wear*, **257**, pp. 721–729, 2004.

[6] Hutchings, I. & Shipway, P., *Tribology: Friction and Wear of Engineering Materials*, Butterworth-Heinemann, 2017.

[7] de Almeida, L.P.F., Falqueto, L.E., Goldenstein, H., Bozzi, A.C. & Scandian, C., Study of sliding wear of the wheel flange: Rail gauge corner contact conditions – Comparative between cast and forged steel wheel materials. *Wear*, **432–433**, 2019.

[8] Sundh, J., Olofsson, U. & Sundvall, K., Seizure and wear rate testing of wheel–rail contacts under lubricated conditions using pin-on-disc methodology. *Wear*, **265**, pp. 1425–1430, 2008. DOI: 10.1016/j.wear.2008.03.025.

[9] Danks, D. & Clayton, P., Comparison of the wear process for eutectoid rail steels: Field and laboratory tests. *Wear*, **120**, pp. 233–250, 1987.

[10] Oliver, W.C. & Pharr, G.M., An improved technique for determining hardness and elastic modulus using load and displacement sensing indentation experiments. *J. Mat. Res.*, **7**, pp. 1564–1583, 1992.

[11] Bastola, A., Stewart, D. & Dini, D., Three-dimensional finite element simulation and experimental validation of sliding wear. *Wear*, 2022.

[12] Hegadekatte, V., Huber, N. & Kraft, O., Finite element-based simulation of dry sliding wear. *Modelling and Simulation in Materials Science and Engineering*, **13**, pp. 57–75, 2005.

[13] Põdra, P. & Andersson, S., Simulating sliding wear with finite element method. *Tribology International*, **32**, pp. 71–81, 1999.

[14] Bortoleto, E.M., Rovani, A.C., Seriacopi, V., Profito, F.J., Zachariadis, D.C., Machado, I.F., Sinatora, A. & Souza, R.M., Experimental and numerical analysis of dry contact in the pin on disc test. *Wear*, **301**, pp. 19–26, 2013.

[15] Archard, J.F., Contact and rubbing of flat surfaces. *Journal of Applied Physics*, **24**(8), pp. 981–988, 1953.

[16] Liu, B., Bruni, S. & Lewis, R., Numerical calculation of wear in rolling contact based on the Archard equation: Effect of contact parameters and consideration of uncertainties. *Wear*, 2021.

[17] Hegadekatte, V., Huber, N. & Kraft, O., Modeling and simulation of wear in a pin on disc tribometer. *Tribology Letters*, **24**, pp. 51–60, 2006.

[18] ASTM G99, Standard Test Method for Wear Testing with a Pin-On-Disk Apparatus, 2017.

[19] Hegadekatte, V. et al., A predictive modeling scheme for wear in tribometers. *Tribology International*, **41**(11), pp. 1020–1031, 2008.
[20] Kurzenhäuser, S., Hegadekatte, V., Schneider, J., Huber, N., Kraft, O. & Zum Gahr, K.-H., Tribological characterization and numerical wear simulation of microcomponents under sliding and rolling conditions. *Microsyst. Technol.*, **14**, pp. 1839–1846, 2008.
[21] Jamari, J., Wear prediction using GIWM (global incremental wear model) method. *ROTASI*, **11**(4), pp. 1–4, 2012.

SECTION 3
OPERATION OF RAIL NETWORKS

POTENTIALITY OF RAIL NETWORKS: INTEGRATED SERVICES ON CONVENTIONAL AND HIGH-SPEED LINES

MASSIMO DI GANGI[1] & FRANCESCO RUSSO[2]
[1]Dipartimento di Ingegneria, Università degli Studi di Messina, Italy
[2]Dipartimento di Ingegneria dell'Informazione, delle Infrastrutture e dell'Energia Sostenibile, Università Mediterranea di Reggio Calabria, Italy

ABSTRACT

56,000 km of high-speed rail lines have been built around the world, and another 74,000 km are being built or planned. During the extension of high-speed infrastructures, it is possible to design services that use high-speed lines and conventional lines, in relation to where high-speed has not yet been fully realized. In fact, there is potentiality in existing rail networks, not used for the realization of integrated services that although not of high speed, are better, in terms of travel time, than the conventional ones. An important example is the rail system in Italy, which covers the central and northern areas of the country with high-speed, but it is absent in the south and in Sicily, the large island separated from Italy by a maritime strait. The current services with their travel times from the metropolitan cities of Sicily to Rome, were analysed. An integration of the services is proposed in the hypothesis of no infrastructural changes to the railway lines and terminals and the use of trains and ships available. The results obtained are useful to public planners and technicians of national public departments and railway, as they are able to know what time reductions are possible without any investment. The method used can be applied in other countries where there are high-speed lines and it is possible to create services that use the existing high-speed network and the conventional one.
Keywords: high speed railway, conventional lines, optimization of rail services, integrated service, zero cost and zero time.

1 INTRODUCTION

According to data updated to 2021 [1], the high-speed rail (HSR) lines in the world are: 56,129 km in operation, 22,562 km under construction, 18,781 km medium term planned, 33,005 km long-term planned, for a total of 130,477 km.

From the analysis of the international framework, the benefits of HSR emerge in a very clear way, so much so that all countries are developing impressive programs for the construction of new lines. High-speed networks are increasingly decisive in the development of territories, particularly those less developed [2]. During the extension of high-speed infrastructures, it is useful to analyze the potentiality of conventional and HSR networks to design services that use high-speed lines and conventional lines, where high-speed has not yet been fully realized.

Italy is one of the countries that first built high-speed railway lines. The transport planning documents drawn up by the national government, on the basis of in-depth analyses [3], have established that the extension of the HSR to southern Italy is one of the priorities of the country [4]–[6]. Priority is also set out in all regional plans of the regions crossed [7].

The construction of the high speed for the south, with the stable crossing of Messina Strait, still takes years, and although starting now it would not be completed before a decade. In this context, it is useful and necessary to make the best use of existing infrastructures, reorganizing some significant services. The case study is that of the HSR connection between the capital and the metropolitan cities of Sicily. From the analyzes carried out it emerges the possibility of reducing the current times without any infrastructural intervention, only by

WIT Transactions on The Built Environment, Vol 213, © 2022 WIT Press
www.witpress.com, ISSN 1743-3509 (on-line)
doi:10.2495/CR220091

optimizing the schedules of the services. There is also the possibility of obtaining further reductions with specific interventions on the compositions of the trains.

This problem is of great interest to the set of countries that build new HSR lines. This set first includes the two large blocks of the European Union [8] and China [9], but extends from Saudi Arabia [10] to Morocco, to the trans-Asian lines up to the new lines in the USA [11].

The aim of the paper is therefore to investigate the possibility of creating services with better times than those that take place exclusively on conventional networks, creating routes that take place partly on high-speed lines and partly on conventional lines. The goal is usually shared theoretically by all users, while in practice it is not often pursued.

The method used operates in two stages. In the first phase, the current state of the services available on the infrastructure lines of the two types is reconstructed. In the second phase, a reorganization is proposed with integration between services currently already available. The proposal for integrated services is made on the assumption that no amount is spent on infrastructures and on means: ships and trains. The proposal, based on these characteristics, can therefore be called zero cost and zero time.

In Section 2 the first phase is described. The current situation is presented with a summary of the infrastructural situation of both the HSR network and the conventional network. The structure of the current services is then recalled considering the best services already active on the high-speed network, on the conventional network and on the maritime arcs. In Section 3 the second phase is described. The plans for the construction of the HSR in the south and for upgrading the conventional network are first briefly recalled. Then hypotheses are introduced for an integration of existing services with their combination. The results are presented, demonstrating that, by integrating the services already available on the different infrastructure networks, it is possible to obtain new services that to reduce the current travel times.

The proposed approach can be easily updated, every year, in the system considered as the high-speed infrastructure network grows. The approach can be implemented in all areas where extensions of high-speed networks are being realized, considering that there are 74,000 km under construction. The issue of service integration is therefore of particular interest both to planners operating at national level in the relevant ministries and to service planners within railway companies. The integration of services is of interest to researchers because it allows on the one hand to formulate general models, and algorithms for the use of networks with different characteristics and because it allows to study during the design of new HSR lines, the commissioning of individual parts of the new HSR and conventional lines.

2 ANALYSIS OF THE CURRENT STATE

This section analyzes the current situation of the railway network in the south of Italy and the available rail services with reference to the main route connecting Rome and Sicily. The first part briefly describes the three infrastructure subsystems involved: the HSR network, the conventional network and the maritime connection that allows the transshipment of trains. The second part describes the rail services that are now available to users for long and medium distances considering: connection services between Rome and the extreme south of the peninsula; crossing services; internal services in Sicily.

2.1 Infrastructures

The railway section considered is part of the Scandinavia–Mediterranean corridor which extends from the Russian–Finnish border and from the Finnish ports of Hamina Kotka,

Helsinki and Turku-Naantali to Stockholm, passing through southern Sweden, Denmark, Germany, western Austria, Italy up to Malta [12]. The part of this corridor that affects Italy is shown in Fig. 1(a). The HSR network reaches Salerno, further south the network is of the conventional double-track type and in Sicily some sections are single-track. There is also a maritime link that allows trains to pass through the Messina Strait. Fig. 1(b) illustrates the parts of the corridor in southern Italy with the peninsular part from Rome to Villa S. Giovanni (the extension of the HSR network in dashed) and the island parts from Messina to Catania and Palermo.

(a) (b)

Figure 1: Scandinavian–Mediterranean corridor intersecting Italy [12], [13].

2.2 Services

The study of rail services must be developed on the basis of the demand for the use of services. Nationwide services have characteristics of high regularity and models that simulate demand pose the regularity of services as a basic element [14], [15]. Based on the demand it is possible to know the impacts [16], [17]. In the present case, there is a large potential demand for the relations considered [18]. It is interesting to consider the complexity of the case study, which also contains sea links [19]. The demand is estimated in relation to the complete HSR line, but a part can manifest itself with the supply of integrated services that allow to reduce the current travel times on the conventional line.

To analyze the current travel times on the railway routes from Sicily (Catania and Palermo) to Rome, the Palermo–Rome and Catania–Rome routes were considered and, for simplicity of presentation, the analysis reported concerns only even trains (south–north and east–west directions), that is, trains that go from Sicily to Rome. For the routes considered, the direct connections without service breakage (i.e. those in which there is no transshipment of travelers) have been deduced from the Trenitalia timetable consulted on 10 March 2021 with reference to trips made on 11 March 2021. The analyses described below have been conducted by disaggregating the relationships into island and continental sections. The abbreviation IC stands for intercity, the abbreviation RV and R for fast regional train and for regional train.

2.2.1 The route Villa S. Giovanni–Rome

Considering the Trenitalia timetable, it emerges that the route is covered in 6 h 44 min by the IC 728 train. The IC 728 is recalled here because it is one of the fastest trains in the connection between Sicily and Rome. The stop times are 2 min except for the stations of Lamezia Terme, Paola and Salerno (3 min) and central Naples (14 min).

The main factors for the different sections, in terms of time from the timetable, and physical and technological characteristics from line sheets [22]–[25], are shown in Table 1.

Table 1: Characteristics of the sections and of the performance of the IC 728 train on the Villa S. Giovanni–Rome Termini line.

Section	Line type	No. tracks	Traction type	Distance (km)	Time (minutes)
Villa S. Giovanni–Gioia Tauro	Conv	2	3kV	36.528	25
Gioia Tauro–Lamezia	Conv	2	3kV	69.703	36
Lamezia–Paola	Conv	2	3kV	56.870	31
Paola–Sapri	Conv	2	3kV	92.212	48
Sapri–Salerno	Conv	2	3kV	124.492	74
Salerno–Napoli Central	Conv	2	3kV	53.090	40
Napoli Central–Aversa	Conv	2	3kV	19.220	16
Aversa–Formia	Conv	2	3kV	50.077	31
Formia–Latina	Conv	2	3kV	67.225	36
Latina–Rome T.ni	Conv	2	3kV	61.018	34

2.2.2 The crossing of Strait of Messina

The evaluation of the crossing time of the Strait of Messina was carried out considering the time between the arrival at the Messina central station and the departure from the Villa S. Giovanni station for direct connections without service breakage (i.e. those in which there is no transshipment of travelers).

The origins from Palermo and Catania were analyzed. The Milazzo–Lamezia Terme and Taormina–Lamezia Terme routes are examined for the pair of trains IC 728–IC 722 and for the pair of trains IC 730–IC 724. The crossing times are summarized in Table 2.

Table 2: Characteristics of the crossing times of the Strait of Messina.

Train number	Time	
	(hours)	(minutes)
728	2	10
722	1	57
730	1	55
724	2	05

2.2.3 The route Palermo–Messina

The analysis shows that the route is covered in 2 h 50 min by train IC 728 and in 2 h 43 min by train RV 5364. So, it is clear that the RV fast regional train makes two intermediate stops more than the IC but takes 7 min less to travel the route. The RV train will therefore be considered in the subsequent integration proposal.

The stopping times at the stops are 2 min for the IC train and 1 min for the RV train with the exception, for the latter of the S. Agata station where it stops for 4 min. Altogether you have 14 min stop for the IC train and 12 min stop for the RV train.

The main factors for the different sections, in terms of time from the timetable, and physical and technological characteristics from line sheet [20], are shown in Table 3.

Table 3: Characteristics of the sections and of the performance of the RV 5364 and IC 728 trains on the Palermo–Messina line.

Section	Line type	No. tracks	Traction type	Distance (km)	Time (minutes)	
					RV 5364	IC 728
Palermo Central–Termini	Conv	2	3kV	36.415	24	23
Termini–Campofelice	Conv	2	3kV	16.378	9	18
Campofelice–Cefalù	Conv	2	3kV	14.001	10	
Cefalù–S. Stefano	Conv	1	3kV	31.219	23	47
S. Stefano–S. Agata	Conv	1	3kV	27.265	20	
S. Agata–Capo d'Orlando	Conv	1	3kV	13.363	9	9
Capo d'Orlando–Patti	Conv	1	3kV	23.705	18	19
Patti–Barcellona	Conv	2	3kV	21.910	11	12
Barcellona–Milazzo	Conv	2	3kV	7.939	5	5
Milazzo–Messina Central	Conv	2	3kV	31.578	22	23

2.2.4 The route Catania–Messina

The analysis shows that the route is traveled in 1 h 12 min from IC 722 train, 1 h 27 min from IC 724 train, 1 h 34 min from train R 5384, 1 h 24 min from the RV 5386 train.

It can be noted that the IC 724 train, while making the same stops with the same duration, takes 15 min longer than the IC 722 train. In addition, the R train makes seven more stops than the IC 722 train and takes only 7 min longer. Finally, the RV train makes three more stops than the IC 724 train and takes 3 min less. Also, in this case the stopping times are 2 min for the IC trains and 1 min for the R and RV trains with the exception, for the R 5384 train, of the Letoianni station where it stops for 5 min and, for the RV 5386 train, of the S. Teresa di Riva station where it stops for 4 min. Altogether you have 6 min stop for the IC trains, 14 min stop for the R train and 9 min for the RV train. Then there are various possibilities for a decisive improvement in services on national routes.

The main factors for the different sections, in terms of time from the timetable, and physical and technological characteristics from line sheet [21] are shown in Tables 4 and 5.

Table 4: Characteristics of the sections and of the performance of the IC 722 and IC 724 trains on the Catania–Messina line.

Section	Line type	No. tracks	Traction type	Distance (km)	Time (minutes)	
					IC 722	IC 724
Catania Central–Acireale	Conv	2	3kV	13.054	10	10
Acireale–Giarre	Conv	2	3kV	16.757	9	10
Giarre–Taormina	Conv	1*	3kV	17.951	12	12
Taormina–Messina Central	Conv	1**	3kV	47.009	35	49

* Partially double track – from Giarre to Fiumefreddo (8.222 km);
** Partially double track – from Giampilieri to Messina (13.354 km).

Table 5: Characteristics of the sections and of the performance of the RV 5384 and RV 5386 trains on the Catania–Messina line.

<table>
<tr><th rowspan="2">Section</th><th rowspan="2">Line type</th><th rowspan="2">No. tracks</th><th rowspan="2">Traction type</th><th rowspan="2">Distance (km)</th><th colspan="2">Time (minutes)</th></tr>
<tr><th>RV 5384</th><th>RV 5386</th></tr>
<tr><td>Catania Central–Acireale</td><td>Conv</td><td>2</td><td>3kV</td><td>13.054</td><td>11</td><td>9</td></tr>
<tr><td>Acireale–Giarre</td><td>Conv</td><td>2</td><td>3kV</td><td>16.757</td><td>9</td><td>10</td></tr>
<tr><td>Giarre–Fiumefreddo</td><td>Conv</td><td>2</td><td>3kV</td><td>8.222</td><td>6</td><td>7</td></tr>
<tr><td>Fiumefreddo–Taormina</td><td>Conv</td><td>1</td><td>3kV</td><td>9.729</td><td>8</td><td>9</td></tr>
<tr><td>Taormina–Letojanni</td><td>Conv</td><td>1</td><td>3kV</td><td>4.943</td><td>7</td><td rowspan="2">13</td></tr>
<tr><td>Letojanni–S. Teresa Riva</td><td>Conv</td><td>1</td><td>3kV</td><td>9.873</td><td>9</td></tr>
<tr><td>S. Teresa Riva–Furci</td><td>Conv</td><td>1</td><td>3kV</td><td>2.226</td><td>2</td><td rowspan="3">7</td></tr>
<tr><td>Furci–Roccalumera</td><td>Conv</td><td>1</td><td>3kV</td><td>1.514</td><td>2</td></tr>
<tr><td>Roccalumera–Alì terme</td><td>Conv</td><td>1</td><td>3kV</td><td>4.643</td><td>4</td></tr>
<tr><td>Alì Terme–Giampilieri</td><td>Conv</td><td>1</td><td>3kV</td><td>8.456</td><td>6</td><td rowspan="2">20</td></tr>
<tr><td>Giampilieri–Messina Central</td><td>Conv</td><td>2</td><td>3kV</td><td>13.354</td><td>16</td></tr>
</table>

3 INTEGRATION OF SERVICES

This section analyzes the planned situation of the HSR and conventional railway infrastructure network in the south of Italy and the proposal for rail services that can immediately be realized with reference to the main route connecting Rome and Sicily. The projects are first briefly recalled. The railway services available today are examined by verifying the upgrades that can be implemented, based on what was seen in Section 2, at no cost and at no time. The macro characteristics of the means necessary to carry out the services are recalled: ships and trains. Then the integration of the overall long-distance services for the connection between Rome and the metropolitan cities of Sicily is studied and the best configuration is reported.

3.1 Strategic infrastructural planning

Currently, some actions are underway aimed at extending the HSR network towards the south of the Italian peninsula by building a new infrastructure from Salerno to Reggio Calabria. To make train ferry times more efficient it is under development the use of locomotives equipped with a buffer battery to allow autonomous entry on ferries and also the use of trains with blocked composition to save the time due to the recomposition of the trains and the verification of the functioning of the braking system after disembarking from the ferries. Regarding the improvement of the Sicilian infrastructural network, work is being done through by completing the doubling of some single-track sections and by improving the speed rank of the currently existing conventional network.

3.2 Operational planning of rail services

Based on what has been seen in the previous section, it is possible to introduce modest changes to existing services by combining their best features. In the following it is then proposed for each service the modification of some attributes:

- *NS* = the number of stops;
- *ST* = the stopping time at the stations;

- *TT* = the time between two stations, i.e. considering the shortest of all the times used by the trains available today.

These changes are fully compatible with the available networks and result only from the composition of the best available features among the services supplied. In this sense, it is an operational planning of rail services.

3.2.1 The route Villa S. Giovanni–Rome

The Villa S. Giovanni–Rome section has two railway lines that proceed almost side by side: a high-speed line and a conventional line. The high-speed line runs from Rome to Salerno. After an initial period in which the services were closely connected to the networks, for some years services have been available that use the HSR network from Rome to Salerno and the conventional network from Salerno to Villa S. Giovanni. In Italy, the services that are carried out on the HSR networks are called Frecciarossa and Frecciargento. The services operating on the HSR networks and on the conventional networks also take the same names: Frecciarossa and Frecciargento.

To choose the best available service, it is considered to modify the three attributes: *NS, ST, TT*. Therefore, the use of the Freccia is proposed.

To evaluate the travel times on the Villa S. Giovanni–Rome route, consider the Frecciargento service already offered by train 8352 in 2017. The train departed at 06.48 from Reggio Calabria and arrived in Rome at 11.35, taking 4 h 47 min, stopping at the stations of Villa San Giovanni, Lamezia Terme Centrale, Paola and Salerno. The number of stops *NS* is then reduced, the time *ST* is reduced, and the fastest train *TT* between two stations is taken. The service to connect Villa with the capital took 4 h 31 min.

The main factors for the different sections, in terms of time from the timetable, and physical and technological characteristics from line sheets [22], [23], [26], are shown in Table 6.

Table 6: Characteristics of the sections on the Villa S. Giovanni–Rome line.

Section	Line type	No. tracks	Traction type	Distance (km)	Time (minutes)
Villa S. Giovanni–Lamezia	Conv	2	3kV	106.231	49
Lamezia–Paola	Conv	2	3kV	56.870	27
Paola–Salerno	Conv	2	3kV	216.712	91
Salerno–Rome T.ni	HSR	2	25kV	264.091	95

3.2.2 The crossing of Strait of Messina

The crossing of the Strait is a central element of the connections between Sicily and Rome. For the crossing of trains, several hypotheses have been studied relating to the realization of a “stable crossing”. Recently, several hypotheses have been developed for the strengthening of the maritime link. These hypotheses have been called “dynamic crossing”.

In this work, in line with what is proposed for the other infrastructural links, two scenarios are considered, both achievable at zero time and zero cost.

The first scenario is called Scenario 1. It is used as a crossing time (time between the arrival of the convoy at the Messina central station and departure from the Villa central station) the best among the current ones: 1 h 55 min, using only the *TT* attribute.

The second scenario is called Scenario 2. It is assumed to use a block-sized train of shorter length than the available ferry. In the case of a blocked composition, the current ferry times would be significantly reduced as the operations of decomposition and recomposition of the train and the related braking checks would not be necessary, then operating on the *TT* and *ST* attributes. In this scenario, it is necessary to consider the timing of the different operations: transfer from central Messina to Maritime Messina; boarding the ferry; crossing the Strait; disembarkation from the ferry; transfer from Villa Maritime to Villa Central.

The total time, considering the estimated average time for each operation, is 55 min.

3.2.3 The route Palermo–Messina

Three changes are envisaged on this route: use of the best times between the different trains and that is modification of *TT*; decrease in the number of intermediate stops, *NS*; reduction of stopping time, *ST*.

In the assumptions made, a total time of 150 min is obtained. The detail is in Table 7.

Table 7: Characteristics of the sections on Palermo–Messina line.

Section	Line type	No. tracks	Traction type	Distance (km)	Time (minutes)
Palermo C.le–Termini	Conv	2	3kV	36,415	22
Termini–Cefalù	Conv	2	3kV	30,379	17
Cefalù–S. Agata	Conv	1	3kV	58,484	42
S. Agata–Barcellona	Conv	1*	3kV	58,969	38
Barcellona–Milazzo	Conv	2	3kV	7,939	6
Milazzo–Messina C.le	Conv	2	3kV	31,578	20

* Partially double track – from Patti to Barcellona (21.910 km).

3.2.4 The route Catania–Messina

On this route, three changes are hypothesized, similar to those proposed for the Palermo–Messina: use of the best times between the different trains and that is modification of *TT*; decrease in the number of intermediate stops, *NS*; reduction of dwell time, *ST*.

In the assumptions made a total time of 55 min is obtained. The detail is in Table 8.

Table 8: Characteristics of the section Catania–Messina.

Section	Line type	No. tracks	Traction type	Distance (km)	Time (minutes)
Catania Central–Taormina	Conv	1*	3kV	47.762	26
Taormina–Messina Central	Conv	1**	3kV	47.009	28

* Partially double track – from Catania to Fiumefreddo (38.033 km);
** Partially double track – from Giampilieri to Messina (13.354 km).

3.2.5 Variation of attributes

To show, in a quantitative way, the differences between the current service and the proposed one, these variations are summarized in Table 9 in terms of the attributes described above.

3.3 The used rolling stock

The hypotheses made for the crossing with the proposal defined Scenario 2, must be compatible with the available means, in order to respect the basic hypothesis of feasibility in zero time and zero cost.

Table 9: Values of the attributes for the current service and for the proposed one.

Section	Current service			Proposed service		
	NS	ST	TT	NS	ST	TT
Catania Central–Messina Central	3	6	66	1	1	54
Palermo Central–Messina Central	7	14	156	5	5	145
Villa S. Giovanni–Rome T.ni	9	33	371	3	9	262

The ship *Messina* currently in service has an average load capacity of 16 carriages of 26.40 m distributed on four tracks. From the track descriptions contained in [20] it can be seen that the maximum length of track that can be occupied by a single train is equal to just over 133 m. As for the usable material, in order to obtain a convoy of less than 133 m, it is necessary to use a railway material available in other Italian lines.

As seen above, the railway material used for the Frecciargento 8352 that carried out the indicated travel times, was ETR485 material. The composition was nine elements with a length of 236.6 m and a maximum speed of 250 km/h. It is proposed to replace the material of the ETR485 series with the material of the ETR400 series, commonly known in Italy as Frecciarossa1000. The Frecciarossa1000 trains can be configured in versions of four, eight, 12 or 16 carriages, with a driving position at each extreme. The standard composition of the ETR 400 train has eight carriages for a total length of 202 m. There is a four carriage composition, used in 2013 for tests, which has a total length of 102.4 m.

As it is easy to see, the convoy in composition of four carriages can be transported in full on a track of the ferry ships currently in service.

3.4 The integration of services

It is possible to integrate the services obtained with the hypotheses for each section and the two crossing scenarios, respecting the basic hypothesis of zero time and zero cost.

Table 10 shows the times for each route and for each scenario, and the times of the current situation. The percentage reductions obtained for each overall scenario are also reported. The times per route and per scenario are pictured in Fig. 2.

Table 10: Connection times of the Sicilian metropolitan cities with Rome.

Scenario	Attributes	City of origin		
		Palermo	Catania	Messina
Current	Travel time	11 h 38 min	9 h 53 min	8 h 24 min
Scenario 1	Travel time	8 h 56 min	7 h 21 min	6 h 26 min
	Reduction	2 h 42 min	2 h 32 min	1 h 58 min
	Reduction %	23.2%	25.6%	23.4%
Scenario 2	Travel time	7 h 56 min	6 h 21 min	5 h 26 min
	Reduction	3 h 24 min	3 h 32 min	2 h 58 min
	Reduction %	31.8%	35.8%	35.3%

From the analysis of the times reported emerge the strong reductions in time immediately obtainable. On the longer connection, Palermo–Rome the reduction is greater than 20% in Scenario 1 and 30% in Scenario 2. On the connection from Catania the reduction is greater than 25% in Scenario 1 and 35% in Scenario 2.

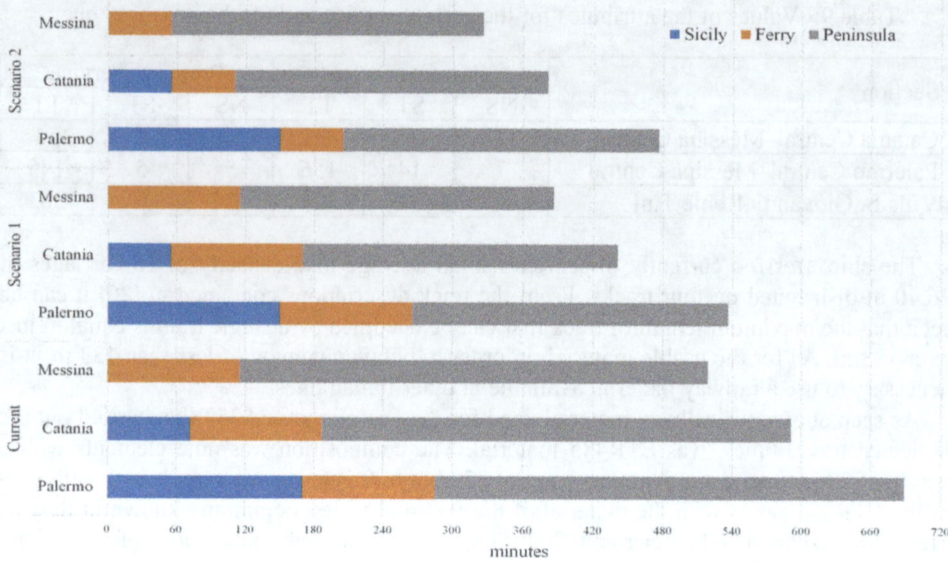

Figure 2: Components of travel times per route and per scenario.

The results obtained are based on the hypothesis of not operating infrastructural intervention and are therefore immediately implementable. Scenario 2 despite being at no cost, because the Frecciarosssa1000 are available to Trenitalia, would still imply a decision by the top management to move some trains on the connection between Sicily and Rome. Scenario 1 does not imply any decision because it would be implemented with the material already available for the connection between Villa S. Giovanni and Rome.

4 CONCLUSIONS

The integration method used is combines exhaustively all the trains currently in operation, first proceeding to local optimizations on three attributes *NS, ST* and *TT*. From the exhaustive combination it is possible to identify the optimal integrated service.

The method is applied to combine existing services on HSR and conventional lines.

The results obtained are interesting in different aspects. On the scientific level they allow: with regard to the supply to investigate and build multi-level optimization models, considering each network as a different layer; with regard to the demand, the ex-ante assessment of the change in the utility of users to the choice of mode of transport. The results can be useful to know what time reductions are possible without any investment. Finally, they are interesting because they constitute the real reference in the evaluation of the alternatives for the realization of the high speed. These times are the ones with which to compare any infrastructure operation proposed for the southern Italy, thus eliminating the use of train times without changes for passengers currently in operation, which are unjustifiably higher and do not respond to the actual current potential.

The proposed method is very simple and can be used by planners and technicians of state departments, in all territorial contexts of any country where the extension of high speed is being planned. The method is also interesting for the technicians and planners of the railway companies that manage the services because they can build new market alternatives to offer to users. Finally, they are interesting for researchers because they allow to develop multi-level optimization models to be applied to the construction of railway timetables.

REFERENCES

[1] UIC, High speed line in the world, 2021. https://uic.org/IMG/pdf/20210601_high_speed_lines_in_the_world.pdf. Accessed on: 24 Aug. 2022.

[2] Chen, Z., Xue, J., Rose, A. & Haynes, E.H., The impact of high-speed rail investment on economic and environmental change in China: A dynamic CGE analysis. *Transp. Res. Part A Policy Pract.*, **92**, pp. 232–245, 2016.

[3] Cascetta, E., Nuzzolo, A., Biggiero, L. & Russo, F., Passenger and freight demand models for the Italian transportation system. *Proceedings of 7th World Conference on Transport Research*, **2**, 1995.

[4] GURI (Gazzetta Ufficiale della Repubblica Italiana), Decreto del Presidente della Repubblica 14 marzo 2001. Nuovo piano generale dei trasporti e della logistica. GU Serie Generale n.163 del 16-07-2001-Suppl. Straordinario. 2001 https://www.gazzettaufficiale.it/eli/id/2001/07/16/001A6017/sg. Accessed on: 24 Aug. 2022.

[5] MIT (Ministero Infrastrutture e Trasporti), Piano generale della mobilita, Linee Guida. Nota Introduttiva Roma, 2007. https://trafficlab.eu/bfd_download/linee-guida-pgm-2007/. Accessed on: 24 Aug. 2022.

[6] Council Presidency of Italy, Piano Nazionale di Ripresa e Resilienza, 2021. https://www.governo.it/sites/governo.it/files/PNRR_0.pdf. Accessed on: 24 Aug. 2022.

[7] Russo, F. & Rindone, C., Regional transport plans: From direction role denied to common rules identified. *Sustainability*, **13**(16), p. 9052. 2021.

[8] De Rus, G., Economic analysis of high speed rail in Europe, Fundacion BBVA/BBVA Foundation, 2012. https://econpapers.repec.org/bookchap/fbbreport/2012126.htm. Accessed on: 24 Aug. 2022.

[9] Wangtu, A.X., Jiangping, Z., Linchuan, Y. & Ling, L., The implications of high-speed rail for Chinese cities: Connectivity and accessibility. *Transp. Res. Part A*, **116**, pp. 308–326, 2018.

[10] Ali, M. & Siegmann, J., Introducing high speed rail system in Middle East (Kingdom of Saudi Arabia): A comparison of past, current and future networks. *Glob. J. Eng. Sci. Res. Manag.*, 2017. http://www.gjesrm.com. Accessed on: 24 Aug. 2022.

[11] Eidlin, E., Making the most of high-speed rail in California: Lessons from France and Germany. Project Report of the German Marshall Fund of the United States, German Marshall Fund of the United States: Washington, DC, 2015.

[12] OJEU (Official Journal of the European Union), Regulation (EU) No 1315/2013 of the European Parliament and of the Council, 11 December 2013. Union Guidelines for the Development of the Trans-European Transport Network and Repealing. Decision No 661/2010/EU. https://eur-lex.europa.eu/legal-content/EN/TXT/?uri=celex%3A32013R1315. Accessed on: 24 Aug. 2022.

[13] European Commission, TENtec interactive map viewer. https://ec.europa.eu/transport/infrastructure/tentec/tentec-portal/map/maps.html. Accessed on: 24 Aug. 2022.

[14] Cascetta, E., Biggiero, L., Nuzzolo, A. & Russo, F., A system of within-day dynamic demand and assignment models for scheduled intercity services. *Proceedings of Seminar D&E on Transportation Planning Methods at the 24th PTRC Summer Annual Meeting*, UK, 1996.

[15] Nuzzolo, A. & Russo, F., Departure time and path choice models for intercity transit assignment. *Travel Behaviour Research: Updating the State of Play*, Elsevier Science, 1998.
[16] Cascetta, E., Cartenì, A., Henke, I. & Pagliara, F., Economic growth, transport accessibility and regional equity impacts of high-speed railways in Italy: Ten years ex post evaluation and future perspectives. *Transp. Res. Part A*, **139**, pp. 412–428, 2020.
[17] Di Gangi, M. & Cirianni, F., A methodology for operative cost and revenue evaluation in transit systems: Application to an Italian extra-urban area. *Proceedings of the European Transport Annual Meeting: Applied Transport Methods*, PTRC: London, 2002.
[18] Russo, F., Which high-speed rail? LARG approach between plan and design. *Future Transportation*, **1**(2), pp. 202–226, 2021.
[19] Di Gangi, M. & Polimeni, A., A model to simulate multimodality in a mesoscopic dynamic network loading framework. *Journal of Advanced Transportation*, 2017.
[20] Fascicolo Circolazione Linea n. 153 (linea Messina C.le–Palermo C.le), Edizione Dicembre 2003 (CT PA 4/2021). https://normativaesercizio.rfi.it/NormativaEsercizio. Accessed on: 22 Mar. 2021.
[21] Fascicolo Circolazione Linea n. 152 (linea Messina C.le–Siracusa), Edizione Dicembre 2003 (CT PA 4/2021). https://normativaesercizio.rfi.it/NormativaEsercizio. Accessed on: 22 Mar. 2021.
[22] Fascicolo Circolazione Linea n. 142 (linea Reggio Calabria–Battipaglia), Edizione Dicembre 2003 C.T. 39/2018. https://normativaesercizio.rfi.it/NormativaEsercizio. Accessed on: 22 Mar. 2021.
[23] Fascicolo Circolazione Linea n. 123 (linea Napoli–Battipaglia), Edizione Dicembre 2003. https://normativaesercizio.rfi.it/NormativaEsercizio. Accessed on: 22 Mar. 2021.
[24] Fascicolo Circolazione Linea n. 122 (linea Formia Gaeta–Napoli C/le), Edizione Dicembre 2003. https://normativaesercizio.rfi.it/NormativaEsercizio. Accessed on: 22 Mar. 2021.
[25] Fascicolo Circolazione Linea n. 117 (linea Roma Termini–Formia Gaeta), Edizione Dicembre 2003. https://normativaesercizio.rfi.it/NormativaEsercizio. Accessed on: 22 Mar. 2021.
[26] Fascicolo Circolazione Linea n. 119 (linea AC/AV Roma–Napoli), Edizione Settembre 2005. https://normativaesercizio.rfi.it/NormativaEsercizio. Accessed on: 22 Mar. 2021.

WEATHER AND TRAIN DISRUPTIONS IN SWEDEN, 2011–2019

MICHELLE OCHSNER[1,2] & CARL-WILLIAM PALMQVIST[1,2]
[1]Department of Technology and Society, Lund University, Sweden
[2]K2 Swedish Knowledge Centre for Public Transport, Sweden

ABSTRACT

The impacts of adverse weather conditions on railway systems can lead to large delays and cancellations across the entire network. In this paper, we aim to understand the relationship between weather and train disruptions (i.e. cancellations and large delays) across the entire Swedish railway network for the years 2011–2019. Using railway operations data and snow depth, temperature, precipitation, and wind data aggregated on a weekly level, we use visual graphical analysis to understand this relationship. The results indicate that the disruption shares increase with higher amounts of snow and rainfall, and wind speeds. Results show that disruptions increase dramatically both at cold temperatures, with high snow depths, and at high wind speeds. High temperatures and precipitation levels also correlate with increased disruptions, but less dramatically. With projected increases in temperatures and precipitation due to climate change, and an increased frequency of storms, some of these relationships are expected to become more significant, while winter-related problems are likely to decrease. The results highlight the importance of increasing the resilience of railways to adverse weather conditions and the need for appropriate adaptation strategies.

Keywords: extreme weather, temperature, precipitation, snow, wind, railway, disruptions.

1 INTRODUCTION

Reliable railway systems are essential to an operating and developing society [1], [2], and weather is one factor that can lead to disruptions in a railway system, decreasing its reliability. When compared with road infrastructure, railways are more vulnerable to disturbances and disruptions due to capacity constraints and limited rerouting alternatives [3]. Adverse weather conditions demonstrate railways' vulnerability to the current climate, and due to climate change this vulnerability is likely to increase [4].

Heavy rain or snowfall can lead to visibility issues, flooding of track and tunnels, blockages on tracks, and also impacts soil stability near slopes and retaining walls which can lead to landslides, mudflows, and other earth flows [4], [5]. Freezing rain can cause ice build-up on infrastructure such as tracks or overhead contact wires, and precipitation deficit may lead to track misalignment due to decreased amounts of groundwater [5]. Low temperatures can lead to problems such as cracking of railway tracks, slippery track conditions, or freezing of overhead lines and signalling equipment; and in contrast, high temperatures can cause problems such as track buckling, or overheating of signalling equipment [4], [5]. Strong winds can also lead to disruptions due to fallen trees blocking tracks, damage to electrical equipment, and decreased train wagon stability [6], [7].

To mitigate the negative effects of climate change on railway systems in the future, increase network resiliency, and to develop subsequent adaptation measures, it is important to understand the past and current effects of adverse weather conditions on railway systems [4]. Hence, the aim of this study is to analyse the past effects of weather on railway disruptions in Sweden (i.e. cancellations or large delays) and consider how these may change along with changing climate conditions.

WIT Transactions on The Built Environment, Vol 213, © 2022 WIT Press
www.witpress.com, ISSN 1743-3509 (on-line)
doi:10.2495/CR220101

2 PREVIOUS RESEARCH

2.1 Past weather and train delays or disruptions

A number of researchers have investigated the connection between various types of weather and train delays or disruptions. Ling et al. [8] found that rail delays in China are strongly correlated with extreme weather conditions related to rain and snowfall. Brazil et al. [9] studied the effects of weather conditions on train delays in Dublin, Ireland and concluded that rainfall is the main variable leading to delays, especially when it occurs together with high winds. Diab and Shalaby [10] studied the impact of weather on outdoor track segments of the metro system in Toronto, Canada and concluded that snow on the ground and rainfall led to more service interruptions.

In the Netherlands, Xia et al. [7] concluded that bad weather accounts for 4–8% of all train disturbances, and that wind gusts of more than 19 m/s have significant effects on disruptions. A study by Ludvigsen and Klæboe [11] analysed the impact of the 2010 winter on freight rail operations in Switzerland, Poland, Sweden, Norway, and Finland. The results indicate that the harsh winter weather conditions of long periods of heavy snowfall, long periods of cold temperatures, and long periods of strong wind played a serious role in the punctuality of freight trains. In Norway, Zakeri and Olsson [12] studied the effects of extreme weather conditions on delays and punctuality between 2007 and 2016 and concluded that harsher winters resulted in more delays compared to more mild winters, and that snow depth was found to be the main weather variable that best explains both daily and weekly punctuality variations. In Sweden, Palmqvist et al. [13] found that punctuality dropped by almost 2% points when a quarter of all trains analysed accumulated at least 30 mm of precipitation, drops by 2% when wind speeds exceed 10 m/s and by 9% when they exceed 23 m/s, and that punctuality decreases exponentially when temperatures fall below 0°C and or reach high temperatures. Wang et al. [14] studied the impacts of winter climate on high-speed passenger trains in Sweden, between Umeå and Stockholm, and found that that low temperatures and high humidity in the winter months decrease train punctuality.

2.2 Future climate change impacts on railway systems

Other studies have been concerned with understanding the future impacts of climate change on railway systems. Palin et al. [15] used future temperature projections to study the impacts of climate change on railways in the UK, and project that an increase in temperatures will not only cause stress on infrastructure such as track buckling or overheating of overhead power lines, but also on operations as heat can cause stress on workers. Similarly, Dobney et al. [16] quantified the effects of high summer temperatures related to climate change on rail buckling and consequently delays in the UK. They concluded that the number of buckles and therefore rail delays per year will increase if tracks are maintained to their current standard. The effect of climate change on the frequency of critical meteorological conditions in Austria was simulated by Kellermann et al. [17], who concluded that extreme cold temperatures and snowfall will become less common but heatwaves and intense rainfall will become more frequent, calling for a shift in adaptation measures.

Chinowsky et al. [18] conducted a study on the impacts of climate change on railway operations in the United States in order to understand the future vulnerabilities. They estimate that the railway network may encounter an increase in delay-minute costs of between $35 and $60 billion over historic costs through to 2100. Forzieri et al. [19] found that damage from heat waves, droughts, flooding, windstorms, and forest fires is expected to increase across Europe as climate change progresses which will result in higher costs of adaptation. Ilalokhoin et al. [20] developed a multi-track model for estimating railway journey impacts from extreme weather events in Great Britain, which highlighted the importance of increasing resilience to flood and storm events that are predicted to become more frequent in the future. Bubeck et al. [21] focused on the impacts of climate change on flood risk around Europe and concluded that currently the annual damage of flooding on railways in Europe is currently €581 million per year, however, this is expected to increase by up to 310% in light of climate change.

3 METHODS

In this study we make use of two datasets, railway operations data and weather data from 2011–2019 across the entire Swedish railway network.

The railway operations data comes from the Swedish Transport Administration and includes about 100 million registered arrivals at stations where the trains stop, not merely pass by. The data covers both passenger and freight trains. In this study, we define disruptions as arrivals that were cancelled or delayed by more than 60 minutes. Overall, about 10 of the 100 million arrivals were cancelled, and slightly less than 1 million delayed by more than 60 minutes. This leads to a baseline rate of disruptions of about 11%. A large part of the cancellations can be explained by freight trains, where operators often apply for more train paths than will be used, because they do not know far in advance exactly which of the paths will be required. Unfortunately, we do not have data on how far in advance trains are cancelled, so all cancellations are included in our data, though we would ideally like to focus on late-stage cancellations. An option would be to focus exclusively on passenger trains, but because freight trains are also important and affected by severe weather, we instead opt to include both types of trains and a higher baseline rate of cancellations.

We made use of the open access weather data provided by the Swedish Meteorological and Hydrological Institute (SMHI). These cover historical meteorological observations of average snow depth, average precipitation, average temperature, and maximum wind speed across the entirety of Sweden. Table 1 provides an overview of the weather variables used in this study. Snow depth, temperature, and precipitation are recorded once a day at each weather station while wind speed was recorded hourly.

Table 1: Overview of studied weather variables.

Weather variable and unit	Number of observations	Observation frequency	Number of weather stations
Snow depth (m)	505,317	Daily	217
Temperature (°C)	692,773	Daily	241
Precipitation (mm)	778,131	Daily	312
Wind speed (m/s)	10,938,298	Hourly	153

Since weather stations are not located at train stations an algorithm was created to match the coordinates of the weather station to the nearest train station on a day-by-day basis. Then the railway operations and weather data were aggregated on a weekly basis to determine the shares of disruptions that occur for each studied weather variable, which was then plotted in order to visually analyse trends.

4 RESULTS

Fig. 1(a) shows the shares disrupted plotted against the average weekly snow depth. The frequency of disruptions begins to increase at about 0.2 m and rises steadily until about 0.7 m, at which point the disruptions level off. At this point, about one in three trains is cancelled or severely delayed, up by about 300% from the baseline rate. Most observations, by far, fall in the range of 0–1 m of snow, and we should not read too much into the fluctuations above 1 m of snow depth.

Fig. 1(b) plots the frequency of disruptions against the level of precipitation. The line is mostly flat, indicating a weak relationship. Towards the far right of the figure, at levels greater than 15 mm/day for a week, we can see a slight increase in disruptions, up to about 17%. This is a modest increase, compared to the extremes of other weather variables, but still up by about 50% from the baseline rate of 11%.

Fig. 1(c) shows the relationship between temperature and disruptions. To the left, we see a steep increase in disruptions as temperatures fall below 0°C. At its most extreme, about 66% of trains suffer from disruptions in connection with cold temperatures, up by about 600% from the baseline rate. To the right in the figure, we see a much more modest but still pronounced increase in disruptions as temperatures rise. At the most extreme, about 18% of trains suffer from disruptions in connection with high temperatures, up by about 60% from the baseline rate. We can see roughly linear increases in both directions.

Finally, Fig. 1(d) illustrates the relationship between the maximum wind speed and the frequency of disruptions. Somewhat surprisingly, we see an elevated rate of disruptions when wind speeds are very low, although periods without any wind for an entire week are rare. More interestingly and reasonably, we see that the frequency of disruptions begins to increase as wind speeds exceed about 20 m/s. The increase is modest at first, but then picks up, and at the most extreme, about two out of every three trains suffer from disruptions, up by about 600% from the baseline rate.

5 DISCUSSION

The results from our graphical visual analysis highlight that the shares disrupted on the Swedish railway network between 2011–2019 increase with temperature, precipitation, snow depth, and wind speed. In regard to temperature, the relationship is stronger when temperatures are below freezing compared to above. Moreover, the relationship between precipitation and disruptions is the weakest when compared to the other weather variables.

Due to climate change, it is expected that Sweden will see a greater increase in precipitation in the winter months compared to summer months [22]. In some regions, this will lead to greater snowfall and depths. In other regions, the increasing temperatures will mean that even in the winter, more of the precipitation will fall as rain rather than snow, and thus lead to lower levels of snow depth and shorter periods of snow cover [6]. On balance, this is likely to lead to less railway disruptions due to snow, but there will be regional variations. The overall increase in precipitation levels may lead to slightly more disruptions, and attention will have to be made to the more extreme cases, which may lead to flooding events and major disruptions.

The mean annual temperature in Sweden will rise, with the highest rises expected to occur during the winter months [6]. We would thus expect the severe disruptions associated with cold temperatures to decrease. The increase in temperatures in the summer months will, on the other hand, likely lead to more disruptions. More trains are also likely to be affected by very high summer temperatures than by the more extreme cold periods, which often happen

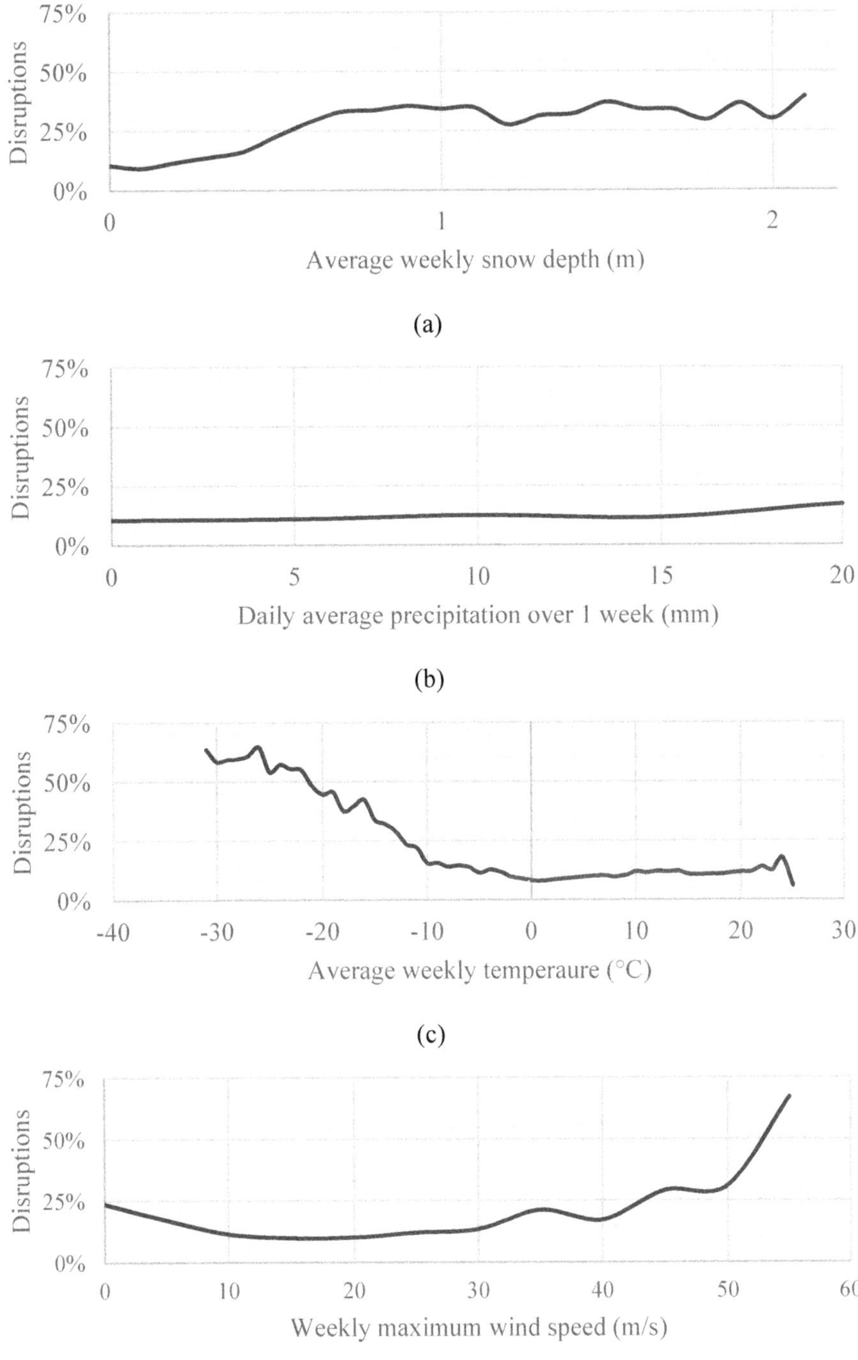

Figure 1: The frequency of disruptions plotted against average (a) Snow depth, (b) Precipitation, (c) Temperature, and (d) Maximum wind speed across a week.

in less densely populated areas of the country. Care must thus be taken so that performance does not suffer too much during the summers.

Future wind climate is challenging to estimate. Thaduri et al. [6] points towards an increase in storms and storm intensity due to increased sea surface temperatures with more water vapour. However, ocean warming may also lead to less low-pressure systems originating in the northern hemisphere. If Sweden sees an increase in frequency and severity of windstorms in the future, we might expect more disruptions caused by high wind speeds, and adaptation measures should be considered to avoid the most severe disruptions.

6 CONCLUSION

In this paper we have studied some 100 million scheduled train arrivals across the entire Swedish railway network during the period 2011–2019. Roughly 10 million of these arrivals were cancelled, and almost 1 million delayed by more than 60 minutes. Considering these two together as disruptions, we see a baseline rate of disruptions at about 11%.

We have seen how this frequency of disruptions is affected by severe weather conditions. Cold temperatures and high winds are both associated with the most severe disruptions, being associated with up to sixfold increases in disruptions. Snow depth also has a strong influence and can lead to threefold increases in disruptions. High temperatures can also be problematic, and we have observed a 60% increase in the rate of disruptions during warm summer weeks. Finally, high levels of precipitation can cause problems, and we have observed up to a 50% increase in the rate of disruptions. Importantly, however, these weather extremes are rather rare, and the effects are usually more modest.

With a changing climate, we would expect some of these conditions to occur more often, and to be even more extreme, than in the past. For instance, temperature, precipitation levels and wind speeds are expected to increase. For snow depths the picture is more complex, where some regions may experience less snow cover, and others experience greater depths but for shorter periods. If the frequency of disruptions is going to be reduced, then adaptation measures will have to be taken to reduce the risks of extreme events. In the context of resiliency, understanding the past patterns is one crucial piece to understanding the vulnerability to extreme weather.

Some future research directions may be to apply machine learning methods to predict disruptions from weather forecasts, to identify particular geographical hotspots, and to explore and develop appropriate adaptation strategies to increase the resiliency of railways.

ACKNOWLEDGEMENTS

This research has been funded by the Swedish Transport Administration through grant numbers TRV2021/99838 and TRV2020/119576. The authors acknowledge the help of Carl Johnsson in downloading and processing of weather data.

REFERENCES

[1] Garmabaki, A.H.S., Thaduri, A., Famurewa, S. & Kumar, U., Adapting railway maintenance to climate change. *Sustainability*, **13**(24), 13856, 2021. DOI: 10.3390/su132413856.

[2] Fabella, V.M. & Szymczak, S., Resilience of railway transport to four types of natural hazards: An analysis of daily train volumes. *Infrastructures*, **6**(12), p. 174, 2021. DOI: 10.3390/infrastructures6120174.

[3] Mattsson, L.G. & Jenelius, E., Vulnerability and resilience of transport systems: A discussion of recent research. *Transportation Research Part A: Policy and Practice*, **81**, pp. 16–34, 2015. DOI: 10.3390/infrastructures6120174.

[4] Kostianaia, E.A., Kostianoy, A.G., Scheglov, M.A., Karelov, A.I. & Vasileisky, A.S., Impact of regional climate change on the infrastructure and operability of railway transport. *Transport and Telecommunication Journal*, **22**(2), pp. 183–195, 2021. DOI: 10.2478/ttj-2021-0014.

[5] Palin, E.J., Stipanovic Oslakovic, I., Gavin, K. & Quinn A., Implications of climate change for railway infrastructure. *Wiley Interdisciplinary Reviews: Climate Change*, **12**(5), 2021. DOI: 10.1002/wcc.728.

[6] Thaduri, A., Garmabaki, A. & Kumar, U., Impact of climate change on railway operation and maintenance in Sweden: A state-of-the-art review. *Maintenance, Reliability and Condition Monitoring,* **1**(2), pp. 52–70, 2021. DOI: 10.21595/mrcm.2021.22136.

[7] Xia, Y., van Ommeren, J.N., Rietveld, P. & Verhagen, W., Railway infrastructure disturbances and train operator performance: The role of weather. *Transportation Research Part D: Transport and Environment*, **18**, pp. 97–102, 2013. DOI: 10.1016/j.trd.2012.09.008.

[8] Ling, X., Peng, Y., Sun, S., Li, P. & Wang, P., Uncovering correlation between train delay and train exposure to bad weather. *Physica A: Statistical Mechanics and its Applications*, **512**, pp. 1152–1159, 2018. DOI: 10.1016/j.physa.2018.07.057.

[9] Brazil, W., White, A., Nogal, M., Caulfield, B., O'Connor, A. & Morton, C., Weather and rail delays: Analysis of metropolitan rail in Dublin. *Journal of Transport Geography*, **59**, pp. 69–76, 2017. DOI: 10.1016/j.jtrangeo.2017.01.008.

[10] Diab, E. & Shalaby, A., Metro transit system resilience: Understanding the impacts of outdoor tracks and weather conditions on metro system interruptions. *International Journal of Sustainable Transportation*, **14**(9), pp. 657–670, 2020. DOI: 10.1080/15568318.2019.1600174.

[11] Ludvigsen, J. & Klæboe, R., Extreme weather impacts on freight railways in Europe. *Natural Hazards*, **70**(1), pp. 767–787, 2014. DOI: 10.1007/s11069-013-0851-3.

[12] Zakeri, G. & Olsson, N.O.E., Investigating the effect of weather on punctuality of Norwegian railways: A case study of the Nordland Line. *Journal of Modern Transportation*, **26**(4), pp. 255–267, 2018. DOI: 10.1007/s40534-018-0169-7.

[13] Palmqvist, C.W., Olsson, N.O.E. & Hiselius, L.W., Some influencing factors for passenger train punctuality in Sweden. *International Journal of Prognostics and Health Management,* **8**(3), 2017. DOI: 10.36001/ijph.201.v8i3.2649.

[14] Wang, J., Granlöf, M. & Yu, J., Effects of winter climate on delays of high speed passenger trains in Botnia-Atlantica region. *Journal of Rail Transport Planning and Management*, **18**, 100251, 2021. DOI: 10.1016/j.jrtpm.2021.100251.

[15] Palin, E.J., Thornton, H.E., Mathison, C.T., McCarthy, R.E., Clark, R.T. & Dora J., Future projections of temperature-related climate change impacts on the railway network of Great Britain. *Climatic Change,* **120**, pp. 71–93, 2013. DOI: 10.1007/s10584-013-0810-8.

[16] Dobney, K., Baker, C.J., Chapman, L. & Quinn, A.D., The future cost to the United Kingdom's railway network of heat-related delays and buckles caused by the predicted increase in high summer temperatures owing to climate change. *Proceedings of the Institution of Mechanical Engineers, Part F: Journal of Rail and Rapid Transit,* **224**(1), pp. 25–34, 2010. DOI:10.1243/09544097JRRT292.

[17] Kellermann, P., Bubeck, P., Kundela, G., Dosio, A. & Thieken, A., Frequency analysis of critical meteorological conditions in a changing climate: Assessing future implications for railway transportation in Austria. *Climate*, **4**(25), 2016. DOI: 10.3390/cli4020025.

[18] Chinowsky, P., Helman, J., Gulati, S., Neumann, J. & Martinich, J., Impacts of climate change on operation of the US rail network. *Transport Policy*, **75**, pp. 183–191, 2019. DOI: 10.1016/j.tranpol.2017.05.007.

[19] Forzieri, G., Bianchi, A., e Silva, F.B., Marin Herrera, M.A., Leblois, A., Lavalle, C., Aerts, J.C.J.H. & Feyen, F., Escalating impacts of climate extremes on critical infrastructures in Europe. *Global Environmental Change*, **48**, pp. 97–107, 2018. DOI: 10.1016/j.gloenvcha.2017.11.007.

[20] Ilalokhoin, O., Pant, R. & Hall, J.W., A multi-track rail model for estimating journey impacts from extreme weather events: A case study of Great Britain's rail network. *International Journal of Rail Transportation*, **10**(2), pp. 133–158, 2021. DOI: 10.1080/23248378.2021.1891582.

[21] Bubeck, P., Dillenardt, L., Alfieri, L., Feyen, L., Thieken, A.H. & Kellermann, P., Global warming to increase flood risk on European railways. *Climatic Change*, **155**, pp. 19–36, 2019. DOI: 10.1007/s10584-019-02434-5.

[22] Lindgren, J., Jonsson, D.K. & Carlsson-Kanyama, A., Climate adaptation of railways: Lessons from Sweden. *European Journal of Transport and Infrastructure Research*, **9**(2), pp. 164–181, 2009.

ARTICULATED TRAIN OF DEEP WELL CARS FOR HIGH-SPEED CONTAINER TRANSPORT

FRIEDER HAFERKORN
Fachhochschule Dortmund, University of Applied Sciences and Arts, Germany

ABSTRACT

A literature search on the length, mass and speed of passenger and freight trains revealed a close connection; particularly high speeds seem to be allowed only trains whose mass is distributed over a correspondingly large length. The product of mass per length (t/m) and speed (m/s) appears in the dimension (t/s) to represent a kind of stress or footprint for the infrastructure of the tracks and bridges. Resonances caused by air flow around the successive vehicles within the train at the same distance can be avoided by the surface design. Resonances caused by wheel–rail vibrations can be damped by unsymmetric chassis such as those under the Talgo and AGV. High board walls prevent containers from detaching from the train due to vibrations. Derailments due to speed that is too high for the track geometry (e.g. track arches that are too narrow, transition arches that are too short) can at least be partially prevented by particularly large wheelbases, semi-permanent couplings between bogies and lateral buffers. In this way, the vehicle frames would be connected by a separable Jacobs bogie, which would transmit rolling torques along the train and prevent individual axles from climbing up. Unfortunately, despite all the safety systems, there are still collisions between trains. The proposed container train is very long for its mass, with only one high-cube container 40 ft per wagon and with a large wheelbase. This length can act like a built-in brake bumper in the event of a collision. In the event of a collision, the container load is protected by shortening the train as necessary. The development of the new high-speed container train is to be supported with data from our own simulations and measurements as well as from previous literature.

Keywords: mass per length, speed, stress for tracks and bridges, footprint, vibration resonances, asymmetric chassis, derailments, detachable Jacobs bogies, simulations, measurements.

1 INTRODUCTION

According to Watson et al. [1], there is a market for transporting priority cargo on high-speed freight trains and in 2020 [2] a vehicle and a fleet of trains were proposed to transport 40 ft high-speed high-cube containers (Fig. 1). The literature on high-speed trains (HS) and interesting freight wagons, in particular container wagons, was reviewed (Table 1). A strong correlation between velocity and a quotient C of the concentration mass per length was found (Fig. 4). All examples from the literature seem to "stick" to the axes below threshold values.

However, the Pocket Wagon [3] is already in use in the UK, which transports high-cube 40 ft containers through the low and narrow loading dimensions of the UK. In order to be able to start the high-speed container service earlier, the Pocket Wagons+ should travel at 201 km/h using the Mark III bogies and locomotives of the now discontinued HST125 fast diesel multiple unit [4].

These were the proposals of 2020, illustrated with simple 2D graphics. In the meantime, the vehicle and train evolved into a new design called the Aero, and its graphic representation evolved as well. Now there is a 3D axonometry (Fig. 2) and even a PowerPoint animation film with a central perspective. Fig. 3 shows a screenshot of it, supplemented by streamlines. In Figs 2 and 3, the cross-section of the Aero is slightly v-shaped, so that cross-wind currents such as those that caused the Tacoma Narrows Bridge to collapse in 1940 [5] do not endanger it.

WIT Transactions on The Built Environment, Vol 213, © 2022 WIT Press
www.witpress.com, ISSN 1743-3509 (on-line)
doi:10.2495/CR220111

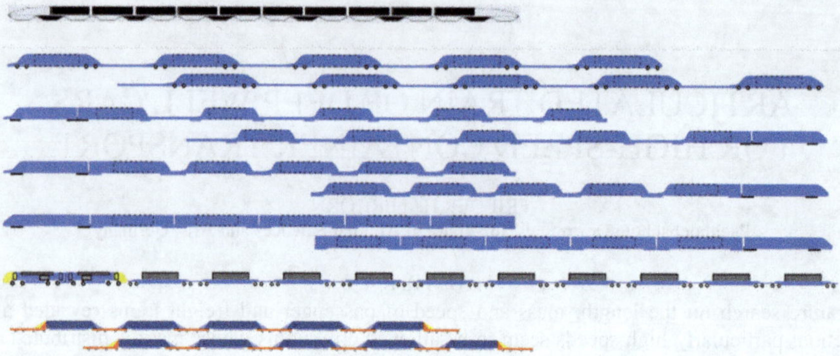

Figure 1: High-speed container train projects (from the top): Aerosprinter2002, four Aeros and Pocket Wagons+2020, Aero2022.

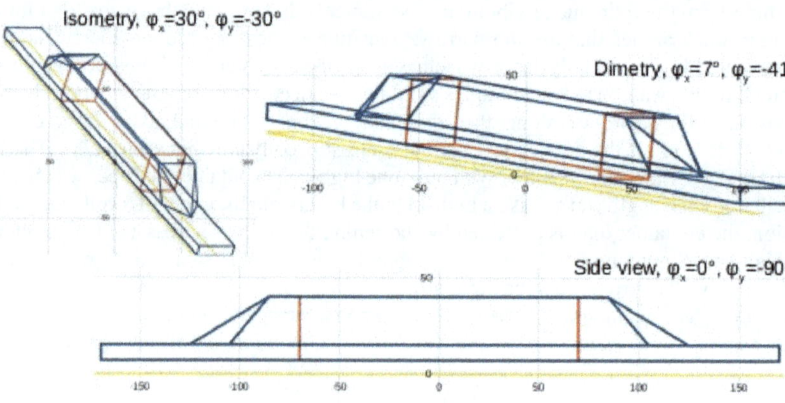

Figure 2: Aero vehicle in 3D axonometry.

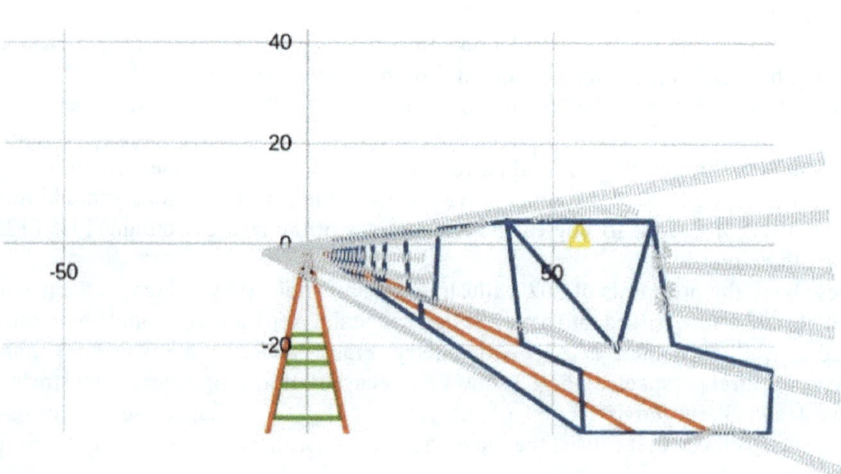

Figure 3: Aero train sketch with headwind and crosswind streamlines.

Table 1: Vehicles and trains.

Type	L (m)	m (t)	C = m/L (t/m)	V (km/h)	A = C × V/3.6 (t/s)
Freight cars DR/DB [8]:					
Fad 169	12.81	64.9	5.07	80	112.66
Hbis 298	14.02	40.8	2.91	100	80.84
Habiss 345	21.70	80.0	3.68	120	122.65
Laae 540	22.12	39.7	1.80	80	40.00
Laeqrss 548	26.24	45.4	1.73	120	57.66
Laaes 549	113.74	151.3	1.33	100	36.95
Saads 704	31.87	126.5	3.97	100	110.29
Sdkms(s) 707	16.44	51.5	3.13	120	104.32
Sahs 711	16.40	95.8	5.84	100	162.24
Sgjs(s) 716	21.08	79.7	3.78	120	125.99
Tefhss	11.74	39.0	3.32	120	110.66
TT.nhhrs 19	16.27	65.5	4.03	100	111.95
Ibblpqrs	14.02	39.7	2.83	100	78.62
Fals 183	12.54	89.8	7.16	100	198.90
Eas 5951	14.04	80	5.70	100	158.35
Soviet Highboard cars [9]:					
4-axles	13.92	83.0	5.96	100	165.57
6-axles	16.40	126.0	7.68	100	213.35
8-axles	20.24	167.8	8.29	100	230.30
Soviet or Russian Railcars [9]:					
DP-01-08	158.7	367	2.31	104	66.74
DP-1-10	78.9	138	1.75	120	58.33
DP-11/12	48.1	90	1.87	125	64.93
DP-14	70.2	161	2.29	160	101.77
DP-15	69.5	161	2.32	160	103.10
DP-21	73.6	165	2.24	120	74.66
ER-200-8	208.0	442	2.13	180	106.50
ER-200-14	364.0	787	2.16	180	108.00
Sokol-250	158.0	356	2.25	250	156.24
TGV family [10]:					
Paris-Sud-Est1	200.2	428	2.14	270	160.50
Paris-Sud-Est2	200.2	409	2.04	300	169.99
Atlantique	237.6	479	2.02	300	168.33
Réseau	200.2	388	1.94	320	172.45
Postal	200.2	345	1.72	270	129.00
Eurostar	394.0	752	1.91	300	159.16
Thalys PBKA	200.2	416	2.08	320	184.89
Duplex	200.2	380	1.90	320	168.89
Est-Européen	200.2	423	2.11	320	187.56

Table 1: Continued.

Type	L (m)	m (t)	C = m/L (t/m)	V (km/h)	A = C × V/3.6 (t/s)
Shinkansen family [10]:					
A	49.5	120	2.42	250	168.04
B	99.5	240	2.41	250	167.35
0, 16 cars	400.3	967	2.42	220	147.89
961	150.3	351	2.34	260	168.99
962	150.3	348	2.32	210	135.33
200, 16 cars	400.3	1.088	2.72	240	181.34
100	402.1	925	2.30	230	146.95
2000	402.1	1.088	2.71	275	207.02
300	402.1	710	1.77	270	132.75
400	128.2	312	2.44	240	162.67
WIN 350	151.6	230	1.52	350	147.77
Others [10]:					
HST/IC-125	220	435	1.98	201	110.54
ICE 1	410.7	911	2.22	250	154.16
ICE 2	205.0	412	2.01	260	145.16
Velaro family	250.0	667	2.67	250	185.40
Special examples:					
300 X	152.0	210	1.38	400	153.33
Parcel-IC	197.4	525	2.66	160	118.21
CS/T-Long	118.2	308	2.61	120	86.99
CS-Light	90.4	233	2.58	120	85.99
CargoSprinter	90.4	281	3.11	100	86.40
Talion-Light	90.4	238	2.63	120	87.66
Talion	90.4	286	3.16	100	87.78
Container Train	259.4	840	3.24	100	90.01
CargoMover Train	259.4	940	3.62	90	90.50
WELL cars (USA)	174.4	830	4.76	112	148.08
FLAT cars (India)	135.6	863	6.36	100	176.68
empty Uaai 839	50.3	263	5.22	80	115.99
Uaai 839	63.8	717	11.23	65	202.81
Projects:					
AeroSprinter-Railcar	407	628	1.54	350	**149.72**
AeroSprinter-Long	370	754	2.04	310	175.66
AeroSprinter-BC	305	716	2.35	270	176.25
AeroSprinter-A	305	736	2.41	230	153.97
Pocket Wagons+	255	871	3.41	160	151.54
AeroSprinter 2002	250	1.001	4.00	230	255.56
AeroSprinter 2020	250	1.001	4.00	100	111.12
Aero 2022	536	750.4	1.4	360	140

A = C × V/3.6 (t/s)	
226.94	ar.mean+2*std.dev.n
181.27	ar.mean+std.dev.n
158.44	ar.mean+1/2*std.dev.n
135.60	ar.mean
45.67	std.dev.n

As a newcomer, Aero will meet with a lot of scepticism and must never be involved in accidents or even cause them. Considerations on accidents and their prevention were already under way in 2020 [2]. Therefore, in Section 3 and 4 it is proposed to experiment with models on a larger scale.

Simultaneously with the container train Aero, a footprint theory had been developed in 2020 based on literature data and inspired by Sato [6]. As explained in Section 2, this has also evolved since then.

2 THE FOOTPRINT THEORY

In Haferkorn [2], literature data of vehicles and trains were defined as "admissible" if they belong to a union set defined by the thresholds maxV ≤ 160 km/h or C = m/L ≤ 2.8 t/m, as shown in Fig. 4. Both thresholds seem arbitrary, but are apparently confirmed by practical experience. A less arbitrary approach is to add another column to Table 1 and let the point cloud data itself decide admissibility.

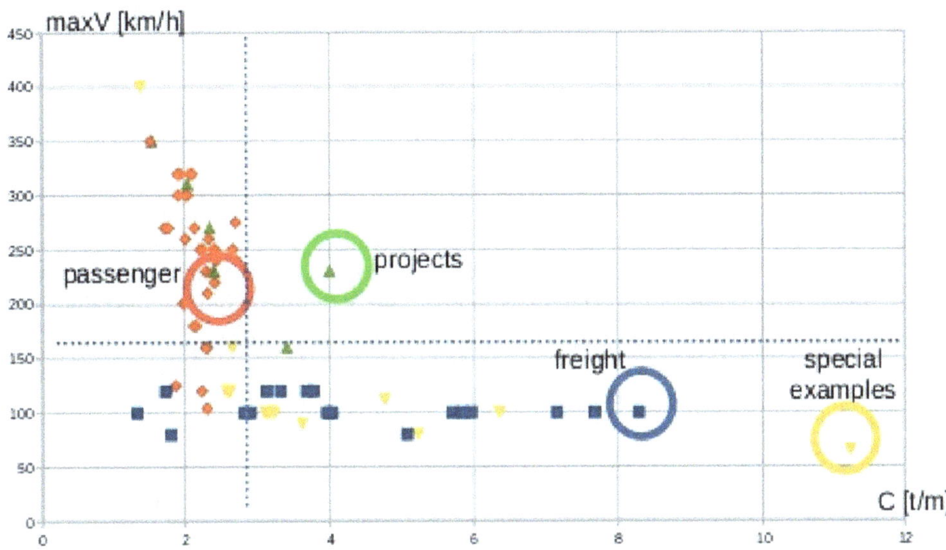

Figure 4: MaxV and mass per length concentration C of vehicles and trains.

Multiplying maxV with C gives a product value A (t/s); A = V × C/3.6. Like the constant c in the hyperbolic formula x × y = c, A is a scalar and statistical value with an arithmetic mean and a standard deviation (Table 1, Fig. 5). So it is quite easy to explain why the AeroSprinter 2002 is not allowed again (the ar.mean + std.dev threshold is clearly exceeded), and the Soviet highboard vehicles with two, three and four axle bogies should be checked for speed. But A is also a meaningful value: it is the stress amplitude, the footprint of a train on the infrastructure. In the early days of the railway, at least one reason for the collapse of the Tay Bridge was that trains often ran over it too fast to keep to the timetable. (Other reasons were the weak bridge construction and the heavy storm at that night [7].)

Figs 6 and 7 show how different tensile masses, lengths and mass per length (mpl) concentrations C have to be compensated by velocities V in order to keep products A = C × V/3.6 at a reasonable level. The mass m (t) is represented by a yellow 3D ball, which

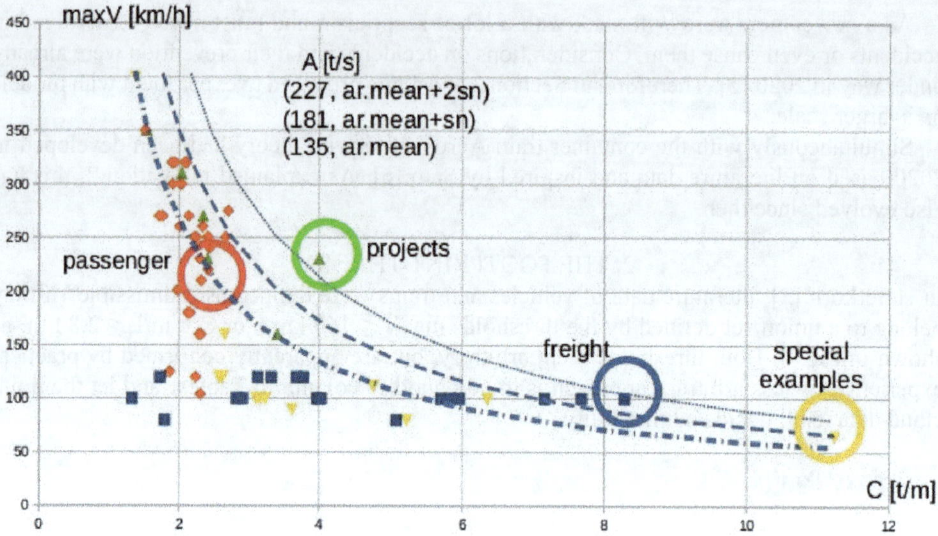

Figure 5: Vehicles and trains, maxV vs mass per length concentration C plus levels of stress amplitude A.

of course has to be distributed over the train length. The speed V (km/h) is represented by two parallel lines, the horizontal distance of which corresponds to the length of the train and the vertical distance of the time. The trains in Fig. 6 seem to run on more or less thick blue lines, which are supposed to represent the respective mpl concentrations C.

In Fig. 7 on the left, the black train lengths and blue mpl concentrations are transferred to the green driving times and the red voltage amplitudes A via the diamonds below. The masses m are shown here as yellow 2D surfaces:

$$C \times L = m \text{ and } v \times A = m.$$

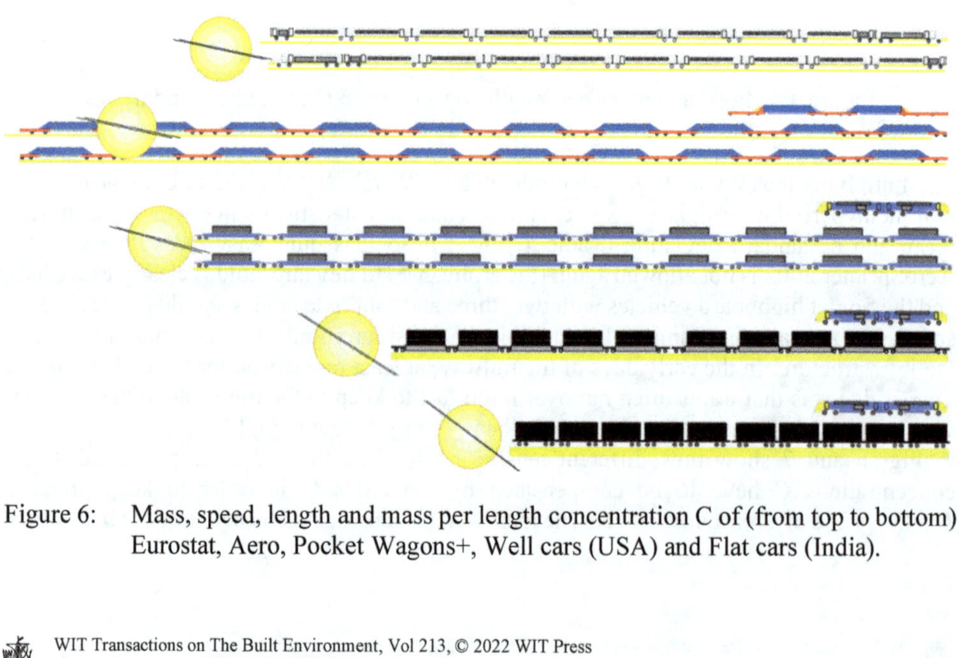

Figure 6: Mass, speed, length and mass per length concentration C of (from top to bottom) Eurostat, Aero, Pocket Wagons+, Well cars (USA) and Flat cars (India).

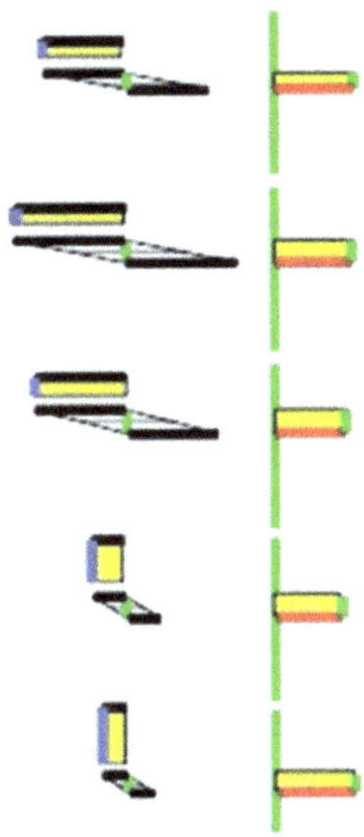

			mass.concentration		stress.amplitude	
	m [t]	L[m]	C [t/m]	V [km/h]	A [t/s]	T [s]
			m/L		C*V/3,6	L/V*3,6
Eurostar	752	394	1.91	360	191	3.94
Aero	750.4	536	1.40	360	140	5.36
Pocket Wagons+	1000	438	2.28	270	171	5.84
WELL cars (USA)	830	161	5.16	112	160	5.18
FLAT cars (India)	863	126	6.85	100	190	4.54

Figure 7: Length, mass-per-length concentration C, speed V and stress amplitude A, the footprint on infrastructure.

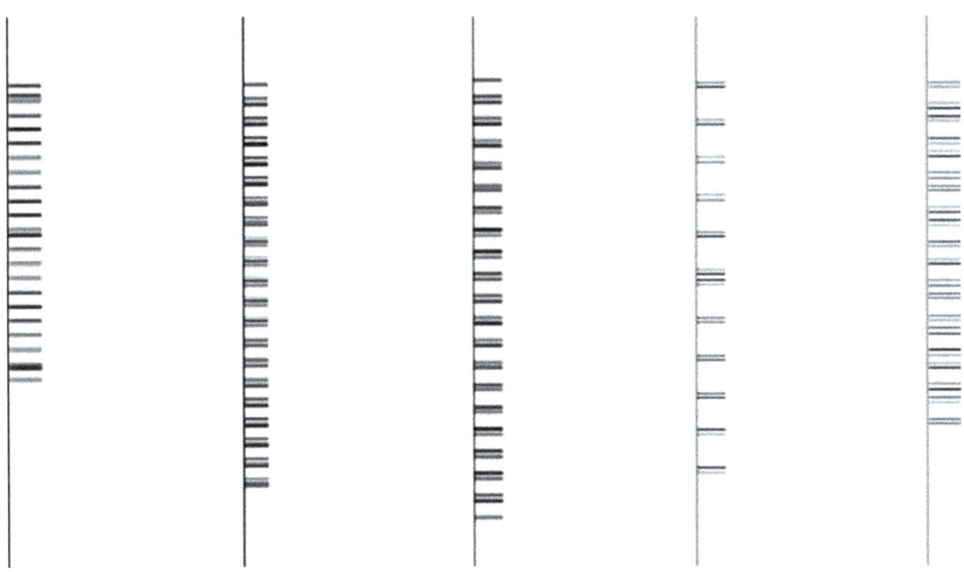

Figure 8: Probable vertical acceleration marks of (from left to right) Eurostar, Aero, Pocket Wagons+, Well cars (USA), and Flat cars (India).

Further right in Fig. 7 the amplitudes A are plotted along the green vertical time axis. The voltage amplitude A seems to act at a certain point in the infrastructure like a short stroke between long rest periods.

As confirmed by the literature [6], [8], [9], the effects of the stress amplitude A of trains on infrastructure, in particular on bridges or switches, can be measured in the form of vertical acceleration. Fig. 8 gives an idea of what A might look like if it was recorded or sounded if it was intercepted. The trains come in very different masses, lengths and speeds. But the corresponding time T, the height of the diagrams, and the corresponding voltage amplitude A, the width of the diagrams, do not differ too much. Fig. 8 is a data visualization that has yet to be confirmed by measurements. However, the individual trains already seem to show the individual footprint of their bogies or even their axles.

3 DESIGN STUDIES, ACCIDENTS PREVENTION, IMPACT MITIGATION

A long list of rail vehicles and even some road vehicles influenced the Aero design. The most important factor, however, was how to prevent accidents or at least mitigate their consequences.

The stress amplitude A has an effect on bridges and track arches, in particular turnouts [6], [8], [9]. Low-voltage amplitude trains such as the Spanish Talgo, the Italian Italo, the British APT, the Swiss light steel high-speed trains [10] and the German Schienenceppelin [11] could have been much faster, but could not have been justified due to accident concerns.

Chen and Guo [12] saw collisions [13] and derailments [14] as the most common types of accidents, and Table 2 tries to get an idea of where to take corrective measures/solutions for a new train as the Aero.

Table 2: Railway accidents, types, causes and remedies/solutions.

Accident types	**Causes**	**Remedies/solutions**
Collision	Lost containers	(Deep) well cars
Collision	Runaway train	Internal buffer stops
Derailing (jackknifing)	Cornering too fast	Articulated/Cardanic coupling
Derailing (capsizing)	Crosswind	Articulated/Cardanic coupling
Derailing	Resonance	
Resonance	Repeated surface shapes	Reversed wing profile
Resonance	Short rails	Continuously welded track
Resonance (hunting)	Rolling system symmetry	Asymmetric rolling system

3.1 Resonance due to flow around the container well and shaking in the chassis

First, flow resonance: In order to separate the containers far from each other, the Aero vehicles became very long, and large distances remained between the container wells, which were supposed to be flow-friendly on their own (Figs 2 and 3). These distances allow streamlines to flow around vehicles and trains without turbulence at high speed. However, the constant return of the same forms can also lead to resonance. Which scenario really occurs has to be clarified in a separate study.

The skeletal structure of the Schienenzeppelin [11] gives an idea of how the Aero wells can become light, long and flow-friendly. However, the silver canvas coating should be replaced by thin steel sheet with stabilising golf ball embossing in order to hold the streamlines together [15].

Alstom AGV [16], Talgo [17], [18] and Hanover's TW 3000 [19] suggest that hunting [20] can also be calmed by an asymmetry of the suspension. Asymmetry is naturally found in all road vehicles [21], so that lightweight components [22] and independent wheels [23] can be derived for rail vehicles.

3.2 Derailments: Shongololo rolling system

Shongololo is a giant millipede [24] and a nickname for trains in the South African isiZulu. Alstoms TGV [25] and AGV [26] use Jacobs bogies to prevent derailments. Like millipedes, they transmit torsion moments between adjacent vehicle frames and thus prevent the climbing of wheel flanges. Fig. 10 shows a TW 3000 [19] as a special edition fife-element articulated shongololo train, which crosses an arc of 50 m diameter without derailing.

However, the Aero requires cardan-coupled bogies or detachable Jacobs-type bogies to transmit the roll moments [27] and to prevent its vehicles from derailing at high speeds. Side buffers are supposed to catch the yaw moments [28].

3.3 Collisions: telescopic drawbars as built-in buffer-stops

In Fig. 11 two variants of the asymmetrical Aero rolling system are shown as a built-in buffer-stop [29]. They combine the rolling system of the (original) Talgo [18] with conventional bogies (Fig. 9), drawbar dollies for truck trailers [21] and railway buffer-stops [29].

The Aero has become unusually long in order to keep the mpl concentration low in favour of the high speeds. In the event of a collision, this additional length in the telescopic drawbar shortens and intercepts the impact like a built-in buffer-stop [29].

4 ENGINEERING: PROTOTOTYPING, TESTING PLANTS AND TESTING DRIVES

It will be a technical task to prove the footprint theory and to develop prototypes of a highspeed container train. In 2020 [2] the tasks were formulated in specifications, in 2022 a list of study assignments will follow.

Simulation and model experiments (1:10) are often combined [30], [31]. Simulation is a great tool to answer questions and will certainly be used. But in the end prototypes have to be built and tested. With regard to derailment, collision, high speed, development time and cost, this should not exclude smaller models [32] or narrow gauge vehicles [33].

The following list of study assignments will be examined:

- Speed and mpl concentration are the factors for the infrastructure stress: $C[t/m] \times v[m/s] = A[t/s]$.
- Low and narrow vehicle cross-section enveloping HC-40ft containers enables the worldwide use of high-speed container trains, even under British loading gauges.
- Low and narrow as well as air-flow friendly container wells between long and low chassis enable low-vibration, high-speed operation even in strong crosswinds.
- Steel sheet with golf ball embossing as outer skin reduces air resistance and mass and increases strength.
- Asymmetric articulated Jacobs bogies ensure smooth running even at high speed.
- Wheel set bogies can replace loose wheels.
- Cardanic (torque-resistant) semi-permanent coupled bogies with side buffers prevent derailments and jackknifing.
- Telescopic chassis mitigate collision impacts.

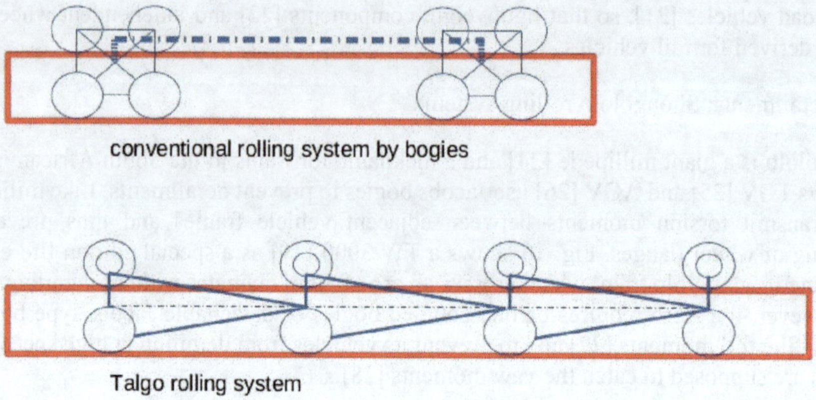

Figure 9: Rolling systems in comparison (Talgo).

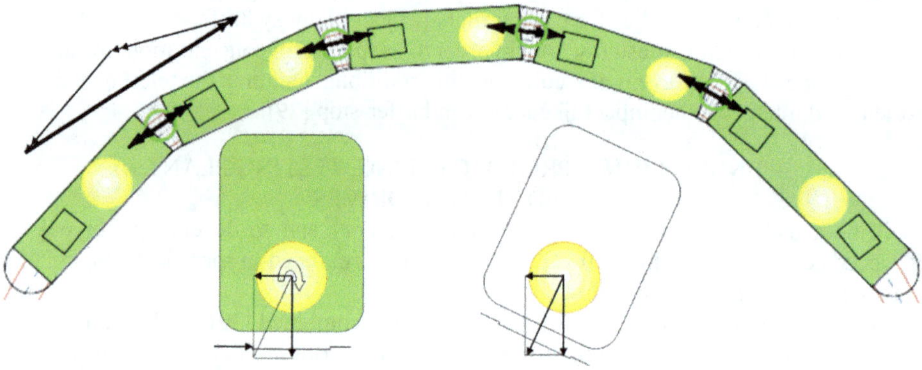

Figure 10: Hannover ÜSTRA's TW3000 is made an asymmetric derailment-resistant "Shongololo" millipede (TW3000).

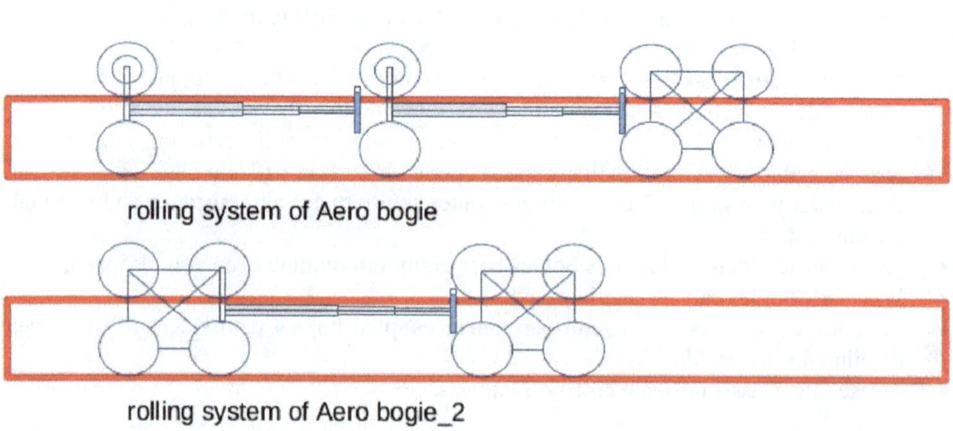

Figure 11: Asymmetric Aero rolling systems with telescopic onboard buffer-stops.

4.1 Testing the footprint theory

Video cameras are already being installed in tiny model trains [34]. The installation of acceleration sensors in trains and also locally (e.g. under track connections) of model railway systems should therefore be possible without any problems, but also in full scale vehicles and rail systems. The on-board sensors measure and send their data to a local receiver where it is combined with the data from the local sensors on the route to determine velocity v, mpl concentration C and stress amplitude A.

4.2 Aero-prototyping

Small prototypes can be tested in a tub-shaped arrangement with gravity drive (Fig. 12). This is tilted by an angle to compensate for the rolling resistance of the prototype. The prototype starts on the left at a height h above the ground, and without the other prototype standing in its way, it would reach the same position on the right. However, both prototypes collide and come to a halt in the middle of the hull with their bogies shortened by the impact.

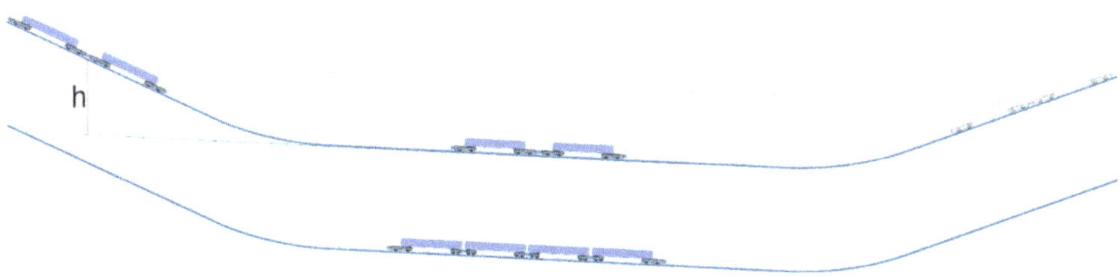

Figure 12: Gravity drive, trains before and after collision.

Another application of gravity drive is the testing of rolling system prototypes. It has to be clarified whether resonance can be soothed by asymmetric suspension or also by independent wheels.

The gravity drive can also be used to determine which speed and track curvature separable and torque-transmitting Jacobs bogies can withstand without derailing. The circular curved track arch is located in the middle part of the hull, where the speed is constant [31].

For H0 models, the 24-hour timetable is reduced to 15 minutes on a scale of 1:87 (and train speeds accordingly), i.e. to 7 1⁄2 minutes day and 7 1⁄2 minutes night. This also means that a world record train in 1:87 scale instead of 574.8 km/h [32] would not go faster than 1.84 m/s in such a 1:87 scene.

In gravity drives the acceleration a = a0 is constant. The velocity v = a0 × t is linear and does not depend on the mass or the gradient. When a vehicle or train runs down from height h, velocity v and altitude h follow the formulae $v = \sqrt{(2 gh)}$ and h = v2/ (2 g).

With a gravity drive, the discharge height h of the record 1/87 scale train would be only 0.17 m.

For large prototypes in scale 1:5 or 1:2 or in narrow gauge [33], a rubber belt drive is required (Figs 13 and 14). The acceleration a(t) (starting with about 5 g) is a quadratic function of time t. Speed v(t) and path s(t) as integrals of a are greater powers of t, and here they are also dependent on the mass of the prototype. Against the path s(t) is a(s) approximately linear. (Ultimately, it's all about speeding up prototypes with limited budgets to impressive speeds.)

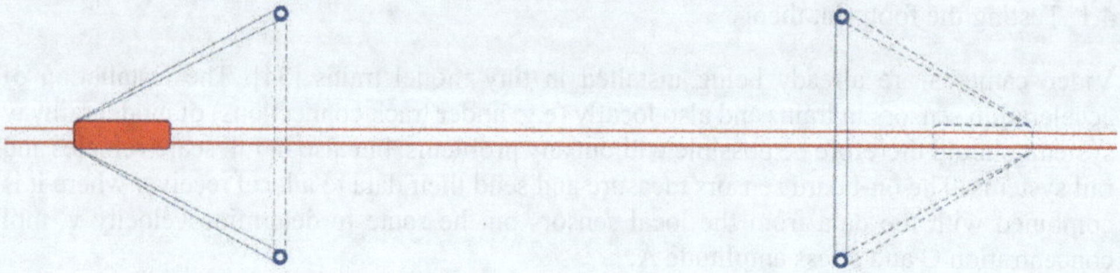

Figure 13: Rubber belt drive. Start = full lines; Stop = dashed lines.

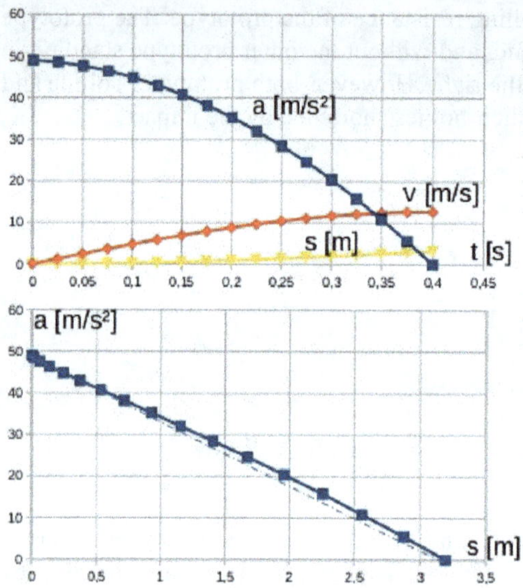

a(t)=(a2*t+a1)*t+a0
v(t)=((a2/3*t+a1/2)*t+a0)*t
s(t)=(((a2/12)*t+a1/6)*t+a0/2)*t²

a0	a1	a2	
49	**-14.5**	**-270**	
t [s]	a [m/s²]	v [m/s]	s [m]
0	49	0	0
…	…	…	…
0.4	**0**	**12.7** (45.72 km/h)	**3.19**

Figure 14: Rubber belt drive functions a(t), v(t), s(t), a(s).

The world speed record on the LEGO tracks is 30.67 km/h = 8.52 m/s [35]. The record holder is an AGV Italo in scale 1:47. (For the "big" train this would be 1,438 km/h.) Even a gravity drive of 3.70 m height could reach 30.67 km/h.

The rubber band drive from Fig. 14 goes even further with V = 45.72 km/h = 12.7 m/s, provided the acceleration a(t) really starts at 5 g. The gravity drive would need a height of 8.22 m to accelerate trains to that speed.

5 CONCLUSIONS AND OUTLOOK

The Japanese concept trains on the island of Kyushu [36] are a good model for the Aero. Even if they are passenger trains and not container trains, they show how ideas are put into plans and plans into full-scale reality.

It looks as if the container train Aero can be used in conjunction with passenger trains and on the same tracks, for example on the HS-2 in Great Britain [37], [38], for reliable (i.e. accident-proof) and sustainable high-speed operation. It will take a lot of time and money to prove this and to develop and manufacture the Aero, even if only models are used as prototypes.

It is not the speed of the container train that is of greatest interest, but the overall speed of the container from door to door. Therefore, the collection and distribution of containers over the last kilometres and metres to and from the terminals should also be investigated. It is to be hoped that other rail systems will take over a large part of this and not leave too much to road transport.

REFERENCES

[1] Watson, I., Ali, A. & Bayyati, A., Freight transport using high-speed railways. *International Journal of Transport Development and Integration*, **3**(2), pp. 103–116, 2019. https://www.witpress.com/elibrary/tdi-volumes/3/2/2417

[2] Haferkorn, F., Deep well cars exclusively for high-cube 40′ containers on high-speed trains. *International Journal of Transport Development and Integration*, **4**(4), pp. 368–378, 2020. https://www.witpress.com/elibrary/tdi-volumes/4/4/2738.

[3] G & W, Our fleet. https://www.gwrr.co.uk/about/fleet/.

[4] Wikipedia, InterCity 125. https://en.wikipedia.org/wiki/InterCity_125.

[5] Wikipedia, Tacoma Narrows Bridge. https://en.wikipedia.org/wiki/Tacoma_Narrows_Bridge.

[6] Sato, Y., Effect of intermediate beam in track on train induced ground vibration. *WIT Transactions on The Built Environment*, vol. 74, WIT Press: Southampton and Boston, 2004. DOI: 10.2495/CR040811.

[7] Wikipedia, Tay Bridge disaster. https://en.wikipedia.org/wiki/Tay_Bridge_disaster.

[8] Fryba, L., Intensive vibration of bridges due to high speed trains. *WIT Transactions on The Built Environment*, vol. 61, WIT Press: Southampton and Boston, 2002. DOI: 10.2495/CR020581.

[9] Droździel, J. & Sowiński, B., Railway car dynamic response to track transition curve and single standard turnout. *WIT Transactions on The Built Environment*, vol. 88, WIT Press: Southampton and Boston, 2006. DOI: 10.2495/CR060831.

[10] Wikipedia, Leichtstahlwagen (SBB). https://de.wikipedia.org/wiki/Leichtstahlwagen_(SBB).

[11] Theoldman777 (YouTube), Propellertriebwagen Kruckenberg Schienenzeppelin (1930) Part 1.mpg. https://www.youtube.com/watch?v=E-ID_ktSoLY.

[12] Chen, R. & Guo, J., Development of the new CBTC system simulation and performance analysis. *WIT Transactions on The Built Environment*, vol. 114, WIT Press: Southampton and Boston, pp. 497–507, 2010. DOI: 10.2495/CR100461.

[13] Deutsche Welle, Germany: 1 killed, over a dozen injured in train collision near Munich. 14 Feb. 2022. https://www.dw.com/en/germany-1-killed-over-a-dozen-injured-in-traincollision-near-munich/a-60776534.

[14] AZATOR (YouTube), Train lego. AGV run on LGV: World speed record. Crash. Brick expo. https://www.youtube.com/watch?v=U8QB91XwZHw.

[15] Hucho, W.-H. (ed.), *Aerodynamik des Automobils*, 3rd ed., Springer, p. 447, Fig. 9.45, 1999. Herwig/v. Löhneysen, Helmtest: Windkanal – Wind-Spiele 1984.

[16] Wikipedia, AGV (train). https://en.wikipedia.org/wiki/AGV_(train).

[17] CoasterFan2105 (YouTube), Amtrak Talgo trains of the northwest. https://www.youtube.com/watch?v=SVKqbsYbGEU.

[18] Talgo, History: Talgo North America. http://web.talgoamerica.com/history.

[19] Wikipedia, TW 3000. https://en.wikipedia.org/wiki/TW_3000.

[20] Stichel, S., The influence of underframe structural flexibility on the hunting behaviour of a freight wagon. *WIT Transactions on The Built Environment*, vol. 50, WIT Press: Southampton and Boston, 2000. DOI: 10.2495/CR000701.

[21] Wikipedia, Semi-trailer truck. https://en.wikipedia.org/wiki/Semi-trailer_truck
[22] TRIPAN Leichtbauteile, https://www.tripan.at/en/.
[23] Wikipedia, Dolly (trailer). https://en.wikipedia.org/wiki/Dolly_(trailer).
[24] Wikipedia, *Archispirostreptus gigas.* https://en.wikipedia.org/wiki/Archispirostreptus_gigas.
[25] 40 Years of TGV. http://www.emdx.org/rail/40ansTGV/index.html.
[26] Spark (YouTube), How train disasters changed the way we build high speed trains: Built from disaster. https://www.youtube.com/watch?v=9571zV6TkQA.
[27] Wikipedia, Roll moment. https://en.wikipedia.org/wiki/Roll_moment.
[28] Wikipedia, Yaw (rotation). https://en.wikipedia.org/wiki/Yaw_(rotation).
[29] Rawie, Buffer-stops. https://www.rawie.de/en/buffer-stops/.
[30] Aki, M. et al., Railway vehicle derailment simulation for derailment detection system in early signs. *5th Asian Conference on Multibody Dynamics 2010*, 23–26 Aug., Kyoto, Japan, 2010. https://www.jstage.jst.go.jp/article/jsmeacmd/2010.5/0/2010.5__63877-1_/_pdf.
[31] Romero Navarrete, J.A. & Otremba, F., A testing facility to assess railway car infrastructure damage: A conceptual design. *International Journal of Transport Development and Integration*, **4**(2), pp. 142–151, 2020. DOI: 10.2495/TDI-V4-N2-142-151.
[32] Märklín, Hochgeschwindigkeitszug TGV Duplex V 150. https://www.maerklin.de/de/produkte/details/article/37797.
[33] Neuhäuser, https://neuhaeuser.com/bergbau25/index.php/de/wagen/.
[34] MisterPersuasion (YouTube), Z-scale cab ride on the Liberty National Modular Layout. https://www.youtube.com/watch?v=G6tJ6VJNA3M.
[35] AZATOR (YouTube), Train lego. AGV run on LGV: World speed record. Crash. Brick expo. https://www.youtube.com/watch?v=U8QB91XwZHw.
[36] Luxury Lifestyle Magazine, Travel Japan in style: Five luxury train journeys around Japan. 8 Jan., 2018. https://www.luxurylifestylemag.co.uk/travel/travel-japan-in-style-five-luxury-train-journeys-around-japan/.
[37] Wikipedia, High Speed 2. https://en.wikipedia.org/wiki/High_Speed_2.
[38] Bidstats, HRS18: Switches and crossings (S&C) for HS2 Ltd: A tender notice by HS2. https://bidstats.uk/tenders/2020/W51/740950221.

PREDICTION OF REAL-TIME TRAIN ARRIVAL TIMES ALONG THE SWEDISH SOUTHERN MAINLINE

KAH YONG TIONG[1], ZHENLIANG MA[2] & CARL-WILLIAM PALMQVIST[1]
[1]Department of Technology and Society, Lund University, Sweden
[2]Department of Civil and Architectural Engineering, KTH Royal Institute of Technology, Sweden

ABSTRACT
Real-time train arrival time prediction is crucial for providing passenger information and timely decision support. The paper develops methods to simultaneously predict train arrival times at downstream stations, including direct multiple output liner regression (DMOLR) and seemingly unrelated regression (SUR) models. To capture correlations of prediction equations, two bias correction terms are tested: (1) one-step prior prediction error and (2) upstream prediction errors. The models are validated on high-speed trains operation data along the Swedish Southern Mainline from 2016 to 2020. The results show that the DMOLR model slightly outperforms the SUR. The DMOLR's prediction performance improves up to 0.32% and 24.03% in term of RMSE and R^2 respectively when upstream prediction errors are considered.
Keywords: train arrival time predictions, direct multiple output liner regression, seemingly unrelated regression.

1 INTRODUCTION

The accurate prediction of train movements is critical to ensure the quality and reliability of railway transport. It provides passengers with reliable decision support, allowing them to take proactive actions to mitigate the impact of train delays. Passengers, for example, can make alternate travel plans if they are informed in advance of any train delays.

In passenger information systems, real-time information is utilised to generate a continuous prediction of train arrival times for multiple downstream stations at arbitrary prediction times. The predictions are updated in real time periodically or when the train arrives at a station. However, most studies developed data-driven approaches to predict train arrival times at the next train station [1]–[5]. The paper aims to model the train arrival time prediction at multiple station and arbitrary times and explores prediction approaches and prediction bias correction methods.

The remaining of the paper is organized as follows: Section 2 examines existing literature on the train delay prediction. Section 3 introduces the model formulation and prediction methodologies. Section 4 presents a case study of the high-speed train (HSR) line in Sweden. Section 5 concludes the findings of the paper and discusses future research directions.

2 LITERATURE REVIEW

With the growing availability of data in the rail industry, a number of studies have been conducted to predict the train delay in real-time. This task is well suited to data-driven methods, which include statistical models, machine learning models, and deep learning models. For statistical methods, Gorman [6] used linear regression to identify factors that contribute to railroad congestion delays. According to Jiang et al. [7], semi-parametric models outperform linear models, weibull distributions, binomial logistic regression, and random forest alone while maintaining interpretability.

Machine learning methods are becoming increasingly popular due to their ability to handle high-dimensional data and nonlinear relationships between dependent and explanatory variables. For example, Oh et al. [8] developed a real-time dwell time prediction model for

WIT Transactions on The Built Environment, Vol 213, © 2022 WIT Press
www.witpress.com, ISSN 1743-3509 (on-line)
doi:10.2495/CR220121

dynamic railway timetables by combining support vector regression (SVR), multiple linear regression, and RF techniques using data from real-time metro operation and smartcard data. Huang et al. [9] adopted Kalman filter to update SVR prediction using real-time information to ensure accurate running time predictions under unexpected situations. Considering passengers have different destinations, Tiang et al. [10] developed an arrival times prediction model for any downstream stations rather than only the next station using direct multi-output light gradient boosting machine. The works of Barbour et al. [11], Li et al. [12], Wen et al. [13] and Gao et al. [14] demonstrated the superiority of RF over other data-driven methods in predicting train events.

In recent years, deep learning methods have also been widely used to predict train delays. For example, Wen et al. [2] and Mou et al. [15] utilised long short-term memory to predict the arrival delay time of the train at the next station. Oneto et al. [16] employed extreme learning machines (ELM) together with train operation data and weather data to build a dynamic train delay prediction model. Li et al. [3] and Bao et al. [17] utilised particle swarm optimization algorithm to optimize hyperparameter of ELM when predicting train delay for real-time train dispatching. To comprehensively account for the temporal and spatial dependence between multiple trains and routes, Zhang et al. [18] proposed a train spatio-temporal graph convolutional network to predict the collective cumulative effect of train delays.

Despite the fact that numerous efforts have been made to develop train delay prediction models using advanced and complex algorithms, little work has been done to improve the model through bias or error adjustment. To address this gap, we propose a prediction framework that uses seemingly unrelated regression (SUR) to account for systematic model bias and prediction residual correlations due to unobserved predictors, as well as bias correction modules to improve model prediction.

3 METHODOLOGY

3.1 Problem formulation

The goal of this paper is to predict train arrival times for multiple downstream stations at arbitrary times. This allows passengers to keep track of their own journey between two points: origin and destination.

Consider a train line with multiple stations $\{i = 0, 1, 2, \ldots, N\}$, with N being the last station. Given the train is located at the current station i at time t, predict the train arrival times at the downstream stations $\{a_{i+1}, a_{i+2}, \ldots, a_N\}$. The prediction model receives real-time train operation data based on the current train location, allowing downstream train arrival time prediction based on the most up-to-date information. When the train arrives at station $i + 1$, predictions for the train arrival times at the downstream stations $\{a_{i+2}, a_{i+3}, \ldots, a_N\}$ are simultaneously updated. The prediction problem is represented as a multi-output regression conditional on the train location.

$$\widehat{\mathbf{y}} = f(X \mid i), \tag{1}$$

where $\widehat{\mathbf{y}}$ is the predicted train arrival time for all the downstream stations; i is the current train station; X is the predictor variables presented in Section 3.4.

Fig. 1 shows the prediction framework.

3.2 Prediction methods

In order to make train arrival time predictions for multiple downstream stations, multiple regression models are generated simultaneously. In this study, linear regression with two

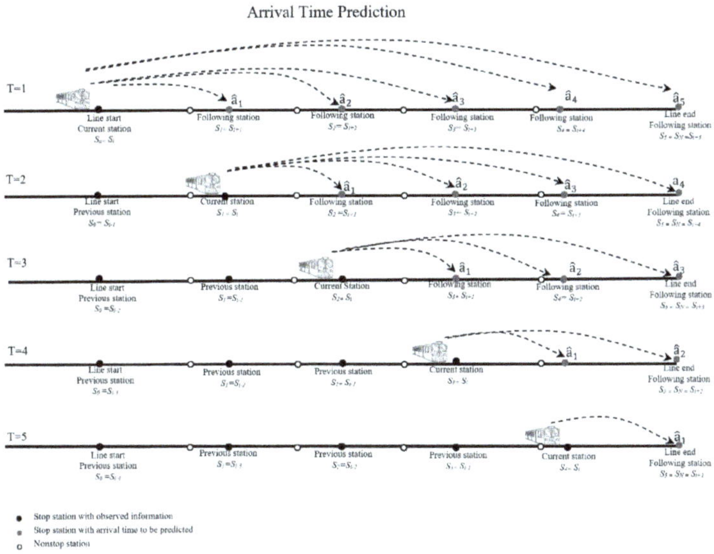

Figure 1: Prediction framework.

different frameworks, that is (1) direct multiple output linear regression (DMOLR) and (2) seemingly unrelated regression (SUR), are proposed to train these regression models.

The DMOLR model train the multiple linear regression equations independently with corresponding sets of explanatory variables. The predictor variables at current station i is inputted into $N - i$ number of regression models to generate prediction for downstream train arrival times $\widehat{a}_{i+1}, \widehat{a}_{i+2}, \ldots, \widehat{a}_N$. The prediction outputs are independent of one another in DMOLR, neglecting contemporaneous correlations between prediction equation error terms.

SUR, on the other hand, is a system of linear regressions that accounts for prediction errors that are correlated across equations [19]. Because there may be correlations between the shared unobserved characteristics, SUR's use of correlated errors terms across multiple regression models may increase the likelihood of prediction. For detailed information on SUR, see Washington et al. [20] and Brownlee [21] for more information on direct multiple output regression.

3.3 Bias correction modules

This section introduces two iterative correction approaches: (1) one-step before prediction error correction and (2) upstream prediction error correction. The purpose of this step is to improve the model's performance by leveraging the real-time observed information (prediction errors at previous stations) along with the predictors in Section 3.4.

The model utilises real time information $X_{i,i}$ at current station i where the train currently located to make prediction for all downstream station $\widehat{y} = \widehat{a}_{i+1,i}, \widehat{a}_{i+2,i}, \ldots, \widehat{a}_{N,i}$. The actual train arrival time $a_{i+1,i+1}$ is observed when the train arrives at the next station $i + 1$, and the prediction error $E_{i+1,i+1}$ can be calculated using eqn (2).

$$E_{i,i} = \widehat{a}_{i,i-1} - a_{i,i}, \tag{2}$$

where $E_{i,i}$ is the prediction error at station i when the train is at station i; $\widehat{a}_{i,i-1}$ is the predicted train arrival times for station i when the train is at station $i-1$; $a_{i,i}$ is the actual train arrival times for station i when the train is at station i.

For one-step before prediction error correction, only prediction error at current station i where the train currently located, $E_{i,i}$, is utilised as a predictor together with predictors $X_{i,i}$ introduced in Section 3.4. For example, in Fig. 2(a), at $T = 3$, the train arrives at station S_2, the model predicts the arrival times for downstream stations $\{S_3, S_4, S_5\}$ to be $\{\widehat{a}_{3,2}, \widehat{a}_{4,2}, \widehat{a}_{5,2}\}$. At $T = 4$, the train arrives at station S_3, the actual arrival times $a_{3,3}$ of station S_3 is observed, the prediction error $E_{3,3}$ is computed and used as predictor with $X_{3,3}$ to make prediction $\{\widehat{a}_{4,3}, \widehat{a}_{5,3}\}$.

For upstream prediction errors correction, all previously determined prediction errors together with prediction errors at the current station, $\{E_{1,1}, \ldots, E_{i-1,i-1}, E_{i,i}\}$, are utilised as predictors together with $X_{i,i}$ as predictors. For example, in Fig. 2(b), at $T = 4$, the train arrives at station S_3, the prediction error $E_{3,3}$ is computed and used together with previously computed prediction errors $\{E_{1,1}, E_{2,2}\}$ and $X_{3,3}$ as predictors to make prediction for $\{\widehat{a}_{4,3}, \widehat{a}_{5,3}\}$.

3.4 Predictor variables

The train operation data is used to define predictor variables utilised in this study. Six common factors that influence train event prediction are selected as potential predictors:

1. The arrival delay $\Delta a_{i,k}$ of the train k at current station i
2. The departure delay $\Delta d_{i,k}$ of the train k at current station i
3. The actual dwell time $dw^r_{i,k}$ of the train k at current station i
4. The scheduled headway $hw^s_{i,k}$ of the train k with previous train $k-1$ at current station i
5. The actual headway $hw^r_{i,k}$ of the train k with previous train $k-1$ at current station i
6. The scheduled running time $r^s_{i,k}$ of the train k from current station i to the next station $i+1$

Y represents the times required for the train to arrive at the targeted stations given the current station where the train is currently located. All the variables in this study are measured in minutes.

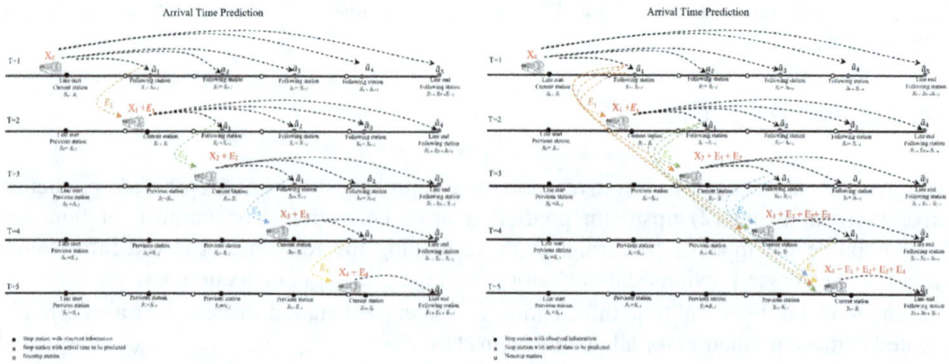

(a) (b)

Figure 2: (a) One-step before prediction error correction; and (b) Upstream prediction errors correction.

To avoid multicollinearity, these variables are first analysed and filtered using Pearson Correlation. $\Delta a_{i,k}$ is excluded since it is highly correlated to $\Delta d_{i,k}$ (with Pearson correlation coefficient (PCC) of 0.96) and has slightly lower importance with Y than $\Delta d_{i,k}$ (with PCC of 0.11 vs. 0.18). Thus, the predictor variables $\Delta a_{i,k}, dw^{r}_{i,k}, hw^{s}_{i,k}, hw^{r}_{i,k}, r^{s}_{i,k}$ are chosen for the final regression model.

4 CASE STUDY

4.1 Data

The train arrival time prediction is applied to the northbound direction of the long-distance HSR along the Swedish Southern Mainline, Sweden, from Lund C station to Linköpings C station (red dashed line with yellow dots in Fig. 3).

We focus on four HSR (train service No. 530, 538, 542, and 546) due to the data availability throughout the time span from December 2016 to December 2020. However, the train headways are calculated by taking into account all types of trains that use the line.

As trains travel along the route toward the final station N, the explanatory variables used to predict arrival times will change in time and space. To model train moving downstream closer toward N, separate datasets with different sets of explanatory variables that reflect different current railway traffic condition in time and space are used to train the prediction models. Since this study area has six stations, five separate datasets are prepared.

4.2 Experimental setting

The data is cleaned before training by removing observations with missing values or the extreme observation that exceeding two standard deviations from the central. The StandardScaler function in the scikit-learn library is then employed to normalized continuous

Figure 3: Swedish Southern Mainline.

variables into [0, 1]. The scikit-learn library's MultiOutputRegressor class extends the linear regression model to build MOLR whereas SUR models are implemented using "systemfit" package in R.

The R-squared is used to determine the model's goodness of fit in this study. The model fits better if R-squared is close to one. The root-mean-square error (RMSE) is used to evaluate the performance of prediction models in terms of estimation errors, as shown in eqn (3).

$$\mathrm{RMSE} = \sqrt{\frac{1}{N}\sum_{k=1}^{N}(\hat{y}_k - y_k)^2}, \tag{3}$$

where y_k and $\hat{y}_k$ respectively represent the actual and predicted arrival times, recorded in minutes. The closer RMSE are to zero, the better the performance of the model.

4.3 Results

First, we compare the performance of SUR and DMOLR in terms of R^2 and RMSE. The SUR is found to not have an obvious advantage compared with DMOLR since DMOLR has a slightly lower RMSE (0.05% lower than DMOLR) and no difference in R^2 on overall. This indicates that taking into account the prediction residual correlations has no significant impact on the subsequent stations' train arrival time prediction. Thus, the direct multi-output regression model structure is used for further analysis.

Then, we attempt to measure the effectiveness of the bias correction approaches in enhancing the prediction accuracy of the prediction models. The % Improvement in RMSE and R^2 is determined through the comparison between DMOLR with correction and the baseline model, that is DMOLR without any correction using eqn (4).

$$\text{Improvement (\%)} = \left(\frac{A_i - B_i}{B_i}\right) \times 100\%, \tag{4}$$

where A_i is the model prediction performance with correction at station i station, B_i is the model prediction performance without correction at station i (baseline model). It is important to note that improvement in RMSE indicates a lower RMSE and opposite is true for R^2.

Table 1 shows the comparison results of prediction models with or without bias correction modules. It shows that the DMOLR model with one-step before prediction error correction performs better than that without correction. This finding gives evidence that iterative prediction error adjustment using real-time information enables the model to constantly adjust itself, thus giving a slightly better prediction effect. DMOLR with upstream prediction errors correction via exhibits a slightly more notable improvement effect over the other models in

Table 1: Percentage improvement using different bias correction modules where baseline model is DMOLR without correction.

Model ($S_{i+1} - S_N$)	Improvement one-step before prediction error correction		Upstream prediction errors correction	
	% Improvement in RMSE	% Improvement in R^2	% Improvement in RMSE	% Improvement in R^2
Model 1 (Hm-Lp)	0.00%	0.00%	0.00%	0.00 %
Model 2 (AV-Lp)	1.34%	5.22%	0.02%	0.09%
Model 3 (N-Lp)	0.00%	0.50%	0.17%	20.90%
Model 4 (My-Lp)	0.09%	0.36%	0.15%	0.62%
Model 5 (Lp)	0.27%	20.34%	0.32%	24.03%

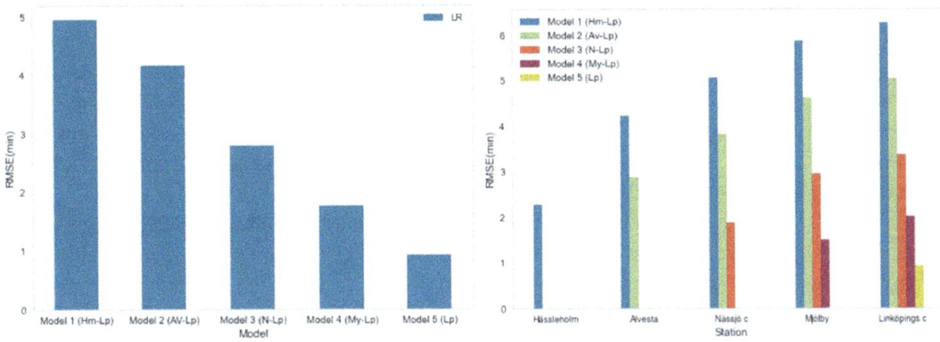

(a) (b)

Figure 4: (a) Average RMSE; and (b) RMSE across stations.

Table 1, showing the importance of both historical and real-time information in enhancing the performance of the models.

On the basis of previous analysis, the performance of DMOLR with upstream prediction error correction is evaluated from other angles, in each space horizon and each evaluation metric. Fig. 4(a) demonstrates average RMSE when moving closer toward the last station, Linköpings c (i is closer to N). We can notice that model 1 (Hm-Lp), which needs to predict the arrival times for more number of stations from i to N, has the largest prediction error with an average RMSE of 4.94 min. This is reasonable since it has more uncertainty and fluctuations in railway traffic conditions when the distance between i and N is longer. Fig. 4(b) explores the changes in RMSE and MAE of DMOLR at each station when the trains move along the route. Linköpings c has the largest prediction errors since the prediction of arrival times is a cumulative measurement. We can also observe that the prediction performance of DMOLR at a station improves with the train moving closer to it since more relevant real-time information that can capture the actual dynamics of traffic is used to make predictions. However, the R^2 values of these models as shown in Fig. 5 are relatively low. This might be attributed to the use of less representative predictor variables.

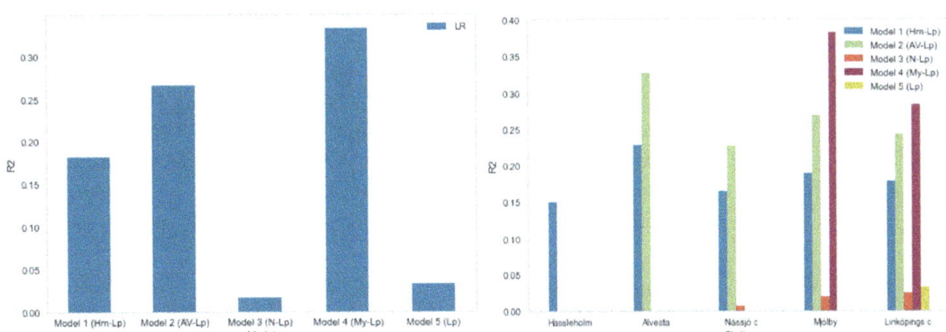

(a) (b)

Figure 5: (a) Average R2; and (b) R2 across stations.

5 CONCLUSION

The paper aims to develop and explore ways to improve train arrival time prediction for multiple downstream stations at arbitrary times in passenger railway systems. Specifically, this paper focuses on two main objectives. First, it examines whether contemporaneous correlations between the error terms across regression equations should be taken into account when developing prediction models. Second, the effectiveness of bias correction modules in enhancing the prediction model performance is assessed.

The case study findings shows that the train arrival time prediction is independent of the prediction residual correlations since the performance of SUR and DMOLR are comparable across stations. The train arrival prediction models taking into consideration of upstream prediction errors correction is found to be an effective in improving the prediction in downstream stations. Future studies will improve the model by exploring deep learning methods that could automatically capture complex interactions of variables. The low R^2 of the model indicates the need to include more predictor variables, such as historical train operational data, passenger data, weather conditions, infrastructure information, to improve the model's overall representative power.

ACKNOWLEDGEMENT

This work was funded by the Swedish Transport Administration, Grant Number TRV2018/139443.

REFERENCES

[1] Barbour, W., Mori, J.C.M., Kuppa, S. & Work, D.B., Prediction of arrival times of freight traffic on us railroads using support vector regression. *Transportation Research Part C: Emerging Technologies*, **93**, pp. 211–227, 2018.

[2] Wen, C., Mou, W., Huang, P. & Li, Z., A predictive model of train delays on a railway line. *Journal of Forecasting*, **39**(3), pp. 470–488, 2020.

[3] Li, Y., Xu, X., Li, J. & Shi, R., A delay prediction model for high-speed railway: an extreme learning machine tuned via particle swarm optimization. *2020 IEEE 23rd International Conference on Intelligent Transportation Systems (ITSC)*, IEEE, pp. 1–5, 2020.

[4] Li, Z., Huang, P., Wen, C., Tang, Y. & Jiang, X., Predictive models for influence of primary delays using high-speed train operation records. *Journal of Forecasting*, **39**(8), pp. 1198–1212, 2020.

[5] Huang, P., Wen, C., Fu, L., Peng, Q. & Tang, Y., A deep learning approach for multi-attribute data: A study of train delay prediction in railway systems. *Information Sciences*, **516**, pp. 234–253, 2020.

[6] Gorman, M.F., Statistical estimation of railroad congestion delay. *Transportation Research Part E: Logistics and Transportation Review*, **45**(3), pp. 446–456, 2009.

[7] Jiang, S., Persson, C. & Akesson, J., Punctuality prediction: Combined probability approach and random forest modelling with railway delay statistics in Sweden. *2019 IEEE Intelligent Transportation Systems Conference (ITSC)*, IEEE, pp. 2797–2802, 2019.

[8] Oh, Y., Byon, Y.J., Song, J.Y., Kwak, H.C. & Kang, S., Dwell time estimation using real-time train operation and smart card-based passenger data: A case study in Seoul, South Korea. *Applied Sciences*, **10**(2), p. 476, 2020.

[9] Huang, P., Wen, C., Fu, L., Peng, Q. & Li, Z., A hybrid model to improve the train running time prediction ability during high-speed railway disruptions. *Safety Science*, **122**, 104510, 2020.

[10] Tiong, K.Y., Ma, Z.L. & Palmqvist, C.W., Real-time train arrival time prediction at multiple stations and arbitrary times. *25th International Conference on Intelligent Transportation Systems (ITSC)*, IEEE, 2022. (Paper submitted.)
[11] Barbour, W., Samal, C., Kuppa, S., Dubey, A. & Work, D.B., On the data-driven prediction of arrival times for freight trains on us railroads. *21st International Conference on Intelligent Transportation Systems (ITSC)*, IEEE, pp. 2289–2296, 2018.
[12] Li, Z., Wen, C., Hu, R., Xu, C., Huang, P. & Jiang, X., Near-term train delay prediction in the Dutch railways network. *International Journal of Rail Transportation*, **9**(6), pp. 520–539, 2021.
[13] Wen, C., Lessan, J., Fu, L., Huang, P. & Jiang, C., Data-driven models for predicting delay recovery in high-speed rail. *4th International Conference on Transportation Information and Safety (ICTIS)*, IEEE, pp. 144–151, 2017.
[14] Gao, B., Ou, D., Dong, D. & Wu, Y., A data-driven two-stage prediction model for train primary-delay recovery time. *International Journal of Software Engineering and Knowledge Engineering*, **30**(7), pp. 921–940, 2020.
[15] Mou, W., Cheng, Z. & Wen, C., Predictive model of train delays in a railway system. *RailNorrköping 2019. 8th International Conference on Railway Operations Modelling and Analysis (ICROMA)*, Norrköping, Sweden, 17–20 Jun., pp. 913–929, 2019.
[16] Oneto, L. et al., Dynamic delay predictions for large-scale railway networks: Deep and shallow extreme learning machines tuned via thresholdout. *IEEE Transactions on Systems, Man, and Cybernetics: Systems*, **47**(10), pp. 2754–2767, 2017.
[17] Bao, X., Li, Y., Li, J., Shi, R. & Ding, X., Prediction of train arrival delay using hybrid ELM-PSO approach. *Journal of Advanced Transportation*, **2021**, 2021.
[18] Zhang, Y., Li, R., Guo, T., Li, Z., Wang, Y. & Chen, F., A conditional Bayesian delay propagation model for large-scale railway traffic networks. *Australasian Transport Research Forum, ATRF 2019-Proceedings*, 2019.
[19] Nasri, A. & Zhang, L., Multi-level urban form and commuting mode share in rail station areas across the United States: A seemingly unrelated regression approach. *Transport Policy*, **81**, pp. 311–319, 2019.
[20] Washington, S., Karlaftis, M., Mannering, F. & Anastasopoulos, P., *Statistical and Econometric Methods for Transportation Data Analysis*, Chapman and Hall/CRC, 2020.
[21] Brownlee, J., How to develop multi-output regression models with Python, 2020.

SECTION 4
ADVANCED TRAIN CONTROL

SPECIFICATION AND DESIGN OF A MODULAR AND EXTENSIBLE ARCHITECTURE FOR TESTING MOVING BLOCK SYSTEMS

ACHILA MAZINI, MOHAMED SAMRA, LEI CHEN, MARCELO BLUMENFELD & GEMMA NICHOLSON
University of Birmingham, UK

ABSTRACT

Testing train control systems is a crucial task to ensure their reliable and safe performance. Although testing systems and strategies for ETCS Level 2 are in place, as moving block/ETCS Level 3 systems are specified, the necessity to appropriately minimise the reliance on on-site tests, in light of increased testing scenarios, highlights the need to extend current testing capabilities to enable the operational paradigm shift of moving block. This paper, which reports on the results of the MOVINGRAIL project funded by the Shift2Rail programme, presents a testing solution for moving block systems to serve as a baseline for increasing the reliability of current laboratory and test practices. To obtain a good understanding of stakeholders' needs and requirements, a workshop was held with key stakeholders from industry and academia who are involved in railway signalling systems to discuss the current capabilities and the challenges that the transition from ETCS Level 2 to moving block may raise in the testing domain. Based on the outputs from the workshop, three important requirements for successful moving block testing formed the foundational assumptions used to define a modular and extensible architecture for testing moving block signalling systems. The components and interfaces of an integrated test system that is backwards compatible, i.e., it applies to all levels of ETCS, including future virtual coupling, regardless of system supplier, are then defined.

Keywords: testing, test architecture, ETCS-L3, moving block systems.

1 INTRODUCTION

In conventional railway systems, train detection and movement authority rely on trackside equipment. In this regime, track lines are strategically divided into predefined sections, also called fixed blocks (FBS), and a long separation between two trains is required, limiting the capacity of the railway line.

Moving block systems (MBS) represents a paradigm shift. Under MBS operation, the train detection no longer relies on trackside equipment. Instead, the safety-critical task of determining whether a section of track is occupied is performed by the on-board computer and the radio block centre (RBC) [1]. As a result, the integrity of trains (i.e., that there are no loose carriages or wagons) must be verified by train-based equipment rather than trackside systems. Another distinguishing characteristic of MBS is that blocks are not defined by pairs of fixed points on the line and movement authorities can be allocated to the next obstruction point on the track (i.e., by the rear of a preceding train) and move with trains.

It logically follows that the introduction of the new paradigm increases the operational complexity, and the challenge is then to guarantee that the system fulfils the safety requirements while operating trains closely to each other. In this scenario, testing plays an important role to guarantee that the quality and reliability of the system are being fulfilled. As moving block systems creates an infinite number of movement authority generation possibilities, it results in the exponential expansion to the number of scenarios that must be tested. Furthermore, as the positioning and train integrity are managed on-board rather than from the trackside, the architecture of both the on-board and trackside components differ between FBS and MBS. Cases where communication is lost, and wagons are unintentionally detached from the train, must also be managed differently. Although testing techniques and

WIT Transactions on The Built Environment, Vol 213, © 2022 WIT Press
www.witpress.com, ISSN 1743-3509 (on-line)
doi:10.2495/CR220131

strategies are currently in place for conventional railway system, as moving block system are introduced, testing techniques and strategies must be appropriately extended to consider the specific differences of MBS.

This paper reports the results of the *Work Package 2: Approaches for Testing Moving Block Systems* [1], [2] of the MOVINGRAIL project funded by the Shift2Rail programme. Here, a testing solution is defined to serve as a baseline to increase the reliability of current laboratory and adapt current test practices to accommodate testing for MBS. This has been approached by holding a workshop with key stakeholders from industry and academia who are involved in railway signalling systems to discuss the current capabilities and the challenges that the transition from conventional railway systems to moving block may raise in the testing domain. Based on the outputs from the workshop, three important principles for successful moving block testing formed the foundational assumptions used to specify a modular and extensible architecture, as well as related interfaces, for testing moving block signalling systems.

2 REQUIREMENTS SPECIFICATION

At a workshop held in May 2019 discussion facilitation sessions were conducted with key stakeholders to elicited requirements for MBS testing. The workshop was attended by 40 experts from industry and academia who are involved in railway signalling systems, including design and development, testing, and regulation. Of the 40 participants, 23 fully completed the 15 questions of the questionnaire, regarding: current testing process and the gap to zero-on-site testing, the format of a realistic moving block testing strategy, and ideas about how to bridge the gap between current testing capability and moving block testing. The full questionnaire and aggregated anonymised results can be found at https://beardatashare.bham.ac.uk/getlink/fiNYac39GLAxPfS7s5WWRvi9/ [1].

Overall, the results from the survey highlighted three important aspects for moving block testing. Firstly, responses emphasised the greater complexity of moving block systems, meaning that a wider array of possible scenarios need to be tested for the system to be deemed reliable. That leads to the second priority, where testing should be automated and conducted off-site whenever possible to avoid escalating costs. This contrasts with the current reality where manual processes are still prevalent in the organisations, from the generation of test cases (62%) to the analysis of results (73.3%). Finally, respondents recognised the greater safety criticality of moving block systems compared to their predecessors. Operating with shorter safety margins inevitably carries higher risks, so test strategies need to cover as many scenarios of degraded operation as possible.

Therefore, as determined from stakeholder interviews and reviews of the literature, the key point to achieve a robust testing solution for moving block systems relies on increasing the reliability in current laboratory test practices and providing a test environment that is able to reproduce relevant operational scenarios and conditions as realistically as possible. The key design principles used for the specification of the testing architecture derived from those premises and have been organised into seven key requirements, as follows.

1. The testing system and strategy shall be backwards compatible with all official ETCS baseline versions, as well as capable of upgrade to support virtual coupling and future versions of ERTMS/ETCS.
2. The architecture shall be a single integrated system that is capable of supporting testing by different stakeholders, suppliers, and with different test objectives.

3. The simulation models shall cover the complete railway system including railway infrastructure, rolling stock, timetables, railway operation rules and simulated train movements
4. The specification of components and interfaces shall cover commonly required functionalities to support a wide range of operational scenarios, to include (1) functionalities and requirements (main objective); (2) potentially safety critical instances; (3) common failures in previous systems
5. The use of hardware-in-the-loop (HIL) solutions shall be implemented to achieve close to real operation as much as possible.
6. The implementation of the functions in the adaptor shall be considered as the responsibility of each company.
7. The testing system shall be capable of running routines of different levels of automation (e.g., manual, fully automated)

3 ARCHITECTURE OVERVIEW

The system architecture shown in Fig. 1 [2] follows the requirements defined in the previous section. The architecture is considered an extension of the test architecture for fixed block systems defined in [3], as it adds up the specific components needed to enable a moving block system including the train integrity monitoring systems, as well as the use of virtual balises for train positioning.

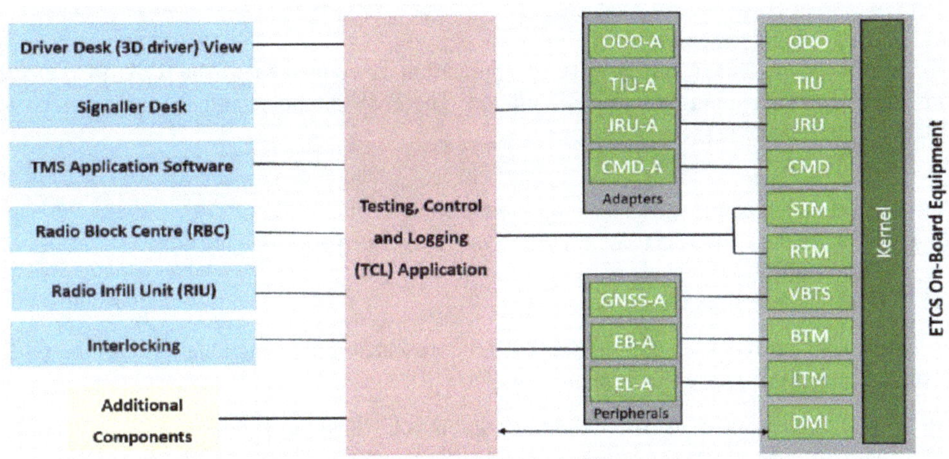

Figure 1: ERTMS test architecture.

The architecture illustrated in Fig. 1 is divided into four principal groups: The first group, in pink box, represents the test execution domain and contains the test control and logging unit (TCL); The green boxes indicate all the onboard related components; The third group, in blue, represents the external entities that are part of the test environment, such as simulators or any hardware-in-the-loop (HIL) components. The fourth and last group is shown in yellow and anticipates the existing of additional components or external tools that can be attached to the architecture as per the stakeholder's needs.

Each component, as well as their interfaces with the testing environment (i.e., TCL) are summarised in the following sections. More details can be found in Deliverable D2.2 [2].

3.1 Testing domain

3.1.1 Testing, control and logging application

The testing, control, and logging application (TCL) is the main component in the testing domain. The TCL manages the simulation and testing configurations and processes to represent the state of the railway network and traffic. It acts as a central unit between the external simulators, HIL components, and the ERTMS/ETCS on-board constituent. This paper summarises the TCL interfaces and functionalities. Further details can be found in [3].

The TCL entity is capable of initiating several distinct functions such as providing multi-train simulation, occupying and clearing train detections based on train movement, feeding coherent train position, speed, and acceleration to the odometry via the intermediate interface, logging data, checking train integrity, generating DMI actions, and simulating a complete railway system with mixed traffic operation (i.e. freight and passenger) and mixed signalling types (i.e. ETCS-fitted and unfitted trains).

Besides, the TCL application allows the setup, execution and analysis of the test scenarios specified in [5]. The TCL is able to fulfil the testing objectives of different stakeholders and provide a compliant Form Fit Function Interface Specification (FFFIS), where defined.

The next sections of this document highlight the distinct functionalities of the TCL entity when connected to each of the components showed in Fig. 1.

3.2 External entities domain

3.2.1 Traffic management system

The traffic management system (TMS) application is connected to the TCL to manage timetables and enable multiple train simulation. The TMS should be able to implement basic features that include [2]:

(i) Train tracking;
(ii) Interlocking commands and/or automatic route setting (ARS);
(iii) Infrastructure controls (e.g., traction system, reduced adhesion areas);
(iv) Train status;
(v) Conflict detection and resolution.

Under moving block operation, the TMS incorporates more functionality than the other levels of operation. These functionalities include [3]:

(i) Setting/clearing areas where the track status is UNKNOWN;
(ii) Moving points within a known area by emergency procedure;
(iii) Providing an estimated train location to the trackside component;
(iv) Providing the Staff Responsible (SR) distance to the trackside;
(v) Validating the SR distance calculated by the trackside;
(vi) Activating and disabling shunting areas;
(vii) Establishing and removing temporary shunting areas;
(viii) Activating and deactivating dynamic radio holes.

The high-level functional requirements of the TMS can be found in [6], while moving block focused requirements are detailed in [7].

The architecture to interface the TMS with the TCL is shown in Fig. 2 [2]. The TCL aims to interface with any TMS provided by an appropriate supplier. In Fig. 2, the TCL forwards the static variables including the network topology and timetable information and the dynamic variables originated from the RBC/interlocking to the TMS. These dynamic variables include the position updates for all trains in the control area being monitored by the TMS. Additionally, TMS sends back the control plans to the TCL including the signalling instructions. Another functionality of the TCL is logging the simulation scenario and the passed variables.

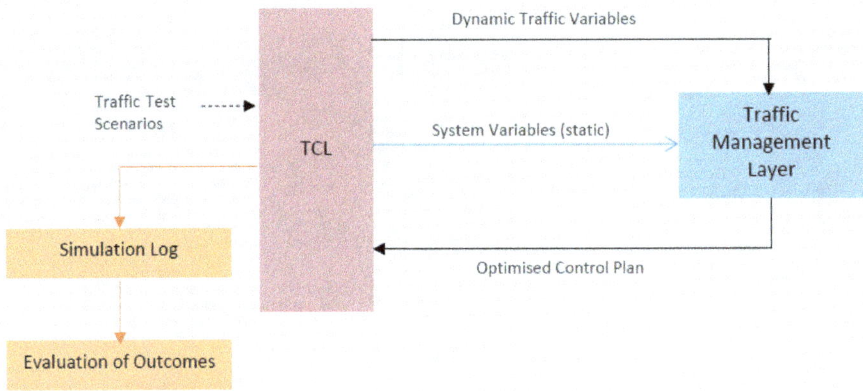

Figure 2: TMS framework.

3.2.2 Signaller desk

The signaller desk is a system that simulates the train traffic control by signallers and dispatchers with a similar UI to a real traffic control room. The signaller desk interface, represented in Fig. 3, requires a large amount of information that is to flow between the TCL application and the signaller desk which includes [2]:

(i) Traffic state including the speed and location of all of the trains in the signaller's area;
(ii) Interlocking state, including route setting, point settings, and signal aspects (based on the ETCS level being tested);
(iii) Train movement authorities.

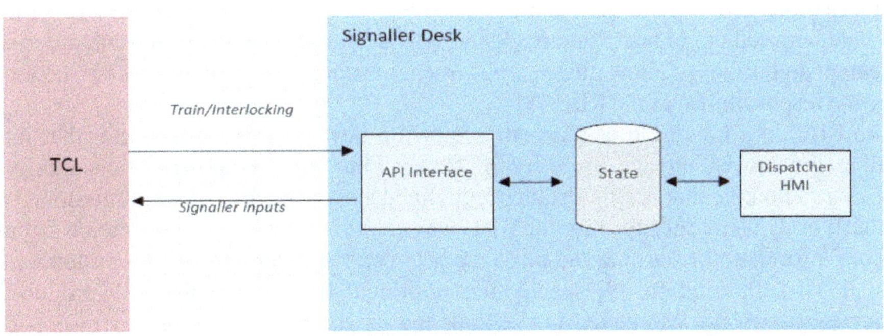

Figure 3: Signaller desk interface.

The TCL works on forwarding the needed information from RBC/Interlocking and TMS to the signaller desk as well as logging the simulation data.

3.2.3 Driver desk with 3D views
The driver desk is an optional element that is able to provide a 3D graphics view of the simulated railway environment. The driver desk consists of two main components with separate user datagram protocols (UDP) interfaces, as shown in the example desk in Fig. 4.

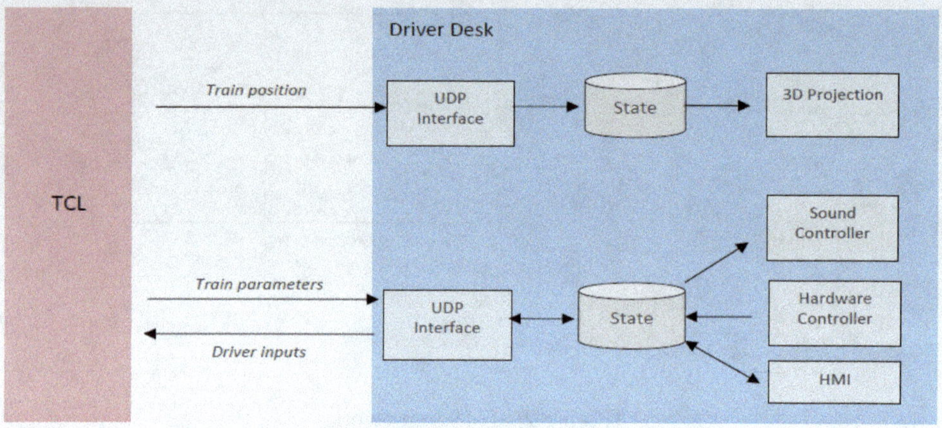

Figure 4: Driver desk architecture.

The first component is the driver 3D view, which represents a common driver's view outside of the train's window, while the cab controller is the second component, formed by a number of sub-components, such as the sound and hardware controller, with data flowing both to and from the TCL components. Both components have a local state object that contains the contextualised state of the train which the driver desk represents. Concomitantly, the TCL works on forwarding the RBC/interlocking data to the driver desk and it logs all of the simulation data.

3.2.4 Radio block centre
The radio block centre (RBC) is a computer-based system responsible for managing the data exchange between the onboard and trackside. The data exchanged is then used to define the movement authorities to allow the safe movement of trains on the railway infrastructure area under the responsibility of the RBC [8].

The RBC in a moving block system acquires a new set of functionalities that include handling the movement and recovery of trains with failed communication, along with managing radio hole that is either static (predefined since the RBC was commissioned (e.g., a tunnel)) or dynamic (occurs after the RBC was commissioned (e.g., base station failure).

More information regarding the interface between radio communication systems can be found in [10]. In addition, [9] specify the additional RBC functionalities introduced for moving block system. Moreover, [11] details the prospect of having one hardware-in-the-loop RBC under test sharing the environment with a simulated RBC.

The interface functionalities between TCL-RBC ate detailed in [12]. The following sections describe the role of the RBC and how it interacts with the other components of the test architecture.

3.2.5 Radio infill unit

As the test architecture is expected to be applicable to various ETCS levels, this section covers the radio infill unit (RIU), which is an optional component that is applicable to ETCS level 1 only. The RIU provides the signalling information in advance to the train by GSM-R transmission. In the test environment, the RIU corresponds to the real equipment provided by the supplier and no functional modifications compared to the commercial version are allowed.

The RBC and RIU equipment will interface with the TCL via the API mechanism, as seen in Fig. 5 [2]. Moreover, the RBC/RIU Adaptor Unit has the potential to enable the attachment of various RBC/RIU constituents to the test environment. More details on that can be found in [3].

Furthermore, the RBC and RIU can be integrated with the onboard radio transmission module (RTM) to constitute the radio base system (RBS). The RBS framework is part of the

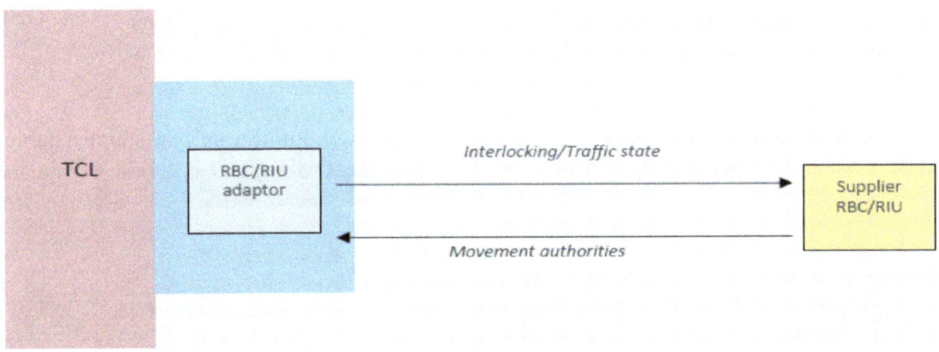

Figure 5: TCL-RBC interface.

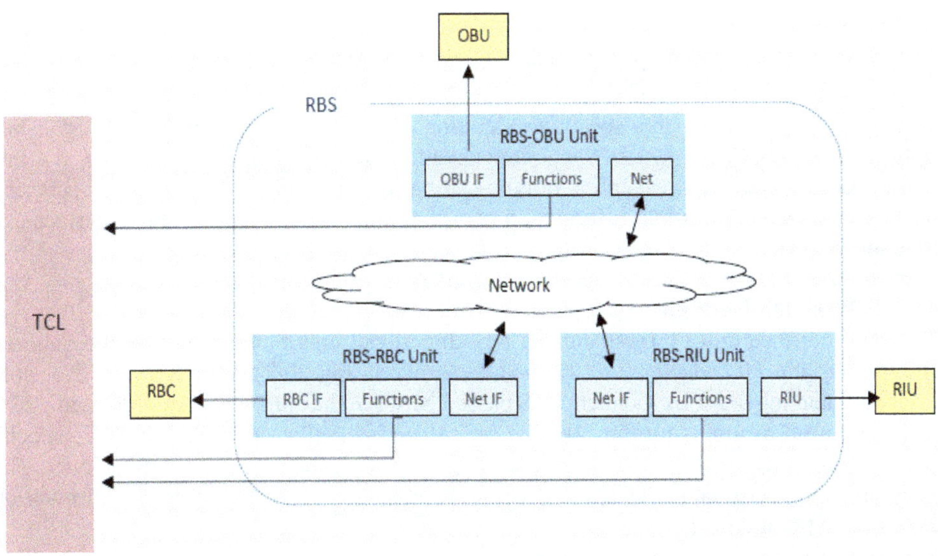

Figure 6: RBS interface.

TCL layer, and its duty corresponds for establishing a connection between its sub-systems while monitoring the message transfer between them, as shown in Fig. 6 [2]. This framework is expandable to accommodate multiple RTM, RBC, and RIU units in the test environment as per the stakeholders' needs.

3.3 Onboard domain

3.3.1 Onboard system

Comprising a combination of hardware and software elements, the main objective of the on-board unit (OBU) is to provide automatic train protection (ATP). Partnering with the ETCS trackside system and data entered by the driver, the OBU monitors the position of the train and determines the safe area in which the train is allowed to move. Should the train surpass this area, then the OBU acts to control the speed of the train and bring it to a stand [13].

In the test architecture, the OBU consists of a number of modules that interface with the TCL, as defined in Fig. 1. The following sections will focus on defining the TCL-OBU constituents interfaces highlighting the TCL functionality in case of OBU absence.

3.3.1.1 Odometry unit

The onboard odometry unit connects with the TCL application through an adapter named ODO-A. The communication between the TCL and the OBU ODO is unidirectional, as shown in Fig. 7 [2].

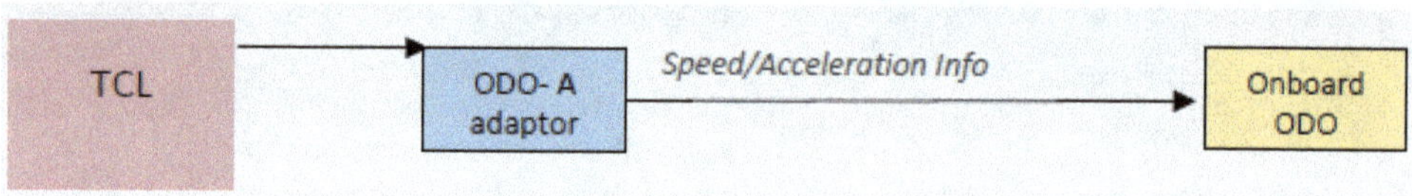

Figure 7: TCL/ODO unit interface.

The TCL layer and ODO-A can either generate multiple signals to make sure that the train is moving within the desired speed, acceleration, and designated area. Alternatively, the ODO-A may feed the desired speed, acceleration, and location uncertainty to the systems, replacing the ODO hardware when convenient. Another approach supported by this configuration includes the execution of type-testing the ODO unit itself without considering the TCL and ODO-A. Further information regarding the characteristics of this interface can be found in [14].

3.3.1.2 Train interface unit

The train interface unit (TIU) maintains a bi-directional communication with the onboard TIU through the TIU adapter (i.e., TIU-A), as shown in Fig. 8 [2]. With it, the TCL is able to forward and log the correspondent data passed between the components. For that, the TCL deals with a set of inputs for the TIU that are categorised either as dependent (e.g., special brake status, traction status) or independent (e.g., train integrity, train data) inputs. The communication between the TCL and TIU should adhere to all the train interface information presented in [4] and [15].

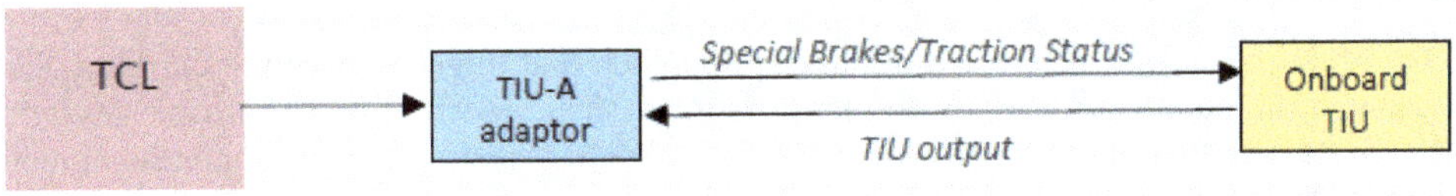

Figure 8: TCL/TIU unit interface.

3.3.1.3 Onboard train integrity

Monitoring the status of the rear of the train to guarantee the movement coherence is the principal feature in the onboard train integrity (OTI) that it is needed for the moving block concept. The OTI is considered as an additional subsystem included to the onboard TIU to replace the trackside train detection equipment in the management of the train integrity functionality.

The OTI is responsible for handling the communication between the master and slave modules to ensure that the train tail status is determined and monitored. Further details regarding the functional requirements and between the OTI and on-board TIU are available in [16].

3.3.1.4 Juridical recording unit (JRU)

The communication between the JRU and TCL is unidirectional through the intermediate adapter (i.e., JRU-A) and the main role of the TCL is to forward and collect the data passed between the JRU and the European virtual computer (EVC). The communication diagram between them is identical to the one shown in Fig. 6.

3.3.1.5 Cold movement detection (CMD)

The communication between the cold movement detection (CMD) and the TCL is unidirectional through the intermediate adapter (i.e., CMD-A). Within it, the duty of the TCL is to provide information to the OBU CMD unit such as: train has moved, train has not moved, or fail state. The communication diagram that represents this it is identical to Fig. 6. Additional information about the CMD and the adapter can be found in [14].

3.3.1.6 Specific transmission module

The TCL is responsible for manage a bidirectional link with the onboard specific transmission module (STM) equipment, and the messages should fir the guidelines provided in [17]. The TCL is also responsible for applying the protocols defined in [18], [19] to encode/decode message exchanges with the equipment.

3.3.1.7 Balise transmission module

The TCL interfaces with the OBU balise transmission module (BTM) and generates a balise telegram that is compliant with the requirements details in [22]. In addition, the TCL manages a group of balise telegrams that can be loaded in the configuration phase or generated dynamically as the simulation is executed. These telegrams contain the balise location information and can be defined by a single balise or balise groups. More details on the TCL functional interface with the BTM can be found in [14].

3.3.1.8 Virtual balise transmission system (VBTS)

The VBTS is considered to be a promising approach that might replace the current balise transmission module for train positioning. As the system is seen as only a prospect system, it was not specified in Fig. 2. However, the TCL should face no problem in interfacing with the VBTS, as it does with the BTM, and supervise the generation of the virtual balise telegram that is compliant with [21]. Also, the TCL is expected to be able to oversee a set of virtual balise telegrams that is either loaded in the configuration phase or updated dynamically as the simulation runs.

3.3.1.9 Loop transmission module (LTM)

The loop transmission module (LTM) is only applied for the L1 instance of ETCS. In terms of connection with the TCL, the test domains interfaces with the LTM to generate an Euroloop message that should fit the specifications in [23]. On top of that, the TCL is also responsible for overseeing a list of Euroloop messages that contains the Euroloop start and end location to be used for the correct loop signal generation. More details on the TCL functional interface with the LTM can be found in [14].

3.3.1.10 Driver machine interface

The test domain interfaces directly with the driver machine interface (DMI) to log every input and output on the DMI device in a digital format. An additional option includes the use of the TCL to automate the DMI inputs without the need of having test engineers performing manual interventions to execute a certain test sequence. Further details on the TCL functional interface with the DMI can be found in [14].

4 IMPLEMENTATION ROADMAP

The key goal of the implementation roadmap is to present the role of the test architecture and interfaces presented in this paper, in addition to the processes and technologies determined in several other projects, in the process of achieving a feasible test environment that can be integrated within the organization(s) current test process.

Fig. 9 summarises the key steps for the development and deployment of a test solution suitable for testing MBS, which includes highlighting the specification of requirements and safety aspects of the target system, in addition to the definition of current testing techniques and strategies available in the industry to guide the definition of a test strategy that considers current test practices.

This paper, which reports the MOVINGRAIL Work Package 2 results, builds on these specifications to specify, and design a modular and extensible architecture to serve as a baseline for different suppliers and organisations.

However, considering the general approach of the architecture, the feasibility analysis and implementation plan now rely on each organisation, as it should consider the organisation's testing and business objectives, as well as the internal assessment of current test capabilities, which includes software, hardware, test cases availability, data, and procedures currently in place for all the test activities.

5 CONCLUSIONS

Testing train control systems is essential to ensure their reliable and safe performance. As moving block/ETCS level 3 systems are specified, testing systems and strategies must be appropriately extended. Therefore, this paper, which reports on the results of the MOVINGRAIL project funded by the Shift2Rail programme, presented a modular and

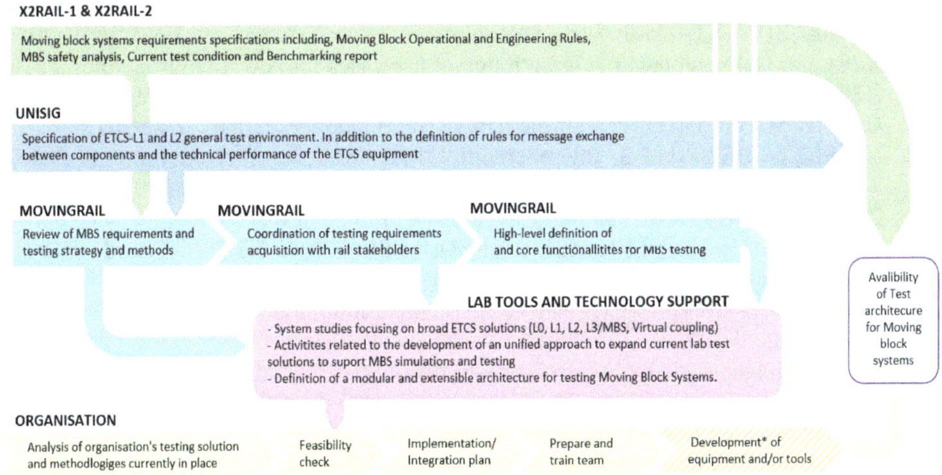

Figure 9: MBS testing architecture roadmap.

extensible architecture for testing of future moving block signalling systems to serve as a baseline for different companies and suppliers. The proposed architecture highlights the extended functionalities of existing sub-systems, including the TMS and the RBC, needed for moving block system operations. Furthermore, the architecture listed the newly added sub-systems that are unique for ETCS-L3 such as the train integrity (as part of the TIU) and prospect systems such as the VBTS for more accurate train positioning. It is expected that the architecture will be also appropriate for the current ETCS-L2 and ETCS-L1. To achieve this, the architecture has maintained the components that are needed for ETCS-L1 such as the LTM and RIU. An implementation roadmap is then presented to discuss the role of test architecture and interfaces presented in this paper to collaborate in the development of a feasible test environment that can be integrated within the organization(s) current test process.

ACKNOWLEDGEMENTS

This project has received funding from the Shift2Rail Joint Undertaking (JU) under grant agreement No. 826347. The authors would also like to thank the support from the Birmingham Centre for Railway Research (BCRRE) and the UK Railway Research and Innovation Network (UKRRIN).

REFERENCES

[1] MOVINGRAIL D2.1, Moving Block Signalling System Test Strategy, rev 2.0.0 29/02/2020.
[2] MOVINGRAIL D2.2, Moving Block Signalling System Test Methods, rev 5.0.0 14/07/2020.
[3] UNISIG SUBSET-111: IOP Test Environment Definition UNISIG, rev 3.5.0, 17/02/2016.
[4] UNISIG SUBSET-026: System Requirements Specification, rev 3.6.0, 25/05/2016.
[5] UNISIG SUBSET-076-6-3: Test Sequences, rev 3.2.0, 30/05/2017.
[6] In2Rail, Deliverable D7.1, State-of-the-Art and High-Level Requirements, 2016.

[7] X2Rail-2, Deliverable D5.1, Moving Block System Specification, 2019.
[8] UNISIG SUBSET-026-2: System Requirements Specification, rev 3.6.0, 13/05/2016.
[9] X2Rail-2, Deliverable D6.3, Description of use-cases for new TMS principles, 2018.
[10] X2Rail-1, Deliverable D6.1 Current test condition and benchmarking report, 2017.
[11] UNISIG SUBSET-039: FIS for the RBC/RBC Handover, v3.2.0, 17/12/2015.
[12] UNISIG SUBSET-111-3: Interoperability Test Environment Definition (FFFIS for TCL-RBC adaptor), rev 3.5.0, 17/02/2016.
[13] Digital Railway, ETCS Onboard System Definition. http://digitalrailway.co.uk/wp-content/uploads/2019/04/153821-NWR-REP-ESE-000005-ETCS-Onboard-SDD_3.0.pdf. Accessed on: 22 Apr. 2020.
[14] UNISIG SUBSET-94: Functional requirements for an onboard reference test facility, rev 3.1.0, 24/04/2017.
[15] UNISIG Subset-034: Train Interface FIS, rev 3.2.0, 17/12/2015.
[16] X2Rail-2, Deliverable D4.1, Train Integrity Concept and Functional Requirement Specification, 2017.
[17] UNISIG SUBSET-058: Application Layer STM FFFIS, rev 3.1.0, 16/12/2015.
[18] UNISIG SUBSET-056: Safe Time Layer STM FFFIS, rev 3.0.0, 29/02/2012.
[19] UNISIG SUBSET-057: Safe Link Layer STM FFFIS, rev 3.1.0, 16/12/2015.
[20] A11 T6001, Radio transmission FFFIS for Euroradio, rev 13.0.0, 18/12/2015.
[21] X2RAIL-2, D3.1, System Requirement Specification of the Fail-Safe Train Positioning Functional Block, 18/12/2018.
[22] UNISIG SUBSET-036: FFFIS FOR Eurobalise, rev 3.1.0, 17/12/2015.
[23] UNISIG SUBSET-044: FFFIS for Euroloop, rev 2.4.0, 29/02/2012.

SAFE DUAL-FREQUENCY EGNSS RECEIVER FOR RAILWAYS: THE TRENI PROJECT

HANAA AL BITAR[1], ANNE-MARIE TOBIE[1], MARCO PUCCITELLI[2], LIVIO MARRADI[2], GIOVANNI GALGANI[3], RODOLFO GUIDI[3] & DANIEL LOPOUR[4]
[1]Thales Alenia Space France, France
[2]Thales Alenia Space Italia, Italy
[3]EikonTech, Italy
[4]EUSPA, Czech Republic

ABSTRACT

The railway signalling system in Europe is currently undergoing a major change, converging towards interoperability and safety to be ensured by the ongoing deployment of the European Rail Traffic Management System (ERTMS). However, at present, ERTMS does not envisage the use of GNSS positioning technology for safety relevant train localization. Introduction of GNSS is an opportunity to contribute towards increasing of both safety and security or simplifying and reducing trackside equipment. It can also contribute to reducing overall signalling system costs which is instrumental especially for keeping the rural capillary lines competitive with other modes of transport. To enable such benefits and to contribute toward green and sustainable transport services the European Commission and European Union Agency for the Space Program (EUSPA) are collaborating with the main rail and space stakeholders on the inclusion of GNSS into the future evolution of ERTMS. This paper presents the TRENI railway GNSS receiver and antenna development, to be used directly or integrated in a train multi-sensor safe positioning platform, suitable for railway safety-related applications.

Keywords: GNSS, EGNOS, Galileo, rail, safety, integrity, CRPA, hybrid-PVT.

1 INTRODUCTION

According to the latest EUSPA GNSS Market Report [1], GNSS plays an important role in many non-safety related applications and the introduction of GNSS in future safety-related applications is expected to increase railway network capacity whilst decreasing operational costs. However, the rail scenario introduces several challenges: it is a dynamic scenario, moving in different environments from rural to urban, with different visibility conditions of the GNSS signals and with varying RF environment conditions. In addition, the criticality of the application requires a GNSS system robust to threats that may occur during operations.

In this context, the TRENI project aims at implementing a double step forward with respect to current state-of-the-art GNSS railway solutions. On the one side, the GNSS receiver will provide a dual-frequency (L1/L5) Galileo/GPS multi-constellation platform, with enhanced robustness and integrity features granted by the capability to autonomously identify and counteract to failures resulting from GNSS constellations faults, RF environment threats or from the receiver itself. Key features in terms of robustness to harsh RF environments will be based on receiver digitally controlled radiation pattern antenna (CRPA) techniques, pre/post-correlation algorithms for Jamming or Spoofing detection and mitigation and lastly PVT hybridization with complementary position navigation timing (PNT) sensors (IMU and odometers) (Fig. 1). On top of this, the integrity information broadcasted by SBAS (EGNOS) will be used for the evaluation of the along-track protection level (ATPL) and solution confidence intervals, with alerts provision in case predefined thresholds for the service are exceeded. The second innovative element brought by the TRENI solution consists in the antenna element design. Indeed, currently only single-band (L1) GNSS antennas certified for rail applications (i.e. designed and tested against EN

WIT Transactions on The Built Environment, Vol 213, © 2022 WIT Press
www.witpress.com, ISSN 1743-3509 (on-line)
doi:10.2495/CR220141

applicable standards) are available on the market, raising the need to develop a dual-band (L1/L5) multi-element CRPA antenna capable to support the interference mitigation functionality and to comply with the EN standards, thus being certifiable for the use in railway environment.

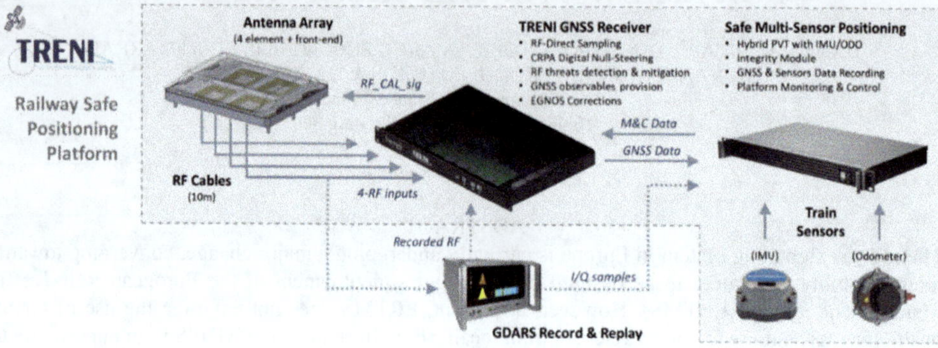

Figure 1: TRENI platform functional diagram.

2 USE CASES AND CONOPS

GNSS may be used to increase the capacity of the railway network by allowing the development of future train operations such as moving block or virtual coupling. These systems are evaluated with the aim of ensuring fail-safe train location and location integrity. Moreover, GNSS is part of the digitalization that is reflected in the development of new applications, such as enhanced passengers information services, but also bringing benefits to railway operators and infrastructure managers because of the improved asset management and maintenance, thereby reducing the operational costs.

Different applications can be hence addressed by the TRENI platform, starting from primary safety systems, where GNSS is involved in direct safety chain of rail operations. As non-exhaustive examples, these primary safety systems encompass:

- Train integrity (i.e. train length monitoring);
- Train control (virtual balises, absolute positioning, guidance and navigation);
- Trains spacing over the line for traffic control systems.

In addition, overlaid safety systems can be considered as a potential use case, in which the GNSS could be to provide information to safety back-up systems, for instance:

- Simplified signalling (back-up) systems, capable of providing safety in operational conditions (e.g. cold movement detectors or level-crossing protection).
- Driving intelligent assistance (e.g. alarms to train driver);

Dealing with non-safety applications examples could be:

- Fixed asset management (e.g. infrastructure surveying and monitoring);
- Rolling stock management (e.g. fleet management, cargo monitoring, etc.);
- Passenger information (e.g. journey assistant, customer information, on-train reservations).

3 DUAL-BAND CRPA ANTENNA

The GNSS antenna for the TRENI project is asked to have features not available in commercial GNSS antennas currently on the market. Indeed the antenna is required to be dual band (i.e. L1/E1+L5/E5a) and to give the possibility to perform null forming by the receiver, in order to maintain integrity in presence of interference and spoofing. This leads to an antenna architecture of a four-element array, necessary to apply beam forming strategies that give the additional requirement of an inter-element spacing within lambda/2 at maximum operating frequency. Another constraint, not related to performance, is the need to design an antenna system keeping the cost within limits compatible with the railway market. An RF front-end (FE), capable to amplify the GNSS signal of about 25 dB and to reject quite demanding near and out-of-band interferences, is part of the antenna system. A calibration circuit allows the equalization of the four FEs. The whole antenna architecture is shown in Fig. 2.

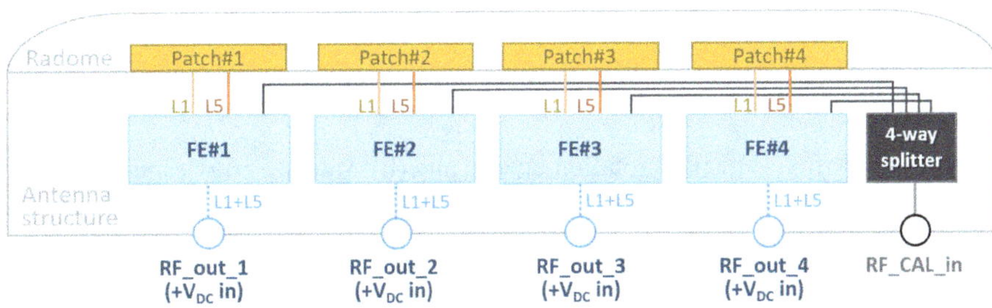

Figure 2: CRPA antenna high-level architecture.

The radiating elements main characteristics are listed below and shown in Fig. 3:

- Patch antenna technology for an easy and cheap manufacturing;
- Grounding pin not interfering with radiative performance, implemented as overvoltage protection from overhead catenary;
- Dual-band self-diplexed with two separated outputs (i.e. one for L1/E1, one for L5/E5), thus optimizing the front-end architecture;
- Sequential rotation applied to array layout, in order to assure axial symmetry during installation.

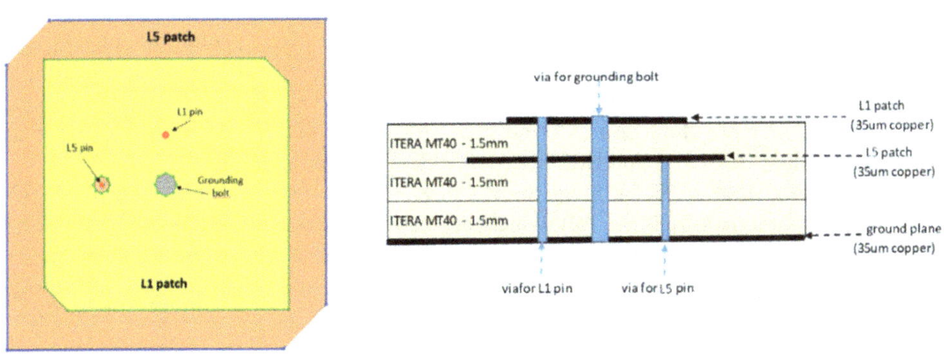

Figure 3: CRPA single antenna radiating element design (left) and stack up (right).

The antenna array return loss (Fig. 4), shows that the −10 dB target in E5/L5 (i.e. in the band 1166–1186 MHz) and E1/L1 (i.e. between 1565 and 1585 MHz) is satisfied with a safe margin, allowing the matching of the requirement also at array level.

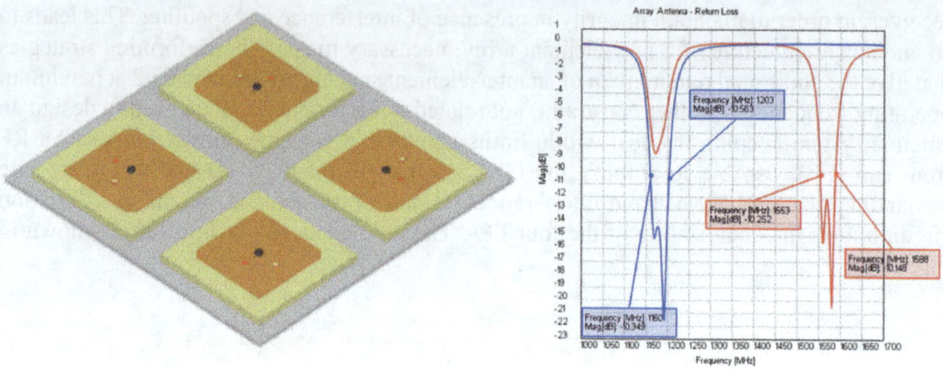

(a) (b)

Figure 4: (a) Array sequential rotation layout; and (b) Antenna array return loss (dB).

Regarding the antenna front-end (FE) architecture, it consists in a single amplification stage based on COTS amplifier components and custom design band-pass filters, with low insertion loss and steep transition regions, specifically tailored to cope with RF interference masks specified by [2], [3]. At the antenna FE level also coupling microstrip sections are foreseen to inject the RF calibration signal, provided by the GNSS receiver for the end-to-end RF chain calibration (amplitude and phase).

4 TRENI GNSS RECEIVER

The TRENI GNSS receiver is a customization of Thales Alenia Space Italia latest test user receiver (TUR) 19”-1U platform, already foreseen to be used for rail applications, as well as for avionic or maritime users. The baseline architecture is adapted to handle and process signals from up to 4 parallel RF inputs, with a future-proof design granted by the RF direct sampling and digital down-conversion approach, intrinsically allowing the receiver to accommodate any GNSS signal scenario evolution in terms of frequency plan and signal modulations by simply updating FPGA FW and receiver application SW.

The high-level architecture of the receiver is presented in Fig. 5, mainly consisting in a power supply module (i.e. a COTS AC/DC converter in the TRL7 prototype), an analogue RF front-end section (for RF signal filtering and antenna elements power feeding), a digital section (in charge of RF sampling, signal acquisition/tracking and navigation processing, calibration signal generation and external communication handling) and an I/O interface expansion module (for 1PPS and ERR/RESET TTL signals provision).

Starting from the TUR building block, the TRENI receiver implements specific functionalities, among which the following ones can be considered the most relevant ones w.r.t. future rail solution:

- GPS/Galileo multi-constellation satellite tracking and combined solution capability for higher position accuracy and availability;
- PVT solution configurability (single to dual-constellation dual-frequency, L1/E1+ L5/E5a);

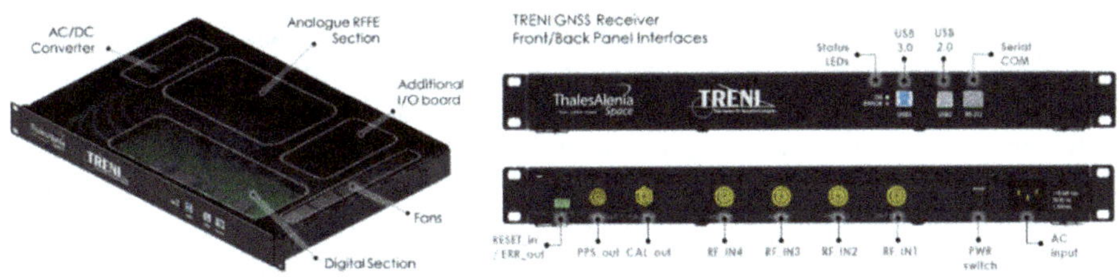

(a) (b)

Figure 5: TRENI DFMC GNSS receiver architecture layout (a) and interfaces (b).

- Application of EGNOS corrections at receiver level based on SBAS MOPS [2] and DFMC [3] standards, provided either by live EGNOS SiS or available through EURORADIO link (e.g. according to EUG-CR1368 guidelines, [4], [5]);
- Techniques for improved receiver resilience with active anti-jamming (i.e. digital pulse blanking in the time domain, excision in the frequency domain), anti-spoofing (including Galileo OSNMA capability) and multipath mitigation (based on multi-correlators DLL discriminators);
- Capability to implement at digital pre-correlation level up to two run-time nulls in the direction of detected interference/jammer sources;
- RAIM algorithm for the mitigation of local threats, with fault detection and exclusion (FDE);
- Provision of accurate 1PPS signal for the synchronization of on-board equipment and sensors;
- Real-time provision of raw observables, navigation data as well as measurements/signal quality monitoring (MQM/SQM) outputs for service level evaluation;
- Compliance to main railway safety standards (EN50126, EN50128, EN50129, EN50159).

Besides the TRENI GNSS receiver HW, the "safe multi-sensor positioning" equipment (i.e. a companion host PC) will be interfaced to allow the receiver monitoring and control, GNSS raw observables real-time visualization and storage (e.g. for post-processing and test replay under different configurations and data-fusion with external sensors data for GNSS-IMU hybrid PVT solution evaluation).

Among pre-correlation techniques considered within the TRENI Receiver for mitigation of unintentional RF interference and/or malicious jammer, a focus is here below proposed w.r.t. the well-known MUltiple SIgnal Classification (MUSIC) [6] and power inversion (PI) [7] methods, applied to antenna pattern digital null-steering. Both the mentioned algorithms can be implemented at receiver FPGA level by conveniently combining the I/Q digital signal samples generated by the digital down-conversion chains (DDCs), associated to the different radiating elements. In particular, the digital board FPGA engine performs the following main tasks associated to the CRPA functionality:

- reception of eight high-speed lanes (carrying I/Q samples from the four RF channels) and feeding of the "covariance matrix" calculation block;
- covariance matrices computation engine and communication with DSP processor for provision of covariance indexes and reception of associated complex weights (computed by DSP for the following I/Q samples digital combination);
- management of the calibration signal synthesis through an external dedicated DAC.

The Eigen value decomposition of the covariance matrix, computed by the DSP processor as described above, gives a perfect interference detector: indeed without interference (i.e. without correlated signal at the antenna array), the correlation of the array matrix will be close to diagonal (signals of each antenna would consist in uncorrelated white noise) and the Eigen values will then correspond to the noise power. Otherwise, in presence for instance of one jammer, one Eigen value will increase to represent the power of the interference source.

Hence starting from the covariance matrix decomposition in eigenvalues and eigenvectors, the null-steered antenna element complex weights (ω^*) are computed with MUSIC or PI method and used to multiply the I/Q signal samples to generate a unique stream as follows:

$$y_{out} = \sum_{n=1}^{N_{ant}} y_n \cdot \omega^*. \tag{1}$$

The effects of a jammer on weighted signals combination, if properly managed, will result mitigated after the null-forming process. In general, despite the superior performance expected for MUSIC algorithm in terms of direction of arrival (DoA) estimation and maximum "peak-to-null" gain ratio (i.e. interference rejection), PI method is typically preferred in GNSS applications due to its simpler implementation based on a "blind" approach (i.e. it does not require a-priori knowledge about antenna array such as antenna element orientation, gain/phase patterns, calibration values, etc.).

Before qualitatively assessing the null-steering capability, by assuming an AWGN only environment (i.e. no interference) as the nominal antenna operating condition, default CRPA weights can be defined, for instance, in order to optimize RHCP gain pattern at zenith. The results for the combination of antenna elements embedded RHCP gain patterns in a single equivalent one are reported in Fig. 6.

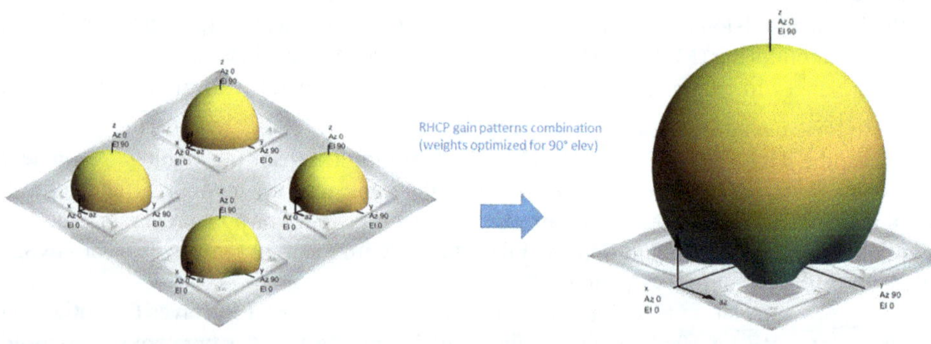

Figure 6: CRPA digitally combined pattern in AWGN only (weights optimized for zenith).

In case environmental conditions are characterized by the presence of EMI source(s), null-steering algorithm can be executed to mitigate interference effects at the receiver level. The maximum number of EMI sources that can be simultaneously (and effectively) mitigated by the current CRPA antenna design is approximately equal to $N_{RFI} \leq N_{ANT}/2 = 2$ (where $N_{ANT} = 4$ is the number of radiating elements).

In order to characterize the null-steering capability, a fixed JNR resulting in −3dB degradation of C/N_0 is considered in Fig. 7, in presence of two terrestrial interference sources simulated at 1176 MHz and with DoA1[azm=60°,elv=20°], DoA2[azm=−110°,elv=5°] (highlighted by red markers).

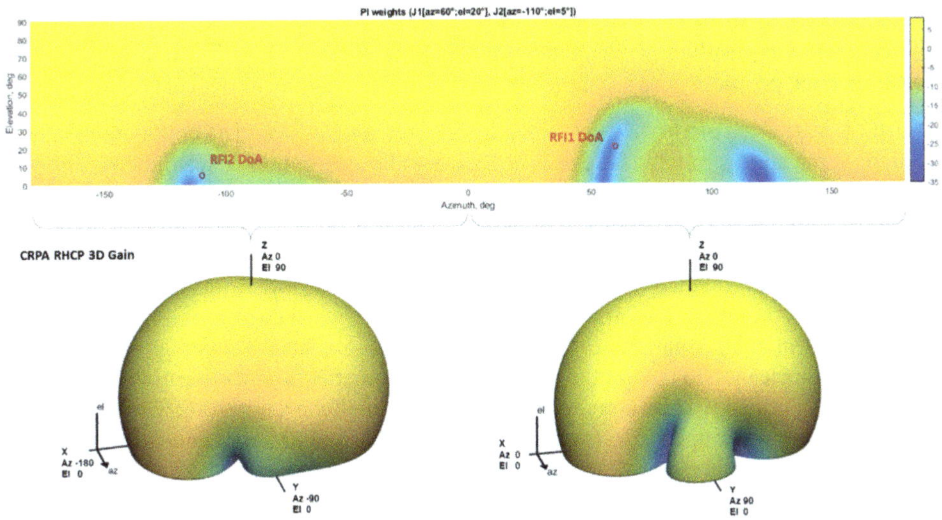

Figure 7: Digital null-steering capability example in presence of two RFI sources.

Similarly to the previous example (i.e. given a fixed JNR resulting in −3dB C/N_0 degradation), the expected null-steering capability for the antenna patterns over L1 and L5 bands have been statistically characterized by simulating different jammers directions of arrival over entire antenna coverage area, with a spatial resolution of 10 deg (i.e. DoA bins defined by azm=[0:10:360] deg, elv=[5:10:85] deg). Simulations results are provided in Fig. 8, showing as expected a higher interference rejection for MUSIC (minimum P2N ratio in the order of 50dB), compared to the PI algorithm one (approx. 20dB).

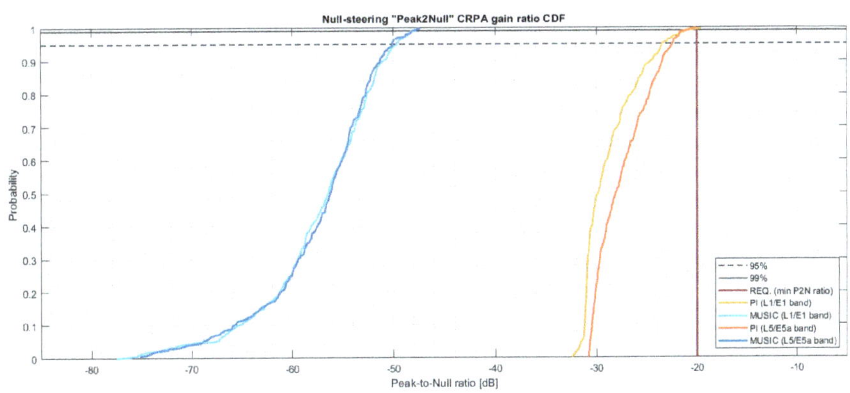

Figure 8: Peak-to-null gain ratio cumulative distributions for MUSIC and PI methods.

5 SAFE MULTI-SENSOR POSITIONING: HYBRID PVT AND INTEGRITY

Hybridized PVT solutions will be implemented and evaluated in order to demonstrate the enhancements brought by GNSS data hybridization with additional sensors installed on the test rolling stock. This integration will allow for:

- FDE capability to remove faulty ranges;
- Accurate train positioning even under GNSS signal limited-visibility conditions;
- Along track position, speed and the associated integrity protection level (ATPL).

Each of these steps are briefly described in this section. An IMU is a complete 3D dead-reckoning navigation system. Therefore, it does not allow to obtain an absolute positioning solution by itself, but can significantly improve the accuracy and the integrity of the positioning solution when combined with other sensors. In the TRENI project, the IMU will be hybridized with GNSS, odometer and possibly 2D maps.

In order to prevent unavailability of maps or unavailability of associated integrity information, it is proposed to limit the impact of the map on the navigation filter design while keeping its potential information useful. If available and associated with integrity, it has been proposed to use the map to correct the navigation solution after the hybridization filter. Since the cartography in the railways domain is expected to be highly accurate (yet with no integrity data associated), it is proposed to assume it fault free for the integrity concept. The method consists in projecting the navigation solution on to the nearest point of the rail in the map. If the map is available, FDE methods will have to be derived to ensure that, in case where 2 rails are side by side but heading in opposite directions, the navigation solution is projected to the correct rail. Therefore, the focus is on the coupling scheme between GNSS, IMU and odometer. According to Groves [8], several hybridization schemes may be considered: loose (LC), tight (TC) and ultra-tight coupling (UTC).

The choice of the coupling strategy is not straightforward. A critical analysis has been performed and the TC is preferred for the TRENI hybridization module. The arguments considered are the following: the TC provides a more accurate solution than a LC and, a PVT can be computed even with less than four GNSS satellites but at the expense of a slightly more complex implementation. In addition, a TC solution requires the knowledge of the ephemeris as well as an accurate synchronization between the integrated navigation systems.

Following the previously defined TC solution, an integrity concept is also proposed. Solutions are designed at several levels (pre-processing techniques, error characterization and measurement rejection approaches) in order to meet the integrity requirements and Key Performance Indicators (KPIs).

The proposed integrity concept is illustrated in Fig. 9. On one side, the IMU is used to propagate the solution, and, on the other side, the odometer and GNSS are the measurements considered to update the solution.

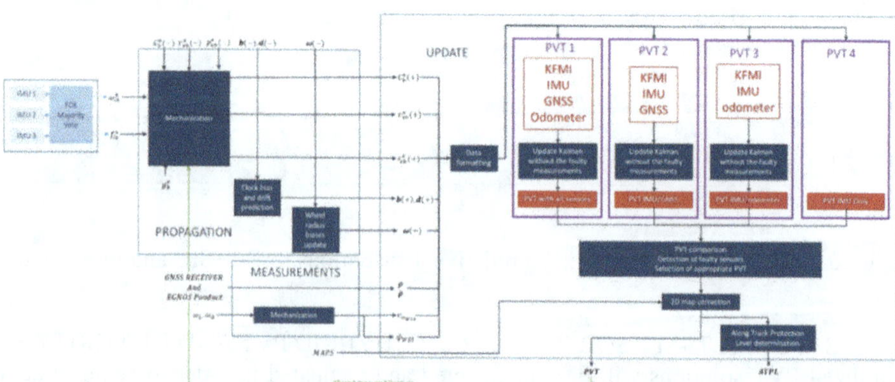

Figure 9: TRENI Integrity concept – architecture overview.

The integrity solution leverages on a mixed use of Kalman filter measurement innovation (KFMI) principle, and majority vote redundancy scheme. The FDE methods are applied both in the pre-processing step and in the update step. Majority vote method is applied in the pre-processing step to ensure the validity of the IMU measurements. Then, the combination of the KFMI based solution with majority vote solution is used to identify and reject potential faulty sensors.

In Fig. 9 four PVT solutions are represented: a hybrid IMU/GNSS/odometer tight coupling filter (PVT 1), a hybrid IMU/GNSS tight coupling filter (PVT 2), a hybrid IMU/odometer tight coupling filter (PVT 3) and an IMU only filter (PVT 4).

- If PVT 2, 3 and 4 provide the same solution (assuming a pre-defined tolerable difference) then the final solution will be PVT 1.
- If PVT 2 and 4 are equal but different from PVT 3, the odometer is detected as faulty, the final solution will be PVT 2.
- If PVT 3 and 4 are equal but different from PVT 2, the GNSS is detected as faulty, the final solution will be PVT 3.

Based on the final PVT choice, the 2D map can be applied to correct the position, to ensure that the train is on the correct rail. As explained above, the map is expected to be use in a post PVT step to correct the PVT, therefore, it is assumed that the map is correct and fulfils integrity requirements to be defined. This association of hybridization with majority voting and GNSS processing techniques is a key enabler for the determination of a navigation solution that is highly available and safe (regarding the target integrity risk).

Finally, the last step of hybridization section is the definition of the PL, as illustrated in Fig. 10. In fact, for the train case, the definition of PL can be simply projected on the train track in order to provide the ATPL (since there are no other degrees of freedom in the train motion, and thus the problem is essentially 1D).

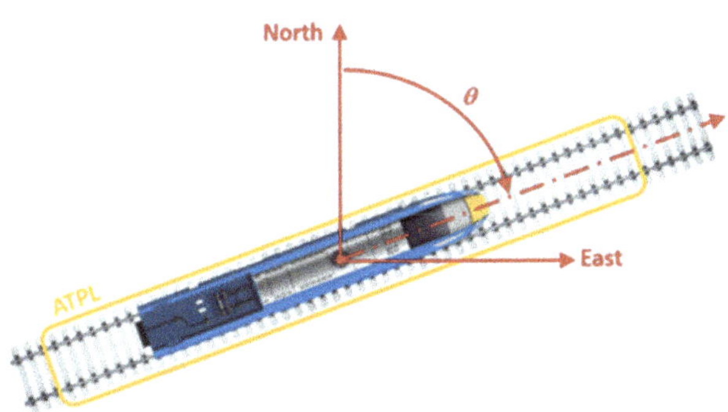

Figure 10: TRENI integrity concept – along track protection level (ATPL).

In this way the horizontal PL "collapses" into a 1D PL in the horizontal plane. Hence the ATPL, computed using all non-excluded measurements, is defined as:

$$ATPL = K_{PMI} \cdot \sigma_{along}, \tag{2}$$

where K_{PMI} is a protection coefficient defined as a function of the integrity risk probability P_{MI}, and σ_{along} is the along track standard deviation defined as:

$$\sigma_{along} = \sigma_E \cdot sin\,(\theta) + \sigma_N \cdot cos\,(\theta), \tag{3}$$

where θ is the azimuth of the track line segment on which the train has been determined to be situated, σ_E and σ_N are the east and north standard deviation components.

In order to complete the integrity concept design, a safety analysis has been performed. It relies on a thorough analysis of the sensor failures.

On one hand, the GNSS failures have been identified and quantified as proposed in Fig. 11(a). As it can be observed, the GNSS safety analysis gathers all local effect related failures as well as signal in space or ground segment failures. It conducted to a tolerable hazard rate (THR) of $THR = 7.2 \cdot 10^{-6}/h$.

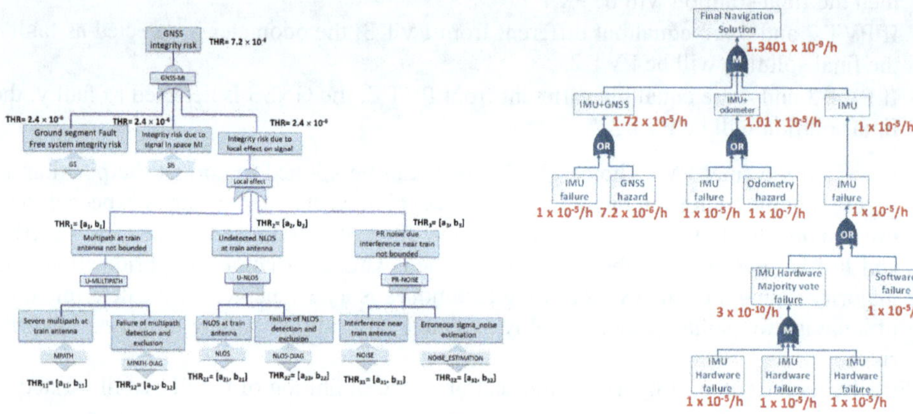

(a) (b)

Figure 11: TRENI integrity concept – safety analysis. (a) GNSS part; and (b) Complete hybrid system.

On the other hand, the INS and odometer failures have been analysed. There is not much information in the literature concerning these sensor failure rates. Nevertheless for both, the TRENI safety analysis relies on a probability of failure given as a function of mean time between failure (MTBF) and expressed as follow:

$$P = 1 - e^{-\frac{1}{MTBF}}. \tag{4}$$

For the INS failures, according to the literature, they come from either hardware or software failures. The hardware failure rate varies generally around $10^{-6}/h$ and $10^{-5}/h$ according to sensor quality (the risky case will be considered in the TRENI analysis). The software failures, or algorithmic failures, strongly depend on the algorithms and the error models used for the INS system. Navarro Madrid et al. [9] proposed that the failure rate due to stochastic modelling of Kalman filter for a GNSS/IMU system is $10^{-5}/h$.

For the odometer, Flammini et al. [10] mentioned that the MTBF of a train-embedded odometer is 10^7 hours. As a result, the corresponding failure rate is $10^{-7}/h$.

Based on the sensor failure analysis and the integrity concept proposed in Fig. 9, the integrity tree illustrated in Fig. 11(b) is proposed. It ends up with a THR of $THR = 1.3401 \times 10^{-9}/h$ which fulfils the requirements for a safety integrity level 4 function, the highest level of safety.

6 WAY FORWARD AND CONCLUSION

In this paper, the different applications addressed by the TRENI platform have been presented; even though safety related applications are a must for the TRENI project, non-safety related applications are also addressed (such as passenger information). Then the need for a specific antenna has been highlighted and its design detailed; as a reminder, the TRENI antenna is required to be dual band (i.e. L1/E1+L5/E5a) and to give the possibility to perform null forming by the receiver, in order to maintain integrity in presence of interference and spoofing. Finally, the TRENI GNSS receiver and the hybrid PVT and integrity software have been presented. This software is designed such that it guarantees that the trains navigation solution fulfils the performance requirement associated to safety-of-life rail applications.

The TRENI platform will go through an extensive verification and validation activity. Different phases are envisaged starting from laboratory subsystems integration and functional verification, validation at Telespazio laboratories in Rome against worst case expected threats models generated by a realistic emulation test bed, and lastly relying on the field test campaign, supported by additional equipment that will record I/Q data streams from the GNSS antenna during the train runs on the Italian national railway line. The gathered data will be very useful to replay the experienced scenario in laboratory and will allow for the characterization of the RF environment during the field test runs, as well as allow for the testing and comparison of the different receiver algorithms and techniques on the replayed data. Moreover GNSS receiver measurements gathered along with the IMU and Odometer sensors data (but also with other external sensors data such as physical balises and geo-located reference points along the track), will finally allow for the definition of an a-posteriori reference "truth" trajectory, that will be exploited for the verification of GNSS performance achieved during the field tests campaign and verification of the hybridized PVT solution and integrity concept performance.

ACKNOWLEDGEMENTS

This project is part of "Fundamental Element" framework and is being conducted under a grant related to the development of a Galileo Receiver for localization in train signalling (GSA/GRANT/05/2019), supported by the European Union Agency for the Space Program (EUSPA) and coordinated by Thales Alenia Space Italia S.p.A (TAS-I), in collaboration with Thales Alenia Space France S.A.S. (TAS-F), MERMEC S.p.A. (Italy), Telespazio Italia S.p.A. (TPZ-I) and Saphyrion Sagl. (Switzerland).

REFERENCES

[1] EUSPA EO and GNSS Market Report issue 1/2022.

[2] Minimum Operational Performance Standards for Global Positioning System Satellite-Based Augmentation System Airborne Equipment, RTCA DO-229, Issue F.

[3] Minimum Operational Performance Specification for Galileo/Global Positioning System/Satellite-Based Augmentation System Airborne Equipment, EUROCAE ED-259, Issue 1.0.

[4] SBAS L1 Receiver Guidelines for Railway On-board Unit, ESSP-TN-25931 Issue 01-00.

[5] SBAS DFMC Receiver Guidelines for Railway On-board Unit, ESSP-TN-26136 Issue 01-00.

[6] Schmidt, R., Multiple emitter location and signal parameter estimation. *IEEE Transactions on Antennas and Propagation*, **34**(3), pp. 276–280, 1986.

[7] Moelker, D.-J., van der Pol, E. & Bar-Ness, Y., Adaptive antenna arrays for interference cancellation in GPS and GLONASS receivers. *Proceedings of Position, Location and Navigation Symposium – PLANS '96*, pp. 191–198, 1996.

[8] Groves, P.D., *Principles of GNSS, Inertial and Multi Sensor Integrated Navigation Systems*, Artech House, 2007.

[9] Navarro Madrid, P.F., Martínez Fernández, L.M. & López, A., PPP integrity for advanced applications, including field trials with Galileo, geodetic and low-cost receivers, and a preliminary safety analysis. *Proceedings of the 29th ITM of The Satellite Division of the Institute of Navigation (ION GNSS+ 2016)*, pp. 3332–3354, 2016.

[10] Flammini, F., Marrone, S., Mazzocca, N. & Vittorini, V., Modelling system reliability aspects of ERTMS/ETCS by fault trees and Bayesian networks. *Proc. European Safety and Reliability Conference, ESREL*, pp. 2675–2683, 2006

DEVELOPMENT OF A NEW LEVEL CROSSING CONTROL SYSTEM UTILIZING COMMERCIAL MOBILE NETWORK AND GNSS

KOSHIRO YANAI, MITSUGU TOMIOKA, HIROSHI ITO & KOJI SUGIURA
East Japan Rail Company, Japan

ABSTRACT

East Japan Railway Company is working to streamline its facilities as the number of workers decreases due to the declining birth-rate and aging population in Japan. The analysis of life cycle costs related to signalling equipment shows that the majority of the costs are for level crossing safety equipment. A new developing level crossing control system depending upon mobile networks and GNSS, will streamline the equipment and improve level crossing safety and reliability by reducing the train detecting sensors, which are usually equipped with track circuits, level crossing emergency signals, which inform danger at level crossings to the driver, and the dedicated cables. There are many issues to be addressed in order to use mobile networks and GNSS before applying to the train control system, and it is necessary to establish methods to ensure safety and required level of availability. In our previous paper, we conducted an FMEA/FTA analysis to identify hazardous events for this system. This paper proposes an advanced method for level crossing control including train speed control and suggests the ways to ensure the safety and reliability of the system according to the previous hazardous analysis. As the running test result of the prototype devices on the Hachiko Line, the probability of mobile network disconnection between the control server and the on-board device was 9.9×10^{-7}/h. Localization error rate using GNSS was calculated as 0.18% to the actual distance. The running test result showed that safety and reliability of the system meet the level required for revenue service. We are targeting to start using this system on the Hachiko Line in 2025 as first revenue service.

Keywords: level crossing, mobile network, GNSS.

1 INTRODUCTION

The electric department of East Japan Railway Company is working to streamline its facilities as the number of workers decreases due to the declining birth-rate and aging population. The Signalling Division in the electric department maintains a variety of equipment, including signal, interlocking system, track circuit, point machine and level crossing equipment. According to the survey, level crossing equipment at local branches cost 34% of the total maintenance costs of all signal facilities, and the number of fault responses to level crossings accounts for 75% of the total number of fault responses. On the other hand, level crossing equipment is required to have the same level of safety in rural areas as in the Tokyo metropolitan area, and investments are continuously being made to improve safety. We have been working since 2018 on a new system development project to streamline level crossing equipment while increasing safety, especially on rural routes that are difficult to maintain [1]. The new system will reduce field equipment and improve safety by utilizing the general-purpose technologies of mobile networks and GNSS for level crossing control. There are many challenges to utilizing general-purpose mobile network and GNSS for railway safety equipment, and it is necessary to establish a methodology to ensure safety and achieve a certain level of availability. In this paper, we propose a new level crossing control method that utilizes general-purpose technology and a concept for ensuring safety. A prototype of the system was developed, and its safety and reliability was verified through running tests on actual trains.

WIT Transactions on The Built Environment, Vol 213, © 2022 WIT Press
www.witpress.com, ISSN 1743-3509 (on-line)
doi:10.2495/CR220151

2 OVERVIEW OF SYSTEM

2.1 Legacy level crossing control system

Fig. 1 shows the configuration of our legacy level crossing control system. In the legacy system, a sensor installed on the side of the railway tracks detects trains approaching or passing through the level crossing and controls the level crossing warning. When an emergency button is pressed due to an obstruction on the level crossing road or an obstruction is detected by the obstacle detector, the system notifies the driver of the abnormality by flickering emergency signal installed far away from the level crossing so that the driver makes arrangement to stop the train to avoid a collision. Each device transmits information via cables, and since sensors and emergency signals are installed far from the level crossing, the length of the cables is enormous. These many devices installed on the side of the railway tracks and the cables that connect them have inflated the cost of maintenance.

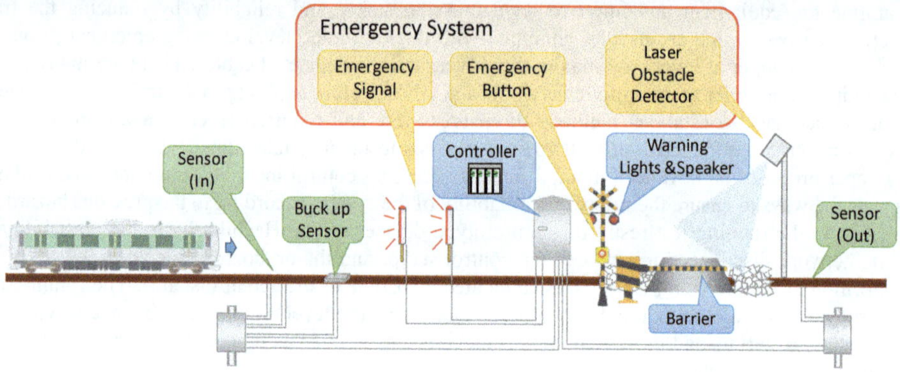

Figure 1: Configuration of legacy level crossing control and emergency system.

2.2 New level crossing control system

In the new system, the concept is to utilize general-purpose technology to reduce field equipment and cables, which are factors that increase maintenance costs in conventional systems. A configuration of the new system is shown in Fig. 2. In the new system, the control server controls level crossings and emergency signal by exchanging information with on-board device, level crossing device, and interface device with interlocking device via mobile networks. The on-board device uses the train position calculated from GNSS speed information to control level crossings and emergency signal.

The features of the new system are listed below.

1. Streamlining of facilities

   - Reduction of sensors
     The on-board device to localize the train position utilizing GNSS reduces the number of sensors which have been used to localize the train position until now.
   - Reduction of emergency signal
     The system in which the driver is notified of a level crossing obstacle by the blinking emergency signal installed at the site as well as the sound of an alarm in the cab reduces the number of emergency signal.

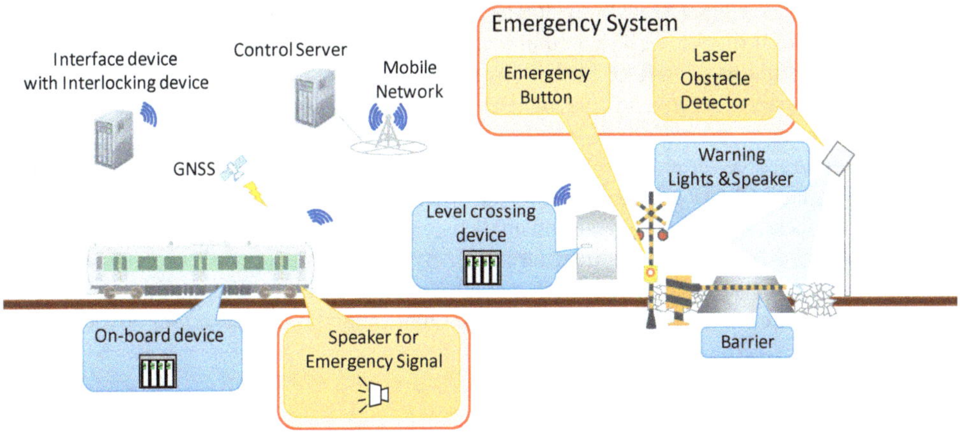

Figure 2: Configuration of new level crossing control and emergency system.

- Reduction of cables
  One server for each control is installed in a train line, and information is transmitted to and from each system (on-board device, level crossing device, and interface device with interlocking device) using mobile networks, thereby reducing the amount of control cables.

2. Improvement of safety

- Train control linked to level crossing status
  By monitoring the level crossing status by a control server and transmitting the status to the train, train control can be performed in accordance with the level crossing status.
  Example 1: Braking a train by identifying a no-barrier condition at a level crossing.
  Example 2: Output a speed profile to stop before a level crossing when an emergency signal is activated.
- Improvement of emergency signal recognition
  By changing the emergency signal at level crossing obstructions to an audible warning signal inside the cab, the system reduces the risk of overlooking or delaying recognition without being affected by poor visibility due to vegetation, fog, or other factors.
- Prevention of no-barrier due to sensor non-detection
  Since the system does not use conventional track circuit type sensors for warnings, it is possible to prevent unstable events due to detection errors such as non-short-circuit.

The introduction of the system will reduce the number of ground facilities, but will require the installation of new on-board device. The life-cycle costs calculated from the installation and maintenance costs on the Hachiko Line were estimated, and it is possible to reduce the life-cycle costs related to level crossing warning control and protective control at level crossing obstruction and obstruction protection by 20–30%, even taking into account the increased costs related to on-board device.

3 CONTROL METHODS AND SAFETY CONCEPTS

Since this system utilizes mobile communications and GNSS for high-risk control of level crossing control and protective control at obstruction, where hazardous events may occur, it is important to analyse safety and control methods based on this analysis. Safety analysis was conducted for the following non-safety events: no warning, insufficient warning time, and failure to send/receive an emergency signal. Hazards were identified and countermeasures were taken using STAMP analysis, an analysis method used to identify non-safety events in the control process, and FTA analysis, an analysis method used to analyse the causes of non-safety events and consider countermeasures [1]. By combining STAMP analysis and FTA analysis, countermeasures were comprehensively examined against non-safety events. This section outlines the basic functions studied based on the analysis and describes how to ensure safety.

3.1 Information transmission

In this system, each device is controlled by exchanging information between the control server and each device via a mobile network. Since the mobile networks utilize other companies' resources and public radio waves, they may be affected by stability due to factors over which we have no control. The mobile networks of two telecommunication companies are used together, and the same information is sent to both lines at the same time, with the first-arrived information being used to ensure stability. The control server sends a polling message to each device every second, and each device exchanges information by sending back an answer message to the control server. If the control server and each device cannot receive a message for three consecutive cycles, the mobile network is assumed to be disconnected and the safety-side operation is performed. As described in Sections 3.3 or 3.4, the safety-side operation at the level crossing device is to warn at the scheduled warning time, and the safety-side operation at the on-board device is immediate stop control. This system is designed to ensure safety even in the event of a mobile network breakdown.

3.2 Train localization

Level crossing waning control is based on the train position calculated by on-board device. The on-board device determines the train position by calculating the distance travelled based on GNSS speed information and adding it to the previous position. Whether GNSS can be valid or not is determined by performing various tests using input information from two antennas installed on the car. This test eliminates incorrect data from the GNSS. As a backup in case GNSS is not available due to structures or other surrounding environments, continuity is ensured by calculating the distance travelled from the speed information obtained from the speed generator as shown in Fig. 3. Position-corrected balises are installed between the rails to correct the position as an absolute position at the time of passage. The train position in the system is added to the train length as a correction value for the error assumed for the distance travelled, thus covering the error included in the GNSS or TG speed information. Each on-board device transmits its own train position to the central unit via a cellular phone line every second, and the central unit manages the position of each train for control.

3.3 Level crossing warning control

Fig. 4 shows an overview of control at the start of a level crossing warning. Level crossing waning start control is performed according to the scheduled alarm time calculated from train

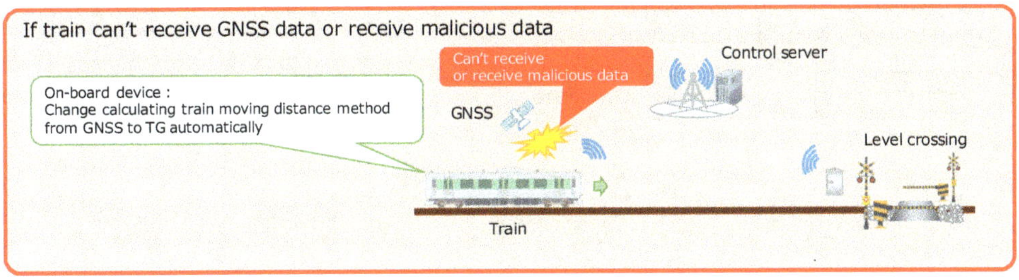

Figure 3: Behaviour when GNSS is not available.

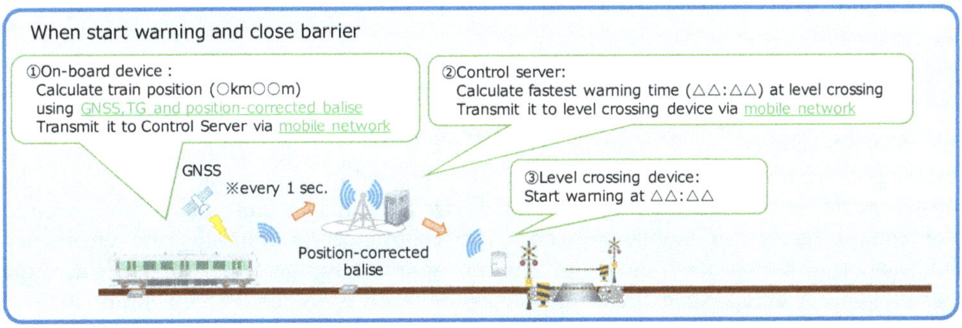

Figure 4: Level crossing warning control (start warning and close barriers).

positions by the control server. The scheduled warning time is the time that the control server calculates based on the train position and the starting position of the level crossing warning in the DB, and is the time that the train would reach the starting position of the warning if it travelled at the maximum speed of the line. The central unit transmits the calculated scheduled warning time to the level crossing device via mobile network, and the level crossing device that receives the information starts warning and closes the barriers when the scheduled warning start time arrives.

If the mobile network between the control server and the on-board device or between the control server and the level crossing device is disconnected and the scheduled warning time is no longer updated, the level crossing device will start warning when the last received scheduled warning time is reached. This ensures that even if the mobile network is interrupted, the level crossing can start warning before the train arrives, so that no interruption or insufficient warning time can occur. Furthermore, trains are prevented from approaching level crossings for which the scheduled warning time has not been set. For example, an indication of progress on the departure signal at the station is issued only when the warning time is set for all level crossing, thereby avoiding the danger of omission of time settings. In addition, the central unit constantly monitors the level crossing warning status, and when a train approaches a level crossing that has not been warned, it transmits information to the on-board device and controls braking to prevent no-barrier.

Fig. 5 shows an overview of the control at the end of the level crossing warning. In the level crossing warning control, the control server determines that the train has moved through the level crossing based on the train position and the location of the level crossing in the DB, and sends an instruction to the level crossing device to terminate warning.

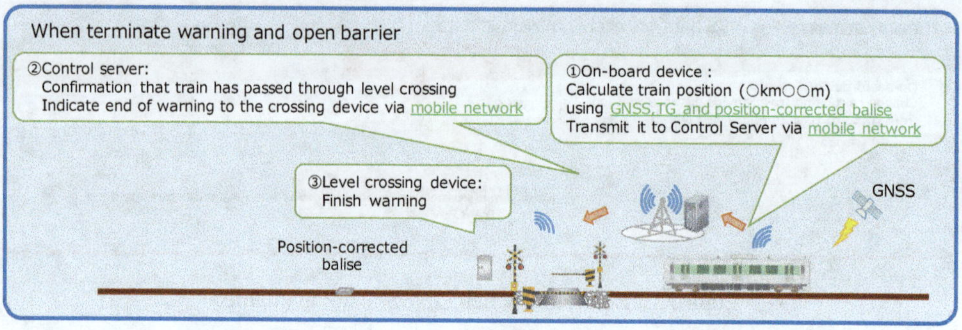

Figure 5: Level crossing warning control (terminate warning and open barriers).

3.4 Protective control at level crossing obstructions

Fig. 6 shows an overview of protective control at a level crossing disturbance. When a level crossing is disturbed and an emergency button is pressed or an obstacle is detected by the obstacle detection device, the level crossing device transmits the emergency information to the control server via mobile network. The control server transmits the emergency information to the on-board device of the train approaching the level crossing where the obstruction occurred. When the on-board device receives the emergency information, it outputs an alarm sound as an emergency signal to warn the driver of the danger. When the driver recognizes the alarm sound, he or she immediately makes arrangements to stop the train. When the on-board device receives the emergency information, it outputs a speed profile that enables the driver to stop before the level crossing. This enables the system to automatically apply the brakes even in the unlikely event that the driver's stopping arrangements are delayed, thereby preventing entry into the obstruction level crossing.

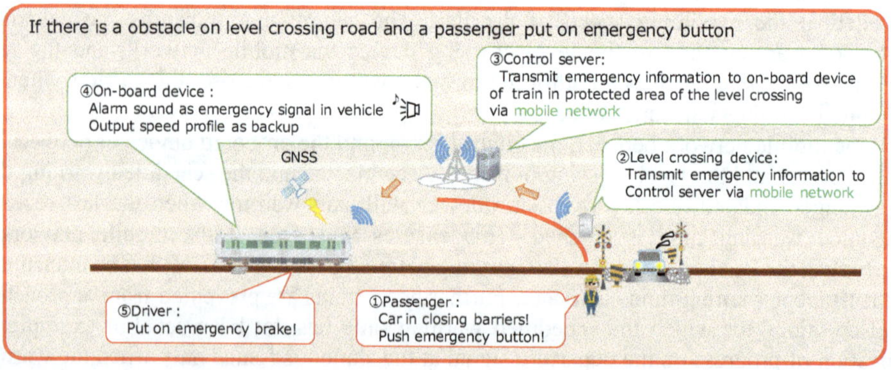

Figure 6: Protective control at level crossing obstructions.

If the communication between the control server and the level crossing device is disconnected, the system assumes that an obstruction is occurring at the crossing and transmits the emergency information to the on-board unit of the approaching train. If communication between the control server and on-board units is disconnected, emergency braking is applied to the train when communication is disabled for three times. This prevents the risk of failure of the obstacle protection due to communication breakdown.

4 TESTING FOR SYSTEM VERIFICATION

A prototype was developed and tested to verify the practicality of the functions of the devised system and the usefulness of the mobile network and GNSS. We conducted a test in the factory and a running test on the test line in advance, followed by a running test on the commercial line to confirm functions and verify data in the commercial environment. The running test in a commercial line on the Hachiko Line were conducted from September 2020 to January 2021. This running test consisted of monitored runs (39 daytime runs, approx.6,000 km) to verify the stability of the mobile network, communication delays, and position detection accuracy when utilizing GNSS, and night time controlled runs (25 night time runs, approx.500 km) to verify basic system functions and safety operation in case of failure. Level crossing devices were installed at two crossings, station devices were installed at two stations (Yorii station and Ogawamachi station), and two test trains were equipped with on-board devices. An overview of the running test is shown in Fig. 7.

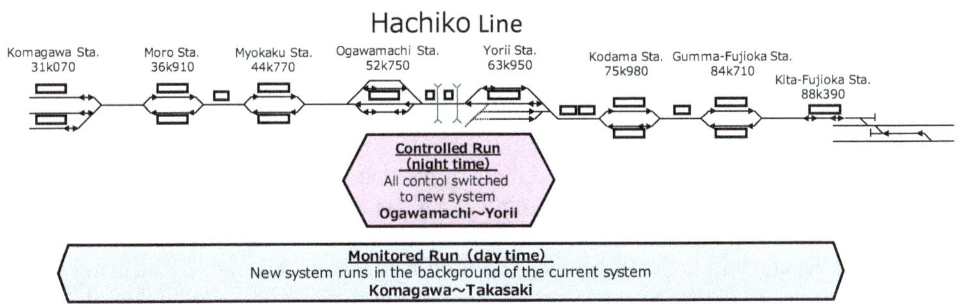

Figure 7: Overview of the running test in Hachiko Line.

5 VERIFICATION RESULTS

5.1 Functional verification

It was confirmed that there were no problems with the basic control functions and the functions to ensure safety in the event of an abnormality by all tests. In the functional verification test, to confirm the safety of the system, it was verified that safety side operations such as emergency stop of trains and blocking of level crossings work in situations where GNSS and mobile networks are not available or when device malfunctions.

5.2 Reliability of mobile networks

The data to be verified was the data transmitted and received by the control server to and from each device in one-second cycles, and the transmission delay and transmission loss were combined to obtain the transmission error rate. Transmission delay occurs when the response time exceeds the time allowed by the system, and 600 ms is used as the threshold value in this test. Transmission loss is considered to occur when there is no response from each device to a transmission from the control server. Table 1 shows the probability of a single transmission error between the control server and ground equipment (level crossing devices and Interface devices with interlocking device) and between the control server and on-board devices, as well as the probability of three consecutive errors that cause the system to operate on the safe side. A frequency of 1.0×10^{-5}/h, which is the frequency of occurrence once every 10 years, was used as the evaluated value of the transmission error rate. If only one company's mobile network is used for both ground devices and on-board devices, the evaluated value will not be met, but by using two companies' evaluated value together, a sufficient connection rate below the evaluated value can be ensured. The results indicate the possibility of utilizing mobile networks for information transmission on Hachiko Line. However, it was found that there are some spots with weak signals in some sections, so implementation of countermeasures will be considered in the future.

Table 1: Transmission error rate in running test.

Transmission error rate with control server (/h)		Mobile network (Company A)	Mobile network (Company B)	Combination of two networks
Grand device	Single	8.76×10^{-2}	5.02×10^{-1}	1.22×10^{-5}
	3 consecutive	1.45×10^{-2}	1.17×10^{-1}	4.72×10^{-7}
On-board device	Single	6.53×10^{-1}	3.47×10^{-2}	2.13×10^{-4}
	3 consecutive	1.17	1.02×10^{-1}	9.89×10^{-7}

5.3 Train localization accuracy by utilizing GNSS

The train localization accuracy was verified by comparing the distance travelled by the system with the distance actually measured from the previous ground station when the position-correcting ground station was detected. Table 2 shows the results of train localization accuracy in the running test. The train localization accuracy by utilizing GNSS was found to be 0.18% as an error rate relative to the distance travelled, which is within the2% accuracy assumed at the time of the test, and therefore, the system was found to detect the position with high accuracy as expected. The adoption rate of GNSS in this case was 95%. Since the accuracy of train localization by utilizing GNSS was 0.63% when position detection was performed only by tacho-generator generators, it is possible to perform train localization with higher accuracy by utilizing GNSS. This system ensures safety by extending the train length relative to the distance travelled according to the assumed accuracy. The reliability of the train position is high because the average accuracy is lower than the assumed accuracy, even when three times the standard deviation is taken into account, and this allows the control of level crossings to be achieved with safety ensured. In addition, it was found that GNSS could be used to localize the position without being affected by idling, slipping or changes in wheel diameter. The results indicate that the use of GNSS may be effective.

Table 2: Accuracy of localization in running test.

Localized method	GNSS+TG (GNSS 95% adopted)	TG only
Total distance	3,713 km	4,890 km
Error distance per 1 km	-1.8 ± 2.4 m	6.3 ± 8.5 m
Accuracy	0.18%	0.63%
Assumed accuracy	2.%	4.0%

6 CONCLUSION

This paper proposes a control method and a concept for ensuring safety for a new level crossing control system by utilizing GNSS and mobile networks to reduce maintenance costs at local line sections. In addition, a running test in Hachiko Line using a prototype of the system was conducted to confirm its functionality and to verify the reliability of the mobile line and the accuracy of position detection by utilizing GNSS. The running test result shows that safety and reliability of the system meet the level required for revenue service. We are targeting to start using this system on the Hachiko Line in 2025 as first revenue service. By implementing this system, we are expected to reduce the lifecycle cost of level crossing equipment by about 20%.

REFERENCES

[1] Komukai, H., Horigome, B., Hattori, T., Sugiura, K. & Kawano, T., Development study on next-generation train control system utilizing GNSS and 5G mobile communication network. *WCRR 2019*, 2019.

SECTION 5
ENERGY-EFFICIENT DESIGN

VERIFICATION OF DC GROUND FAULT DETECTOR FOR THE SIGNAL EQUIPMENT ROOM

HIDEKI NAKAZAWA[1], DAISUKE TAKAISHI[1], TAKUYA TAKEMATSU[1], MAKOTO NEZAKI[1], MASAHIRO NAKAYAMA[1], RYUUICHI KOMA[1] & MASAKAZU TAGUCHI[2]
[1]East Japan Railway Company, Japan
[2]Eiraku Electric Co. Ltd., Japan

ABSTRACT

The feeder circuit protection system of the DC substation is protected by the DC overcurrent device, DC fault selective relay and ground fault overvoltage relay. The DC overcurrent device detects an accident when a current exceeds the set value, and the feeder fault selective relay detects a sudden change in the current during the fluctuation time. In addition, the ground fault overvoltage relay detects an accident when the potential between the rail and the ground of the substation mesh earth exceeds the set value and continues for a certain period of time. However, high-resistance ground faults flow only several hundred amperes. Therefore, the high-resistance ground faults cannot be detected by the DC overcurrent device and feeder fault selection relay installed in the substation. In addition, the rail potential is too small to be detected by ground fault overvoltage relay. If the high resistance ground fault continues, the signal equipment will burn out and transport disorder will occur. There was no way to protect the signal equipment room from high-resistance ground faults. Therefore, we have developed a DC ground fault detector with the aim of protecting the signal equipment room from high-resistance ground faults and preventing defect in transport. This time, a field test was conducted to determine the protection set value of the DC ground fault detector and evaluate the weather resistance. In conclusion, it was confirmed that the developed DC ground fault detector for the signal equipment room was no malfunction. Also, considering that the operating voltage of the signal protector operates at 470V DC ± 20%, the major fault setting value was set to 350V DC so that the ground fault current can be cut off due to a serious fault before the protector operates.

Keywords: high-resistance ground fault, DC ground fault detection method, rail potential, signal equipment room.

1 INTRODUCTION

The high-resistance ground fault that could not be detected by the protection system of the substation occurred in the electrical equipment inside the station in the JR East, and the ground fault current flowed from the 1,500V DC feeder circuit to the signal equipment and burned out. It is difficult to distinguish between the load current of a train (several hundred to several thousand amperes) and the high resistance ground fault current (several hundred amps) at a substation in the electric power system using 1,500 V DC [1]. There was no way to protect the signal equipment room from high-resistance ground faults. Therefore, we have developed a DC ground fault detection relay with the aim of protecting the signal equipment room from high-resistance ground faults and preventing large-scale transport disorder.

This time, a field test was performed using this DC ground fault detector to confirm protection settings and weather resistance.

2 SUBSTATION PROTECTION SYSTEM

The DC substation's power circuit protection system is protected by DC overcurrent device, DC fault selective device and voltage detection method using the ground fault overvoltage relay. DC overcurrent device detects an accident when a current exceeds the set value. DC fault selective relay detects an accident when a steep change (ΔI) occur in the current during the fluctuation time (Δt). In addition, ground fault overvoltage relay detects an accident when

WIT Transactions on The Built Environment, Vol 213, © 2022 WIT Press
www.witpress.com, ISSN 1743-3509 (on-line)
doi:10.2495/CR220161

the potential between the rail and the substation mesh grounding (rail potential) exceeds the set value and continues for a certain period of time. However, high-resistance ground faults cannot be detected by the DC overcurrent device and instantaneous rate of rise relay installed in substations because only a ground fault current of several hundred amps flows. In addition, the rail potential too small to be detected by ground fault overvoltage relay. If a high resistance ground fault cannot be detected, dielectric breakdown in protective device will occur due to the potential difference between the signal equipment room and the ground. And ground fault current flows, leads to burning. Detection of high resistance ground fault accidents in DC feeder circuits has been a long-standing issue (Fig. 1).

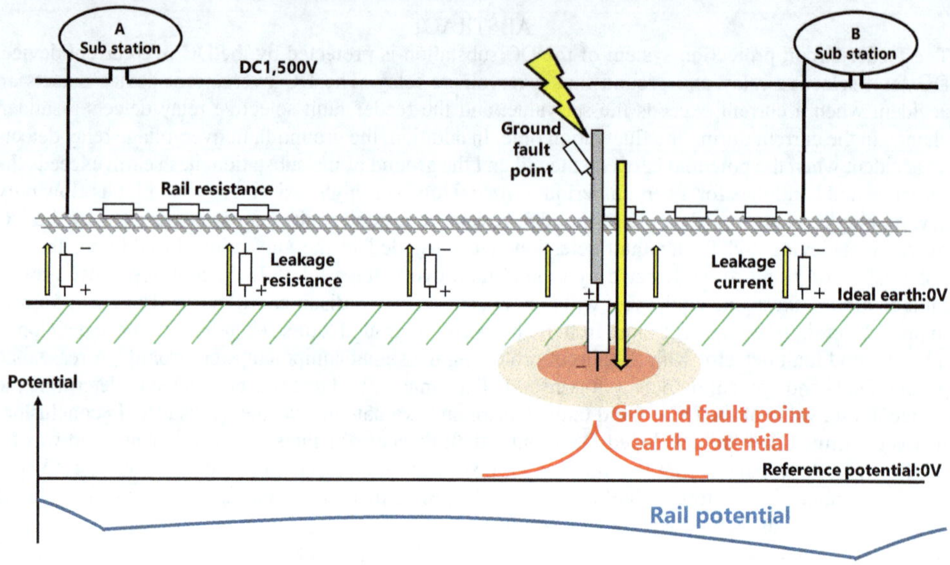

Figure 1: Rail potential at ground fault.

3 HIGH RESISTANCE GROUND FAULT DETECTION PRINCIPLE AND OUTLINE OF DETECTION DEVICE

In order to protect the signal equipment room from high-resistance ground faults, we select the method to detect the ground surface potential rise around the signal equipment room when high resistance ground fault occur and to open the DC high speed circuit breaker of the substation. This method uses ground fault overvoltage relay to detect the rail potential and the potential difference between the grounds near the signal equipment room. There are two types of detection, minor fault and major fault. For minor faults, the operating voltage is 100V/150V DC, and the operating time is variable from 0 to 30 s. For serious fault, a 50V DC step selection system with an operating voltage of 250 to 500V DC was used, and the operating time limit was a fixed value of 15 ms. In addition, polarity discrimination function is provided for the operating voltage. The reason for this is that at the time of a high-resistance ground fault, the rail potential is always negative with respect to the ground. When a high-resistance ground fault is detected by this detector, a signal that detects a high-resistance ground fault is transmitted by transmitting a cut-off signal from the power command to the DC high-speed circuit breaker of the substation via a communication facility provided separately. Stop feeding in the equipment room section (Fig. 2).

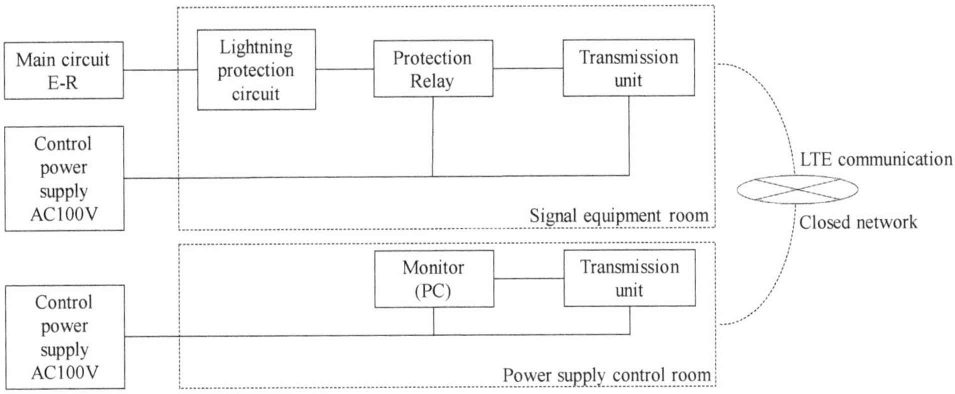

Figure 2: Detection device configuration.

4 FIELD TEST

4.1 Test environment

The DC ground fault detection device was installed near the signal equipment room at Shiraoka Station on the Tohoku Main Line, and ground of 10 ohm or less was placed near the signal equipment room to measure the potential difference between the rail potential and the ground in the signal equipment room. The shape of the detector has been reduced in size and weight so that it can be installed on a utility pole, and has length of 890 mm, width of 500 mm, depth of 565 mm, and weight of 70 kg.

4.2 Weather ability measurement

The temperature and humidity inside the DC ground fault detector were measured from 21 April to 4 November 2020. In order to prevent the temperature inside the panel from rising, the housing of this detection device has a double structure and has a light-shielding property. As a result, the maximum ambient temperature was 3°C, the maximum temperature inside the detector was 45°C, and the maximum humidity was 62%, and the results were good. In the factory, the test was conducted at an ambient temperature of –20 to 60°C. As a results, weather ability measurement was got good results. (Fig. 3).

4.3 Rail potential measurement

The rail potential due to the train load current was measured by sampling 1 s from 30 May to 4 November 2020. The reason is to confirm that the rail potential due to the train load current is equal to or less than the minor fault settling value of this detection device. As a result, the maximum negative rail potential was 69.5V DC and the duration of 60V DC was 0.8 s, so the minor fault settling value was 100V DC or less and the operating time was 10 s or less. Therefore, it was confirmed that there is no risk of malfunction due to rail potential fluctuation due to train load current (Fig. 4).

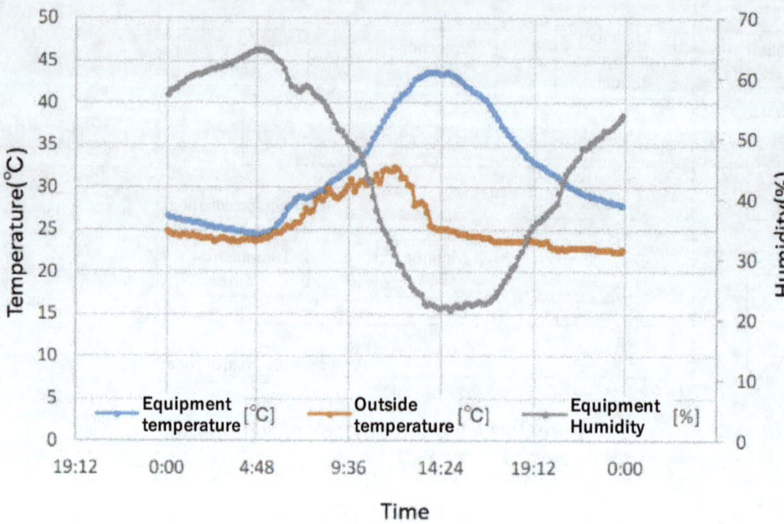

Figure 3: Temperature and humidity measurement results.

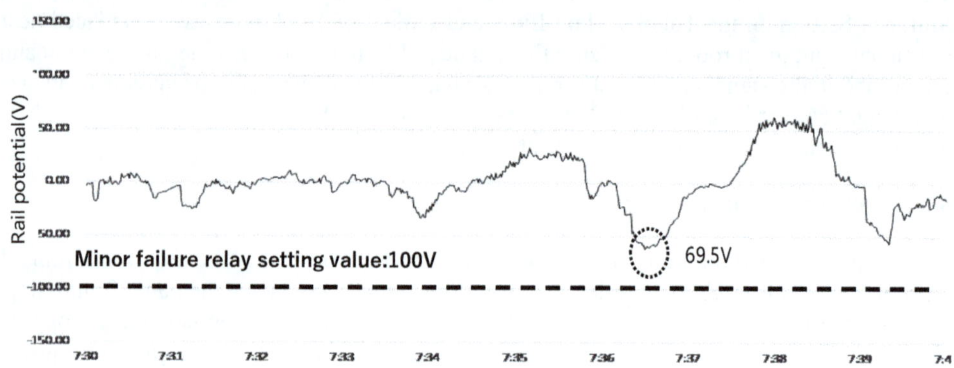

Figure 4: Rail potential measurement results.

5 CONCLUSIONS

The field test was conducted at Shiraoka Station on the Tohoku Main Line regarding the developed DC ground fault detector for the signal equipment room, and as a result of environmental resistance measurement and rail potential measurement, it was confirmed that there was no risk of malfunction. Also, considering that the operating voltage of the signal protector operates at 470V DC ± 20%, the major fault setting value was determined to be 350V DC so that the ground fault current can be cut-off due to a serious fault before the protector operates [2] (Table 1). The feature of this detection device is that the fluctuation range of the rail potential differs depending on the environment such as train load and rail leakage resistance. So the specifications are such that the settling value can be flexibly determined. On the other hand, when this detection device is introduced, it is necessary to measure the rail potential due to the train load for a certain period of time in advance to grasp the negative maximum rail potential in order to prevent erroneous detection.

Table 1: Relay setting value.

Fault item	Relay setting value	Note
Minor fault	Operating voltage: 100V DC Operation time limit: 10s	No cut-off signal
Serious fault	Operating voltage: 350V DC Operation time limit: 15ms (fixed)	With cut-off signal

REFERENCES

[1] Morimoto, D., Higuchi, Y. & Akagi, M., Detection method for DC high resistance ground fault with large current arc. *Railway Technical Research Institute Report*, **34**(9), 2020.

[2] Yoshii, K., Damage to signal equipment during an AC feeder circuit ground fault: Part 1. *Railway Research Institute Electric Power News*, **111**, 2019.

STUDY FOR THE INTRODUCTION OF DIGITAL COMMUNICATION USING OPTICAL FIBRE CABLES BETWEEN CONTROL ROOMS AND SWITCHYARD

DAISUKE TAKAISHI[1], HIDEKI NAKAZAWA[1], TAKUYA TAKEMATSU[1], NAOKI YAMANAKA[1], HIDEYUKI YOSHIOKA[2], YOSHITAKA TAKEMOTO[2] & TAKAMICHI ENDO[2]
[1]East Japan Railway Company, Japan
[2]Hitachi Ltd., Japan

ABSTRACT

Many copper cables for supervision, trip, measurements and control commands are laid between the switchyard equipment and the control room in the conventional substation. Therefore, it is difficult to remove the existing cables when the equipment is renewed, and to arrange the cable pits when the equipment is newly installed. In addition, since a large number of cables are connected, there is a problem that the construction period becomes longer. Therefore, to update the equipment easily, we studied the system configuration and information exchange method by digital communication technology reducing the number of cables between the switchyard equipment and the control room. We developed a prototype system, and field tests were conducted for the practical application of inter-equipment optical digital communication in a substation of the East Japan Railway Company. In the field test, we evaluated the prototype system compared to the conventional system not only by the performance test such as operation and transmission, but also by noise resistance performance test, workability check, and weather resistance check. We applied optical fibre cables to connect among the developed protection relay unit and field unit, instead of copper cables. In the substation, we evaluated abnormalities in power supply voltage, transmission line, CPU, etc. in outdoor environment. Also, we confirmed that trip signals and VT information are properly acquired by simulating relay operation, and we evaluated the redundancy in system configuration and protection performance. In conclusion, by using optical fibre cables for control cables except power supplies such as equipment and lighting, we confirmed that it is possible to significantly reduce the number of cables, and that work would become more efficient. We also confirmed that there were no problems about noise resistance, redundancy, and weather resistance.

Keywords: optical fibre cable, protection relay unit, field unit.

1 INTRODUCTION

Many copper cables for supervision, trip, measurements and control commands are laid throughout the substation between the switchyard equipment at the substation and the switchboard, and when updating the equipment. It is difficult to remove the existing cables or arrange the cable pits at the time of new installation. In addition, since a large number of cables are connected, there is a problem that the construction period becomes longer. Therefore, we decided to proceed with the development of a system configuration and transmission method in consideration of the ease of equipment update by digitally transmitting information technology for the purpose of reducing the number of cables between field equipment and switchboards.

A prototype was manufactured and field tests were conducted at the substation for the practical application of inter-equipment optical digital at the substation. In the field test, in addition to the operation test and transmission test for evaluating the performance of the prototype, the noise resistance performance, workability and weather resistance from the existing equipment were tested, and the conventional system configuration and the developed system configuration were evaluated. The equipment configuration was such that the developed protection relay unit and field unit were replaced with optical fibre cables via

WIT Transactions on The Built Environment, Vol 213, © 2022 WIT Press
www.witpress.com, ISSN 1743-3509 (on-line)
doi:10.2495/CR220171

L2SW from multiple metal cables. For Musashisakai substation of bulk power supply substation in the East Japan Railway Company (Fig. 1), check for abnormalities in power supply voltage, transmission line, CPU, etc. in outdoor environment, acquire trip information and VT information from existing equipment by simulating relay operation, and system configuration Issues were extracted from the confirmation of redundancy and protection performance.

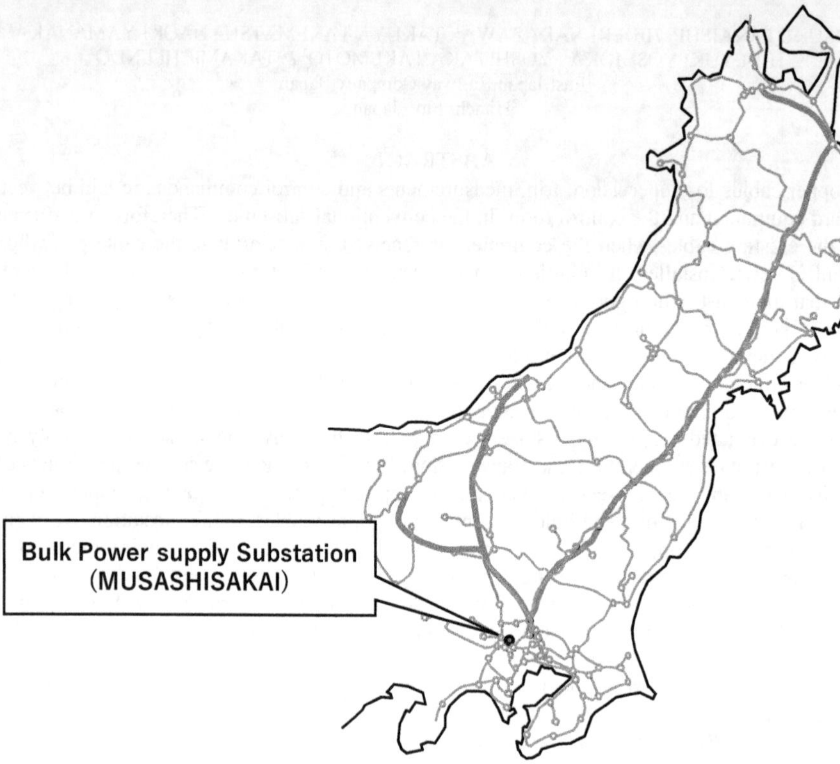

Figure 1: Location of the Musashisakai substation.

2 COMPARISON WITH THE CURRENT SYSTEM CONFIGURATION

2.1 Current system configuration

There are many cables between the field equipment and the switchboard, and there are a lot of issues such as electric shock risk due to incorrect wiring, cost increase due to the use of the switchboard, long construction period, noise intrusion into the control circuit due to opening/closing surge and lightning damage (Fig. 2).

2.2 Optical digital system configuration

Digital transmission is used between the field unit and the switchboard. This enables multiplex transmission, so the number of wires can be significantly reduced. Furthermore,

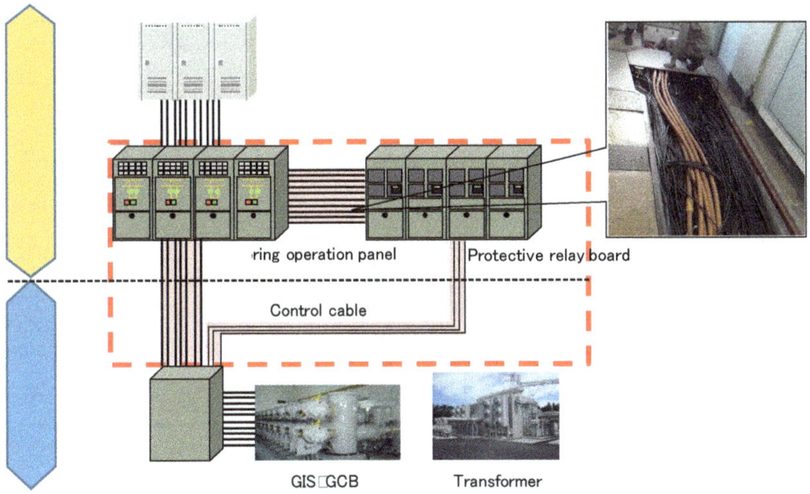

Figure 2: Current system configuration.

by insulating with optical fibre cables, there are many things compared to the current system configuration, such as reduction of electric shock risk, cost reduction due to reduction of the number of control cables, shortening of construction period, reduction of influence of opening/closing surge, securing of renewal space, etc. Therefore, this system is competent. In addition, the PRP (parallel redundancy protocol) method compliant with IEC62439-3 was adopted as the communication method to ensure the redundancy of the transmission line [1]–[3] (Figs 3 and 4).

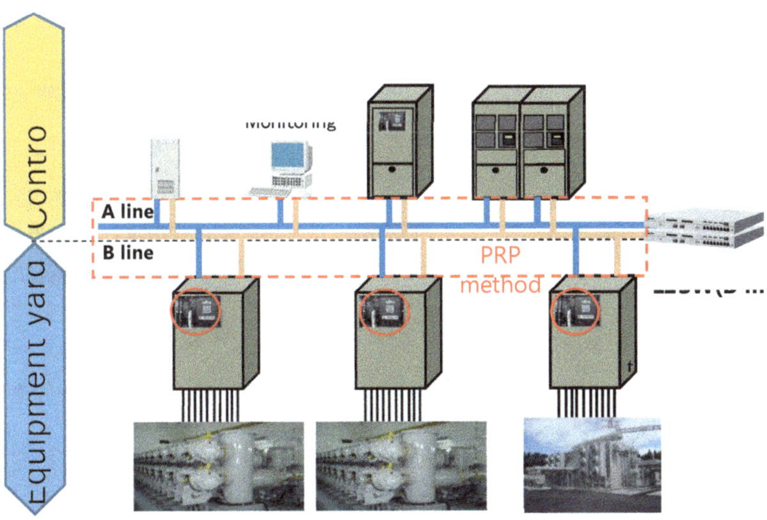

Figure 3: Optical digital system overview.

WIT Transactions on The Built Environment, Vol 213, © 2022 WIT Press
www.witpress.com, ISSN 1743-3509 (on-line)

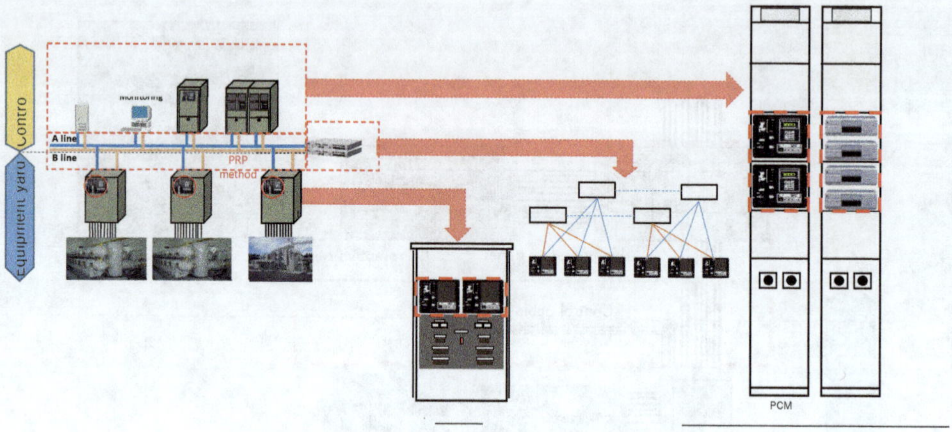

Figure 4: Optical digital system configuration.

3 FIELD TEST CONFIGURATION

The field test was conducted at the Musashisakai Substation. As a test configuration, a protection relay unit and a master clock were installed in the optical digital transmission switchboard. An optical digital transmission site unit was installed at the site, and L2SW was connected between by the PRP method, and various tests were conducted. The master clock is installed to time synchronization between distributed field units. As PRP communication path monitoring (transmission route monitoring), monitoring packets are sent from the master clock to all field units and protection relay units for each route A and B, and the reply is monitored to identify the location of the failure. In addition to the optical fibre cable, each unit is also duplicated to ensure redundancy (Fig. 5).

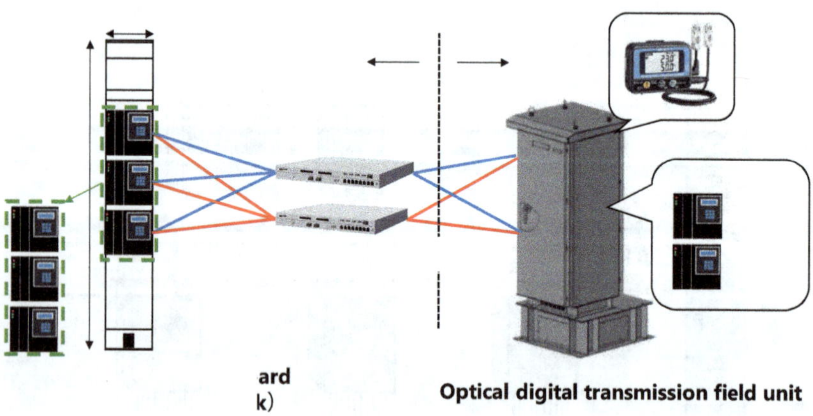

Figure 5: Field test configuration.

4 FIELD TEST CONTENT

4.1 Transmission abnormality test

In order to ensure redundancy, the transmission line is always a dual system, and it was confirmed that the protection function can be continued in the event of an abnormality in the single system transmission line. Specifically, the optical fibre cables from ① to ⑩ in Fig. 6 were connected and disconnected to simulate transmission abnormalities. As a result, the test results of ① to ④, ⑨ and ⑩ were able to get good results. However, after disconnecting the optical fibre cable from ⑤ to ⑧ (between the field unit and L2SW) and confirming that the protection is continued, when the optical fibre cable is reconnected to L2SW, the transmission error item GOOSE (generic object oriented substation events) on the field unit side. The reception error has occurred. GOOSE indicates a general-purpose object-oriented substation event defined in IEC61850 [4], and is a high-speed and highly reliable message. It is mainly used for information transmission such as circuit breaker cut-off command, operation command, field equipment status, and failure information. In order to identify the cause of the GOOSE reception abnormality, the same transmission abnormality simulation pattern was carried out, and the detailed monitoring items on the site unit side were directly confirmed on the debug PC. In order to check the soundness of the sender, we used a LAN monitor to check whether the GOOSE transmission operation was normal. We also confirmed whether there was any influence on the L2SW side. As a result, the GOOSE reception error detection process was operating normally, but in the software process on the site unit side linked to the master clock transmission route monitoring function, a transmission error was detected when the optical fibre cable was repeatedly inserted and removed in a short time. It turned out that the software processing continues abnormally. In the factory, when we simulated the abnormal mode when inserting and removing the optical fibre cable that occurred in the field, we confirmed that the transmission abnormality continued in the same way as in the field, and repaired the software.

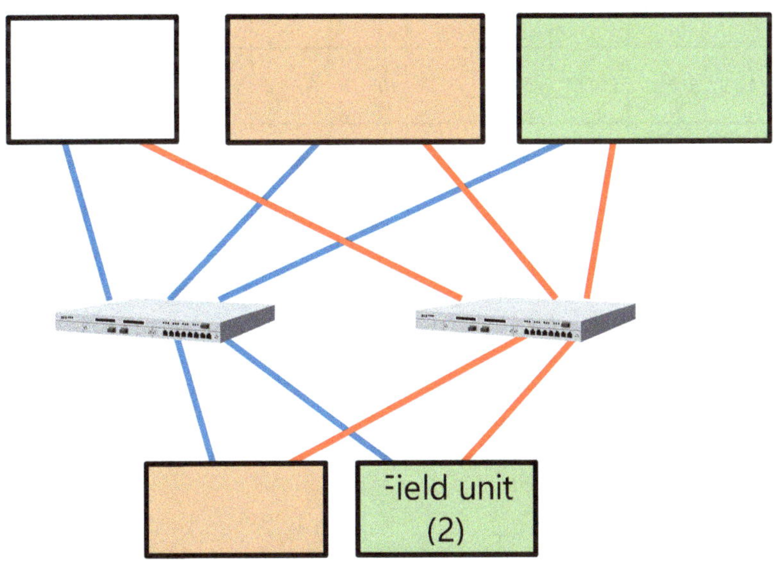

Figure 6: Transmission abnormality test contents.

When analysing the cause of this event, by implementing a memory dump function that captures the memory contents at the time of occurrence in an external file, it became possible to identify the cause of the abnormality and shorten the response time. In addition, it is effective to visualize the software operation so that debugging and software operation confirmation can be confirmed more easily and quickly.

4.2 Circuit breaker open/close surge test

In the past, a substation in the JR East had an event that affected the equipment due to noise caused by an opening/closing surge of the circuit breaker. The opening of circuit breaker operation was performed, and the presence or absence of system failure and the surge voltage were measured. The measurements sampling was set to 5 μs. For the measurement points, total of four items were measured: field unit power supply-reference ground, field unit-reference ground, switchboard power supply-reference ground, and switchboard-reference ground. As a test procedure, the circuit breaker of the 22 kV line was repeatedly turned on and off three times. As a result, the surge was larger on the field unit side than on the switchboard side because it was closer to the circuit breaker (Table 1). The potential difference of about 80 V was generated between the field unit and the switchboard side (Fig. 7), Fibre optic cables do not affect transmission information. It was also confirmed that the switchyard unit responded normally before and after the opening/closing surge test. For the protection of field unit electronic components, it is necessary to reduce the ground impedance and consider installing in a place away from GIS equipment.

Table 1: Circuit breaker open/close surge test results.

	Field unit power supply-reference ground			Field unit-reference ground			Switchboard power supply-reference ground			Switchboard-reference ground		
	Min	Max	P-P	Min	Max	P-P	Min	Max	P-P	Min	Max	P-P
CB close 1st	−50.8V	124.8V	175.6V	−99.9V	89.5V	189.4V	18.3V	89.6V	71.3V	−34.7V	34.4V	69.1V
CB close 2nd	−4.3V	106.3V	110.6V	−57.0V	48.7V	105.7V	32.9V	76.3V	43.4V	−20.8V	22.4V	43.2V
CB close 3rd	−27.4V	124.8V	152.2V	−83.2V	78.5V	161.7V	25.6V	98.0V	72.4V	−28.4V	38.6V	67.0V
Average	−82.5V	63.6V	146.1V	−80.0V	72.2V	152.3V	−29.4V	33.0V	62.4V	−28.0V	31.8V	59.8V

4.3 TCB on/off test

In order to operate the keep relay (TCB) that imitates the circuit breaker once every 10 days, the circuit breaker on/off command is transmitted from the protection relay unit to the site unit, the TCB is operated, and the TCB on/off information is transmitted to the protection relay unit. By transmitting to the side, it was confirmed that there was no abnormality in the entire system including the trip circuit. As a result, it was confirmed that there was no abnormality due to TCB operation.

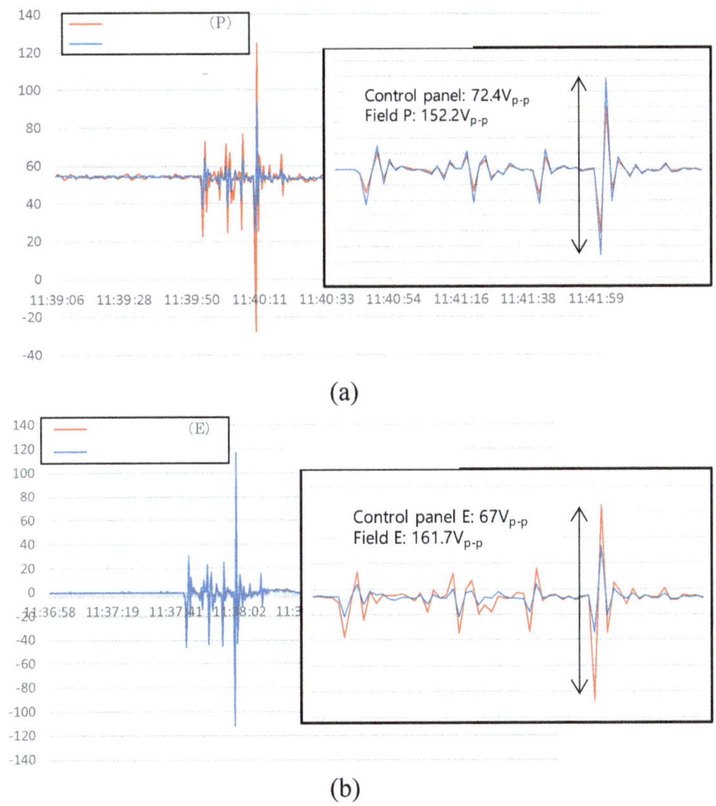

Figure 7: Circuit breaker open/close surge test waveform. (a) Field unit-reference grounding; and (b) Switchboard-reference ground.

4.4 Input electric energy test

The single-phase 100V AC voltage (device power supply) was taken into the field unit and sampled, and it was confirmed that the input electricity amount was always displayed correctly in the digital transmission and protection relay unit. As a result, it was confirmed that the AC voltage can be input normally (Fig. 8).

Figure 8: Input electric energy test result.

4.5 Bypass circuit test

As a system configuration, all units are duplicated, the protection relay operating conditions are transmitted from the protection unit to the site unit, the conditions of the site unit 1 system and 2 system are configured by the hard circuit, and the AND condition is output. It was configured. In addition, the circuit configuration is also equipped with a function (bypass circuit) for bypassing the faulty system break circuit in the event of a single system failure among the field unit or protection unit. This time, we simulated the power failure of one system of the protection relay unit, and confirmed that the bypass circuit was established by the operation of the security lock (86) of the same system, and the final output was normally performed only by the cut-off command of the sound system (Fig. 9).

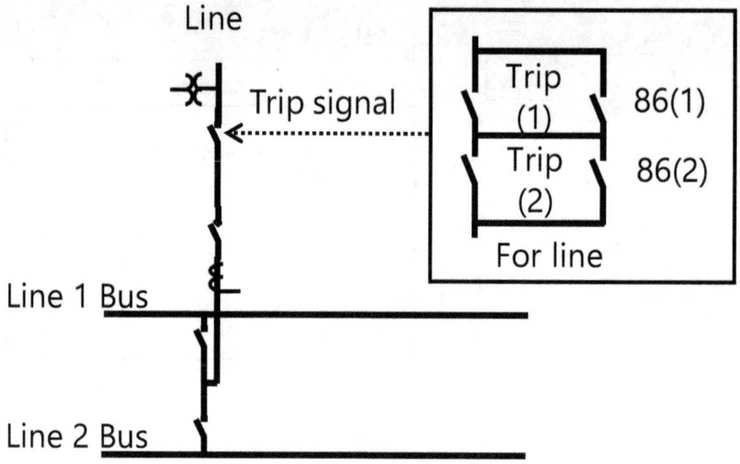

Figure 9: Operation/trip circuit.

4.6 Temperature/humidity environment evaluation test

For the cubicle equipped with the switchyard unit, the temperature rise was calculated based on the outside air temperature, the exhaust heat of the unit, the shape of the cubicle, etc. The specifications were set to be within the upper limit of the temperature specifications (Table 2). As a result, the maximum temperature inside the cubicle was 49.2°C, which did not reach the unit operating temperature upper limit of +50°C. This is because in the heat calculation at the design stage, the maximum power consumption of the unit was taken into consideration, and the light-shielding plate was attached so that the temperature did not exceed +50°C, and the width and position of the vents were designed (Table 3).

Table 2: Temperature and humidity performance.

Performance temperature	0 to + 40°C
Operating temperature	–10 to +50°C
Restoration temperature	–20 to + 60°C
Humidity	30 to 80% (however, does not condense)

Table 3: Temperature and humidity measurement results.

	Maximum		Minimum	
	Temperature (°C)	Daily average relative humidity (%)	Temperature (°C)	Daily average relative humidity (%)
Cubicle	49.2	76.5	1.2	22.8
Outside	44.2	100.0	–2.5	34.1
Difference	5.0	–23.4	3.7	–11.3

4.7 Consideration for accidental failure

By detecting a system abnormality (serious failure) during the field test, the failure history was confirmed on the board of the field unit and the protection relay unit. The log of each unit was acquired, and it was confirmed that the cause of the failure was a transmission error between field unit and the protection relay unit. When checking the equipment operation records at the Musashisakai Substation, it was found that the equipment supplying power to the substation premises was stopped at the same time as the failure occurred. The power supply in the substation is a dual system. This time, the regular power supply system was stopped. Therefore, it was found that the cause was a momentary power outage when switching from the regular system to the standby system. Specifically, since the L2SW power supply used in the field test was 100V AC, the L2SW power supply was temporarily lost due to a momentary power failure of the power supply in the substation, and communication became impossible, resulting in a transmission error in field unit and the protection relay unit. As a finding obtained from this event, the L2SW and the power supply for the master clock, which are the common parts of the substation system, are DC with the backup of the storage battery and the power cable is duplicated to ensure sufficient reliability as in the transmission part.

5 CONCLUSIONS

With the aim of reducing cables between switchyard equipment and switchboards. We produced prototypes of system configurations and transmission methods that take into consideration the ease of equipment update by digitally transmitting information. We conducted field tests at the Musashisakai Substation. From the results, it was possible to significantly reduce the number of cables by using optical fibre cables for control cables other than power supplies such as equipment and lighting, and it was confirmed that workability was improved. It was also confirmed that there were no problems with noise resistance, redundancy, and weather resistance. Since the prototype equipment is a part of the equipment required for the substation configuration, we will continue to develop and verify it for practical use. In addition, the transmission method conforms to international standards to ensure the redundancy of the transmission line, which is a shared part, and the unit redundancy ensures high reliability in the system, so that various power systems can be used. It is expected to be introduced in. In the future, based on the results of this research, specifications will be formulated with an eye on the realization of digitalization of the entire control and protection system of the substation.

REFERENCES

[1] IEC 62439-3, Industrial communication networks: High availability automation networks – Part 3: Parallel Redundancy Protocol (PRP) and High-availability Seamless Redundancy (HSR), 2016.

[2] Ueraku, Y., Nishizawa, K., Tanaka, Y., Endo, T. & Yoshioka, H., Development of transmission line protection relay device using PRP redundant communication. PRP-17-013, 2017.

[3] IEC 61850-9-2 Ed.2.0, Communication networks and systems for power utility automation: Part 9-2: Specific communication service mapping (SCSM) – Sampled values over ISO/IEC8802-3, 2011.

[4] IEC 61850-8-1 Ed.2.1, Communication networks and systems for power utility automation: Part 8-1: Specific communication service mapping (SCSM) – Mappings to MMS (ISO 9506-1 and ISO 9506-2) and to ISO/IEC 8802-3, 2020.

SUSTAINABLE DEVELOPMENT OF FREIGHT TRANSPORT USING A FASTER AND MORE ECO-FRIENDLY MODE

HAMAD ALMUJIBAH
Department of Civil Engineering, College of Engineering, Taif University, Saudi Arabia

ABSTRACT

Especially in developing countries such as Saudi Arabia, when considering an increase in rail lines it is vital to examine the freight sector's sustainable development. The aim is to transfer freight from slow modes of transport (trucks) to the faster and more eco-friendly mode of rail. This paper predicts two economic impacts from the transfer: less wear on the pavement structure of the highways, and changes in terms of time, cost, infrastructure capacity, and so on, compared to shipment by heavy trucks. Using rail can prevent damage to roads and the costs relating to heavy trucks, as well as accidents and air pollution. Various parameters are considered, such as loading and the longitudinal tire forces of trucks, the materials used in the construction of roads (e.g. asphalt) and their thickness. In this case, a 950-km length of the Riyadh–Jeddah line is used as a case study, determining the cost and time taken both before and after introducing a freight rail system. This method can be applied to the military sector to move heavy haulage and to transport minerals all over Saudi Arabia. In this case, the just-in-time (JIT) or door to door (DTD) method of delivery services is adopted, as trucks still have to drive the first and/ or last few kilometers of each railway journey. It is based on a comparative model to calculate and compare total shipping costs and transport time for road and rail transport. As a result, the total cost of transporting military vehicles/freight by rail transport is about $11,423, resulting from $1,272, $8,695, and $1,456 of fuel, labor wages, and drivers' wages, respectively, which is lower than by road transport of about $12,634, resulting from $606, $661, $8,695, and $2,672 for the fuel cost, road user charge/express tolls, labor wages, and drivers' wage, respectively.

Keywords: sustainable, freight, rail, vehicle trucks, just-in-time, door-to-door, Riyadh, Jeddah.

1 INTRODUCTION

Freight transport is the movement of goods by inland transport modes such as roads and railways on a given network, and is a key feature of supply chain management. In this case, goods can be transported through various units of transportation such as pallets, crates, containers, or cages [1]. Rail transport is regarded as one of the most environmentally friendly modes of transport, and receives attention from policy-makers due to increasing volumes of freight. It is considered as a sustainable mode of freight transport in terms of reliability, efficiency, and resilience with respect to economic factors; accessible and safe with respect to social factors; and ability to reduce pollution, climate change, and greenhouse gas emissions [2].

In Saudi Arabia, improved efficiency in the freight sector and increased regional connectivity will give the country a more central logistics role within the countries of the Gulf Cooperation Council (GCC). For example, the Landbridge railway project (Riyadh to Jeddah) could reduce the country's CO_2 emissions by 19% and fuel consumption by 17%, leading to decreases in freight transport by road and increases in delivery by rail. In 2018, around 50% of containerized goods were transported from Saudi Arabia's Red Sea ports via Makkah Province to Riyadh Province by roadway connections, as the country relies heavily on its road network, which covers 68,000 km, compared with only 4,175 km of freight rail network. There are only two important freight railways in the Kingdom: connecting the

WIT Transactions on The Built Environment, Vol 213, © 2022 WIT Press
www.witpress.com, ISSN 1743-3509 (on-line)
doi:10.2495/CR220181

commercial port of Dammam in the east to the main hub in Riyadh, and to the north-eastern mineral deposits.

2 LITERATURE REVIEW

In European Union (EU) countries, in 2020 road transport accounted for more than 77.4% of total inland freight transport, followed by rail freight and inland waterways at 16.8% and 5.8%, respectively. However, the performance of road transport increased by 12% from 2010 to 2020, while the performance of rail remained stable at 0.9% and for inland waterways decreased by 15.2% [3]. The shift of freight to rail transport will require an huge change to the railway transport sector in terms of infrastructure capacities, cost efficiency and productivity, and so on [3]. The performance of rail freight transport in various European countries is presented in Table 1, and shows a decrease in Spain, France, Italy, Switzerland, and Poland of 23%, 19%, 2%, 2%, and 3%, respectively, from 2015 to 2020. On the other hand, in Turkey, Croatia, and Finland it increased by 42%, 51%, and 15%, respectively [3].

Table 1: Performance of freight transport by rail (million tonne-km) [3].

Year	**2015**	**2016**	**2017**	**2018**	**2019**	**2020**
Spain	28,960	26,504	27,654	27,161	26,268	22,254
France	102,743	96,702	98,573	89,457	91,997	83,143
Italy	92,273	92,949	94,287	97,197	94,295	90,529
Turkey	24,286	24,546	28,287	28,484	33,285	34,374
Switzerland	66,089	67,846	67,157	68,719	68,658	64,987
Poland	224,320	222,523	239,501	249,260	233,744	218,381
Croatia	9,939	9,985	12,178	13,444	14,449	14,992
Finland	33,392	36,162	38,468	40,721	38,464	38,406

Turkey connects Europe and Asia by virtue of its location, involving an increase in freight flows in this region, and the country aims to be in the world's top 10 economies by 2023. The railway sector has seen the largest growth, as it is the primary sector and many railway reforms have taken place in the country to increase productivity [4]. With over 19 billion tonnes of goods shipped every year, freight transport accounts for 6% of GDP in Europe, as 75% of all freight transport is now undertaken by road. Moreover, an estimated annual emission of 275 million tonnes of CO_2 accounts for 30% of total transport emissions for both passenger and freight transport. By 2030, freight transport is expected to increase by 30%, adding a million trucks to European roads over the next decade [5].

2.1 Rail and road transport

Rail transport plays a crucial role in constructing a more sustainable freight sector, leading to an increase in the economy of €100 billion. For example, an estimated 5000 fatalities and 40,000 premature deaths will be prevented due to fewer truck accidents and less pollution. Shifting goods from road to rail can help to reduce the negative impacts of freight transport on climate, environment, and mobility [6].

A comparative study of road and rail transport with respect to unit costs for Switzerland and the European Union (EU) countries focused on factors such as the costs of a transport corridor, depreciation of vehicles, electricity and diesel fuel, and salaries and labor for handling. For the input data of the model, road freight transport costs have independent fixed variables for the type and size of cargo, such as cost of vehicle maintenance, road tax and mandatory insurance, vehicle depreciation, driver salary, and loading and haulage fees. Also, the carrier's overhead costs include central services, management, and dispatch. The dependent variables on transport distance and the type and size of cargo include the cost of tire consumption, fuel, drivers' mandatory safety breaks, and fees for use of roads [7]. In general, more challenges are faced by rail freight transport than by road, such as flexibility, price, transport time, frequency, reliability, and so on, as shown in Table 2. By contrast, road transport has no choice to be made in advance regarding the route, yet a driver is needed for each truck, and it also involves a significant number of road transport companies.

Table 2: Comparison of the challenges for rail freight and road [8].

Category	Rail	Road
Flexibility	Path requested in advance	No request needed in advance
Flexibility and price	One locomotive and one driver for each country	One truck and one driver for the whole EU
	No door-to-door transport	Door-to-door transport
Frequency, customer service and price	Limited number of railway undertakings	Significant number of road transport companies
Price	Use of every km of track is charged	In some countries for free
Reliability and transport time	Freight is disadvantaged in terms of priority on tracks	Freight is not disadvantaged
Transport time	Trains generally need to stop to change locomotive, driver, etc.	Less frequent stops

On the other hand, the independent variables for rail transport costs include vehicle maintenance, train crew salaries, vehicle depreciation, handling fees, and overhead costs of carrier in terms of salaries of other rail employees, management, central services, building the rains, and so on. The dependent variables of rail transport costs include traction energy and the fees for using the rail route, such as those associated with the train's mileage and access [7]. Rail freight challenges involve requesting a route in advance over a limited number of railway undertakings, as it is not door-to-door transport mode. Also, there is a charge for using each kilometer of track, and freight is disadvantaged in terms of priority on the tracks, as trains need to stop often to change locomotive, drivers, and so on, compared to trucks [8].

In general, there is a trade-off between cost and service quality factors in the choice of transport mode. For any freight, the quality factors include transit time, service availability or frequency, and reliability, as the transit time offer may include express, economy, general and customized. In this case, road and rail are competitors, according to freight studies, as the price elasticities of long-distance corridors are estimated for freight across short-, medium-, and long-distance corridors [9].

Service quality elasticity is of a magnitude of 0.33 to 0.66, as shown in Table 3 with respect to medium- and long-distance transport, respectively, implying that rail freight has a limited sensitivity to service quality changes [9].

With respect to the elasticities of road and freight market, 17 freight studies from UK, Asia-Pacific, and North America were examined to estimate all major commodity groups and grain only. The price elasticities regarding grains are between −0.52 and −1.18, whereas those

Table 3: Long-run price elasticities for road and rail freight, by corridor [9].

Mode	Freight rate (short-distance corridors)		Freight rate (medium-distance corridors)		Freight rate (long-distance corridors)		Freight rate (all corridors)	
	Road	Rail	Road	Rail	Road	Rail	Road	Rail
Road	−0.36	0.35	−0.43	0.33	−1.08	0.66	−0.46	0.58
Rail	0.88	−0.93	1.08	−1.15	0.42	−0.78	1.04	−1.66

of all commodities are −0.60 to −1.52. For rail freight demand, the cross-price elasticity with respect to trucking cost is positive and significant at 10%, as the freight rate and aggregate economic activity for short-run of rail freight transport are 0.51 and −0.28, while the same elasticities in the long run are 0.84 and −0.39 [10].

Depending on the length of transport route and shipping price, users have the opportunity to optimize their transport by their choice of route within and across the countries by total transport time. In this case, the general relationship between average transit time and distance, and between average freight costs and distance, is shown in Fig. 1 for road and rail freight in Australia.

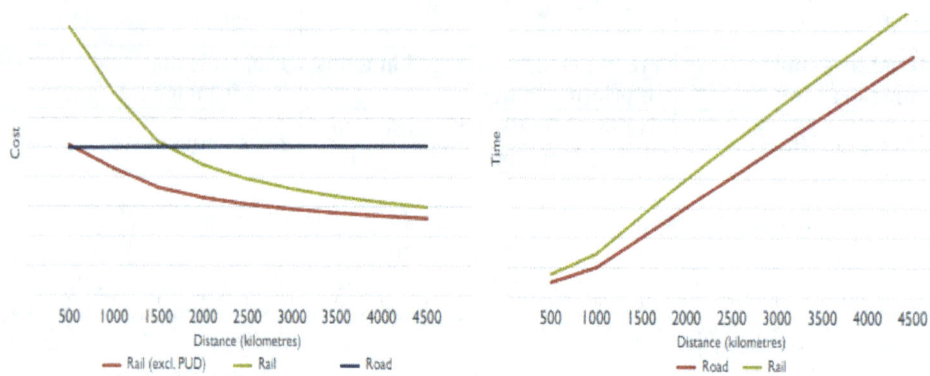

Figure 1: Average freight costs and transit times for Australian road and rail freight [9].

Over short distances, road freight was found to be the highest-cost transport mode, as the average freight cost per kilometer of road is less or more constant with respect to distance. In general, road has higher line–haul costs over longer distance and for large volumes than rail, which shows that rail is cheaper for door-to door freight haulage, especially for distances above 1000 km. In terms of handling long-haul freight, rail is the preferred mode of transport due to less damage to environmental quality [9]. In the United States, using trucks to transport coal along public road networks may have an advantage over rail in terms of negotiating more severe gradients and curves, moreover roads can be constructed more readily, at less capital investment [11].

2.2 Military logistics

Rail transport plays an important role in the military logistics system, and was used for the first time during the American Civil War between 1861 and 1865, providing efficient movement of large items over long distances. Afterwards, the advantages of trail transport started to disappear because of the development of road transport. One of the reasons behind the disappearance of rapid-movement military loads is the number of legal, physical, and regulatory barriers. The use of mass rail transport is necessitated by the movement of oversize loads and contributes to the poor condition of the road infrastructure because the first and last few km are by road [12]. The movement of military by rail transport is inherently safer and less expensive than by road. In terms of effectiveness, one rail car has the loading capacity of up to four truckloads, and it is the most cost-efficient shipping option [13]. In the United States, the movement of army vehicles by rail as shown in Fig. 2 through a Chicago suburb is a normal part of the country's training operations and equipment deliveries, as the army needs many trains to move large numbers of troops.

Figure 2: Army vehicles moving by rail across the United States [14].

The services of rail transport are mainly carried out for the Army by commercial carriers, essential to the development of overweight and oversized military equipment, including artillery and heavy tanks. During World War II, the Russian Army needed 2981 rail transports between 1940 and 1945, consisting of 22,934 railway wagons. There were used to move more than 56,000 soldiers from Poland, 47,500 personnel and family members, 952 armored fighting vehicles, and 390 mortars and howitzers, together with 202 aircraft and 144 helicopters [12].

Due to the huge capacity of military transport, rail transport can be used over medium and long distances, and is characterized by low sensitivity to weather conditions and by high efficiency and regularity. Specialist types of military rolling stock are in use, as they are usually built and operated by railway troops. The special loads demand unusual rolling stock, such as for battle tanks, which has to be determined well in advance. In this case, trains may be switched onto regional and national networks with separate regulations and standards, such as track width, heights of platforms and bridge, and speed limits [12].

For heavy equipment loaded at the military railhead by rail, the minimum transport distance is 50 km, according to the Polish Armed Forces procedures, and this is associated with higher costs. The weight and length of a military train depends on parameters related to the railway line, and it cannot exceed 600 m long with an average weight of 1,200 tons, and it has an average practical speed of 20 to 30 km/h. According to data from the Polish National Movement Coordination Centre (PLNMCC), the annual number of domestic military rail transports is between 120 and 180 trains formed of 3,000 to 4,000 carriages, compared to international transport of three to eight trains formed of 50 to 160 carriages. In this case, the types of wagons used by the army include first- and second-class passenger cars (e.g. medical evacuation, troops movement, convoys), tank cars (e.g. chemicals, fuel, water), flatcars (e.g. containers, vehicles, oversize loads), covered cars (e.g. medical equipment, ammunition, food), and other equipment (e.g. cranes and mobile ramps) [12].

2.3 Railway and mining sector

Transportation is a key aspect of every industrial project, advantageously located to have mineral products delivered by truck, railway, or other mode of transport. Rail infrastructure is often essential if a mining operation to be effective and economically feasible, and a priority in this industry is to move freight safely with optimal efficiency and capacity. In this case, Bombardier's INTERFLO system is the optimal choice for heavy haulage lines, and is supplied to the mining sector worldwide [15]. Over long distances, rail transport is the most common mode of transport for moving prepared coal from the mine to the market, and it is the most attractive for long-term and high-volume movement of coal. For example, a unit train in the United States usually has a capacity of 100 or more cars and transports 17,400 tons per 1,200 km for the round trip from mine to plant, which takes 72 hours, including 4 and 10 hours for loading and hauling coal [11]. In terms of trucks causing road damage, a study in the United States found that the impact of 9,600 cars is equivalent to that of a single 18-wheeler, and a fully loaded tractor-trailer weighs about 80,000 lb, far more than a typical passenger car at 4,000 lb. The maintenance costs of roads in the United States have risen due to freight-hauling trucks, which cause 99% of the wear and tear, as pavement damage from vehicle traffic generally depends on the number of axles and their weight [16], [17].

In Saudi Arabia, the Ministry of Industrial and Mineral Resources (MoIMR) decided to set an opening budget to support the transformation of the country's mining sector to match its national program leading to Vision 2030. The mining sector is the third pillar of Saudi industry, developing mining investment and achieving optimal utilization of mineral resources, especially with the intention to auction off 45 mining sites to investors. The Saudi goal for the mining sector is to reach a GDP contribution of $64 billion, raising the country's revenue by more than $2.3 billion and generating 219,000 new jobs by 2030 [18]. For example, the north–south train freight line is one of the two freight lines in the country as shown in Fig. 3, running 1,550 km from Al-Jalamid mine in Northern Province to Ras AlKhair in Eastern Province via Al-Jouf, Hail, AlBaithah Junction in Qassim [19].

Figure 3: Saudi minerals being transported by train [14].

The north–south freight fleet consists of 16 locomotives with a capacity of 16,000 tons, including 523 wagons dedicated to transportation of phosphates, 562 for molten sulfur, 240 for bauxite, and 589 for phosphoric acid (MGA). The East cargo line is 556 km long, starting at King Abdulaziz Port in Dammam to Riyadh, passing Al-Ahsa, Abqaiq, AlKharj, Haradh, and Al-Tawdhihiyah. It has total fleet of 2,596 cars in various sizes and types, including 858 for double-stacking containers, 135 for grain hauling, 201 for cement transportation, 60 for hauling rocks, and 47 flatbeds for transporting vehicles [19].

3 METHODOLOGY

This study estimates the total time and cost of using road trucks or rail to transport freight, and to apply it to a case study of military logistics in Saudi Arabia for the Riyadh and Jeddah corridor, using cost and time models mainly based on Microsoft Excel. The Saudi freight railways have displaced 230,000 trucks from the roads, reducing the number of trucks, improving the quality of roads, and contributing to reduce traffic accident rates. As a result, carbon emissions have been reduced by an amount equivalent to 197,000 tonnes, also saving more than 900,000 barrels of diesel for trucks' fuel, achieving environmental returns representing a reduction in CO_2 emissions. In this case, the models are integrated and can be categorized into three equations: weight, time, and cost. Each equation has components as follows.

3.1 Weight limit equation

The total weight limit of both vehicle and freight carried on a truck or train is determined using eqn (1):

$$\mathrm{W_{all}} = W_V + W_F, \tag{1}$$

where $\mathrm{W_{all}}$ = total weight of vehicle and carried freight; W_V = weight of truck or train car in tonnes. W_F = weight of carried freight in tonnes.

In this case, the weight of the train includes the weight of locomotive and the weight of cars, as shown in eqn (2):

$$\mathrm{W_V} = W_L + W_C, \tag{2}$$

where W_L = weight of locomotive in tonnes; W_C = weight of cars in tonnes.

The weight per axle is based on the weight of cars and the number of axles, as shown in eqn (3):

$$\mathrm{w} = \mathrm{W_V}/N, \tag{3}$$

where w = weight of truck or train truck per axle in tonnes; N = number of axles.

By combining the three equations above, the total weight equation is determined as shown in eqn (4).

$$\mathrm{W_{all}} = W_F + (W_L + W_C)/N. \tag{4}$$

3.2 Time equation

In the time equation, access/egress time, in-vehicle travel time, and loading/hauling time are the main components, as presented in eqn (5). In this case, access time is the time from the origin point to the main freight hub, while egress time is that from the final freight hub to the destination. The in-vehicle travel time or journey time is highly dependent on the length of the route and the operating speed of the train/truck.

$$TT_{\mathrm{OD}} = AET_{OD} + IVT_{OD} + LUT_{OD}, \tag{5}$$

where TT_{OD} = total time of freight shipping by rail or road from origin to destination; AET_{OD} = access and egress time taken for transporting freight by each mode from origin to destination; IVT_{OD} = in-vehicle time (travel time) taken by each mode from origin to destination; LUT_{OD} = loading and hauling time taken by each mode in origin and destination.

In terms of loading and hauling, the time is based on the time taken to leave the production sectors and reach the destination, and is dependent on the number of laborers, number of working hours and type of gantry crane, and its operating time.

3.3 Cost equation

The cost for each transport freight is the sum of the expenditure on the inputs of fuel price, expressway toll, labor, and external impacts, as shown in eqn (6). In this case, the cost is dependent on components such as vehicle type, distance travelled, time in use (hours), loading and hauling time (hours), carrying capacity, and average tonnage (tonne).

$$C_{OD} = F_{OD} + T_{OD} + L_{OD} + D_{OD}, \tag{6}$$

where C_{OD} = total cost of shipment by rail or road from origin to destination; F_{OD} = fuel price needed for operating each mode from origin to destination; T_{OD} = express toll paid though the journey by each mode from origin to destination; L_{OD} = cost of labor worked for operating each mode from origin to destination; D_{OD} = driver cost for operating each mode from origin to destination.

The fuel consumption of a train or truck depends on multiple variables, such as speed, engine fuel consumption, engine power, and dimensions. For road transport, paying an express toll is necessary if trucks are to access the road infrastructure, especially heavy goods vehicles, in order for the country to recover the cost of constructing, operating, and developing the infrastructure, and the toll is based on the average loaded weight of the vehicle. In rail and road freight transport the cost for labor and drivers consists of wages, accommodation, and minor expenses related to drivers. Moreover, the cost of parameters is based on secondary data, such as the price of gasoline, express toll, number of laborers needed to transfer freight from origin to destination by either rail or truck.

The flowchart presents the integration of weight, time, and cost, as shown in Fig. 4, and the methods used in this study are explained.

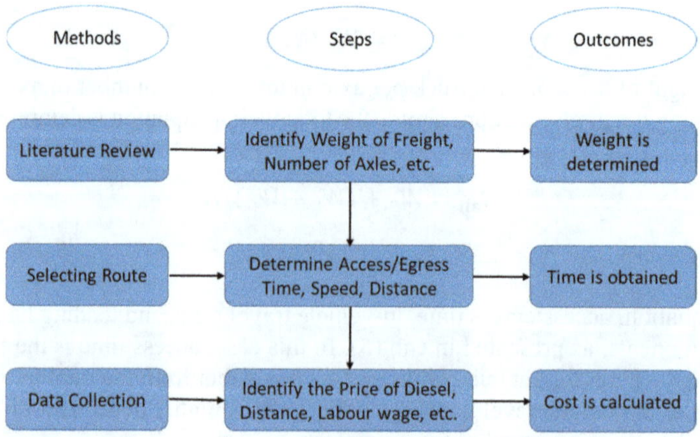

Figure 4: Flowchart of steps performed in the study.

- Sources were used to identify the weight of cars and freight carried by both rail and road transport, as well as the number of axles for trucks.
- A selection of components was needed to determine time, such as access/egress time and in-vehicle travel time, throughout the route between two cities (e.g. Riyadh and Jeddah) and determination of the corridor's length and speed for both truck and train.
- Data were collected to identify the price of diesel, distance, and wages, based on the selection of the case study of the Riyadh–Jeddah corridor.

In this case, the weight, time, and cost of both rail and road transport are determined by following the previous steps and integrating the various equations.

4 RESULTS AND DISCUSSION

To determine the estimated time and cost for transporting freight from origin to destination, the total weight of the freight rail/truck was required, based on components such as capacity, weight in tonnes, fuel price (e.g. diesel), speed, and wages. A freight train commonly carries a considerable weight from origin to destination, dependent on the length of the entire train. Efficiency is limited by the locomotive's capabilities and the railway landscape. Railway freight wagons are used to transport all types of equipment, bulky products, wheeled and tracked vehicles, containers, and so on.

This study shows that the weight of a wagon ranges from 40 to 58 tonnes, based on the length of boxes, around 11 to 15 m, while the weight of the locomotive is 215 tonnes with an assumed speed of 60 km/h. In this case, the weight of an empty freight wagon is 30 tonnes, and each can be loaded with an additional 100 to 130 tonnes. The average weight loaded is estimated at 65 tonnes per wagon, from a range of 63 and 67 tonnes. In military logistics, the weight of vehicles is divided into the classes of light (up to 20 tonnes), medium (20 to 50 tonnes), heavy (up to 100 tonnes), and super-heavy (above 100 tonnes). In this case, the average weight of these types of military vehicle is regarded as 60 tonnes, resulting from a range of 20 to 100 tonnes.

As a result, the weight of rail freight was determined on the basis of the type of freight plus the weight of the locomotive and wagon. The weight of one locomotive was assumed to be 215 tonnes and the weight of a wagon, for a flatcar, 30 tonnes, giving a total of 1,470 tonnes for 49 wagons. In terms of goods and military vehicles, the weight of goods per wagon is 65 tonnes, giving a total weight of 3,185 tonnes for 49 wagons, while the weight of a military vehicle is 60 tonnes, giving a total of 2,940 tonnes for 49 wagons. Therefore, the total weight when transporting military vehicles is 4,625 tonnes, resulting from the weight of the locomotive (215 tonnes), flatcar wagons (1,685 tonnes), and the weight of the military vehicles themselves (2,940 tonnes).

For rail freight, access and egress times are the first and last leg of a journey, and these assumed to be 10 and 15 minutes, respectively, from Riyadh to Jeddah. Travel time was calculated by dividing the distance (950 km) by the estimated speed (50 km/h), while total loading and hauling time was assumed to be the same value as on road transport, at 2.5 hours. Slower speeds by a train prevents buckling and puts less stress on the track, therefore the total travel time for rail freight transportation from Riyadh to Jeddah is about 22 hours, resulting from 0.42 hour, 19 hours, and 2.45 hours of access/egress time, travel time, and loading/hauling time, respectively.

In terms of cost for freight rail transport, there are four components: the fuel for the journey, fees for using track, if any, labor, and drivers' wages. In this case, the cost of fuel per liter was determined with respect to distance, to cover the journey from origin to destination, and diesel in Saudi Arabia costs $0.168 per liter. However, the fuel tanks of diesel locomotives can hold only between 5000 and 6000 liters, which may be insufficient for the route. As the length of the Riyadh–Jeddah corridor is 950 km, a rail locomotive needs about 7,572 liters of diesel, at a cost of around $1272 for the whole journey. It was assumed that there are no fees in Saudi Arabia for using the track to transport freight or military vehicles from Riyadh to Jeddah. As a result, the total cost of transporting military vehicles/freight by rail transport is about $11423, resulting from $1272, $8695, and $1456 of fuel, labor wages, and drivers' wages, respectively.

For road transport, the weight of truck freight was based only on the weight of the truck itself and the actual freight. In this study, a flatbed heavy duty truck of an average weight of 16.5 tonnes was used for the comparison, resulting from values of 11.79 and 21.5 tonnes. Moreover, the weight of the goods was assumed to be the same as for rail freight transport, with the same military vehicles. The weight of the goods and the military vehicle is 65 tonnes and 60 tonnes, respectively, as each duty truck can carry only one vehicle. Therefore, the total weight of goods or military vehicle transporting by heavy duty truck is 3,994 and 3,749 tonnes, respectively, as 49 heavy trucks are needed. So, the weight of vehicle was divided by five axles to achieve a 937-tonne axle load. To determine the in-vehicle travel time for trucks, an average speed is required, and this was taken to be about 48.68 km/h, 60.45 km/h, and 45.39 km/h, respectively, for unloaded, fully loaded, and overloaded [20].

In this case, access and egress times were assumed to be zero for freight road transport, while travel speed was taken to be 60.45 km/h for fully loaded trucks within 950 km of the two cities of Riyadh and Jeddah in Saudi Arabia, giving a travel time of 15.7 hours. In order to determine the time for loading and hauling, the production rate was defined as the units of work made by a unit of equipment or a person within a specified unit of time. Loading and hauling time was found to be 2.45 hours, resulting from 2.22 hours of loading and 0.23 hours for haulage, with a production rate value of 0.75. Therefore, total time was found to be 18.2 hours, resulting from 15.7 hours, 2.2 hours, and 0.23 hour, respectively, for travel time, loading, and hauling time.

The cost of truck fuel mainly depends on the price of diesel in Saudi Arabia, at $0.168 per liter, and the length of corridor, and it costs around $607 for the whole journey. In terms of road user charges, the truck type was assumed to be powered vehicles with five or more axles, and the cost of $661 was based on the distance and the weight of military vehicles (60 tonnes), and secondary data were used. In Saudi Arabia, a truck driver typically earns around $1,336 per month and two truck drivers are needed, so the cost was doubled to give a total cost of $2,672 per month for the entire journey. It was assumed that five laborers are needed at the freight hub for loading and haulage, at a cost of $8,695 per month. As a result, the total cost of transporting military vehicles/freight by road transport is about $12,634, resulting from $606, $661, $8,695, and $2,672 for the fuel cost, road user charge/express tolls, labor wages, and drivers' wage, respectively.

5 CONCLUSION

The Saudi Arabia government plans to reduce fuel consumption by 2030 and increase deliveries by rail, reducing road freight transport. In this case, rail freight is to become an economically attractive mode of transport, giving improved connectivity, security, and efficiency. In summary, the total freight to be transported by road and rail between Riyadh and Jeddah will be 2.7 thousand tonnes and 4.6 thousand tonnes, respectively.

Rail transport takes slightly longer, at 3.7 hours slower than by truck, but the entire load of freight carrying 49 vehicles arrives at the exact same time, whereas 49 vehicles need 49 trucks. Extra time may need to be allowed to transport vehicles by road due to environmental factors such as accidents, weather (e.g. floods caused by heavy rain or sandstorms), and so on.

In terms of the total cost of transporting vehicles/goods, rail has the benefit of a lower cost of $11.4 thousands as transportation by road is $12.6 due to the total labor wages of $8.7 thousands for five laborers. The development of the freight rail sector in Saudi Arabia will help to increase the efficiency of freight transport activities, decrease fuel consumption, and reduce emissions of greenhouse gases and other pollutants, as well as reduce the damage caused to roads by heavy trucks, thereby meeting the targets for economic reform in Saudi Vision 2030.

ACKNOWLEDGEMENT

I would like to thank the Deanship of Scientific Research, Taif University, Saudi Arabia for supporting this research.

REFERENCES

[1] Archetti, C., Peirano, L. & Speranza, M.G., Optimization in multimodal freight transportation problems: A survey. *European Journal of Operational Research*, 2021.

[2] Economic and Social Commission for Asia and the Pacific, Enhancing the sustainability of freight transport in the decade of action for the sustainable development goals. https://www.unescap.org/sites/default/d8files/event-documents/ESCAP-TARN-WG-2021-4-E.pdf. Accessed on: 21 May 2021.

[3] European Court of Auditors, *Rail Freight Transport in the EU: Still not on the right* track. https://www.eca.europa.eu/Lists/ECADocuments/SR16_08/SR_RAIL_FREIGHT_EN.pdf.

[4] Railway Pro, Turkey prioritizes railway transport to increase freight flows. https://www.railwaypro.com/wp/turkey-prioritizes-railway-transport-to-increase-freight-flows/. Accessed on: 23 Jan. 2013.

[5] Union International Railways, Making international freight products and services more competitive by harmonising business, operational and information processes. https://uic.org/freight/.

[6] Rail Freight Forward, 30 by 2030: How rail freight achieves its goals. https://www.railfreightforward.eu/sites/default/files/downloadcenter/rff_cer_position_paper.pdf. Accessed on: 2 Jul. 2020.

[7] Bína, L., Bínová, H., Březina, E., Kumpošt, P. & Padělek, T., Comparative model of unit costs of road and rail freight transport for selected European countries. *European Journal of Business and Social Sciences*, **3**(4), pp. 127–136, 2014.

[8] Wang, X., Song, G., Zhai, Z., Wu, Y., Yin, H. & Yu, L., Effects of vehicle load on emissions of heavy-duty diesel trucks: A study based on real-world data. *International Journal of Environmental Research and Public Health*, **18**(8), p. 3877, 2021.

[9] Department of Infrastructure, Transport, Regional Development and Local Government, Road and Rail Freight: Competitors or complements? https://www.bitre.gov.au/sites/default/files/is_034.pdf.

[10] Khan, M.Z. & Khan, F.N., Estimating the demand for rail freight transport in Pakistan: A time series analysis. *Journal of Rail Transport Planning and Management*, **1**(14), 100176, 2020.

[11] *Britannica*, Coal transportation. https://www.britannica.com/technology/coal-mining/Coal-transportation. Accessed on: 1 May 2020.

[12] Biernikowicz, W., Rail transport in NATO's logistics system: The case of Poland. *European Research Studies*, **24**, pp. 748–761, 2021.

[13] *Building America, Proud to Serve the Military*. https://www.up.com/customers/ind-prod/military/index.htm. Accessed on 01 Jan. 2021. Eurostat Statistics, Freight transport statistics: modal split. https://ec.europa.eu/eurostat/statistics-explained/index.php?title=Freight_transport_statistics_-_modal_split.
[14] Rempfer, K., That army equipment moving by rail? Not a sign of looming martial law. *Army Times*. https://www.armytimes.com/news/your-army/2020/03/22/that-army-equipment-moving-by-rail-not-a-sign-of-looming-martial-law/. Accessed on: 22 Mar. 2020.
[15] *Railway Technology*, Industrial and mining applications. https://www.railway-technology.com/products/industrial-mining-applications/. Accessed on: 1 Dec. 2017.
[16] Murphy, B., How trucks destroy our roads and how a fee on trucks could solve state's transportation problem. https://urbanmilwaukee.com/2017/06/22/murphys-law-how-trucks-destroy-our-roads/#:~:text=An%20off%2Dquoted%20federal%20study,the%20truck%20is%20exponentially%20greater. Accessed on: 22 Jun. 2017.
[17] Luskin, D. & Walton, C.M., Effects of Truck Size and Weights on Highway Infrastructure and Operations: A synthesis report. Center for Transportation Research, Bureau of Engineering Research, University of Texas at Austin, 2001.
[18] *Asharq Al-awsat*, Saudi mineral exploration saves 25% of global spending. https://english.aawsat.com/home/article/2273561/saudi-mineral-exploration-saves-25-global-spending. Accessed on: 8 May 2020.
[19] *Saudi Arabia Railway*, Our network connectivity across the Kingdom. https://www.sar.com.sa/about-sar/ournetwork/.
[20] *Saudi Arabia Railway*, SAR trains are possible industrial. https://SARSaudiRailway/status/1531277285520711680.

SECTION 6
TRAFFIC MODELLING AND SIMULATION

IMPROVING RAIL NETWORK SIMULATIONS WITH DISCRETE DISTRIBUTIONS IN ONTIME

BURKHARD FRANKE, DAN BURKOLTER & BERNHARD SEYBOLD
TrafIT Solutions GmbH, Switzerland

ABSTRACT

To analyse a rail network's punctuality and the operational quality of a timetable on a network-wide scale an advanced simulation is needed. Whereas most simulations use a Monte Carlo approach, we calculate delay distributions analytically and thus need only a single calculation run. Previously we used exponential distribution functions as they map the status in railway operations well and are suited for efficient calculation of delays. The resulting delay distributions due to primary delays along a train's itinerary as well as delay propagation from other trains is handled by convolution of these distribution functions. However, as the resulting distributions become more complex, a simplification step is needed from time to time to keep calculation times reasonable. Increased requirements for the accuracy of the simulation model and improvements in the computational potential led us to remodel the delays with discrete distributions. This has two main advantages. First, restrictions on the possible form of primary delays are much smaller compared to the previous exponential distributions and second, the simplification step is no longer needed, which increases accuracy considerably. We discuss the different options of distribution modelling and their use in railway applications.
Keywords: railway, simulation, delay distribution modelling, operational quality, punctuality.

1 INTRODUCTION

The analysis of the operational quality of a timetable is usually based on the examination of operational data covering the trains and their respective delays in a time interval. Common quality parameters to describe the performance of railways are key figures like punctuality, mean delays, or the variation of arrival times. Looking at the whole set of data reveals the stochastic nature of delays: The deviations can be best described as distributions as Fig. 1 shows for the example of the graphic timetable of planned and realised train runs over several weeks. The actual train runs are distributed around the scheduled train path depending on their delay characteristics on any recorded day.

The characteristics of the delay distributions will be different for every train, station, and time of day or time of year, as the underlying reasons for delays vary. Those reasons can be differentiated in primary delays (caused by external sources) and secondary delays (passed on due to train interaction), which will be discussed in Section 2.

Based on our experience with delay analysis and timetable improvement, our principal insight is that a railway timetable will unavoidably experience a certain level of disturbance and this level of disturbance can best be described as distributions of (primary) delays. It is therefore reasonable to assess the operational quality of a future timetable on a given infrastructure by applying distributions of (primary) delays on every train and simulate delay propagation and delays reduction, as this replicates the situation a timetable will experience during its existence (the timetable period). This idea was developed amongst others in the thesis of Büker [2] and is the basis of what was implemented as the tool OnTime. A description of OnTime and its methodical advantages is part of Section 3. The main topic of this paper is the modelling of distributions in OnTime's calculation kernel. Section 4 outlines the development of the modelling and reviews the reasons for and the implementation of a discrete modelling of distributions in OnTime. The paper is concluded in Section 5.

WIT Transactions on The Built Environment, Vol 213, © 2022 WIT Press
www.witpress.com, ISSN 1743-3509 (on-line)
doi:10.2495/CR220191

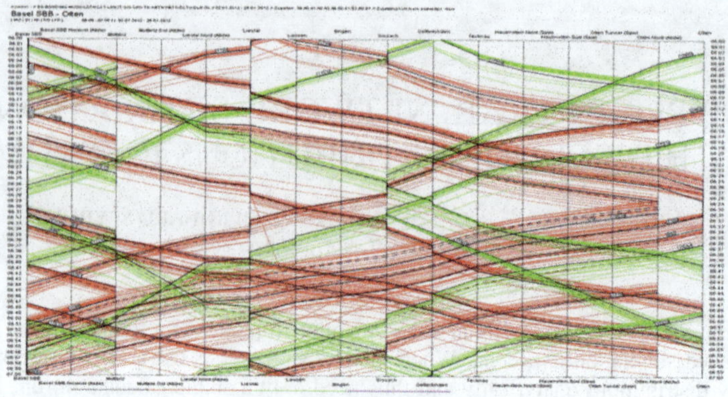

Figure 1: Visualisation of operational data [1].

2 ON DELAYS AND OPERATIONAL QUALITY

Railway operations are vulnerable to delays as variability in operational process times and unexpected disruptive events lead to deviations from the planned timetable [3]. These deviations are called primary delays to discern them from secondary delays, which result from the interaction of trains and the propagation of delays. This differentiation helps to understand and counteract train delays. It is also the conceptual basis for the simulation tool described in the next section since a model cannot deduce the primary delays but must reproduce the interaction of trains and the consequences thereof.

However, these thoughts on primary and secondary delays do have the problem that operational delay data as presented in Fig. 1 do not differentiate between delay reasons as only the resulting delay can be directly measured. From our experience only few railways are able to identify primary delays, best known to us are studies in Switzerland by Labermeier [4] and Schranil [5]. The latter analysed the distribution of primary and total delays in the SBB network.

Although the shape of the distribution is probably SBB-specific, two findings are common to both papers:

- Small (primary) delays are frequent, large delays are rare.
- Very small delays are often recorded incorrectly or even neglected.

The first statement seems trivial, but even data presented in Fig. 2 does not support this completely. Whereas primary delays of 3 minutes are more frequent than primary delays of 4, 5 or more minutes, delays of 1 or 2 minutes hardly seem to occur at all. Our explanation for this phenomenon is given in the second statement: the recording of such small delays is often not correct. This is partly due to railway companies' regulations on how to record delays in the first place and partly due to difficulties in measuring small delays as records are often a spin-off product of the rail control system. Reports usually rely on the delay causes given by railway operators who are obliged to record a delay cause for delays exceeding a defined threshold. What happens below the threshold mostly stays in the dark.

Common sense says that the declining tendency of the frequency of larger delays has its continuation with smaller delays being more frequent: severe weather conditions causing a minute of running delay are less likely than weather conditions causing 30 seconds of delay. Large crowds of passengers delaying departure by 40 seconds are less frequent than crowds

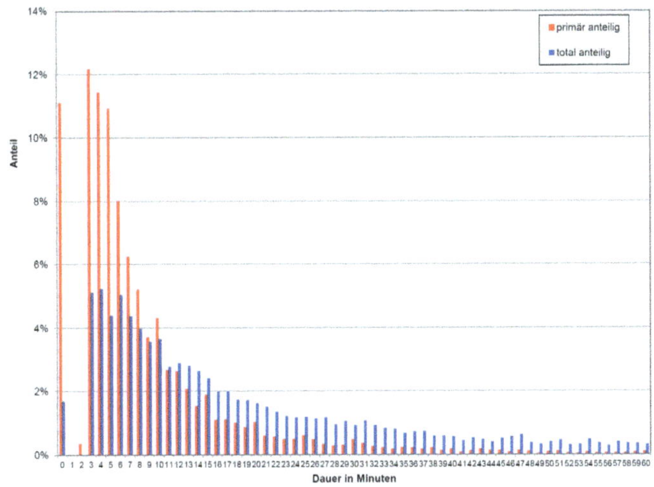

Figure 2: Density function of primary and total delays according to Schranil [5].

of passengers delaying a train by 20 seconds. This is backed by detailed analysis for instance by Yuan [6], who investigated train movement on the level of the rail control system. A similar approach was used by Labermeier [4], and both analyses end up focussing on delays in the range of seconds to few minutes, as these are the most frequent ones.
If we break down the general findings to particular locations or trains, the pattern is repeated as is shown in Fig. 3, small delays and – depending on the amount and allocation of margins – even small early arrivals are more frequent than larger deviations.

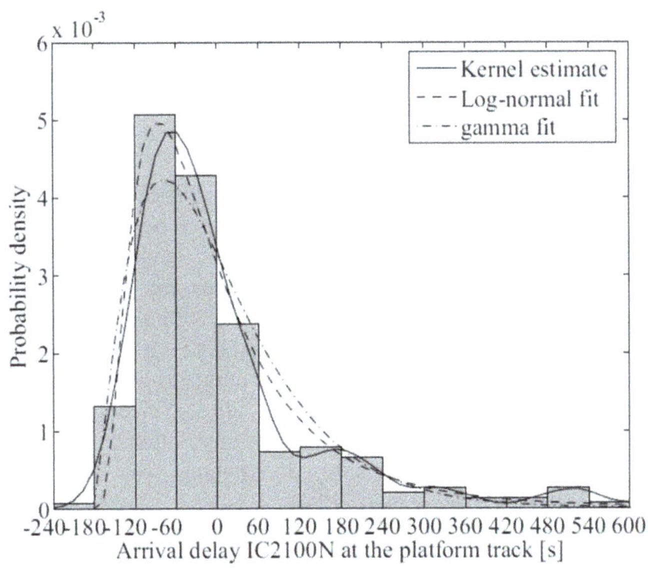

Figure 3: Histogram, fitting curves, and kernel estimate for arrival delays of a train [6].

Fig. 3 also shows some fitting curves for modelling the delays mathematically, a topic we cover in Section 4.

So, although individual disturbances cause discrete primary delays, the timetable over a timetable period is subject to a kind of random noise of disturbance. The distribution of this random noise is characteristic for each railway – a product of weather conditions, maintenance level, and other historic and current circumstances. For a realistic reproduction of operational quality, we need to use proper distributions of primary delays. As we do not know where disturbances will occur and which trains will be affected in a future timetable, we must apply a delay distribution on every train everywhere on its itinerary. This is the idea behind the stochastic simulation tool OnTime.

3 THE TOOL ONTIME

In 2011 SBB commissioned the development of a tool to complement their existing microscopic, deterministic simulation tool. The so-called "Stabilitätsmodell" (stability model) was meant to simulate the complete network to evaluate timetables and infrastructural measures for short- to long-term planning. This tool should not construct or change a timetable but evaluate a given timetable in its entirety regarding chosen punctuality measures. To win the tender the two companies TrafIT Solutions GmbH, Zurich, and VIA Consulting & Development GmbH, Aachen, joined forces to implement the tool OnTime based on research at RWTH Aachen by Weidner and Büker [7] and later Büker [2] and in use at railways such as SBB or DB

3.1 The application

OnTime (see Fig. 4) is designed to work as a complement to an existing timetabling tool as it imports timetables via standardized exchange formats and has no integrated planning capabilities or running time calculator. This is mostly because the first railways using the tool did not want to have "another running time calculator", as keeping all necessary data up to date in several tools is quite costly and different calculators will always differ in running times at least to some degree. OnTime therefore depends on a timetable system to export a timetable with all the necessary data, most notably the differentiation between minimal running times and running time reserves, which can be used to reduce delays. Information on connections and turn-arounds are either imported or generated in a preprocessing step. OnTime uses a rule-based modelling [8] to represent the infrastructure properties, which allows working with the different microscopic or macroscopic levels of detail in different planning horizons for infrastructure. Primary delays can be provided either as default distributions for the whole network or specified for certain stations and sections, times, and trains or types of trains. The primary delay distributions are simply defined by giving a probability of delay and the average delay in case of delay and are differentiated between stopping, departing, and running delays. A set of input data – a scenario – forms an activity graph [1] for a selected day of operation. Trains accumulate delays incurred from primary delays as well as delays propagated from other trains. Since delays are modelled as distributions, the accumulated delay is calculated as a convolution of delay distributions. This delay is reduced by the amount of running or stopping time reserves present, which corresponds to a left shift of the delay distribution.

A single calculation of a scenario produces the results, which can be used to evaluate a timetable or to compare variants of timetables or infrastructure changes based on network-wide operational key figures. All resulting delays are modelled as distributions which enables

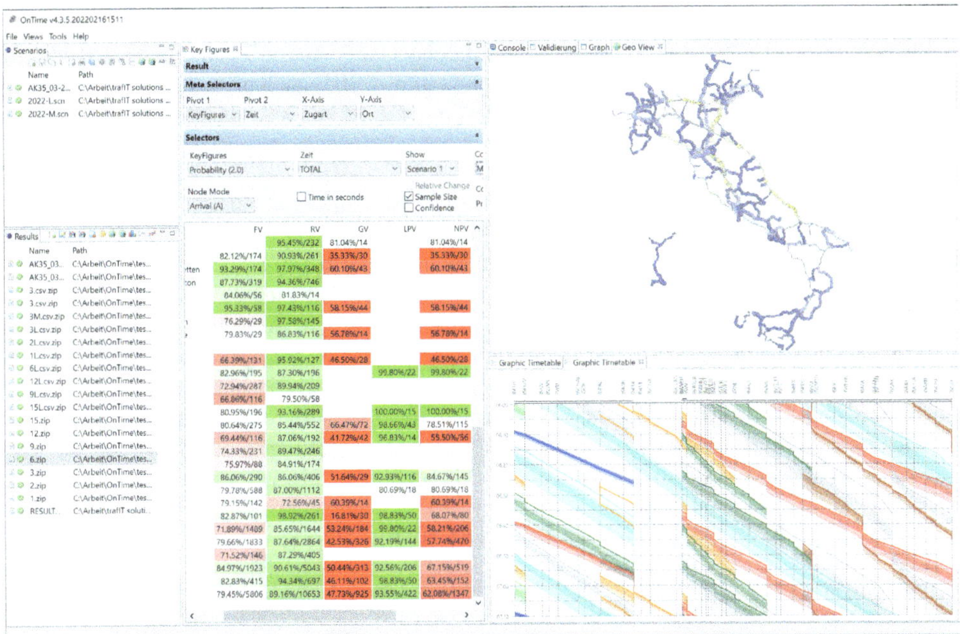

Figure 4: The application OnTime and some views on results.

calculating (almost) any desired key figure. As an example, since OnTime calculates the resulting probability distribution for every train and station, it is possible to determine the frequency of arrivals and departures within the chosen punctuality threshold, e.g. the 5 minute punctuality is given by the integral of the probability density function up to the 5 minute threshold.

3.2 Methodical advantages

Using distributions to model delays in a simulation has significant advantages over a Monte Carlo approach that uses individual disturbances in a (series of) deterministic simulations.

3.2.1 Real world key figures

Traditional tools of railway operation science do not use the same key figures that are common for describing railway operation quality. As Bär et al. [9] pointed out, analytical approaches and simulations do not match in their respective statements and even simulations often do not match empirical analysis of operation. This is mostly because simulations are restricted to parts of a network, so key figures are limited in scope or of a derivational nature. The ability of OnTime to simulate whole networks and to reproduce the operational quality of an average day or a timetable period makes it possible to forecast a future timetable's punctuality. Effects of timetable or infrastructure changes can be assessed consistently for the whole network to compare and prioritise measures.

3.2.2 Calibration

The verification and calibration of a simulation model is a long and laborious process. Using a Monte Carlo approach with repeated simulation runs to mimic all disturbance situations makes this task almost impossible. The fact that disturbances can (and do) occur everywhere in the network and cause a wide range of initial delays (see Section 2) should be reproduced by the tool, which is possible with OnTime. For example, SBB used primary delays extracted as described by Labermeier [4] to verify the OnTime model and as a starting point for a finer calibration.

3.2.3 Combination with demand models to evaluate passenger punctuality

Evaluating the operational quality of a timetable from a passenger's perspective is often quite demanding: a train delay of a few minutes can be just a nuisance, but if it results in missing a connection, the passenger's delay could become an hour or more. For example, Landex [10] described ways to assess passenger delays. Some of the previous problems are resolved when using the stochastic simulation in OnTime as all delays and the probabilities of catching or missing connections are available for the whole network as distributions. This suits the needs of demand modelling tools. In 2016 a project together with SBB showed the feasibility of the combination of OnTime and SBB's demand modelling tool SIMBA [11]. The combination allows for a holistic evaluation of timetable and infrastructural measures [12].

4 MODELLING DISTRIBUTIONS

4.1 Exponential

Exponential distributions are widely used for modelling delays since on the one hand they fit measured delays quite well [6], [13] and on the other hand their convolution is very easy to calculate, which makes calculating delay propagation fast. However, in order to better fit measured delays, Büker [2] introduced delay distributions with segment-wise exponential distributions, with cumulative distribution functions of the following form:

$$F_V(t) = \begin{cases} c^0 - \sum_{i=1}^{n^0} a_i^0 \cdot t^{d_i^0} \cdot e^{(-\lambda_i^0 \cdot t)} & t < g^1 \\ \vdots & \\ c^s - \sum_{i=1}^{n^s} a_i^s \cdot t^{d_i^s} \cdot e^{(-\lambda_i^s \cdot t)} & g^s \leq t \end{cases}$$

Thus, the probability of a delay $\leq$ t is a constant c^n reduced by an exponentially decreasing part for every segment of the distribution.

In theory, delays can be fit arbitrarily accurately using this type of delay distributions by adding more segments. However, though the main mathematical advantage of exponential distributions – namely that the convolution is again an exponential distribution – is retained, the number of segments grows exponentially. This leads to severe limitations in practical applications due to running times becoming too large. Therefore, Büker [2] developed methods for simplifying these distributions by reducing the number of segments. This method is implemented in OnTime. Initially, delay distributions have up to three exponential segments. During calculation the number of segments will quickly grow, thus, when a distribution becomes too large a simplification will be triggered, which reduces the number of segments again.

The approach has worked fine in OnTime and is still widely used, yet it has two drawbacks:

1. Obviously, a simplification of a delay distribution does not fit the original exactly leading to small inaccuracies, which do not matter when a whole railway network is simulated. However, they can become an issue if two simulation runs of the same network with slightly changed parameters are compared. In this case, it is not always easy to distinguish whether the differences in the results are real, in the sense that they are caused due to different parameters, or just a result of simplifications taking place at different stages of the simulation. An example is shown in Fig. 8.
2. The simplification step is numerically very sensitive, which makes using a higher floating-point precision than double necessary. Unfortunately, this increases the running time for a simulation considerably.

With increased requirements on the accuracy of the simulation and increased computational potential changes were made to alleviate these issues. Yet, as raising the number of segments and increasing the floating-point precision did not solve the problems satisfactorily, a new approach became necessary.

4.2 Discrete modelling

In order to tackle the two drawbacks to the exponential distribution approach, we have implemented delay distributions modelled as discrete distributions (Fig. 5) with a fixed step size s, a minimum delay d_{min} (which can be negative, i.e., an earliness), and a maximum delay d_{max}. Delay distributions modelled this way fulfil the necessary requirement of their convolution again being a discrete distribution. Additionally, the step size is not changed by convolution. And though the values of the minimum and maximum delays would decrease or increase respectively, we avoid this by cutting of delays with a probability lower than a chosen minimum probability, e.g., one in a million. This leads to the main advantage of the discrete distribution modelling compared to segment-wise exponential distributions: no simplification steps are needed. Consequently, a floating-point accuracy of double proved to be sufficient for the implementation in OnTime.

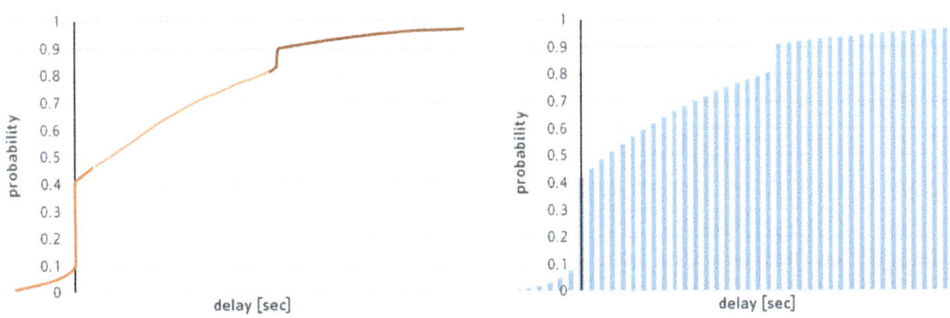

Figure 5: Delay distribution as a segment-wise exponential distribution compared to a discrete distribution. The exponential segments are indicated by the different shades of orange.

A further advantage of modelling delays with discrete distributions is that practically any form can be fitted very accurately further increasing the accuracy of the delay prognosis. As an example, delay distributions often contain discontinuities due to dispatching decisions, which can be better fitted with discrete distributions.

4.3 Experimental results

Since the step size *s* plays a crucial role both for running time and accuracy, we investigated the delay prognosis for test data of a large national network. All calculations were conducted on a standard laptop with an Intel i7 hexa-core CPU and 32 GB RAM.

Fig. 6 shows the calculation time and derived punctuality measures for several step sizes. As expected, the calculation time decreases quadratically with the step size *s* as the calculation time increases quadratically for the main driver of running time – calculating convolutions – in the number of supporting points of the discrete distributions. However, after a step size of 9 s no more improvement in running time can be realised since pre- and postprocessing steps independent of the step size *s* become dominant. On the other hand, the chosen punctuality measures are very robust with respect to changes in the step size. The results are nearly independent of *s* up to 6 s when they start to rise slightly, i.e., the prognosis starts to show higher punctuality values.

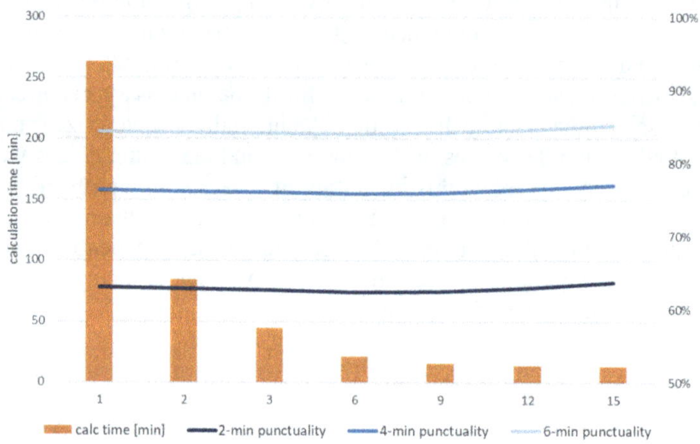

Figure 6: Increment versus punctuality.

Fig. 7 shows the resulting delay measures for several values of *s*. Again, the measured values do not change much up to a step size of 6 s, where measured values start to decrease a bit. As a result of these tests, OnTime now uses a step size of 3 s for the discrete distributions, which we feel results in a good balance between running time and accuracy.

Table 1 compares the calculation time for the same test scenario using either segment-wise exponential distributions or discrete distributions. The calculation time needed using discrete distributions is down to about a quarter.

Finally, Fig. 8 shows the unwanted changes in punctuality values due to the first drawback mentioned in Section 4.1. The figure shows the difference between two simulation runs, where the input is equal except for a small timetable improvement in the centre of the network. The result of the improvement is visualised by the green areas. However, on the left-hand side where the simulations were calculated using segment-wise exponential

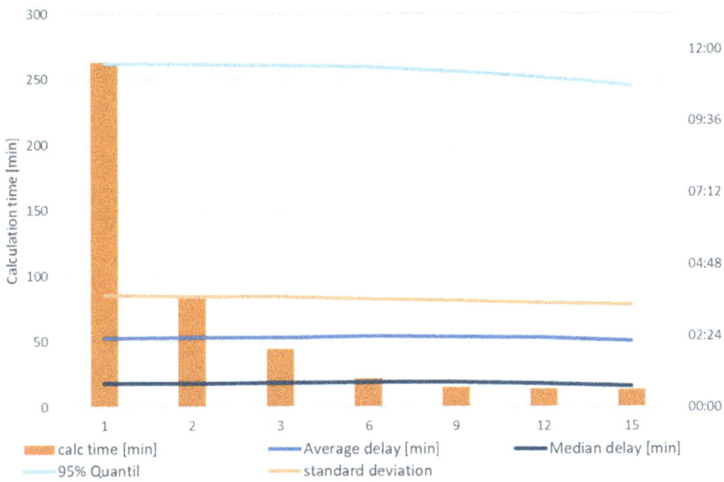

Figure 7: Increment versus delay.

Table 1: Calculation time.

Exemplary network	Calculation time (min)	
	Exponential	Discrete
Germany	220’	60’
Switzerland	125’	30’

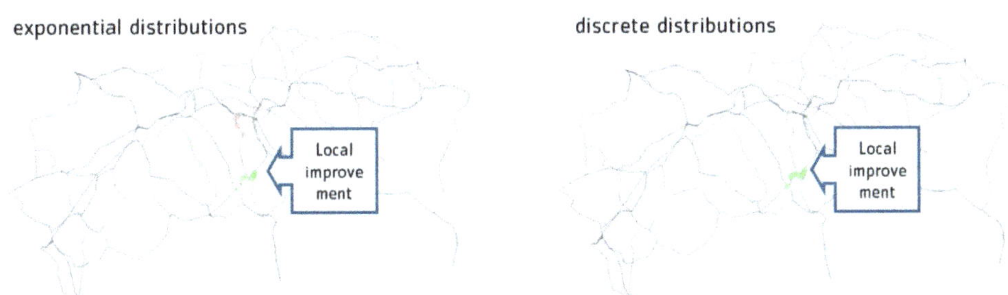

Figure 8: Comparison of difference in punctuality for two simulation runs that are equal up to a local timetable improvement. Green areas show improvements and red areas declines in operational quality.

distributions, some negative effects on operational quality visualised by red areas appear. This change is not caused by the difference of the two inputs of the simulations but are caused by simplification steps happening at different stages of the calculation. As shown on the right-hand side, no such effects occur if the simulation is calculated using discrete distributions.

5 CONCLUSIONS

OnTime is a simulation tool for calculating a delay prognosis for a timetable. While most tools apply a Monte Carlo simulation approach, OnTime calculates resulting delay distributions analytically, thus reducing calculation time considerably and enabling simulations of much larger railway networks. In addition to the previous delay modelling with exponential distributions, we have implemented calculations using discrete distributions. Comparisons between the two approaches have shown that on the one hand calculation time is reduced fourfold and on the other hand accuracy for small changes in the input data is much improved.

REFERENCES

[1] Büker, T. & Seybold, B., Stochastic modelling of delay propagation in large networks. *Journal of Rail Transport Planning and Management*, **2**(1), pp. 34–50, 2012.

[2] Büker, T., Ausgewählte Aspekte der Verspätungsfortpflanzung in Netzen. PhD thesis, RWTH Aachen, Germany, 2010.

[3] Spanninger, T., Trivella, A., Büchel, B. & Corman, F. A review of train delay prediction approaches. *Journal of Rail Transport Planning and Management*, **22**, 2022.

[4] Labermeier, H., On the dynamic of primary and secondary delay. *Proceedings of IAROR,* Copenhagen, 2013.

[5] Schranil, S., Prognose der Dauer von Störungen des Bahnbetriebs. PhD thesis, ETH Zurich, 2013.

[6] Yuan, J., Stochastic modelling of train delays and delay propagation in stations. Dissertation, Delft, Technical University Delft, 2006.

[7] Weidner, T. & Büker, T., Stochastische Simulationen zur Beurteilung der Stabilität von Personenverkehrsfahrplänen. *21. Verkehrswissenschaftliche Tage: Innovation und Investition*, Technische Universität Dresden, 2007.

[8] Seybold, B. & Kuckelberg, A., Adaptive rule-based infrastructure modelling. *Proceedings of IAROR,* Copenhagen, 2013.

[9] Bär, M., Lenze, W., Eisold, J. & Nießen, N., Benchmark von Qualitätsmaßstäben für Kapazitätsermittlungen. *Proceedings of the 2nd International Railway Symposium Aachen,* 2019.

[10] Landex, A., Methods to estimate railway capacity and passenger delays. Dissertation, TU of Denmark Lyngby, 2008.

[11] Olesen, A., Bützberger, P. & Lieberherr, J., Modellierung und Bewertung von Fahrplanangeboten der Zukunft. *Schweizer Eisenbahn-Revue,* **1**, pp. 16–19, 2016.

[12] Franke, B. & Lieberherr, J., Kombinierte betriebliche und verkehrliche Bewertung von Bahn-Angeboten. *Proceedings of the 1st International Railway Symposium Aachen,* 2017.

[13] Engelhardt-Funke, O. & Kolonko, M., Simulating delays for realistic time-table optimization. *International Conference on Operations Research 2001*, 2002.

ATO OVER ETCS: MODEL-BASED SYSTEM AND ARCHITECTURE ANALYSIS WITH ARCADIA AND EVENT-B

ROBERT ESCHBACH*
Railway Technology, ITK Engineering GmbH, Germany

ABSTRACT
The European Railway Traffic Management System (ERTMS) is intended to replace incompatible national rail traffic management systems in Europe and thus simplify cross-border rail traffic. A part of ERTMS is the European Train Control System (ETCS). ETCS is an automatic train protection system and can collaborate with an automatic train operation system (ATO). ATO can control and monitor the braking, traction and door system of a train. This collaboration is called ATO over ETCS. In this paper we describe the experiences gained in the integrated application of the model-based systems and architecture engineering method ARCADIA and the formal method Event-B to the system requirements of ATO over ETCS. A central part of the system requirements is related to the operational modes, mode transitions and mode properties of the ATO onboard unit (ATO-OB). Mode properties are system requirements that must be satisfied whenever the ATO-OB enters a mode or stays within a mode. Especially modes, in which the ATO-OB automatically drives the train, are of utter importance. The main goal of the analysis was to check consistency and completeness of the system requirements related to modes, mode transitions and mode properties. Within the ARCADIA phase "System Analysis" a so-called "Mode/State Model", a special ARCADIA model, was systematically derived from the system requirements. In order to guarantee consistency, especially to guarantee that mode properties will not be violated by mode transitions, a formal Event-B specification was derived and formally analyzed. This analysis approach identified several critical inconsistencies of the system requirements.
Keywords: ATO over ETCS, MBSE, formal methods, ARCADIA, Event-B.

1 INTRODUCTION

The European Railway Traffic Management System (ERTMS) aims at the replacement of incompatible national railway traffic management systems in Europe. A central part of ERTMS is ETCS. In this paper we will focus on the collaboration of ETCS with ATO called ATO over ETCS. The system requirements for ATO over ETCS have been specified within the Shift2Rail research project X2RAIL-1. Further information can be obtained from `https://projects.shift2rail.org` (accessed July 12, 2022). The system requirements are specified in SUBSET-125. (Technical specifications for ETCS are published in the Control Command and Signalling Technical Specification for Interoperability hosted by the European Rail Agency. These specifications are grouped into several uniquely numbered subsets.) As can be seen in the reference architecture of ATO over ETCS depicted in Fig. 2 the ATO is divided in ATO onboard unit (ATO-OB) and ATO trackside unit (ATO-TS). A main part of the system requirements is related to ATO-OB operation modes, mode transitions and mode properties. Mode properties must be satisfied whenever the ATO-OB enters a mode or stays within a mode. They can be modelled as invariants of the ATO-OB. Modes, in which the ATO-OB automatically drives the train, are critical and hence important. The main goal of the presented analysis was to check consistency and completeness of the system requirements related to modes, mode transitions and mode properties.

* *ORCID: https://orcid.org/0000-0002-2789-1873*

WIT Transactions on The Built Environment, Vol 213, © 2022 WIT Press
www.witpress.com, ISSN 1743-3509 (on-line)
doi:10.2495/CR220201

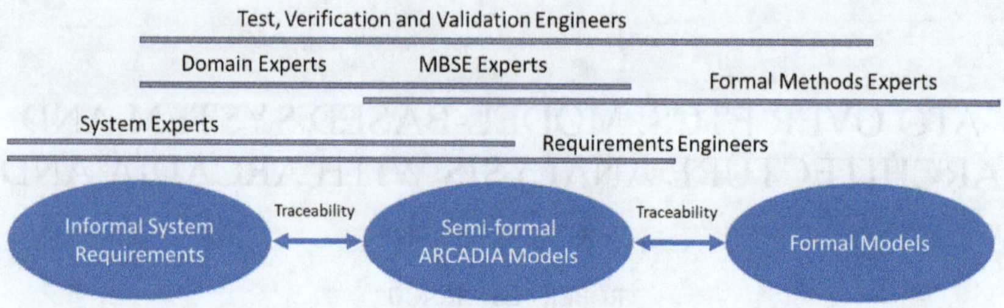

Figure 1: Development roles and scope.

In order to achieve this goal, an analysis basis was defined suited for different stakeholders, especially for the development roles involved in the overall system and software development (the engineering team). This basis was used to enable the analysis of completeness and consistency issues on different formality levels. The analysis involves different kinds of work items: informal requirements, semi-formal ARCADIA models and formal models (more precisely Event-B models). The objectives of the analysis are the following: The analysis basis should be understandable to all stakeholders and should be suitable for their expert knowledge and engineering skills,so that expert knowledge of all stakeholders has the highest influence on the overall system quality. Different work items with different degrees of formality are needed in order to address different types of completeness and consistency issues which require different analysis depths. The higher the degree of formality, the deeper is the formal analysis, but the more expert knowledge related of formal methods is needed. Usually, only a small part of the engineering team is able to peform this kind of formal analysis. Several critical issues regarding consistency and completeness were found in the formal model and could be transferred to the semi-formal ARCADIA models successfully. The formal analysis revealed 23 ambiguities and missing requirements. The anaysis approach and the obtained results will be presented in more detail in the following.

The paper is structured as follows: In Section 2 the underlying analysis approach will be presented. In Section 3 the semi-formal analysis consisting of reviewing system requirements, establishing a bidirectional traceability, analyzing the activation of system functions, verification and validation activities will be explained in more detail. Section 4 focusses on the formal analysis which consists of the identification of components (system, environment), the derivation of so-called function and variable tables, the creation of an Event-B specification together with its verification and validation. Obtained results and experiences gained in the application of the analysis approach are given in Section 5. Concluding remarks, the main results, and some perspectives related the presented study will be summarized in Section 6.

1.1 Related work

Basile et al. [1] present the rationale for designing the formal methods demonstrator for the 4SECURail project. The project 4SECURail is a research project funded by the Shift2Rail Innovation Programme (IP). Thereby they consider the usefulness of the application of formal methods from the infrastructure managers perspective. They show how SysML state machines can be used for execution and simulations and how they can be translated into formal Event-B specifications that can be formally analyzed using model checkers or theorem provers. Graves and Bijan [2] embed SysML into a formal logic to maintain an evolving consistency during design activities. Design decisions may depend on assumptions

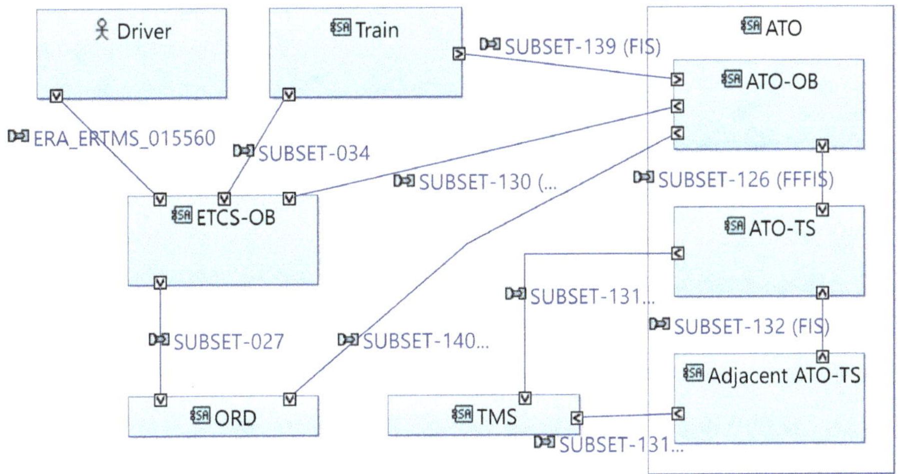

Figure 2: ATO over ETCS reference architecture.

which may introduce inconsistencies during a typical model-based development process. The embedding supports developer by formally verifying consistency when adding new mode assumptions and thus avoid potential rework. Pétin et al. [3] present a methodology how to use formal methods on top of SysML models to formally prove safety properties of heterogeneous safety-critical systems involving software, mechanical, electrical, and pneumatic components. Ahlbrecht and Durak [4] present a holistic application of Model-Based Systems Engineering, System-Theoretic Process Analysis, and formal methods in the area of Urban Air Mobility. The overall goal is to guarantee safety-by-construction within an agile development process. The approach is applied on a simplified Collision Avoidance System architecture. ter Beek et al. [5] present a detailed report on the convergence of FM related studies carried out in the Shift2Rail projects X2Rail-2 and ASTRail. In both projects a systematic survey of the state of the art of formal methods application in railway industry and related best practices was carried out. Basile et al. [6] present the results of a questionnaire which was part of the analysis phase of ASTRail research project. One of the most important results is that classical B and Event-B with the respective tools Atelier-B, ProB and Rodin were used most often in projects. Fitzgerald et al. [7] the authors present an approach to formal model-based systems-of-systems engineering based on different and complementary notations for functional, interaction and architectural aspects.

2 ANALYSIS APPROACH

The overall goal of the model-based system and architecture analysis was the creation of an analysis basis suited for different stakeholders and development roles involved in the overall system and software development as required by railway standards like [8], [9] or [10] (see Fig. 1). This analysis basis consists of the following interconnected work items:

- informal system requirements (as stated for example in SUBSET-125),
- semi-formal ARCADIA models like Mode/State models, sequence diagrams and models for functional chain analysis, and
- formal models as basis for formal verification related to consistency and completeness issues.

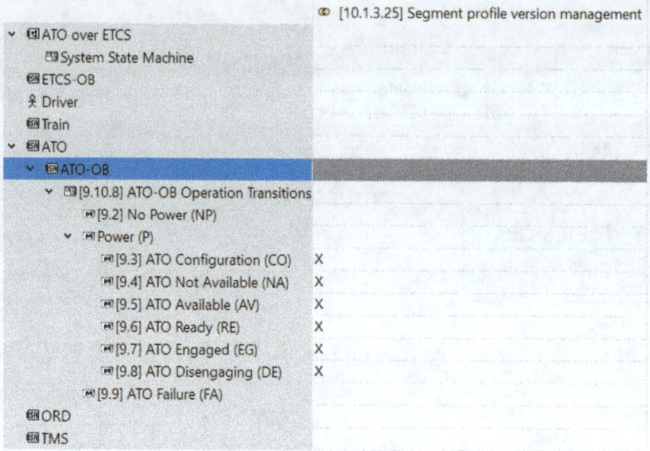

Figure 3: ARCADIA capabilities matrix (excerpt).

Different development roles with different scopes are usually involved in the model-based system development as depicted in Fig. 1. System experts with their system expertise as well as domain experts can support requirements engineers to formulate and analyze system requirements on an informal level. The MBSE experts are needed to extract semi-formal ARCADIA models from the system requirements. A bidirectional traceability between system requirements and ARACDIA models enables the information transfer between requirements and models. For example, inconsistency or incompleteness issues identified in requirements can be related to models and model elements using the traceability information. Vice versa, issues identified in models can be related to system requirements. Test, verification and validation engineers can make use of requirements and models in order to create relevant documents like test plan, test report, verification plan, verification report, validation plan, and validation report. Furthermore, system requirements, especially those expressed by tabular specification methods, or specified as ARCADIA Mode/State models and sequence diagrams are useful for the derivation of appropriate system test cases.

3 SEMI-FORMAL ANALYSIS

The semi-formal analysis consists of the following steps:

- Review system requirements
- Establish bidirectional traceability
- Analyze system function activation
- Verify system properties
- Validate against stakeholder expectations

The analysis approach started with a review of the system requirements related to modes, mode transitions and mode properties of the ATO Onboard Unit (ATO-OB). An ARCADIA Mode/State Model was systematically extracted from the system requirements and a bidirectional traceability between requirements and model elements was established. Modes as well as transition conditions are enriched with traceability information. For example, mode "[9.6] ATO Ready (RE)" refers to Section 6.1 of SUBSET-125, which specifies the system requirements of ATO over ETCS. The transition from mode "[9.6]

```
TRACE [9.10.8, 5>-p5-]
   - section 9.10.8
   - transition condition 5
   - priority p5
CONDITION
  AND
   - Driver has selected 'ATO Engage'.
   - ETCS-OB is in AD Mode.
   - TBL is in neutral or traction position.
```

Figure 4: Transition condition "ATO ready" to "ATO engaged" (excerpt).

ATO Ready (RE)" to mode "[9.7] ATO Engaged (EG)" is enabled whenever the transition condition 4 is satisfied.

Example The traceability condition of transition from mode "ATO Ready" to "ATO Engaged", shown in Fig. 4, refers to Section 9.10.8 of SUBSET-125. The flag `5>-p5` refers to transition condition 5 specified in Section 9.10.8, which, whenever enabled, is carried out with priority 5 ("p5").

The system requirements also specify which functions can be activated a mode. To analyze these activation requirements a so-called capability matrix, a special ARCADIA model, was extracted from the system requirements and analyzed w.r.t. completeness and consistency (see Fig. 3).

The Mode/State Model can be used to verify system properties as well as to validate the model against stakeholder expectations.

4 FORMAL ANALYSIS

The systematic formalization transforms in several steps system requirements as well as the extracted ARCADIA Mode/State Model into a formal Event-B specification. The formalization approach consists of the following steps (see Fig. 5):

- Identify components
- Derive function tables
- Derive variable table
- Derive Event-B specification
- Validation
- Verification

4.1 Identify components

In step *Identify components* components (system, environment) specified in SUBSET-125 are systematically identified. Since most of the requirements in SUBSET-125 are related to the ATO-OB the decision was made to choose the ATO-OB as system. As can bee seen in the reference architecture (see Fig. 1) the following environmental components were identified: Driver, Train, ETCS-OB, ATO-TS, ORD. In step *Derive function tables* conditions and actions related to modes like *ATO Engaged*, *ATO Disengaging* of the ATO-OB and its associated mode transitions and transition conditions (see Fig. 4) will be identified

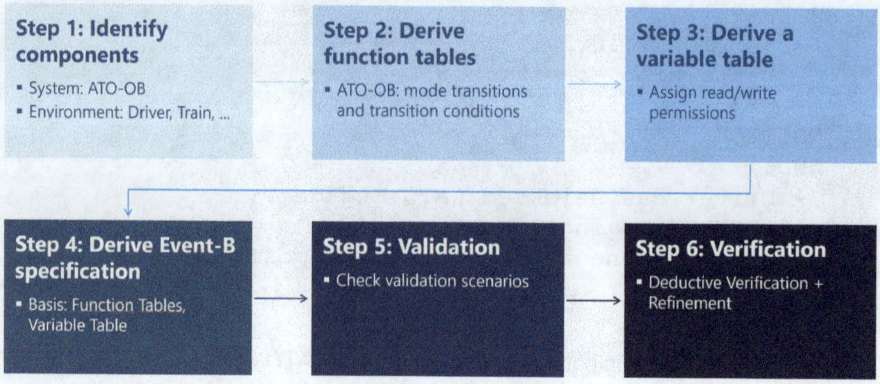

Figure 5: Formal analysis.

and extracted. All conditions and actions were placed in a special table called function table. Function tables were proposed by Dave Parnas (see [11]). Subsequently, traceability information links the requirements with elements of the function tables. A coverage analysis has been performed to ensure that all relevant requirements have been covered in the function tables.

4.2 Derive variable table

In step *Derive variable table* variables in the conditions and actions were identified so that conditions and actions can be specified formally. After analyzing the requirements types (like bool or enumeration types) were assigned to the identified variables. This step involves the analysis of relevant interface specifications SUBSET-139, SUBSET130, SUBSET-126, ... (see reference architecture Fig. 1), especially the interface between ATO-OB and ETCS-OB and the interface between ATO-OB and train, respectively. For each variable and for each component (system, environment) read/write permissions were assigned. traceability information related to both the interface and system requirements and events of the Event-B specification were added.

4.3 Derive Event-B specification

In step *Derive Event-B specification* an Event-B specification was derived on the basis of function tables and identified variables. Each Column of a function table was represented as an event in the Event-B Specification. Mode properties were formalized as Event-B invariants. The derived Event-B Specification has 25 variables, 30 invariants and 41 events.

Example In Fig. 6 the formal Event-B transition from mode "[9.6] ATO Ready" to mode "[9.7] ATO Engaged" ([9.6] and [9.7] are traceability information related to SUBSET-125). The transition can also be found in the ARCADIA Mode/State model.

4.4 Validation

In step *Validation* the use scenarios specified in SUBSET-125 were executed step-by-step with the ProB tool (see for example [12] for an application of ProB in the railway domain).

```
ato_ob_mode_re_6
any
  ato_ob
where
  ato_ob ∈ ATO_OB
  ato_ob_mode(ato_ob) = RE
  ato_ob_operational_conditions(ato_ob) = TRUE
  ato_ob_engagement_conditions(ato_ob) = TRUE
  ato_ob_etcs_ob_in_ad_mode(ato_ob) = TRUE
  ...
then
  ato_ob_mode(ato_ob) = EG
  ...
end
```

Figure 6: Event-B Transition from mode “ATO Ready” to mode “ATO Engaged”.

For example, Section 9.10.2 of SUBSET-125 describes the nominal scenario in which the ATO will be engaged by the driver for each so-called journey segment.

4.5 Verification

In step *Verification* theorem prover of Rodin, SMT solvers and ProB plugins were used for the formal verification. Deductive verification (see proof tree depicted in Fig. 7) was the main proof technique used in the formal verification. Several critical safety properties could be verified by refinement steps and additional constraints on the environment. For example, it could be formally verified that the ATO-OB is never in mode *ATO Engaged (EG)* or *ATO Disengaging (DE)* (the only modes in which ATO is engaged), whenever the driver never selects “ATO Engage”.

The formalization concept and formal analysis approach has been described in more detail in Eschbach [13].

5 RESULTS

Different stakeholders are usually involved in the overall systems engineering process. All of these stakeholders have different views on the system to be designed. All of them use different languages to speak about the system to be designed and to understand the corresponding system properties. Model-based systems and architecture engineering helps to bring all of these different views and languages together by providing common models as a basis for communication and alignment between different stakeholders. Since this common basis should be understandable to all stakeholders these models often lack formality, but formality is needed to ensure completeness and consistency in a mathematical sense. In the project described in this paper the formal method Event-B was used to specify a mathematical model and to formally verify properties of this model. The overall idea was to create a formal model closely related to some relevant ARCADIA models in order to ensure their completeness and consistency. A bidirectional traceability relates the semi-formal ARCADIA models with the formal model and allowed a transfer between the semi-formal and the formal layer. Especially issues regarding consistency and completeness found in the formal model could be transferred to the semi-formal ARCADIA models. The formal analysis revealed 23 ambiguities and

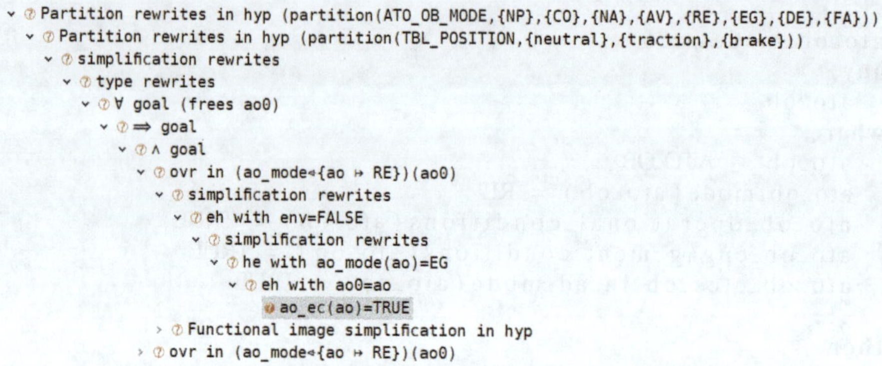

Figure 7: Deductive verification: Proof tree shown in Rodin.

missing requirements. Furthermore, a critical mode invariant violation has been discovered and was transferred to the ARCADIA models, successfully.

6 CONCLUSION

In this paper we have presented the experiences gained in the application of a model-based system and architecture analysis based on informal system requirements, the ARCADIA method and the formal method Event-B. We have shown how a bidirectional traceability between system requirements, ARCADIA models and model elements, and Event-B specifications can be used to involve different stakeholders and technical experts within the overall model-based system and software engineering development. Different levels of formality and a strong traceability between these levels helps to transfer knowledge and insights between stakeholders, technical experts and other roles involved in the overall system and software development. The formal analysis of the mode transition requirements revealed 23 ambiguities and missing requirements and will be continued in the future. Further ATO functions related to journey and segment profiles will be addressed. The current focus is on Grade of Automation Level 2 (GoA2), but will be extended the highest level of automation, namely Grade of Automation Level 4 where more sophisticated sensor technology and innovative algorithms are required.

ACKNOWLEDGEMENT

I thank the anonymous reviewers for their valuable suggestions to improve the paper.

REFERENCES

[1] Basile, D., ter Beek, M.H., Fantechi, A., Ferrari, A., Gnesi, S., Masullo, L., Mazzanti, F., Piattino, A. & Trentini, D., Designing a demonstrator of formal methods for railways infrastructure managers. *Leveraging Applications of Formal Methods, Verification and Validation: Applications*, eds T. Margaria & B. Steffen, Springer International Publishing, volume 12478 of *Lecture Notes in Computer Science*, pp. 467–485, 2020.

[2] Graves, H. & Bijan, Y., Using formal methods with SysML in aerospace design and engineering. *Annals of Mathematics and Artificial Intelligence*, **63**(1), pp. 53–102, 2011.

[3] Pétin, J.F., Evrot, D., Morel, G. & Lamy, P., Combining sysml and formal methods for safety requirements verification. *22nd International Conference on Software and Systems Engineering and Their Applications*, p. 11, 2010.

[4] Ahlbrecht, A. & Durak, U., Integrating safety into mbse processes with formal methods. *2021 IEEE/AIAA 40th Digital Avionics Systems Conference (DASC)*, pp. 1–9, 2021.
[5] ter Beek, M.H., Borälv, A., Fantechi, A., Ferrari, A., Gnesi, S., Löfving, C. & Mazzanti, F., Adopting formal methods in an industrial setting: The railways case. *Formal Methods: The Next 30 Years*, eds M.H. ter Beek, A. McIver & J.N. Oliveira, Springer International Publishing, volume 11800 of *Lecture Notes in Computer Science*, pp. 762–772, 2019.
[6] Basile, D., ter Beek, M.H., Fantechi, A., Gnesi, S., Mazzanti, F., Piattino, A., Trentini, D. & Ferrari, A., On the industrial uptake of formal methods in the railway domain: A survey with stakeholders. *Integrated Formal Methods*, eds C.A. Furia & K. Winter, Springer International Publishing, volume 11023 of *Lecture Notes in Computer Science*, pp. 20–29, 2018.
[7] Fitzgerald, J., Bryans, J. & Payne, R., A formal model-based approach to engineering systems-of-systems. *Collaborative Networks in the Internet of Services*, eds L.M. Camarinha-Matos, L. Xu & H. Afsarmanesh, Springer: Berlin, Heidelberg, pp. 53–62, 2012.
[8] EN 50155:2021 Railway applications – Rolling stock – Electronic equipment, 2021.
[9] EN 50657:2017 Railways applications – Rolling stock applications – Software on board rolling stock, 2017.
[10] EN 50128:2011/A2:2020 Railway applications – Communication, signalling and processing systems – Software for railway control and protection systems, 2020.
[11] Parnas, D.L., Inspection of safety-critical software using program-function tables. *Linkage and Developing Countries, Information Processing '94, Volume 3, Proceedings of the IFIP 13th World Computer Congress*, Hamburg, Germany, 28 Aug.–2 Sep., IFIP Transactions, pp. 270–277, 1994.
[12] Hansen, D., Leuschel, M., Schneider, D., Krings, S., Körner, P., Naulin, T., Nayeri, N. & Skowron, F., Using a formal B model at runtime in a demonstration of the ETCS hybrid level 3 concept with real trains. *Abstract State Machines, Alloy, B, TLA, VDM, and Z*, eds M. Butler, A. Raschke, T.S. Hoang & K. Reichl, Springer International Publishing, pp. 292–306, 2018.
[13] Eschbach, R., Formalizing and analyzing system requirements of automatic train operation over ETCS using Event-B. *Rigorous State-Based Methods*, eds A. Raschke & D. Méry, Springer International Publishing, volume 12709 of *Lecture Notes in Computer Science*, pp. 137–142, 2021.

ENHANCE RAILWAY DIGITAL MAP FOR SLAM: FEASIBILITY STUDY

NADIA CHOUCHANI[1] & IBAN LOPETEGI ZINKUNEGI[2]
[1]RAILENIUM Technological Research Institute, France
[2]CAF J.M. Iturrioz, Spain

ABSTRACT

Safe train positioning is a challenging task that boosts the traffic capabilities and the quality of train localization and integrity information, but above all enables cost reductions in infrastructure train detection systems such as balises and track circuits. Prominent technologies, namely, global navigation satellite system and inertial measurement unit sensors are arising to incorporate in train positioning. Typically, trains run on harsh railway environments including interference, insufficient satellite availability and signal blockages in specific areas like tunnels and urban canyons or due to meteorological conditions changes. Currently, these problems are solved with the use of balises for full supervision modes and drivers for staff responsible/shunting modes. However, autonomous trains with fully automatic driving and without drivers will need to deal these issues. Simultaneously localization and mapping algorithms based on radar and/or lidar sensors have shown great potential of being candidate positioning solutions for future train transportation. This paper presents a state of the art on these techniques and a testing architecture as part of a study on the feasibility of candidate sensors for safe autonomous train positioning in order to assess the viability of absolute positioning without need on infrastructure devices.

Keywords: SLAM, mapping, autonomous driving, railway, sensors.

1 INTRODUCTION

Autonomous driving systems navigation requires a precise mapping and localization solution. In this context, simultaneous localization and mapping (SLAM) is a suited and popular solution [1]. For solving the navigation problem, there are two major questions to be answered. First the environment on which the system is located needs to be identified and secondly the system must be localised within this environment. There are therefore two problems to address; localization means estimating the pose; and mapping which is building a map. It is challenging because there is a dependency between the two tasks: a map is needed for localization and a location estimate is needed for mapping. SLAM is addressing these two problems jointly. It computes the positions and at the same point in time while estimating these poses, a map of the environment is built. A map is a model of what the environment looks like. It can be a dense 3D model or specific positions of landmarks (distinct points or features) in the environment extracted from the sensor data.

The objective of this paper is twofold: firstly, to summarise the state of the art of the SLAM algorithms and their digital map usage, and secondly to describe a testing architecture that allows recording all required sensor's information with high precision and low delay under the railway domain. The recorded data will be part of the feasibility study of a positioning system based on extended maps focused on the proposed sensors.

This document is structured as follows: first, a background on railway maps modelling, sensors and positioning algorithms is presented. Then, relevant SLAM techniques are detailed. In the next section, the identified testing architecture is presented. Finally, the document concludes with discussion and conclusion sections.

doi:10.2495/CR220211

2 BACKGROUND

2.1 Positioning algorithms

Localization represents an elemental requirement for autonomous systems navigation. It is the task of determining the system geo-position relatively to a reference frame in an environment. In this section, the most common localization approaches are presented.

2.1.1 GNSS

Global navigation satellite system (GNSS) represents a widely used pervasive technology in autonomous driving systems for navigation. It rose in the 1980s and is widely used up to now. It presents a solution for absolute positioning [2]. It determines the absolute position of a point using only the measurements made in the associated station based on simple data processing algorithms. No restrictions are sustained by the GNSS receiver antenna position. This solution remains insufficient by itself because of the availability issues, thus not enough accurate.

2.1.2 GNSS and IMU

For positioning autonomous systems, GNSS solutions cannot be used as a stand-alone system. In order to remedy dead reckoning errors in intervals with absolute position readings, GNSS-IMU fusion systems are proposed [3]. IMU captures and measures the changes in position and orientation. This information is processed when localizing the system with dead reckoning. The GPS readings are used in addition to the map information for correction of accumulated errors. The accuracy required for autonomous driving systems represents a major challenge for this solution.

2.1.3 GNSS with IMU and odometry

For bridging the GNSS outages, IMU solutions are coupled with odometry [4]. In addition to fusing GNSS with IMU, wheel speed sensors are used as a backup or alternative to GNSS-based positioning. Unlike GNSS, odometry measurements are available and generally don't suffer from environmental influences, except wheel pulse generators and radars output errors which depend on environmental conditions like wet leaves and snow.

Reuper et al. [5] concluded that thanks to the integration of odometry model, more accurate measurements are obtained into the localization algorithm comparing to GNSS-IMU based results.

2.1.4 Simultaneous localization and mapping

Autonomous trains are safety critical systems. Their localization is a challenging task. An appropriate approach should be able to determine the absolute position measured with on-board sensors and the relative topological position. The mapping approach aim then to generate an automated map and maintain it based on measurements of sensors. Another challenge for railway applications, is that the near field environment is very similar (same objects such as trach rails, catenary, and signs for many kilometres). So, the opportunity to discriminate the position is harder than other environments such as roads for cars. Among the possible solutions that can face these challenges, we distinguish the SLAM approaches which attracted more and more research and industrial attention in recent years.

SLAM is a problem initiated in 1986 by Smith and Cheeseman, and get more popular during the 1990s [1]. Solving a SLAM problem amounts to estimating a system's position in the environment and constructing a map of the surroundings simultaneously. The research in this field involves many topics such as data analysis, sensor data extraction and primitive search and map storage. The availability of new and different sensors have created new data representations and consequently new mapping systems. Nowadays, SLAM is used for various applications ranging from autonomous driving to spatial exploration. SLAM is an estimation problem of both the trajectory or pose of the system and the position of landmarks in the environment [6]. The estimation techniques can be categorized into two main classes: filter-based and optimization-based approaches; which will be detailed in the next section.

2.2 Sensors and hardware

Sensor technologies have experienced remarkable progress in recent years. They now play a crucial role in the development of autonomous driving systems. Various sensors are widely used in different applications such as environment perception, geo-data analysis, mapping and localization [7]. In the following, we present three main types of exteroceptive sensors, which are cameras, radars and lidars.

Cameras are passive sensors because they do not emit any signals. They can sense colour and provide rich information of the environment. However, their performance is affected by illumination and weather conditions. Also, from a single camera, it is difficult to obtain depth information. 360° 2D vision can be assured by omnidirectional cameras. In fact, panoramic views can be exploited for navigation, localization, and mapping.

Radars can cover the cameras' drawbacks since they provide depth information. That is distance to objects can be measured effectively. Contrary to cameras, they are active sensors. They emit radio waves that can interfere with other systems. Similarly to radars, and instead of radio waves, lidars emit infrared light waves. These electromagnetic waves are used to detect objects in the near field environment by a light beam and measure the distance and angle of the reflecting objects. They allow then to measure the distance between the object and the sensor in addition to other physical properties. 3D points highly accurate represent the result of the measurement. The coordinates of these points are provided in local coordinate systems according to the lidar system type and usage area. Coordinates in global positioning systems can be obtained if we dispose of stationary use with known position. Otherwise, further sensors are needed.

Table 1 summarizes the advantages and disadvantages of each of these sensors.

Table 1: Sensor's comparison.

	Advantages	Drawbacks
Lidar	Rotativity 360 degrees Mature technology (used since the late 1980s) High accuracy	Medium range (<200m) Affected by weather (such as fog or snow having a negative impact on their performance) Large size High cost
Radar	High range Small size Medium cost	Interference with other systems (it is an active sensor which emits radio waves) Affected by weather (such as rain or clouds)
Camera	Passive sensor (does not interfere with other systems) Colour Low cost Small/medium size	Affected by illumination Affected by weather Low accuracy

3 RELEVANT SLAM TECHNIQUES

A SLAM system architecture comprises two main components: the front-end and the back-end. The first component performs sensor data abstraction into models. However, the second component deals with inference on the abstracted data produced from the front-end.

There are two formulations of the SLAM problem [1]. In the first one, known as full SLAM, the whole trajectory and the map are estimated based given all control inputs and measurements. The goal is to compute the map and the joint posterior over all poses based on the total sensor data. Given the system's controls $u_{i:t}$ and observations $z_{i:t}$, construct a map of the environment m and a path of the system $x_{0:t}$. Since the observations and motions are uncertain, probability theory is used to express uncertainty. Then full SLAM refers to the full trajectory of all locations $x_{0:t}$ and the map m:

$$p(x_{0:t}, m|z_{0:t}, u_{0:t}). \quad (1)$$

The complexity of the full SLAM grows with the considered variables number; thus it is difficult to compute. Therefore, the second formulation is about the online SLAM. Its goal is to estimate the current position based on the last sensor data. Then the online SLAM refers to the estimation of the current location state x_k and the map m:

$$p(z_k|x_k, m). \quad (2)$$

The goal of SLAM is to estimate the pose and model the environment simultaneously. However, the matching between the observations and the map is unknown because the path and the map are both unknown and the map and pose estimates are correlated. It is then a hard problem and is the typical case for lidar based sensors. However, radar based sensors, the digital map is computed in advance or in a recording process and then they do the matching.

3.1 Filter-based SLAM

Filter-based SLAM techniques derive from Bayesian filtering and are based on two steps that iterate and integrate sensor data to estimate the system pose on the map [1]. The first step predicts the map states using an evolution model and control inputs. In the second step, the observation coming from the sensor data is compared to the map to correct the predicted state. The model that matches the observation against the map is called an observation model. There exist four sub-categories of filter-based techniques, which are:

3.1.1 Extended Kalman filter

These methods are derived from the Kalman filter (KF). KFs handle linear systems and assume that data are affected by Gaussian noises [6]. They present high convergence properties but are rarely used for SLAM. However, the extended Kalman filtering is common in SLAM for non-linear filtering. Its principle is to add linearization step for non-linear models. The current position is performed using the linearization through a first order Taylor expansion. EKF is based on five steps, which are:

- Pose prediction: predict the state given the previous pose;
- Observation: take the real measurement;
- Measurement prediction: predict the expected measurement given the belief state;
- Matching or data association: associate the obtained measurement of the landmarks (based on the map) with the predicted observation;

- Estimation: compute the difference between the obtained measurement and the predicted measurement and update the state (mean and covariance matrix) via the Kalman gain.

The disadvantage of KF based SLAM algorithms is that the computational complexity increases with the environment landmarks added to the state vector [14]. Moreover, matching the observations and landmarks in the state vector may cause filter to diverge when data association is wrong. Some works proposed to improve EKF by reducing complexity and memory usage. Alternatives such as CEKF were proposed [8]. They consider local areas of the stochastic map. CEKF, in contrast with EKF, don't perform full SLAM update since it is working in a local area; however this reduces the computation complexity.

3.1.2 Unscented Kalman filter

Initiated by Julier et al., UKF method got popular during the 2000s. It tried to address the problem of EKF with highly non-linear systems by avoiding the computation of Jacobian matrices. They introduced the concept of sigma points, which are sample particles weighted around the expected measurements thanks to likelihood functions. They are used as input to the non-linear function to update the estimate. UKF reduces estimation errors, but the main disadvantage of this method is its high computational complexity $O(k^3)$, where k is the number of landmarks.

3.1.3 Information filter

Information filter is a variant of Kalman filter. Its principle is to use the inverse of the covariance matrix as information matrix [1]. But converting every measure to its inverse form is costly. However, the main advantage of this method is a near constant-time update step by making the information matrix sparser. The update is then additive and no longer dependent of the observation's integration order.

3.1.4 Particle filter

Particle filter-based algorithms assume that a state is sampled with a set of particles depending on its probability density [1]. As Kalman filter, measurement prediction and update according to the observation are performed. However, the particles are updated by weighting them with reference to their likelihood regarding the measures. For each update step, particles are handled as follows: some are kept (the most likely), the others are eliminated, and new particles are generated. The main drawback of this method is the requirement of a set of particles per landmark. However, its advantage is that it can accommodate with any distribution and does not require an assumption of Gaussian noise.

3.2 Optimization-based SLAM

As in filter-based techniques, optimization-based SLAM approaches are composed of two steps. In the first step, the sensor data are leveraged to identify the constraints of the localization problem by matching the new observations against the map. In the second step, the system pose and the map are computed and refined. Two main sub-categories can be identified; bundle adjustment and graph SLAM.

3.2.1 Bundle adjustment

BA is a visual feature-based SLAM. Based on images and camera parameters, it refines the visual reconstruction of the map based on a number of 3D points [1]. The goal is to estimate the location of the camera and the 3D points locations jointly so that the error where the point is projected to is minimized.

3.2.2 Graph SLAM

3.2.2.1 Pose graph-based SLAM

The idea is to use a graph to represent the SLAM problem where a node corresponds to a pose during the mapping and an edge between two nodes correspond to a spatial constraint between them. A graph-based SLAM problem amounts to build a graph and find the nodes configuration that minimizes the error introduced by the constraints. The principle is to have an interplay between the front-end where the graph is constructed from raw data and back-end where the output graph is optimized; then the node configuration is updated. The configuration is such that the real and predicted observations are as similar as possible. The difference value between the predicted and actual measurements is the error. The goal is to find the state that minimizes the error given all measurements.

3.2.2.2 Graph with landmarks

Nodes can represent poses or landmark locations and edges can represent landmarks observations or odometry measurements [1]. The optimization goal corresponds to minimizing the landmark locations and system poses. The minimization is generally simplified by a local approximation using methods such as Gauss–Newton, Gauss–Seidel relaxation, Levenberg–Marquardt or gradient descent.

Autonomous driving systems designed to perform SLAM are using exteroceptive sensors. lidar can provide accurate 3D mapping of the environment comparing to radar. Applied to a SLAM technique, this sensor can achieve a low drift motion estimation for an acceptable computational complexity. The main solution is the scan-matching approach followed by a graph optimization. Scan-matching is a process used for creating 3D maps with lidar data, giving precise information on motion. Iterative closest point (ICP) is the most common technique for registering 3D point clouds. It is an iterative algorithm for local scan matching.

Table 2: Main algorithms complexity and scalability.

Criterion \ Algorithm	EKF	Information filter	Particle filter	Graph SLAM
Computational complexity	$O(n^2)$	Constant	M.log(n)	Edges
Large scale	–	+	+	+

n = number of landmarks; M = number of particles.

4 TESTING ARCHITECTURE

4.1 Candidate sensors

To assess SLAM algorithm on railway environment two main technologies are proposed, radar and lidar. Both sensors have been widely used in SLAM algorithms as it is described in Bresson et al. [1].

4.1.1 Radar

The proposed radar sensor is an automotive radar sensor, which is already in-service for automotive passenger and commercial vehicle applications especially for the functions adaptive cruise control (ACC) and emergency brake assist (EBA). In Fig. 1 it can be seen the field of view of the proposed sensor. It is based on a 77 GHz frequency with digital beam-forming scanning antenna, which offers two independent scans for far (FRS) and near range

(NRS), as described in Fig. 1. The sensor uses a pulse compression radar modulation to avoid the drawbacks of both the classical Pulse–Doppler and the frequency-modulated continuous wave radar (FMCW) approach. Since the radar sensor is a sensor that could potentially be used for object detection and collision avoidance purposes, it is foreseen to install three radars per cab. One radar per side and one at the centre of the cab facing forward. In this way, a coverage of all three radars would reach to 260°. Notice, that this angle would need to be verified with final train set up. Fig. 2 shows a view of the radars installed at the front of the train cab.

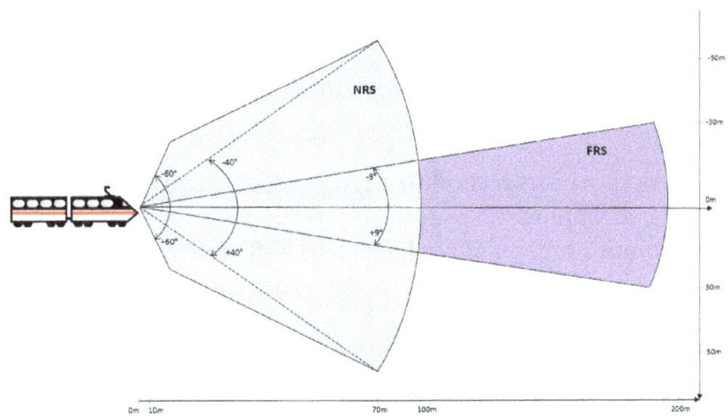

Figure 1: Radar horizontal field of detection.

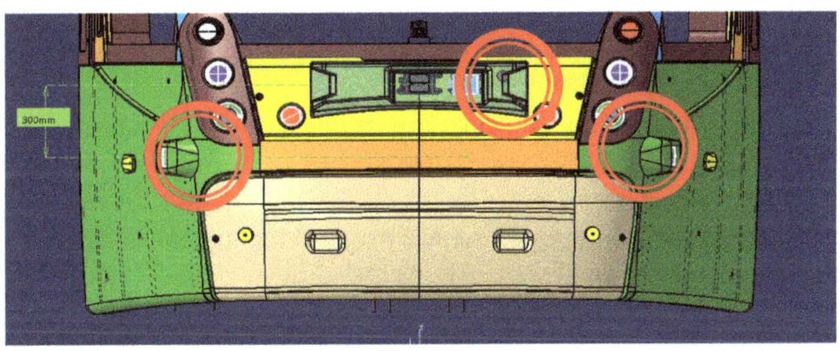

Figure 2: Radar location on train (surrounded objects).

4.1.2 Lidar

The proposed lidar sensor is an automotive sensor. In Fig. 3 the lidar location at the front of the train cab can be seen. The sensor is a time-of-flight sensor, operating at a near-infrared (IR), 1064 nm, wavelength that consists of a single laser illumination module and sensor receiver module (both build-in the HFL118 sensor head).

Laser illumination module, periodically (e.g. every 40 ms) emits a single, very short (~ 3 ns), laser pulse, that is spatially diffused (both horizontally and vertically), to provide the illumination in the full FOI (field of illumination) region (e.g. 120° (horizontal) × 30° (vertical)).

Sensor receiver module captures, and samples all return signals (reflections from targets) that were illuminated in FOI, returned within FOV (field of view), and received within the

Figure 3: Lidar location on train (surrounded object).

shutter open-time period. Receiver module optics is specifically designed to match the FOV with FOI, exactly. And shutter open time (together with lidar link budget calculations) determines the maximum range of flash lidar. HFL118 shutter open time is set to ~400 ns. These extremely fast shutter speeds provide the instantaneous "Flash" mapping of the 3D environment. Fig. 3 shows the view of the lidar installed at the train cab.

4.1.3 Other sensors

It is worth to notice that the full system for positioning may not be able to perform without the inputs from other sensors than radar and lidar. For such, the idea is to complement the recording scheme by using the following additional sensors:

- GNSS receiver
  - Dual constellation dual frequency receiver and antenna are proposed.
- Inertial measurement unit (IMU)
  - Six degrees of freedom sensors are proposed with both accelerometers and gyroscopes.
- Speed sensor (tachometers)
  - Tachometers based on Hall effect are proposed as part of the speed measurement system.
- Camera
  - Fish-eye cameras are set as part of the validation of the sensor set-up and as visual inspection tool for the performance.

Since the additional sensors are not considered as the core of the SLAM problem, their detailed description is considered out of the scope.

4.2 Test recording architecture

The test recording architecture is the hardware/software set-up required to fit in the train for the purpose. Fig. 4 presents an illustration of the proposed architecture for the set-up. This architecture comprises on one side the three radars per cab, one lidar and one fisheye camera. The idea is that the three radars set-up allow to have a full field of view of the train environment increasing the likelihood for positioning algorithms. All these sensors provide their information to the railway certified recording platform, which is based on a UNIX operative system over an ARM architecture. In addition, GNSS receiver data, IMUs and Speed values are also provided to the recording platform so that all the components to measure the train position based on SLAM algorithms are ready to assess.

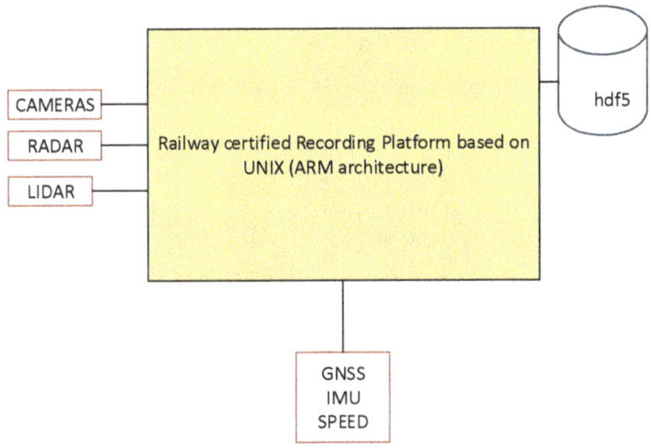

Figure 4: High level architecture set-up for testing.

Based on the testing architecture the appropriate recordings can be carried out and in post-processing mode the expected feasibility study of positioning algorithm can be analysed.

4.3 Test environment

The test recording scenario will be installed in the tram of Zaragoza. The Urbos 3 model, manufactured by CAF in their plant in Zaragoza, uses the very latest technology, aiming to offer a service which is effective, comfortable and environmentally friendly. The design comes from the Fabrizio Giugiario School, which is responsible for the different models of Ferrari and Maserati. From the outset, CAF worked with ONCE and the DFA Foundation to make the Tram fully accessible to all (https://www.tranviasdezaragoza.es/en/informacion/nuestro-tranvia). The tram consists of five modules with a total length of 32.314 m, 296 passenger capacity and a maximum speed of 70 km/h (https://www.caf.net/en/productos-servicios/proyectos/proyecto-detalle.php?p=61).

The tram circulates over the city of Zaragoza where there is mainly an urban environment but also there are shunting yard environments. Both are considered challenging environment for localization purposes and interesting for the TAURO project. The following figure is an illustration from Open Street Maps (https://www.openstreetmap.org) from the expected lines at which the tram is operating.

4.4 Test performance evaluation

In order to evaluate the feasibility study of the proposed SLAM algorithm a ground truth (GT) of the recorded data must be provided. A GT is the absolute true of the train's position used as a reference to validate the outcome of the positioning performance. In order to illustrate this process Fig. 5 depicts the performance evaluation methodology to be carried. On one hand, the SLAM algorithm is executed using an extended digital map based on radars and lidars plus the other sensors. On the other hand, the GT of the train is carried out by using balises, speed sensors, IMU sensor and a geographical digital map. The digital map is based on balise data information plus track segmentation with reference to absolute positions, so that the GT algorithm can always tell you in which track and which position within the track the train is located on. With both sides providing a positioning algorithm a comparison of both is the key for the feasibility study.

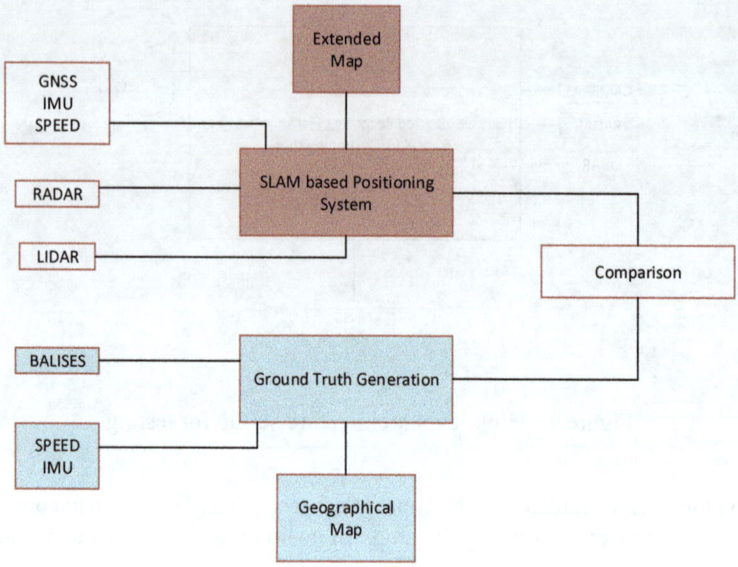

Figure 5: Test performance evaluation diagram block.

5 DISCUSSION

Recent works proposed new customised map formats in order to meet the need for autonomous driving. They aim to include geometric information to topological maps. Enhanced map (Emap) [10] is a customized map format designed for a lane-level localization. A series of straight lines, circles and clothoids represent the lanes. This representation is based on GNSS and dead reckoning measurements. The average lane accuracy was in order of 1m. Czerwionka et al [11] proposed a graph representation of the lanes and the relationships between them. RNDFGraph is based on the route network definition file format (RNDF). It is used to generate splines based on waypoints for ensuring a smooth trajectory. This representation was used in German highways for path planning and can be used for localization purposes. Graph SLAM in addition to line-segment features extracted from 3D lidar were combined with an OpenStreetMap map [12]. The Emap consists of a set of segments that describe the geometry in addition to the topological information of these segments (3D coordinates). The segments are linked to their neighbour's contrary to standard maps where the topology of the map is associated to the nodes. The lane estimation integrated to the map was performed using particle filter. An average accuracy of 5 cm was reached.

A huge amount of data is gathered thanks to sensors and several online resources (panoramas, geographic maps, etc.). Leveraging the available resources can be used to create knowledge supporting the autonomous driving functions' needs such as localization and mapping.

The safety of localization algorithms is a challenging issue. Failures and their impact on localization, must be considered for ensuring that an autonomous driving system operates safely.

6 CONCLUSION AND FUTURE WORK

A state of the art on SLAM methods for autonomous driving systems was presented in this document. In addition to the techniques of building maps, conceptual modelling and standards of railway maps were detailed. They include geometric and topological representation of infrastructure and environment features. These features are obtained thanks to the amount of available data extracted from the various sensors generally used for autonomous driving. A comparison of the main exteroceptive sensors was carried out in this document. Leveraging sensor data using the appropriate mapping algorithms can enhance the representation of the digital track maps.

This document describes the test architecture and the test environment set-up to test SLAM algorithms. The proposed system is based on multipurpose sensorisation and it aims to provide to bases for the further analysis to be carried out within Task 1.3 on the feasibility study of these sensor as part of the extended digital map. In addition, the performance evaluation methodology is also described in the document to allow the reader to understand how the process of feasibility study is going to be carried out.

ACKNOWLEDGEMENTS

This work was accomplished within the framework of the TAURO (Technologies for the Autonomous Rail Operation) project. This project has received funding from the Shift2Rail JU under the European Union's Horizon 2020 research and innovation programme. Grant agreement no. 101014984.

REFERENCES

[1] Bresson, G., Alsayed, Z., Yu, L., & Glaser, S., Simultaneous localization and mapping: A survey of current trends in autonomous driving. *IEEE Trans. Intell. Veh.*, **2**(3), pp. 194–220, 2017. DOI: 10.1109/TIV.2017.2749181.

[2] Bento, L.C., Bonnifait, P. & Nunes, U.J., Cooperative GNSS positioning aided by road-features measurements. *Transp. Res. Part C Emerg. Technol.*, **79**, pp. 42–57, 2017. DOI: 10.1016/j.trc.2017.01.002.

[3] Crocoll, P., Caselitz, T., Hettich, B., Langer, M. & Trommer, G.F., Laser-aided navigation with loop closure capabilities for micro aerial vehicles in indoor and urban environments. *2014 IEEE/ION Position, Location and Navigation Symposium: PLANS 2014*, Monterey, CA, USA, pp. 373–384, 2014. DOI: 10.1109/PLANS.2014.6851395.

[4] Reitbauer, E. & Schmied, C., Bridging GNSS outages with IMU and odometry: A case study for agricultural vehicles. *Sensors*, **21**(13), p. 4467, 2021. DOI: 10.3390/s21134467.

[5] Reuper, B., Becker, M. & Leinen, S., Benefits of multi-constellation/multi-frequency GNSS in a tightly coupled GNSS/IMU/odometry integration algorithm. *Sensors*, **18**(9), p. 3052, 2018. DOI: 10.3390/s18093052.

[6] Debeunne, C. & Vivet, D., *A Review of Visual-LiDAR Fusion Based Simultaneous Localization and Mapping*, p. 20, 2020.

[7] Yurtsever, E., Lambert, J., Carballo, A. & Takeda, K., A survey of autonomous driving: Common practices and emerging technologies. ArXiv190605113 Cs Eess, 2020. DOI: 10.1109/ACCESS.2020.2983149.

[8] Wang, H., Li, C., Lv, H. & Chen, X., Research on compressed EKF based SLAM algorithm for unmanned underwater vehicle. *2012 15th International IEEE Conference on Intelligent Transportation Systems*, Anchorage, AK, USA, pp. 1402–1406, 2012. DOI: 10.1109/ITSC.2012.6338834.

[9] Tuna, G., Gulez, K., Cagri Gungor, V. & Veli Mumcu, T., Evaluations of different simultaneous localization and mapping (SLAM) algorithms. *IECON 2012: 38th Annual Conference on IEEE Industrial Electronics Society*, Montreal, QC, Canada, pp. 2693-2698, 2012. DOI: 10.1109/IECON.2012.6389151.

[10] Betaille, D. & Toledo-Moreo, R., Creating enhanced maps for lane-level vehicle navigation. *IEEE Trans. Intell. Transp. Syst.*, **11**(4), pp. 786–798, 2010. DOI: 10.1109/TITS.2010.2050689.
[11] Czerwionka, P., Wang, M. & Wiesel, F., Optimized route network graph as map reference for autonomous cars operating on German autobahn. *The 5th International Conference on Automation, Robotics and Applications*, Wellington, New Zealand, pp. 78–83, 2011. DOI: 10.1109/ICARA.2011.6144860.
[12] Joshi, A. & James, M.R., Generation of accurate lane-level maps from coarse prior maps and lidar. *IEEE Intell. Transp. Syst. Mag.*, 7(1), pp. 19–29, 2015. DOI: 10.1109/MITS.2014.2364081.

TRAINRUNS.JL: AN OPEN-SOURCE TOOL FOR RUNNING TIME ESTIMATION

MARTIN SCHEIDT* & MAX KANNENBERG
TU Braunschweig, Institute of Railway Systems Engineering and Traffic Safety, Germany

ABSTRACT
Open science requires open-source tools that produce verifiable results. Nevertheless, a universal open-source tool in railway engineering is still missing. This paper presents an open-source tool for running time estimation to promote a change toward more open tools. Besides the tool's implementation, the need for simple data formats and data sources is discussed. The tool was tested against a commercial tool and revealed variations in the computation. Nonetheless, the tool can already deliver valuable results for simple investigations.
Keywords: driving dynamics, run time, railway, railroad, open science, driving mode, railml, railtoolkit, julia programming language.

1 INTRODUCTION

Computations for train runs in simulation, analytical assessments, or timetabling have become indispensable in railway engineering. However, the available standard software is closed source and, thus, a black box; therefore, it is difficult or even impossible to retrace exactly how the computations are performed. Furthermore, dynamic driving behaviors can only be investigated with standard simulation software at its given level. In addition, the high costs of software limit its uses in research and teaching.

The open-source tool TrainRuns.jl (TR) [1] presented in this paper has been developed to address this issue. Its functionality is based on state-of-the-art running time estimation equations. However, different approaches can be taken when converting the equations into software code. Therefore, the running time estimation implementation must be considered and compared against an already-established implementation. For such a comparison, train and path data must be loaded in a suitable format. For the use case of TR, RailML has proven to be impractical and too verbose, so a more straightforward custom schema based upon YAML was developed. For the test, routes and train data were chosen that push the limits in the computation.

In this paper, we present and discuss the following contributions:

- the importance of open sources for open science (Section 3),
- the tool TR (Sections 4 and 5),
- the YAML/railtoolkit schema (Section 6), and
- the testing of the tool against a commercial tool (Section 7).

2 RUNNING TIME ESTIMATION

Running time estimation is used to compute the position, speed, and time of a train run. This computed train run is used for many railway operation calculations; therefore, it is generally well known. In addition to scheduling, this estimation is used to optimize energy consumption, calculate capacity consumption, or run simulations. Therefore, the running time estimation is the basis for engineering and scientific investigation for running trains

* *ORCID: https://orcid.org/0000-0002-9384-8945*

doi:10.2495/CR220221

(significant studies include Lehmann [2] and Wende [3]). In addition, the summary of calculating a train run is presented in Brűnger and Dahlhaus [4].

A computed train run rarely directly corresponds to an observed train run. Heppe et al. [5] closely examined a specific path section and searched for explanations to investigate the discrepancy between the computed and observed train runs. Other researchers, such as Hertel and Steckel [6] and Medeossi et al. [7], have tried to map distributions for the discrepancy. Kecman and Goverde [8] went a step further by not computing the train run but derivating future running times by parameterizing past train runs. The idea is tempting, but this idea may only be realized with proper data management, sufficiently busy sections, and no new vehicles. Wen et al. [9] provided an overview of the prediction of running time from the existing data.

Several input parameters for the train and track are required for the running time estimation. The train data determine the propulsion force and braking behavior. The opposing resistances are determined by the train and track data. The track parameters, which might change rapidly, and the complex acceleration behavior of the train make a continuous analytical calculation of the train run impractical. The iterations, number of parameters, and assumptions do not allow an exact calculation of the running time but only an estimation. Therefore, the acceleration and resistance computations are conducted using the algorithms implemented in software tools.

The general literature divides driving into four modes: accelerating, constant speed/cruising, coasting, and braking [10, p. 45] (see Fig. 1 ①–④). However, these four driving modes are simplistic and only cover cases under the assumption of a low constant

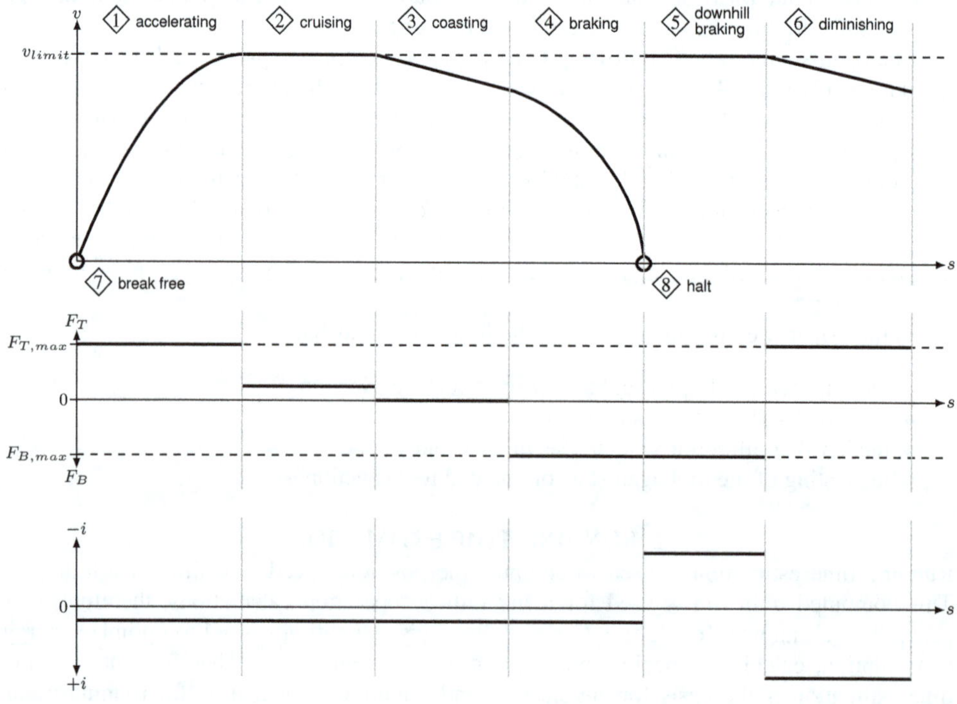

Figure 1: Eight driving modes with qualitative dimensions: Position (s), speed (v), force (traction F_T and braking F_B), and resistance (i).

resistance due to the track. Therefore, Monecke et al. [11] differentiated driving into six movement phases (see Fig. 1 ⟨5⟩, ⟨6⟩). The two additional movement phases are downhill braking and decreasing speed/diminishing. These additional modes account for cases when the train accelerates due to the track slope (downhill braking) or the train does not have enough power to hold its speed due to the slope (diminishing). Adding two more driving modes for the algorithmic computation is also helpful: halt and break free (see Fig. 1 ⟨7⟩, ⟨8⟩). Halt is used when the train is standing still. Break free represents the moment when the train wheels start moving and must overcome the momentum and resistance of the train as an initial state for the computation.

The algorithms for running time estimation are usually embedded in larger software packages. The primary purpose of these software packages is to construct a timetable or simulate operations for stability assessments. Many software packages implement the running time estimation. Some are not citable, and others are presented in a citable form at scientific conferences. A small overview of existing software is presented by Medeossi and de Fabris [12]. Currently, these software packages are used heavily in research and scientific studies. Even if it can be assumed that most of the studies were conducted conscientiously, the results are not independently verifiable because the raw data, parameters, and tools are not openly available.

3 STATEMENT OF NEED

Research results should be freely accessible to all online, particularly if the research has been funded by public money. Besides the results, research methods, or tools, the research process, raw data, and collaborative data processing should also be published. While the publication of raw data, parameters, and processes is a matter of domain culture, the accessibility of tools is dependent on whether the tools are open source. However, most mentioned software packages can only be used to a limited extent for transparent and reproducible research, as they are black boxes due to the unpublished source code.

Figure 2 illustrates the black-box problem for developing a software tool in a scientific context. First, the object of study is from the real world (A). In the example of running time estimation, the train behavior under different conditions. These conditions were identified using statistical methods ⟨1⟩. However, assumptions must also be made ⟨2⟩. For example, air resistance calculation assumes a constant headwind at 15 km/h [4, p. 70]. While air resistance is only a minor factor, the load and load distribution are essential. Assumptions must be made for the load most of the time. Nevertheless, these observations and assumptions form a model ⟨8⟩ that must be implemented with a programming language that introduces the need for adaptation and abstraction ⟨3⟩. In addition to the unintentional errors, this implementation can contain other simplifications and gimmicks that appear necessary from a computer science perspective. The implemented working model generates raw data ⟨4⟩, with which the model's plausibility can be checked ⟨7⟩. However, the raw data must be aggregated for further processing (D). The aggregation is performed by indicators that have proven helpful in the past. If the model does not sufficiently characterize the aggregation result ⟨5⟩ and the desired indicators, the model can be changed through fitting ⟨6⟩. The existing software packages are assumed to have been implemented conscientiously. However, in a scientific context, and in a context that evolves through constant verification of models and assumptions, it is problematic that the implementation cannot be verified. Furthermore, the black box does not allow the model to be changed independently when assumptions or indicators change.

Furthermore, the black-box property makes it challenging to understand how results were achieved. Many parameters are required in the running time estimation, usually computed over long distances, and the implementation can be conducted using different step procedures.

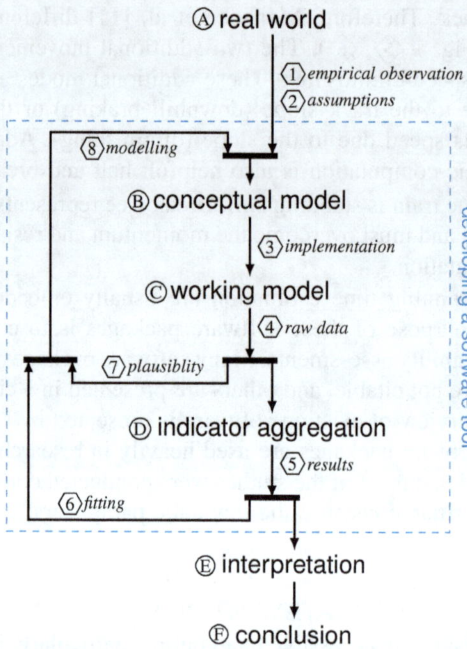

Figure 2: Observations are shaped into models that are used to generate indicators in the development of software tools.

These issues inevitably result in deviations. Because of the numerous parameters, two different implementations never produce the same result. The difference is relatively small, but if one takes the Japanese high-speed network as an example, where the timing is accurate to a few seconds, these deviations from the implementations are relevant.

Three software packages illustrate what is currently needed: OpenTrack [13], RailSys [14], and PULSim [15].

1. The "Open" in OpenTrack suggests that this is open-source software. Although OpenTrack is well suited for research [12], it has not yet been used to generate open science due to the unpublished source code. The "Open" in OpenTrack stands instead for the user-interface framework OpenStep, from which the Cocoa Framework for Mac OS X emerged over several further developments.
2. RailSys has a long history traced back to Völz [16]. However, the remarkable aspect of RailSys is a subprogram called Dynamis [17], [18]. Dynamis is integrated into RailSys and takes over the running time estimation. This example demonstrates that even a comprehensive software package contains smaller components that have a utility independent of the entire package and are worth marketing. It also reveals how much development time must be put into such software packages.
3. PULSim is currently the only open-source software for simulating railway operations. However, being open source is insufficient: the repository is currently unsuitable for potential users. There is no explanation of how the software can be used, modified, or further developed. With this current basis, no community can take care of the project, and the initiator only maintains it without considerable change. However, given the

long development time, having a single person taking care of the code is problematic, as perspectives can change quickly in an academic environment.

Open-source code is needed to overcome the black-box problem of tools in science. Besides the open-source code property, additional tool properties are needed for transparent and reproducible research. The code should be platform-independent so that the code can be run even after changes to user-interface frameworks or runtime environments. Furthermore, it should integrate into an environment for other research, such as computer-aided design, statistics, or simulation. The code should also be readable for advanced beginners in programming so that changes are efficient and transparently possible. A modular structure provides for this purpose, where individual modules can be exchanged, and the individual module already has sufficient utility. Moreover, it takes time and long-term development to meet the expectations of a robust tool.

4 WHAT CAN TRAINRUNS.JL DO OR CANNOT DO?

This paper should contribute to making open science in railway engineering possible. The running time estimation is the basis for these methods; thus, it is logical to start with this matter and create a tool to estimate running time. The tool must be interoperable with other tools or workflows. For the implementation to be as interoperable as possible, a package-oriented scripting language is needed that allows a combination of packages from different scientific domains. Furthermore, a suitable programming language for technical computation must be chosen. Likewise, an interactive language shell is also helpful for beginning programmers.

Currently, the programming languages Julia, MATLAB, Python, and R meet these criteria. All come with a package manager and are scriptable and used for scientific computation. However, MATLAB can be ruled out because of its commercial license and closed source, which are unsuitable for open science. The other three programming languages are a matter of taste. We decided on the newcomer, a fresh approach: the Julia programming language [19]. The naming convention for packages in Julia is to include the file extension *.jl* in the package repository name. The extension is omitted inside the Julia domain. In addition, TR is available as a package in Julia and can be installed via the package manager. The following minimal working example presents the usage.

```
using TrainRuns                         # load the module
train   = Train("freight.yaml")         # load train data from file
path    = Path("east_saxony.yaml")      # load moving section from file
runtime = trainrun(train, path)[end,:t] # returns run time in seconds
```

Three base variables are offered for the computation steps during the use of traction force (see Fig. 1 ⟨1⟩–⟨3⟩, ⟨6⟩): distance, time, and speed. For the braking computation (see Fig. 1 ⟨4⟩, ⟨5⟩), only the simplest method with constant deceleration is currently offered. The detail level of the computation and output can be set via optional settings.

5 IMPLEMENTATION

The package TR consists of a Julia module in several files and is roughly divided into the interfaces and core. Fig. 3 illustrates the package structure. The interfaces provide the means to transfer the necessary data to the core for computation. The settings can be used to select the model for calculating the acceleration. The stepping variable and step size can be selected for distance, time, and speed. Currently, both point masses and mass bands are supported. However, only constant deceleration is currently implemented for braking.

With the given path data, TR assumes that a train run to be computed starts with the first point and ends with the last point. Therefore, the path data must resemble a moving

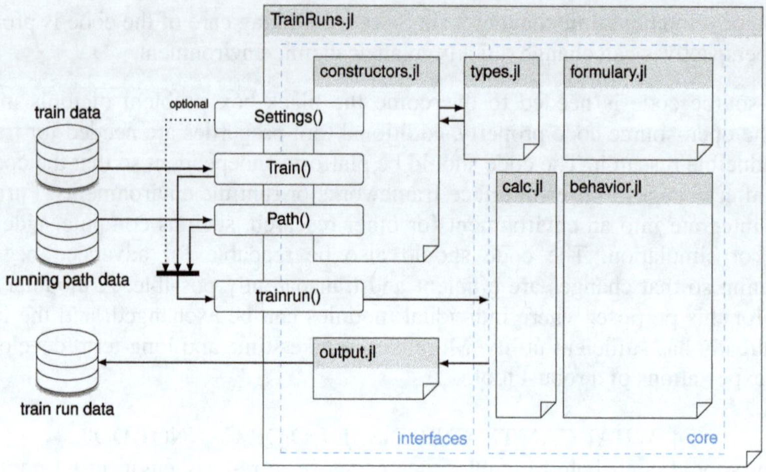

Figure 3: Architectural structure of the module.

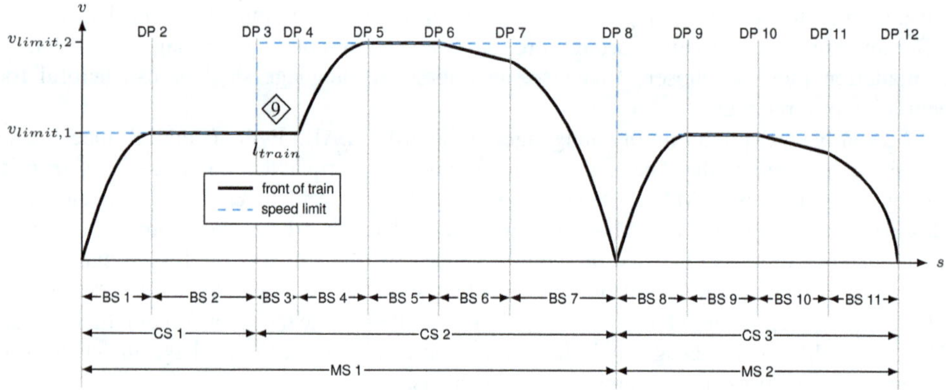

Figure 4: Division of a train run into different sections: Moving sections (MSs), characteristic sections (CSs), and behavioral sections (BSs) results in data points (DPs). The characteristic sections (CSs) are formed from the changes in the properties of the line. The BSs are the driving modes from Fig. 1 with the addition of clearing for the train length l_{train} (BS 3).

section (MS), as presented in Fig. 4. If computing one or more stops along the path data, a preprocessor must first divide the path data at the intended halts and pass the data individually to TR.

The core divides the given path data into characteristic sections (CSs) and behavioral sections (BSs) (cf. [20, p. 80 ff.]). The CSs are sections within the property, such as permitted speed or track resistances, of the infrastructure that do not change (see Fig. 4). A CS is then further divided into one or more BSs. The eight driving modes from Fig. 1 are used for the BS. Furthermore, an additional ninth mode in which the train must maintain a lower speed from a previous section until it has completely cleared the previous section is added (see Fig. 4, ⑨). The ninth mode is not a true BS but a simple implementation of clearing a speed restriction with a train length. The forces for calculating the accelerations in the BS are computed using the classical equations from Wende [3] and Brünger and Dahlhaus [4]. These equations are assembled in the formulary.jl (see Fig. 3).

6 INPUT FORMAT

The train and path data are loaded via files. In addition, YAML with the railtoolkit schema [22] is supported as the file format. The popular XML format with the RailML schema is currently not supported. The YAML format is typically easier to read than XML. Furthermore, RailML data can only be manually created with significant effort. However, it must be possible to collect the train and path data using simple means to study them, especially for a scientific study. Nevertheless, besides readability and writability, other criteria exist where RailML is more reasonable than YAML/railtoolkit.

Like RailML, the YAML/railtoolkit schema is an interchange format with definitions for attributes and properties in the rail context. The YAML/railtoolkit schema is a reduced and simplified set compared to RailML and currently only captures rolling stock and a characteristic sequence of line resistances. Consider the following example of a running path in Fig. 5 to illustrate the readability between YAML/railtoolkit and RailML. The information in Fig. 5 is coded in the YAML/railtoolkit format as follows:

```yaml
%YAML 1.2
schema: "https://railtoolkit.org/schema/running-path.json"
schema_version: "2022.05"
paths:
  - name: "Example running path"
    id: example
    points_of_interest:
      # [ station in m,              label, measure front or rear ]
      - [       850.00,       view_point_1,                front ]
      - [      1000.00,    distant_signal_1,               front ]
      - [      2000.00,       main_signal_1,               front ]
      - [      9000.00,       main_signal_3,               front ]
      - [      9050.00,    clearing_point_1,                rear ]
    characteristic_sections:
      # [ station in m, speed limit in km/h,  resistance in permil ]
      - [          0.0,                 160,                  0.00 ]
      - [       5000.0,                 160,                  5.00 ]
      - [       6000.0,                 160,                -10.00 ]
      - [       7000.0,                  80,                 15.00 ]
      - [       8000.0,                 120,                -10.00 ]
```

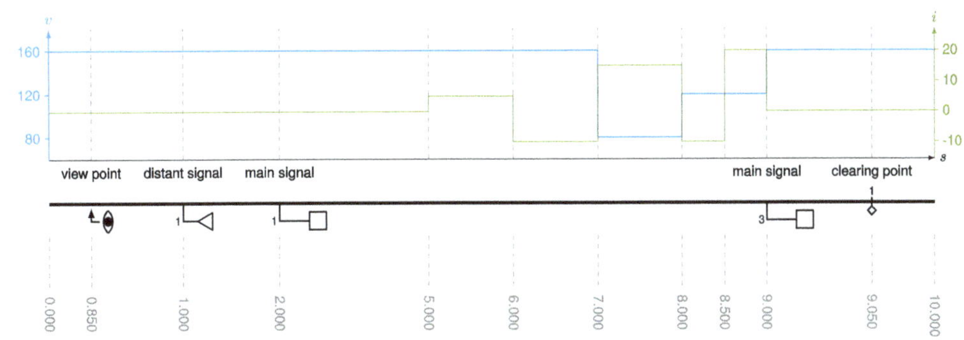

Figure 5: Example running path with symbology from Scheidt and Pachl [21], allowed speed v, and slope i.

```
- [     8500.0,                120,                   20.00 ]
- [     9000.0,                160,                    0.00 ]
- [    10000.0,                160,                    0.00 ]
```

The same information from Fig. 5 encoded in RailML:

```
<?xml version="1.0" encoding="UTF-8"?>
<railml xmlns="https://www.railml.org/schemas/2021" version="2.5">
  <infrastructure id="example" name="Example running path">
    <tracks>
      <track id="01">
        <trackTopology>
          <trackBegin pos="0" id="01_tb">
            <openEnd id="01_start"/>
          </trackBegin>
          <trackEnd pos="10000" id="01_te">
            <openEnd id="01_end"/>
          </trackEnd>
        </trackTopology>
        <trackElements>
          <speedChanges>
            <speedChange id="01_sc01" pos="0"    vMax="160"/>
            <speedChange id="01_sc02" pos="7000" vMax="80"/>
            <speedChange id="01_sc03" pos="8000" vMax="120"/>
            <speedChange id="01_sc04" pos="9000" vMax="160"/>
          </speedChanges>
          <gradientChanges>
            <gradientChange id="01_gc01" pos="0"    slope="0.00"/>
            <gradientChange id="01_gc06" pos="5000" slope="5.00"/>
            <gradientChange id="01_gc07" pos="6000" slope="-10.00"/>
            <gradientChange id="01_gc08" pos="7000" slope="15.00"/>
            <gradientChange id="01_gc09" pos="8000" slope="-10.00"/>
            <gradientChange id="01_gc10" pos="8500" slope="20.00"/>
            <gradientChange id="01_gc11" pos="9000" slope="0.00"/>
          </gradientChanges>
        </trackElements>
        <ocsElements>
          <signals>
            <signal id="01_poi01" pos="850"  name="view_point_1"
                    virtual="true" switchable="false">
            </signal>
            <signal id="01_poi02" pos="1000" name="distant_signal_1"
                    virtual="false" switchable="true">
            </signal>
            <signal id="01_poi03" pos="2000" name="main_signal_1"
                    virtual="false" switchable="true">
            </signal>
            <signal id="01_poi04" pos="9000" name="main_signal_3"
                    virtual="false" switchable="true">
            </signal>
          </signals>
          <trainDetectionElements>
            <trainDetector id="01_poi05" pos="9050" name="clearing_point_1"/>
          </trainDetectionElements>
        </ocsElements>
      </track>
    </tracks>
  </infrastructure>
</railml>
```

Once train data and running path data are loaded, TR computes the run time for the train with the first location on the running path as the departure point and the last location on the running path as the destination. Together with supplementary information, the run time is provided in tabular form as a DataFrame. The tabular DataFrame output was chosen for easy further processing because Julia's DataFrames are suitable for statistical evaluations, visualization, and exporting into comma-separated value files. The total run time, points of interest, data points (see Fig. 4), or all calculated support points from the step procedure can be returned depending on the settings.

7 TEST CASE AND COMPARISON

A test case was generated to compare the computation of TR with an existing tool. As test data, published path data from railML.org with the east Saxony line [24], generated by the software "Fahrplanbearbeitungssystem" (FBS), was utilized. The FBS software is primarily used to generate timetables [23] and provides a good reference. As test train data, two trains, a local and a freight train, were used to show the range of the computation differences. The standard local train for the line and a heavy freight train, which was heavy enough to handle the line at its power limit, was used. The train and path data are found in Scheidt and Kannenberg [25]. The standard local train is suitable to show the similarities, and the power limit of the freight train is suitable for clearly presenting the differences in computations.

Figure 6 depicts the test case for both trains. FBS has a continuous run time increase compared to TR, especially for the freight train. In addition, TR always reaches a slightly higher speed than FBS. When the speed limit is reached, the difference disappears for both trains, making it clear that the tools calculate different tractive forces. At the destination, compared to the beginning, it becomes apparent that TR is still missing a braking model that uses more than only a constant deceleration. Despite all the differences, with a few exceptions, TR follows the characteristic pattern of the speed of both trains by FBS.

In particular, the higher speed at kilometer 4 with a significant slope for the freight train affects the run time because the section clears much faster with TR. The relative difference is also most remarkable at that location as a result. The difference of 15 min is enormous, but the extreme example explains this because a 12-min difference is built up by kilometer 4. The remaining 3-min difference at about 100 km of distance is again acceptable.

The local train accelerates to its maximum with TR, while FBS is cut off beforehand (seen at kilometers 6 and 8). The FBS commuter train also seems to be more sensitive to slope, which could explain the slight dampening of the speed. However, there is hardly any difference between TR and FBS regarding the travel time required for the local train. Nevertheless, the difference raises questions about the implementation, which cannot be clarified lightly because of the closed source of FBS, making it clear that it is insufficient only to implement the equations from the literature.

8 CONCLUSION AND RESULTS

The discrepancy in Fig. 6 highlights the importance of an open-source implementation of the running time estimation. This open implementation is required for the reproducibility of results in open science. In addition to the open implementation, the accessibility of data for computation is another necessary aspect of reproducibility. The available data should follow the findable, accessible, interoperable, and reusable (FAIR) principles [26] for reproducible open science. In most cases, the infrastructure managers do not have FAIR infrastructure data. However, OpenStreetMap (OSM) can help. Considerable information on railway infrastructure can be found on OSM. However, data on the slope are currently lacking on OSM. Nevertheless, the OSM data are growing daily due to the many volunteers.

The situation is different for rolling stock data. Although considerable general data exist on both older and newer vehicles, many essential factors for calculating the run time can only be found as tables in books or, like for tractive effort, must first be determined and computed. As a remedy for a missing open collection, a database for TR was started in Scheidt [27].

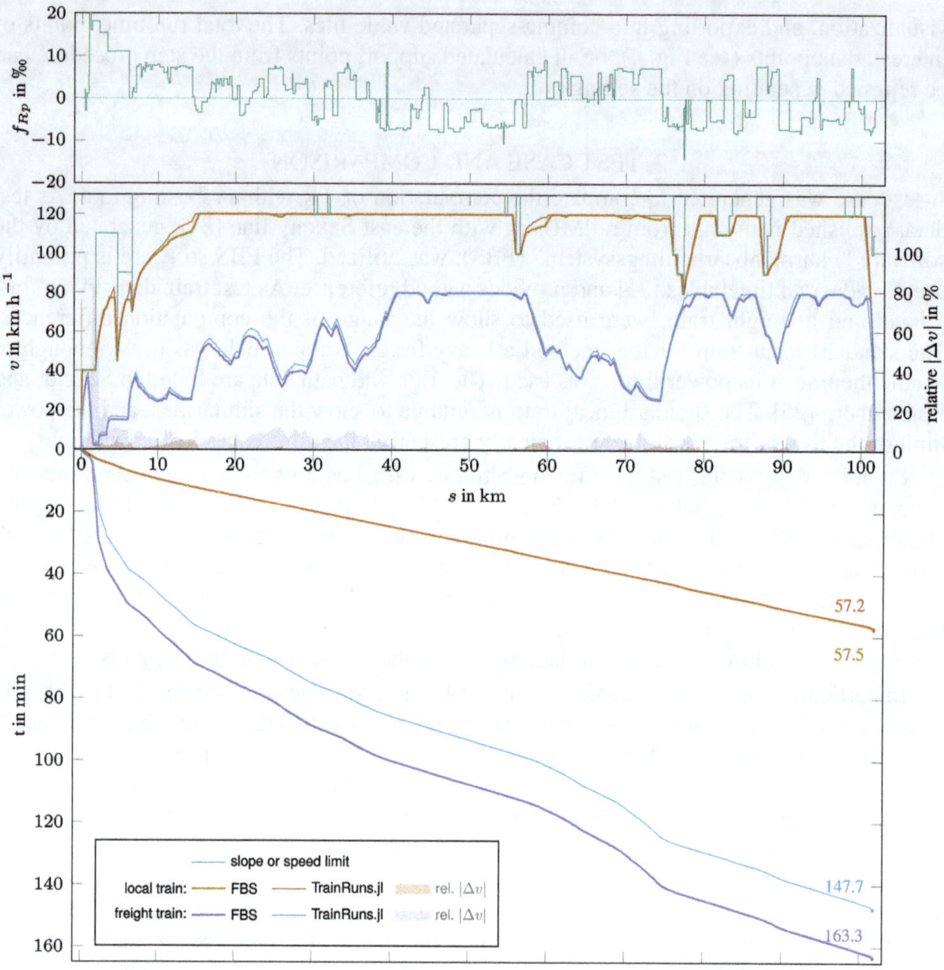

Figure 6: Comparison of the calculation between FBS [23] and TrainRuns.jl for a local train and a freight train on an east Saxony line [24] with a slope (f_{Rp}), showing time (t), speed (v), distance (s), and the relative difference between the two computed speeds for a tain with base to FBS (rel. $|\Delta v|$) are shown. The data are found in Scheidt and Kannenberg [25].

However, TR is not yet fully developed and will be continuously refined over its lifetime. Currently, the emphasis has been on the acceleration phase. Nevertheless, TR is a step toward open science and open data in railway engineering. This tool is suitable for qualitative calculations to compare different trains and is publicly available. We invite others to collaborate. The further development of TR is determined by whether it succeeds in forming a community around the tool and ensuring its usability for its purpose in research and teaching. The following is planned for the further development of TR: a braking model, energy-efficient driving, and visualization.

ACKNOWLEDGEMENTS

We acknowledge support by the German Research Foundation and the Open Access Publication Funds of the Technische Universität Braunschweig.

REFERENCES

[1] Kannenberg, M. & Scheidt, M., Trainruns.jl, Version: v1.0.1, 2022. DOI: 10.5281/zenodo.6448563.

[2] Lehmann, H., *Fahrdynamik der Zugfahrt Theorie und Anwendung*, Shaker: Aachen, 2005.

[3] Wende, D., *Fahrdynamik des Schienenverkehrs*, Springer-Verlag: Wiesbaden, 2003.

[4] Brünger, O. & Dahlhaus, E., Running time estimation. *Railway Timetabling and Operations*, eds I. A. Hansen & J. Pachl, Eurailpress DVV Media Group, pp. 65–89, 2014.

[5] Heppe, A., Fengler, W. & Mersiovsky, J., Untersuchungen der fahrweise von zügen anhand von betriebsdaten und fahrtenschrieben. *ETR Eisenbahntechnische Rundschau*, **2012**(10), pp. 52–57, 2012.

[6] Hertel, G. & Steckel, J., Eine neue Philosophie der Fahrzeitberechnung für Zugfahrten. *Wissenschaftliche Zeitschrift Hochschule für Verkehrswesen Friedrich List*, pp. 104–111, 1992.

[7] Medeossi, G., Longo, G. & de Fabris, S., A method for using stochastic blocking times to improve timetable planning. *Journal of Rail Transport Planning and Management*, **1**(1), pp. 1–13, 2011.

[8] Kecman, P. & Goverde, R.M.P., Predictive modelling of running and dwell times in railway traffic. *Public Transport*, **7**(3), pp. 295–319, 2015. DOI: 10.1007/s12469-015-0106-7.

[9] Wen, C., Mou, W., Huang, P. & Li, Z., A predictive model of train delays on a railway line. *Journal of Forecasting*, **39**(3), pp. 470–488, 2019. DOI: 10.1002/for.2639.

[10] Pachl, J., *Railway Operation Control*, 4th ed., VTD Rail Publishing: Mountlake Terrace (USA), 2018.

[11] Monecke, L., Müller, L. & Anthes, R., Dynamisonline-train run simulation via the internet. *World Congress Railway Research, 4th*, UIC: Köln, Germany, 2001.

[12] Medeossi, G. & de Fabris, S., Simulation of rail operations. *Handbook of Optimization in the Railway Industry*, Springer International Publishing, pp. 1–24, 2018. DOI: 10.1007/978-3-319-72153-8_1.

[13] Nash, A. & Huerlimann, D., Railroad simulation using OpenTrack. *WIT Transactions on The Built Environment, Computers in Railways IX*, vol. 74, WIT Press: Southampton and Boston, 2004. DOI: 10.2495/CR040641.

[14] Bendfeldt, J.P., Mohr, U. & Müller, L., RailSys, A system to plan future railway needs. *WIT Transactions on The Built Environment, Computers in Railways VII*, vol. 50, WIT Press: Southampton and Boston, 2000. DOI: 10.2495/CR000241.

[15] Cui, Y., Martin, U. & Liang, J., PULSim: User-based adaptable simulation tool for railway planning and operations. *Journal of Advanced Transportation*, **2018**, pp. 1–11, 2018. DOI: 10.1155/2018/7284815.

[16] Völz, W.D., Ermittlung der Leistungsfähigkeit von Knotenpunkten spurgeführter Verkehrssysteme mittels Graphentheorie, PhD thesis, Hannover: Lehrstuhl und Institut für Verkehrswesen, Eisenbahnbau und-betrieb; Technische Universität Hannover, 1976.

[17] Habich, G. & Eickmann, F., Dynamis – ein simulationsmodell zur bearbeitung fahrdynamischer fragestellungen. *ETR Eisenbahntechnische Rundschau*, **39**, pp. 83–87, 1990.

[18] Radtke, A., Müller, L. & Schumacher, A., Dynamis: a model for the calculation of running times for an efficient time-table construction. *WIT Transactions on The Built Environment, Computers in Railways VI*, WIT Press, vol. 37, WIT Press: Southampton and Boston, 1998. DOI: 10.2495/CR980301.

[19] Bezanson, J., Karpinski, S., Shah, V.B. & Edelman, A., *Julia: A Fast Dynamic Language for Technical Computing*, 2012. DOI: 10.48550/ARXIV.1209.5145.

[20] Cui, Y., *User-Based Adaptable High Performance Simulation Modelling and Design for Railway Planning and Operations*, Habilitation, Stuttgart: Technische Universität Stuttgart, 2017.

[21] Scheidt, M. & Pachl, J., TikZ-trackschematic library: A symbology towards a universal graphical description for operational scenarios in railway research. *RailBeijing 2021 – the 9th International Conference on Railway Operations Modelling and Analysis (ICROMA)*, 2021. DOI: 10.24355/dbbs.084-202204140847-0.

[22] Scheidt, M., railtoolkit/schema, Version: 2022.05, 2022. DOI: 10.5281/zenodo.6522824.

[23] iRFP – Institut für Regional- und Fernverkehrsplanung, Das fahrplanbearbeitungssystem FBS, Version: 1.7.9. www.irfp.de/das-fahrplanbearbeitungssystem-fbs.html. Accessed on: 29 May 2022.

[24] railML.org e.V., East Saxony railway network by FBS (railml 2.0, 2.2; timetable, infrastructure, rolling stock), available after login, 2016. www.railml.org/en/user/exampledata.html. Accessed on: 29 May 2022.

[25] Scheidt, M. & Kannenberg, M., *Supplement Data – Trainruns.jl: An Open-Source Tool for Running Time Estimation*, Zenodo, 2022. DOI: 10.5281/zenodo.6842604.

[26] Wilkinson, M.D. et al., The FAIR Guiding Principles for Scientific Data Management and Stewardship. *Scientific Data*, **3**(160018), 2016. DOI: 10.1038/sdata.2016.18.

[27] Scheidt, M., Rolling-stock-data, Version: 2022.06, Zenodo, 2022. DOI: 10.5281/zenodo.6467449.

Author index

www.ingramcontent.com/pod-product-compliance
Lightning Source LLC
LaVergne TN
LVHW062228200926
848484LV00006B/1496